PE:

THE A

SIMON GATHERCOLE received a double First in Classics and Theology at King's College, Cambridge, and studied further at the Jewish Theological Seminary in New York and the Universities of Tübingen and Durham. He has written several books on the New Testament and apocryphal Christian literature, and is editor of the journal *New Testament Studies*. He is Professor of New Testament and Early Christianity at the University of Cambridge, and a Fellow of Fitzwilliam College, Cambridge.

The Apocryphal Gospels

Translated with an Introduction by
SIMON GATHERCOLE

PENGUIN BOOKS

PENGUIN CLASSICS

UK | USA | Canada | Ireland | Australia
India | New Zealand | South Africa

Penguin Books is part of the Penguin Random House group of companies
whose addresses can be found at global.penguinrandomhouse.com

First published in Penguin Classics 2021

003

Translation and editorial material copyright © Simon Gathercole, 2021

Translation of *The Epistle of the Apostles* copyright © Francis Watson, 2021

The moral rights of the translator have been asserted

Set in 10.25/12.25pt Sabon LT Std
Typeset by Jouve (UK), Milton Keynes
Printed and bound in Great Britain by Clays Ltd, Elcograf S.p.A.

The authorized representative in the EEA is Penguin Random House Ireland,
Morrison Chambers, 32 Nassau Street, Dublin D02 YH68

A CIP catalogue record for this book is available from the British Library

ISBN: 978-0-241-34055-4

www.greenpenguin.co.uk

Penguin Random House is committed to a
sustainable future for our business, our readers
and our planet. This book is made from Forest
Stewardship Council® certified paper.

Contents

III ACCOUNTS OF JESUS' TRIAL AND DEATH

IV DIALOGUES WITH THE RISEN JESUS

V OTHER GOSPEL TEXTS

VI TWO MODERN FORGERIES

Introduction

'The Gospels could not possibly be either more or less in number than they are.' So wrote St Irenaeus, Bishop of Lyons, around 180 CE. This statement is no mere platitude, but a sharply combative insistence that the four 'canonical' Gospels of Matthew, Mark, Luke and John were the only path to the truth. In Irenaeus' line of fire were some rival groups who used fewer than four Gospels – only a mutilated version of Luke, for example, or an amalgam of the four Gospels rolled into one. At the same time, he was targeting 'heretics' who had minted additional Gospels such as the *Gospel of Truth* or the *Gospel of Judas*. In Irenaeus' view, to deviate in either direction from the fourfold nature of the Gospel was to invite the curse spelled out in the closing words of the Book of Revelation: 'If anyone adds anything to them, God will add to that person the plagues described in this scroll. And if anyone takes words away from this scroll of prophecy, God will take away from that person any share in the tree of life and in the Holy City.'

For Irenaeus and others like him, the books in the fourfold Gospel collection went hand in hand with the way many in the early church understood the message of the 'good news' which they preached. These Gospels now in our New Testament were the four accounts understood to encapsulate the truth of the incarnation, death and resurrection of Jesus Christ. These four had been handed down from the time of Jesus' apostles, in contrast to recent arrivals produced by unorthodox sects. Perhaps above all, since Irenaeus was writing in the midst of vicious Roman persecution, the canonical Gospels provided not just group solidarity but the message of eternal life with

God. Many agreed with the Bishop of Lyons: the canonical
Gospels were generally the most widely copied and quoted,
and in Irenaeus' time many across the breadth of the Roman
Empire had adopted the same fourfold Gospel.[1]

Popular though the four Gospel collection may have been,
however, Irenaeus and the other church leaders of his day
could not enforce it. In the first three centuries CE, Christians
had no legal mandate or military muscle enabling the church
to insist on four, and only four, Gospels. Even under Constan-
tine (emperor 306–337 CE), orthodox Christianity was not the
official religion of the Roman Empire as is sometimes thought.
The so-called Edict of Milan in 313 merely granted Christianity tolerated legal status. It was not until the Edict of
Thessalonica in 380 that the three co-emperors of the time
decreed: 'It is our will that all peoples, over whom the measure
of our mercy reigns, abide in the religion which the divine
apostle Peter passed down to the Romans.' Before this time,
there were no enforceable punishments that could be meted
out to dissident religious groups.

Despite Irenaeus' solemn declaration, then, various groups in
early Christian times produced 'apocrypha'. This term, from the
Greek *apokruphos*, meaning 'hidden' or 'secret', came to refer to
any books which exercised undue allure or which trespassed on
the contents of the Bible by supplementing or replacing the ground
it covered. These apocrypha came in various forms. There were
apocryphal epistles attributed to disciples of Jesus, and other
apocalypses besides the Revelation of St John in the New Testament. The label 'Gospel' was especially potent, however, since it
laid claim to the 'good news', the literal meaning of the Greek
word for Gospel, *euangelion*.[2] Calling a book a Gospel was a
claim to have the truth about Jesus and the message of new life.

Having this label did not necessarily mean that a Gospel
author would rewrite the historical story of Jesus in Galilee
and Judaea *c.* 30 CE, however. 'Gospel' on its own is not a literary genre, but a title referring to the good news of salvation
by Jesus. The form that the text took depended on what kind
of salvation the author considered Jesus to have brought.
Some apocryphal Gospels do imitate the canonical Gospels

of Matthew, Mark, Luke and John. Marcion's Gospel, the *Gospel of Peter* and Tatian's *Diatessaron* all adopt the established biographical, narrative form and so see the good news as rooted in Jesus' activity in history. Other works strike out in different directions, consisting of dialogues between the risen Jesus and certain disciples, or setting out the divine plan of salvation in pithy oracles. In a Gospel which is a catalogue of sayings, like the *Gospel of Thomas*, the medium is the message: interpreting Jesus' enigmatic utterances is what brings salvation. Still other Gospels resemble myths about the genesis of the Greek pantheon, with Jesus revealing the redemptive knowledge of how the different parts of the divine realm came into being.

Alongside the texts called 'Gospels' in their manuscripts or by other writers, there is also a large body of other Gospel material. Some works are not designed to contain the message of salvation as such, but speculate on additional details of the life of Jesus not included in the New Testament Gospels. 'Infancy Gospels' imagine what Jesus got up to as a child, for example. 'Passion' texts, centred on the trial and death of Jesus, offer conjectures on the legal wranglings behind the decision to sentence Jesus to death, or supply further dialogue between Jesus and the criminals crucified with him. Like the theologians of the early church, modern scholars classify these texts as 'apocryphal Gospels' as well. A particular problem arises with very small manuscript fragments referring to Jesus and his disciples. These tend to be labelled immediately as Gospels, but they could equally be fragments of sermons or commentaries or some other genre. The translations in this edition encompass all these kinds of apocryphal Gospel texts, which cover a very diverse array of material by many different authors. The literature included here is not intended to present 'the other Jesus', as if the apocryphal Gospels all joined forces to recount an alternative life of Christ. Rather, the aim of this volume is to present the earliest apocryphal Gospel literature (mostly from before 300 CE) in all its different styles, theologies and perspectives heavenly or earthly.

PURPOSE

A good deal of the apocryphal literature has no particularly subversive purpose. It is pious legendary material supplying *complementary* narratives to the existing canonical Gospels. The Gospel material in this category does not in any sense seek to challenge the conventional picture of Jesus, and indeed in some respects it emphasizes or exaggerates the orthodox view. This is the case for the two most important infancy Gospels, the *Protevangelium of James* and the *Infancy Gospel of Thomas*. The *Protevangelium* stresses the incarnation as the coming of a Christ who is both fully human and fully divine. It also develops the portrayal of Mary, whose own birth and early life is described, with an emphasis on her virginity both before and after the birth of Jesus. Additional dialogue between the angel Gabriel and Mary makes it clear that Mary does not conceive in the normal manner, and she is told by the angel, 'You will conceive by his Word' (*Prot.* 11). In addition, there is a rather lurid scene in which Salome, a sceptical friend of Mary's midwife, insists on examining Mary to check she is still a *virgo intacta* after Jesus' birth: 'As surely as the Lord my God lives, unless I insert my finger and examine her hymen, I will not believe that the virgin has given birth' (*Prot.* 19). When she does so, her hand gets burned off, but God shows mercy and miraculously heals her. The *Infancy Gospel of Thomas* contains similar legendary material to that in the *Protevangelium*, but has more of a single focus on the young Jesus who even before the start of his public ministry possessed miraculous powers which confounded the religious authorities.

At the other end of Jesus' biography, there is an abundance of literature which focuses on the mechanics of Jesus' trial: in the *Gospel of Nicodemus* and the *Narrative of Joseph of Arimathaea*, for example, there is an unsavoury emphasis on the guilt of the Jews involved in the process. The *Gospel of Peter* reports that Jesus redeemed the Old Testament saints from hell on Holy Saturday by going down to rescue them, and the *Questions of Bartholomew* describes the event in detail. After

Easter, the *Epistle of the Apostles* offers a post-resurrection dialogue with Jesus which stresses his fleshly corporeality, countering an unorthodox tendency to question Jesus' bodily humanity. Both these infancy Gospels and the 'Easter' works, then, seek not so much to challenge the established portrait of Jesus, as to bolster it by emphasizing and developing existing features, and providing new ways of shoring up the doctrines of the incarnation, cross and resurrection.

Much more defiant, on the other hand, is a work like the Coptic *Gospel of the Egyptians*. Its form is that of a heavenly mythological narrative which is influenced partly by Greek philosophy, and partly by Egyptian myth. Instead of Galilee and Judaea, the setting is the heavenly realm. Gone are Mary, Joseph and the disciples; instead the cast of characters includes figures with names such as Domedon Doxomedon and Telmael Telmachael Eli Eli Machar Machar Seth. It scarcely seems to touch down on planet earth until the very end, where there is an account of the mysterious baptismal ritual of the 'Gnostics', along with a polemical statement that any other purported accounts of the truth by Old Testament prophets or Christian apostles are simply spurious. It is clearly intended to undercut a conventional understanding of Jesus – and indeed any understanding of Jesus which appealed to his disciples, the apostles.

The Gospels of Judas and Thomas are no less subversive, but – unlike the *Gospel of the Egyptians* – they do seek to undercut the New Testament Gospels on their own terms, that is, by presenting accounts which resemble the canonical four to some degree. The *Gospel of Judas* uses a mythological style similar to that of the Coptic *Gospel of the Egyptians*, but here the episodes in the myth are recounted by Jesus in speeches delivered in the days leading up to Easter. *Thomas* sets out a series of sayings of Jesus, many of which are identical to, or resemble, those in the canonical Gospels. Interspersed among familiar material like the parable of the sower and the saying about the blind leading the blind, however, are more esoteric utterances which reflect the distinctive interests of the author: parables about a woman who loses a jar of meal, and of an assassin (*Gos. Thom.* 97–98), and sayings about the world being a corpse and the person who consumes the lion being blessed (*Gos. Thom.* 7, 56). Even though a good deal of the Jesus tradition in the *Gospel of Thomas* is known in other Gospels, *Thomas* is highly critical of the most influential Gospel name in the second century, Matthew (*Gos. Thom.* 13).

Similarly, *Marcion's Gospel* is also subversive, while imitating even more exactly the canonical Gospel format. While its wording is almost all derived from Luke's Gospel, Marcion's version is highly selective, portraying a kind of 'liberal' Jesus, extracted from his Jewish roots, and relieved of the task of judging the world. Marcion describes Jesus in terms of 'the Good' as defined in a Greek (especially Platonic) philosophical context. He removes from the Gospel any sense that Israel's scripture foresaw or foreshadowed the work of Jesus; indeed, the Old Testament god and the God of Jesus were according to Marcion two entirely separate and unrelated deities. Here, then, we are a considerable distance away from the canonical Gospels, and yet Marcion sets out this radical theological vision through the quite conventional means of narrating Jesus' ministry, death and resurrection, just as Matthew, Mark, Luke and John do.

Between the near-opposites of the conventional Gospels at one end and the confrontational and subversive ones at the other, there is other Gospel literature across the spectrum. Some of this literature appears to provide advanced theological teaching complementary to the canonical Gospels. The *Gospel of Truth* and the *Gospel of Philip*, for example, appear to have this intention. It seems very likely that they belong to the Valentinian school. (See discussion of 'Theology' below.) This movement used the Gospels of Matthew, Mark, Luke and John, but seems also to have employed the other two Gospels (*Truth*, and *Philip*) alongside them. The *Gospel of Truth* supplements the canonical Gospels by providing an elaborate cosmological backdrop, and applying its metaphysics to the work of Jesus. There is no trace of any polemic in the *Gospel of Truth*, and the work is peppered with faint allusions to the New Testament, though without quoting it or acknowledging its sources. The *Gospel of Philip* is also aware of the canonical Gospels, and explicitly and approvingly quotes from them. *Philip* writes, for example: 'For this reason the Word says, "Already the axe is laid at the root of the trees"' (Mt. 3:10; Lk. 3:9), and, 'That is why he said, "Whoever does not eat my flesh and drink my blood has no life in him."' (Jn 6:53). On the other hand, *Philip* takes up a negative stance against some of the standard tenets of those same canonical Gospels. There is criticism of Matthew and Luke in *Philip*'s particular view of Jesus' birth: 'Some say that Mary conceived by the Holy Spirit. They are deceived!' This Valentinian Gospel's unconventional approach to Jesus' death leads to a paradoxical criticism of the standard narrative: 'Those who say that the Lord first died and then rose are wrong. For he first rose and then died.' The *Gospel of Philip*'s attitude to the canonical Gospels therefore is neither whole-hearted acceptance nor rejection, but correction. Some of the post-resurrection dialogues, whether more 'orthodox' works like the *Questions of Bartholomew* or more sectarian works like the *Gospel of Mary*, presuppose knowledge of the canonical Gospels while building further theological edifices upon them. The *Gospel of Mary* is also an interesting case of a work which provides a Jesus who is both reassuringly familiar at points, but innovative in other ways.

Finally, off the spectrum altogether is a work like the *Gospel of the Lots of Mary*. This horoscope-like text announces itself at the beginning as a Gospel, seemingly using the term 'Gospel' merely in an attempt to acquire authority. In this respect, however, it is only an extreme case of what has been happening all along in much of this literature. It illustrates how compelling the label 'Gospel' is, and how contested the subject matter of Jesus and his significance.

MANUSCRIPTS

When we come to consider the earliest period of the apocryphal Gospels, the problem which immediately faces us is the small number of manuscripts which survive. This is sometimes explained as the consequence of the orthodox suppressing or burning the texts of the heretics, but the scarcity of copies is not the result of any kind of systematic destruction. The main reference to the ecclesiastical hierarchy collecting up copies of an apocryphal Gospel comes in the fifth century. While Theodoret was bishop of Cyr (423–457 CE), he found over two hundred copies of the *Diatessaron*, a conflation of all four canonical Gospels; these volumes he 'collected and put away, and introduced instead of them the Gospels of the four evangelists'. But such references are few and far between.

There are other explanations for the limited numbers of apocryphal Gospel manuscripts which we possess. In the first place, it is unlikely that large numbers of the manuscripts were produced, given the cost of both the materials (papyrus being expensive) and labour (involving copying every text by hand). Many of the apocryphal Gospels which reveal a particular sectarian outlook no doubt hailed from small groups. The *Gospel of Thomas* at one point records Jesus as saying: 'I will choose you, one out of a thousand, two out of ten thousand', evoking to some degree the sense of the movement as a small, embattled group (*Gos. Thom.* 23). Some of the more elaborate works probably circulated only in elite intellectual circles. No doubt some apocryphal works have left no trace at all, while others are known to us as mere names. Most of the ancient apocryphal texts which have survived come down to us in fragments and/or in translation, as is the case with the *Gospel of Thomas*.

The paucity of copies, then, is probably primarily a result of not many having been made. There was such a disproportionate amount of copying of canonical biblical books that even orthodox non-canonical books are relatively poorly attested. We can take as an example the corpus which has the modern name of 'The Apostolic Fathers'. These are some of the earliest Christian writings after the New Testament and were in general regarded in the early church as having sound theological credentials. One part of this corpus, the *Didache* or *Teaching of the Twelve Apostles*, is an early document of church order from the beginning or middle of the second century that survives in just one complete Greek manuscript from 1056 CE and two small fragments of medieval translations. The *Epistle to Diognetus*, a letter from a Christian to a pagan interested in knowing about Christianity, was preserved in one thirteenth- or fourteenth-century manuscript, but even this has been lost – in a fire from shelling during the Franco-Prussian war. It was first noticed in Constantinople in 1436 by one Thomas d'Arezzo, who rescued it from a pile of papers to be used for packaging in a fish-shop, so its survival was a result of pure happenstance. Among the earliest 'Apologies', pleas written to the emperor on behalf of Christianity, those of Quadratus of Athens and Melito of Sardis survive in only a few quotations. Justin Martyr's great *Apology* survives complete in three medieval manuscripts, but since one of these is the source of the other two, this means that there is only one independent manuscript. As the German scholar of the early church Christoph Markschies has calculated, of the second-century Christian works whose titles are known to us, only about 15 per cent have survived – and that does not, of course, include the works whose names are lost.[3] For an ancient work, whatever its theological orientation, being copied repeatedly was the only survival strategy.

As a result, the only manuscripts which survive in high quantities are those of 'canonical' books. Here, canonical is used in a broad sense, to refer to any works which were ascribed status by substantial numbers of people. Much as Harold Bloom did in *The Western Canon*, ancient scholars compiled 'canons' of model Greek speakers and writers. There were lists, for example, of the nine great lyrical poets, and of the ten great Attic orators. These canonical authors tend to be those authors who are best preserved. Outside of the Bible, the ancient works extant in the most copies from the ancient world are Homer's *Iliad* and *Odyssey* (the former more than the latter). Hundreds of manuscripts of Homer survive, because the *Iliad* and the *Odyssey* were taught in schools and regarded as essential reading for any educated person. We still have plays of the three great authors of classical Greek tragedy, Aeschylus, Sophocles and Euripides, although nothing like their entire bodies of work.

Against this background, we can better understand the attestation of books like the *Gospel of Thomas* (three Greek fragments; one complete Coptic translation), the *Gospel of*

Judas (one Coptic manuscript) and the *Gospel of Mary* (one fragmentary Coptic manuscript, and two small Greek fragments). The most popular apocryphal Gospels were probably the infancy texts, which were often reworked and incorporated into larger blocks of material: the *Protevangelium* and *Infancy Thomas* were edited and combined to form a *Gospel of Pseudo-Matthew* (probably in the seventh century), which in turn was reworked into other infancy texts. The *Protevangelium of James* and the *Infancy Gospel of Thomas* themselves survive in many manuscripts, and both were translated into Latin, Coptic, Syriac, Armenian, Georgian, Ethiopic and Slavonic. They left footprints in other ways as well. The *Protevangelium*'s depiction of Mary spinning purple and scarlet thread for the veil of the temple (*Prot.* 10) is picked up in a number of late-antique and medieval images of the Annunciation.[4] The *Infancy Gospel of Thomas*'s account of Jesus moulding clay birds and enlivening them (*IGT* 2) is referred to in the Qur'an, according to which Jesus said: 'I have come to you with a sign from your Lord: I will make the shape of a bird for you out of clay, then breathe into it and, with God's permission, it will become a real bird' (*Qur'an* 3:49; cf. 5:110). An image of this scene can be found on the medieval ceiling (*c.* 1100) of the church of St Martin in Zillis in Switzerland.

RECEPTION IN THE CHURCH

During to the relative lack of manuscript evidence, most of what we know about the fate of apocryphal Gospels in the early period comes from the church fathers. While some of these theologians had an entirely negative attitude to such 'heretical' works, others saw them as curates' eggs. Bishop Serapion, patriarch of Antioch at the end of the second century, is highly critical of the *Gospel of Peter*, but this is because it is a mixed bag, rather than wholly awful. In his treatise written in response to it, he remarks: 'I have been able . . . to go through it and discover a majority of the right teaching about the Saviour, but also what was inserted.'[5] Jerome, the translator of the standard Latin version of the Bible, could also concede in 403 CE that in some apocryphal Gospels one might find *aurum in luto*, 'gold in amongst the muck'.[6]

The gold did not stop these texts from being prohibited, however. The fourth-century Alexandrian theologian Didymus the Blind cites an early authority: 'One ancient bishop of the church has put it well: "We prevent the study of the apocrypha," he says, "because of those who are not able to distinguish what has been combined in them by heretics." '[7] Some orthodox theologians studied them on the grounds of wanting to know what tunes the devil was playing. Around the same time as Didymus was writing, St Augustine's teacher Bishop Ambrose of Milan wrote:

> There is another Gospel in circulation, which the Twelve are said to have written. Basilides has also ventured to write a Gospel, which is called 'According to Basilides'. There is also in circulation another Gospel, which is entitled 'According to Thomas'. I know of another entitled 'According to Matthias'. We have read some of them [i.e. privately] not so that they may be read [i.e. publicly, in church]; we have read them so that we may not be ignorant of them; we have read them not in order to hold to them, but to reject them and to know the nature of these books in which those prideful men have elevated their hearts.[8]

Increasingly, the fathers and church documents take this line and prohibit the reading of apocryphal Gospels – at least publicly in church. In fact, we only hear one account of a non-canonical Gospel being read publicly. As noted above, Serapion of Antioch came to a very negative conclusion about the *Gospel of Peter*; initially, however, he had allowed a church to read it in worship before realizing his mistake. Eusebius takes an uncompromising position: some apocryphal writings have not been handed down in the orthodox succession and so are 'to be rejected'. This is not because they contain both good and bad which the unlearned might not be able to distinguish, but on the grounds that such works are, as he puts it, 'completely wicked and impious'.[9]

One official church document, the so-called Gelasian Decree from around the seventh century, catalogues the acknowledged biblical books, and then proceeds with a long list of other Gospels or Gospel-like books – attaching to each of them the Latin word *apocryphum*. Notably here, even the relatively innocuous infancy Gospels appear on the index of prohibited books, the last two titles referring to the *Infancy Gospel of Thomas* and the *Protevangelium of James* respectively:

Gospel in the name of Matthias:	apocryphal
Gospel in the name of Barnabas:	apocryphal
Gospel in the name of James the younger:	apocryphal
Gospel in the name of the apostle Peter:	apocryphal
Gospel in the name of Thomas, which the Manichees use:	apocryphal
Gospel in the name of Bartholomew:	apocryphal
Gospel in the name of Andrew:	apocryphal
Gospel which Lucian forged:	apocryphal
Gospel which Hesychius forged:	apocryphal
Book about the childhood of the redeemer:	apocryphal
Book about the birth of the redeemer, about Mary or the midwife:	apocryphal

... and what has been taught or written by all the disciples of heresy and of heretics or schismatics whose names we have hardly liked to preserve, we acknowledge is not merely to be rejected but is to be excluded from the whole Roman Catholic and Apostolic Church, and damned along with its authors in the inextricable shackles of anathema for ever.[10]

In late antiquity from about 400 CE, and into the medieval period, the main survival of apocryphal works was in lists such as this. There are a few exceptions. Some texts continued to be copied; the surviving manuscript of the *Gospel of Peter*, for example, may have been copied as late as the ninth century. There are also some paths off the beaten track where faint footprints of apocryphal Gospels can be detected. One such place is the literature of the Manichees, a sect which began in the third century CE under the leadership of the Persian prophet Mani, and survived long into the Middle Ages. Some of its writings have quotations from or allusions to apocryphal Gospels: the *Kephalaia of the Teacher*, a third-century Manichaean text, quotes from the *Gospel of Thomas*, as does a late-first-millennium copy of a work written in the central Asian language of Sogdian. A similar Gnostic group known as the Mandaeans alludes to some of the same sayings as do the Manichees: they both refer to *Thomas*'s saying about Jesus choosing 'one out of a thousand, two out of ten thousand', resonating with the sense of being part of an elite few (*Gos. Thom.* 23). Similar esoteric material emerges from the medieval inquisitions of heretics in south-western France, the subject of Emmanuel Le Roy Ladurie's acclaimed historical monograph *Montaillou*.[11] According to some of the mass of detailed inquisition records which survive, certain heretics confessed that women were unable to enter Paradise, and so had to be made male in order to be saved. This corresponds precisely with what Jesus says according to the climax of the *Gospel of Thomas*: 'Behold, I will draw her [i.e. Mary Magdalene] in order to make her male, so that she also might be a living spirit resembling you males. For every woman who makes herself male will enter the kingdom of heaven' (*Gos. Thom.* 114). The *Thomas* saying in turn goes back to an ancient conception of gender, according to which the female spiritual nature is defective (see also the Greek *Gospel of the Egyptians*).[12]

As in late antiquity, however, for most authors in the middle ages and the Reformation era the apocryphal Gospels are no longer known except as mere names. In the thirteenth century, Thomas Aquinas made a catalogue of extra-canonical Gospels, but it is entirely derived from St Jerome's work of nearly a millennium earlier.[13] Canon lists of biblical books often continued to append inventories of forbidden books, but there was rarely any danger of readers using such long-lost heretical texts. Many were itemized purely out of antiquarian interest.

In the early modern period, with the advent of printing, knowledge of the Christian apocrypha became more widespread. Oddly enough, the first issue of a collection of Christian apocrypha is appended to a posthumous edition, published by Michael

Neander in 1567, of Martin Luther's *Small Catechism*.[14] This contains the *Protevangelium of James* and the apocryphal correspondence (from the middle ages) of Pontius Pilate with Tiberius, as well as various extracts from Jewish authors and from church fathers about Jesus. Where there is text of a Greek original, this appears on the left-hand page, with a Latin translation on the right. The editor's introductory letter gives a long list of apocryphal Gospels, almost all of which were lost to him. An exception is the *Gospel of Nicodemus*, to which he appends the words *quod adhuc* – 'which still survives'. Other collections followed, mostly following Neander's very closely, and which by today's standards would probably be judged as plagiarized.

The first volume to resemble a modern collection of Christian apocrypha was published in 1703 by the German scholar Johann Albert Fabricius (1668–1736) – with a subtitle describing the apocryphal literature as 'collected and castigated' in his book.[15] Alongside the original Greek texts and Latin translations of the *Protevangelium of James* and the other works already published by Neander, Fabricius included the *Infancy Gospel of Thomas*, as well as apocryphal epistles such as the purported correspondence between St Paul (*c.* 5–64 CE) and his contemporary the Roman philosopher Seneca (*c.* 4 BCE–65 CE) which dates from the fourth century. Fabricius' collection was also the first modern scholarly work to assemble lists of non-canonical sayings of Jesus found quoted in the church fathers, and his catalogue of apocryphal Gospels therefore contains collections of the material belonging to the Greek *Gospel of the Egyptians*, the *Gospel of the Ebionites* and the *Gospel according to the Hebrews*.

In the absence of new discoveries, the apocryphal publishing industry stagnated for the next couple of hundred years. This all changed at the end of the nineteenth century, when excavations in Egypt transformed our understanding of early Christian literature.

NEW DISCOVERIES

The damp climate of Europe means that very few documents survive from Greece and Italy, the places we most readily associate with ancient classical literature. Public inscriptions on stone abound, as do curses and spells which were often inscribed on strips of metal. The same cannot be said for literary texts written on papyrus. A rare exception is a collection of papyri that are preserved from Herculaneum, which survived because they were baked and turned into almost pure carbon by the nearby eruption of Mount Vesuvius in 79 CE. We do, however, have an enormous quantity of both literary and administrative papyri from Egypt, where the climate is more conducive to their survival. Apocryphal Gospel material, like ancient tax documents and the earliest manuscript fragments of classical literature, is known primarily from there.

One of the first excavations of a new Gospel text was the unearthing of the *Gospel of Peter*, in a dig by the French Archaeological Mission in Cairo during the winter of 1886–7. One Cambridge scholar recorded his amazement at the event: 'We may expect anything, in the world of Christian letters, after such an astonishing discovery; if we do not realise our expectations, it will certainly be because, either at home or abroad, in labours philological or archaeological, we are wicked and slothful servants.'[16]

Neither diggers nor scholars were wicked or slothful, because the following decade witnessed the discovery of the most impressive collection of classical and Christian fragments ever found. This is the hoard of texts from a rubbish dump in the ancient Egyptian town of Oxyrhynchus, modern El-Behnesa. At the time of writing, eighty-four volumes containing nearly 5,000 manuscript fragments from Oxyrhynchus have been published, and this only scratches the surface of the surviving papyri, some scholars estimating that only about 1 per cent of the texts has yet been published. The scholars initially involved in sorting and editing the papyri could not believe their luck, with the very first season of excavation turning up treasures from the classical Greek poetess Sappho as well as apocryphal sayings of Jesus.

Grenfell and Hunt, the Oxford scholars publishing the finds, were so bowled over by the discovery of these sayings of Jesus that they commented, in Volume 1 of the Oxyrhynchus Papyri publication series: 'It is not very likely that we shall find another poem of Sappho, still less that we shall come across another page of the "Logia".'[17] Hence their remark several years later in 1904: 'By a curious stroke of good fortune our second excavations at Oxyrhynchus were, like the first, signalized by the discovery of a fragment of a collection of Sayings of Jesus.'[18] These particular logia, or sayings of Jesus, turned out to be from the *Gospel of Thomas*, and many other logia (as well as manuscripts of Sappho's poetry) have subsequently been discovered as well. In addition to these, dozens of manuscripts of the New Testament, and of the Greek Old Testament, have surfaced there. The Oxyrhynchus harvest of apocryphal Gospels (all in Greek) also includes a manuscript of the *Gospel of Mary*, a short fragment of the *Gospel of Peter* and various otherwise unknown Gospels translated in this volume with such unsensational titles as 'Oxyrhynchus Papyrus 1224' or 'Oxyrhynchus Papyrus 4009'.

The three different fragments of the *Gospel of Thomas* found at Oxyrhynchus were not clearly identified as parts of *Thomas*, or even as parts of the same work, until a complete manuscript of the text appeared. This came as part of another very important discovery of a cache of manuscripts in 1945–6, near the town of Nag Hammadi, approximately halfway between Cairo in the north and Lake Nasser in the south, in the eastern-central part of Egypt. Like the first Greek Oxyrhynchus fragment of *Thomas*, the manuscripts were in the form of codices, or bound books, rather than scrolls. Unlike the Oxyrhynchus texts mentioned, these Nag Hammadi books were written in Coptic, the hieroglyphic language of ancient Egypt transliterated using the Greek alphabet.

It is an ingrained part of the mythology of scholarship on the Nag Hammadi codices that an Egyptian peasant named Muhammad Ali discovered the codices in a jar while digging for *sabakh*, a kind of fertilizer, shortly after the end of the Second World War. Ali allegedly remembers the date with some accuracy because the find coincided with a momentous family event. Ali's father had worked as a night-watchman, and one night had killed an intruder. In revenge, Ali's father was shot dead the next day by a member of the intruder's family. In counter-reprisal, Ali and his brothers planned to murder their father's killer. Eventually, around the time of Coptic Christmas (7 January), Muhammad Ali and his brothers were told of the location of their target, killed him, cut out his heart and each ate a share. Ali's account is that the discovery of the Nag Hammadi codices took place shortly before this blood feud. At least some of this story is questionable. Different tellings of the story have yielded different results. One scholar has noted that the height of the jar containing the manuscripts can range from 2 feet to 6 feet. Others have commented that finding the jar when digging in an area containing fertilizer is hard to imagine, given that papyrus would be unlikely to survive centuries of inundations of the Nile there. Whatever the truth about the discovery, however, there has never been any doubt about the genuine antiquity of the Nag Hammadi codices. Wherever they may have been found, dated letters reused in the binding of the manuscripts indicate that the codices go back to the fourth or fifth century CE.

Among the works preserved from Nag Hammadi are a number which have not captured the public imagination, perhaps because of their uninspiring or unintelligible names – such as the *Discourse on the Eighth and Ninth*, or the *Trimorphic Protennoia*. Others are very widely known. Undoubtedly the most famous is the *Gospel of Philip*, some of whose contents were mediated to a wide audience, in admittedly garbled form, through Dan Brown's *The Da Vinci Code*. The *Gospel of Thomas* similarly has been important, especially to scholars who have tried – albeit unsuccessfully – to argue that it may preserve some of the sayings of Jesus in a more pristine form than do the canonical Gospels, or that it may contain some previously unknown sayings that go back to Jesus.

Probably found in a location near Nag Hammadi was the

Gospel of Judas, although its precise find-spot is now unknown. What is known is a good deal of its recent history, and how before its publication in 2006 it passed through the hands of various dealers, some of whom broke it up into pieces to maximize profit from it. The manuscript spent some years in a bank vault in a town rejoicing in the name of Hicksville, on Long Island in New York State. One dealer even stored it for a time in a freezer, which did not have a salubrious effect on the papyrus. Because the text makes Judas a central character in the Gospel narrative and a confidant of Jesus, its publication caused a sensation in the press. The British *Mail on Sunday*, not without some overstatement, hailed it as the 'greatest archaeological discovery of all time', and a 'threat to 2,000 years of Christian teaching'.

Even since 2006 there have been more discoveries, including the identification by AnneMarie Luijendijk of the *Gospel of the Lots of Mary*, a manuscript found in the Sackler Museum at Harvard University. A further Gospel or Gospel-like text from Oxyrhynchus has been published (Papyrus 5072). Perhaps the best known, which also hit the headlines of national newspapers, is a pseudo-discovery – that of the 'Gospel of Jesus' Wife'. A carefully contrived press release and a lengthy journal article in the *Harvard Theological Review* announced this as a genuine ancient Gospel. Shortly afterwards, however, a combination of technical scholarly analysis and brilliant investigative journalism showed that the text was a forgery: around the year 2010, a confidence trickster wrote on a piece of genuinely ancient papyrus some lines of Coptic which were largely based on a copy of the *Gospel of Thomas* on the internet. Unfortunately, the webpage happened to have a copying mistake in its transcription of *Thomas* – a mistake which the hapless author of the *Gospel of Jesus' Wife* reproduced.[19]

THEOLOGY IN THE
APOCRYPHAL GOSPELS

The *Gospel of Judas* and three of the Nag Hammadi Gospels are significant because they reflect two different, 'heretical' systems of thought. Both these theological worldviews were hotly discussed by Christian scholars in antiquity, and they still elicit interest from scholars today.

Sometimes apocryphal Gospels are generally labelled as 'Gnostic', which is in fact a narrower, more technical term applying to a particular school of thought sometimes called the 'classical Gnostic' or 'Sethian Gnostic' movement. Among the Gospels in this anthology, the *Gospel of Judas* and the *Gospel of the Egyptians* are relatively complete examples, and the Greek *Gospel of Philip* and that of *Eve* are fragmentary survivals of Gnostic Gospels. The Gnostics have always been known to us not just from the church fathers but also from the circle of Neo-Platonist philosophers around Plotinus in Rome in the third century CE. These philosophers, like the church fathers, embarked on an extensive anti-Gnostic project. One particularly zealous disciple of Plotinus, Amelius Gentilianus, composed a treatise against a single Gnostic work (*Zostrianus*), his refutation running to forty books or scrolls in length. Another disciple of this school, Porphyry of Tyre, summarized Gnostic teaching under the two headings: 'the creator of the world is evil' and 'the world is evil' – doctrines which were just as abhorrent to these Neo-Platonists as they were to Christians. Porphyry's two-part summary is naturally an abbreviation or simplification, but is useful nonetheless, and matches what we know from elsewhere. The *Gospel of Judas*, identified as a Gnostic Gospel by Irenaeus in the second century CE, depicts the creators and overlords of this world as demonic in the text that survives. In the other complete Gnostic Gospel translated in this volume, the Coptic *Gospel of the Egyptians*, the world is described as 'the image of night', and has a similar cast of demonic characters presiding over it. The lists of these sentinels of Chaos coincide across the various Gnostic works: 'Harmathoth, Galila, Iobel and Adonaios' (in the *Gospel of Judas*), 'Athoth, Harmas, Iobel and Adonaios' (in the Coptic *Gospel of the Egyptians*) and 'Athoth, Harmas, Galila, Iobel and Adonaios' (in the *Apocryphon of John*).

Long lists of higher heavenly beings are also a feature of the distinctive style of Gnostic theologizing. One of the alternative titles of the Coptic *Gospel of the Egyptians* is *The Holy Book of the 'Great Invisible Spirit'*, and this designation of the supreme divine figure as the Great Invisible Spirit is found frequently in other works with a similar theological outlook, such as *Zostrianus*, the *Apocryphon of John*, the *Hypostasis of the Archons* and, again, the *Gospel of Judas*. The character 'Barbelo' also appears frequently as a kind of heavenly female consort for the Invisible Spirit.

These figures – divine and demonic alike – all constitute part of the Gnostic 'myth'. This myth typically begins with a principal, transcendent figure who generates or emanates additional deities, who in turn generate further heavenly figures. At some point in the sequence, there is a lapse in the process which means that evil creeps in. Sometimes a female deity, Sophia ('Wisdom'), decides to create on her own without male assistance. Sometimes it is just that, after a long sequence of emanations, the derivative divinities are so far removed from their ultimate source that malevolent deities spring up and, seeking to make an imitation of the higher heavenly echelons above, create their own inferior, evil world. This lower world is the world we currently inhabit. At this point, however, a higher deity sows spirit into this lower world, and this spiritual matter resides in the true Gnostic disciples. The process of history consists in the regathering of the spiritual matter back into the divine realm.

A similar, though slightly less stark myth is shared by another important group in early Christianity, the school of Valentinus, one of the most notorious heretics of the second century CE. The Valentinians were probably a kind of reform movement, seeking to reconcile parts of the Gnostic philosophy with a more Christian theological framework. They used the four canonical Gospels, but also – as noted above – produced two

Gospels of their own which reflect their distinctive theological emphases.

The first of these texts, the *Gospel of Truth*, comes in Nag Hammadi Codex I, a volume which at one time was in the possession of the famed psychoanalyst Carl Jung. The *Gospel of Truth* was written around 150 CE, and – as already noted – has a close relationship to the *Gospel of Philip*. In the Valentinian theological systems of these two Gospels, creation of the material world was not part of the plan of the supreme divine Father: 'The world came into being by a mistake. For its creator wanted to make it imperishable and immortal, but failed, and did not manage what he had hoped' (*Gos. Phil.* 99). Because this was a presumptuous creation with no endorsement from the top, it was a cosmos mired in deficiency and ignorance. (In this the Valentinians differed both from more mainstream Christian views and also from the Gnostics who held an even more negative view of creator and creation.) As in more conventional forms of Christianity, Jesus, the Son of the divine Father, is the saviour figure, although in the *Gospel of Philip* and the *Gospel of Truth* the salvation consists in the provision of plenitude or fulness (the solution to deficiency) and of knowledge or revelation (the solution to ignorance).

A further feature of the Valentinian school is a certain theological style, rooted especially in linguistic scholarship. For the *Gospel of Philip*, the word 'messiah' has a double meaning. The conventional sense is 'anointed', but there is also the less common, alternative meaning of 'measure' or 'measured', which would perhaps identify Jesus as the visible, comprehensible, 'measurable' revelation of the invisible, ineffable and immeasurable Father (logion 47). There is word-play in the naming of positive and negative wisdom, personified in the figure Sophia (Greek for wisdom). 'Echamoth' is Sophia, but 'Echmoth' is the negative, deadly Sophia (logion 39): Echamoth sounds like the Aramaic word for 'wisdom' (*hokmatha*), while Echmoth can be heard as the Aramaic for 'like death' (*eyk moth*). In the *Gospel of Truth*, the etymologizing is less playful: 'gospel' means 'the revelation of hope', because of the two components of the Greek-Coptic word *eu-angelion* – 'good' and 'announcement'

(*Gos. Tr.* introduction). The explanation that the 'ointment' is 'the Father's mercy' (*Gos. Tr.* 28) may go back to a Greek pun on *elaion* ('oil', 'ointment') and *eleos* ('mercy').

A very common feature in apocryphal literature, especially of a Gnostic or Valentinian orientation, is the explanation of how to navigate one's way through demonic interrogation as one ascends to the higher spiritual realms after death (and perhaps in mystical experiences during the present life as well). Just as some Greeks thought it necessary to pay the ferryman Charon to take the dead across the rivers Styx and Acheron to Hades, similarly in Egypt it was thought that the 'Books of the Dead' would equip the dead person with the necessary spells to pass the respective doorkeepers to the afterlife. Apocryphal texts appear to be influenced in particular by Egyptian afterlife themes. Hence, the *Gospel of Thomas* (in logion 50) instructs the reader in how to answer questions about the disciple's true identity and place of origin, and much of the *Gospel of Mary* contains Jesus' explanation to Mary Magdalene of how her soul can overcome successive demonic obstacles. Egyptian myth is also influential in some texts' constructions of the heavenly world, as in the case of the 'Octads' or 'Ogdoads' in the Coptic *Gospel of Egyptians* (discussed further in the introduction to that text).

Not all apocryphal Gospels can be neatly sorted under a particular theological label. The *Gospel of Thomas* is, as far as we can tell, *sui generis*. Some have classified the *Gospel of Peter* as a 'Jewish-Christian' Gospel, but this is a problematic term, and the work is at the same time also highly *anti*-Jewish. The same Jewish-Christian label has also been applied to the *Gospel of the Hebrews* and the *Gospel of the Ebionites*, but they are both too fragmentary for us to be able to identify their theological profiles. (Some scholars also suppose the existence of a *Gospel of the Nazoreans* in addition to these two; others, whom I follow here, assume only two such 'Jewish Christian' Gospels.) Although we can come to some conclusions in assigning the apocryphal Gospels to different schools, there are, as always in ancient history, a number of loose ends.

CURRENT STUDY

In addition to theological analysis, a great deal of scholarly work on apocryphal writings is taken up with basic questions of when and where they were written, questions often very difficult to answer precisely. Many ancient books (like, for example, the canonical Gospels) refer to historical events and place-names, and these allusions can be helpful in determining the origins of a work. A good deal of the most significant apocrypha, however, contain precious little. The *Gospel of Thomas* probably refers to the finality of the destruction of the Jerusalem temple which some relate to the aftermath of the failed Jewish revolt by Simon bar Kokhba against the Romans of 132–135 CE, but in the case of the *Gospel of Philip* and the *Gospel of Judas* there are really no references to external events except those of the life of Jesus. The only place names employed in the Gospels of *Judas* and *Thomas*, for example, are 'Judaea' and 'the world'. The authors are almost all unknown. Only Marcion and Tatian can be identified clearly as authors of substantial apocryphal Gospels, and no scholar imagines that any of the apocryphal Gospels are really written by Thomas, Judas, Peter or Mary.

Many of these texts therefore can only be dated by a combination of factors. First, there is carbon dating, which can calculate the age of the papyrus on which the text is written. While a papyrus plant is alive, the proportion of carbon-14 to carbon-12 in it – as in all living things – is constant, but when it dies, the unstable carbon-14 decays. When a piece of a papyrus manuscript is tested, scientific analysis measures how much of the carbon-14 has decayed: because the rate of decay is known, the time elapsed since the papyrus' harvesting can be calculated. There are nevertheless a number of disadvantages to carbon dating. It destroys some of the papyrus. It is also very expensive, and therefore only a very small number of ancient manuscripts have been dated this way. Of the apocryphal Gospels, only the *Gospel of Judas* and the so-called *Gospel of Jesus' Wife* have been carbon dated. *Judas* was dated to

280 CE ± 60 years, and the *Jesus' Wife* papyrus was first dated, impossibly, to sometime between 404 BCE and 209 BCE because the sample was contaminated. (A subsequent carbon analysis was useful in establishing the date of the papyrus in the seventh or eighth centuries CE, but the dialect of Coptic in which the text was written was no longer in use by that time.) And, of course, carbon dating provides a time-frame only for the papyrus, not for the original composition.

The most effective way of dating a papyrus copy is by analysis of its handwriting. This has an important role, but is still fraught with difficulty. Coptic handwriting is difficult to date, as some copying styles can remain very constant over centuries. It is easier to establish the time-frame of Greek handwriting, but this cannot be fixed more securely than within a margin of about a century. Although the discipline is currently being set on a surer footing, scholars previously have come to wildly different conclusions about such matters. While one scholar dated the Oxyrhynchus fragments of the *Gospel of Thomas* to 100–150 CE, another considered 250–300 CE to be the best estimate.

Also very useful for dating an original composition are the literary relations between the text and other roughly contemporaneous writings. In the case of the *Gospel of Judas*, for example, were it not for Irenaeus' reference to it, we would only have the carbon dating to provide the latest possible date (i.e. *c.* 340 CE). Since Irenaeus refers to it in about 180 CE, we know that that is the upper limit before which it must have been written (the so-called *terminus ante quem*). We also know that the *Gospel of Judas* is familiar with the Gospel of Matthew, and probably also the book of Acts, which probably pushes the date of *Judas* out of the first century and into the second. This is confirmed by the presence of second-century Gnostic ideas like 'the aeon of Barbelo' and 'the Great Invisible Spirit'.

Debate continues, however, especially in the case of the *Gospel of Thomas*, which has received the most attention of all the apocrypha. Some have argued that *Thomas* is very early, perhaps even from roughly the same time as the canonical Gospels, and so might provide authentic new sayings of Jesus, or more original versions of sayings of Jesus known already from the canonical Gospels. This optimism has recently declined, as scholars have demonstrated now fairly conclusively that *Thomas* is a product of the second century and is already influenced by Matthew and Luke to a considerable degree.

Although scholars have been very sceptical of taking apocryphal Gospels as historical evidence for Jesus, there has been considerable interest in how such literature opens a window onto the times in the second and third centuries when much of it was composed. To take one example, we have always known that there was controversy in early Christianity about whether Jesus can really be classed as a human being. Statements as early as the New Testament Epistles of John (*c.* 80 CE) and the letters of Ignatius (*c.* 110 CE) strongly warn against those who take the view that Jesus did not really come in the flesh but – as Ignatius puts it – only appeared to do so. This side of the conversation is attested widely in the literature of the church fathers (and in the *Epistle of the Apostles* translated in this edition). With the discoveries of the late nineteenth century onwards, we now have the other side: texts like the *Gospel of Judas*, where Jesus refers to 'the man who carries him about', give voice to that other side. In other similar cases, we can identify clearly the differences between the two opposing viewpoints, or when one side has perhaps caricatured the other.

Scholars have also recently become more interested in what one author has labelled 'the second church', that is, Christianity in its popular forms, rather than as it is manifested in the literature of elite, educated theologians.[20] Some apocryphal Gospels probably reflect views or versions of Gospel stories assumed by ordinary Christians in antiquity even if such accounts were not approved of by church authorities. The doctrine of Mary's perpetual virginity is reflected in the widely popular *Protevangelium of James*, written in the late second century, but only became official Catholic dogma at the Synod of Milan in 390 CE. Similarly, the apocrypha contain a number of the legends especially surrounding Jesus' birth, early life, trial and the 'harrowing of hell' – the idea that Jesus at or after his crucifixion went down to the underworld to redeem those who had believed in him before his coming to earth. These legends appear particularly in works which were very widely distributed – this is true of both the infancy Gospels and the *Gospel of Nicodemus*, which was very influential in medieval Europe, being translated into various vernacular languages including Old English. This popular legendary material consists largely of orthodox material designed to supplement the contents of the canonical Gospels.

The significance of the more esoteric Gospels, by contrast, lies in the evidence it provides for the diversity of early Christianity. Marcionites, Valentinians and Gnostics are all represented by Gospels in the collection here, as is the movement whose lodestar was the *Gospel of Thomas*. The apocryphal Gospels are important evidence for the views of these fringe movements. In addition to the distinctive teachings which they set out, they also respond to orthodox positions, and thereby reciprocate the criticism they had received from church fathers like Irenaeus.

PRESENTATION OF THE TRANSLATIONS

It may be helpful for the reader to understand some of the choices that have been made in the process of translating the works included in this volume. There is no attempt here at a standardized form for the different works. Indeed, the opposite is the case. Unlike in previous translations of the apocryphal Gospels, the aim here has rather been to give a sense of the literary register of the original. Hence the Greek of the *Protevangelium of James* is 'Bible-ese', so I have sought to render it in an English which has the same biblical resonances. By contrast, the *Gospel of Truth* is a highly sophisticated work which is written in the form of a philosophical treatise, and so demands a different style of translation.

One particular difficulty in the translation of Coptic is that the antecedents or referents of pronouns like 'he'/'she' and 'him'/'her' are often rather underdetermined. This can lead to some confusion, especially in complex texts like the *Gospel of Truth*. Where I think it is clear what the pronoun refers to, I have tried to express this in the translation. Often, however, there is considerable ambiguity and so I have attempted to retain this ambiguity in the translation.

It will also be apparent that in some of the translations the text is interrupted with ellipses [. . .]. This indicates that the manuscript is fragmentary and has broken off at this point. The reader should therefore beware of logically linking material that is separated by a [. . .], because some of the intervals are short and some are rather long. Sometimes, as in the case of the rather fragmentary *Gospel of Philip*, the reader will encounter a string of lacunae, where all that can be divined in the text is some kind of continuity of theme. In other places, however, the hole in the papyrus is brief, and there is little doubt about how to fill the gap.

Finally, especially in the dialogue, the translation in particular departs from a 'literal' approach. Ancient works often present dialogue mechanically in a 'X said . . . Y said . . . X said . . . Y said . . .' structure. This is partly because ancient manuscripts generally had no punctuation or spaces between words, so there is no other way to indicate speech or a change of speaker. Modern English literature, of course, has quotation marks and line-breaks at its disposal, and the translation here makes use of these rather than reproducing woodenly the word 'said'. All centred headings, and chapter, verse and logion numbers are modern additions not parts of the ancient texts.

NOTES

1. At the end of the second century, in addition to Irenaeus himself in Gaul in the west, the four-Gospel collection is taken for granted by Tertullian in modern Tunisia, Clement of Alexandria in Egypt and in a list of New Testament books from Rome.
2. This Greek term was so iconic that it was also borrowed by Latin, Syriac and Coptic.
3. Christoph Markschies, *Christian Theology and Its Institutions in the Early Roman Empire*, translated by Wayne Coppins (BMSEC, Waco: Baylor University Press, 2015), 21.
4. See some examples listed in D. R. Cartlidge and J. K. Elliott, *Art and the Christian Apocrypha* (London: Routledge, 2001), 79–80.

5. Serapion of Antioch, quoted in Eusebius, *Ecclesiastical History* 6.12.6.

6. Jerome, *Letter to Laeta* 12.

7. Didymus, *Commentary on Ecclesiastes* 8.3–7.

8. Ambrose, *Exposition of the Gospel according to Luke*, 1.2 (*c.* 389 CE).

9. Eusebius, *Ecclesiastical History* 3.25.6–7.

10. *Gelasian Decree* 5.3.

11. Emmanuel Le Roy Ladurie, *Montaillou: The Promised Land of Error*, translated by Barbara Bray (New York: Vintage Books, 1978).

12. See further the introduction to the translation of the *Sophia of Jesus Christ*.

13. Thomas Aquinas, *Catena aurea on Matthew*, Preface.

14. Michael Neander, *Catechesis Martini Lutheri parua* ... (Basileae: Per Ioannem Oporinum, 1567).

15. Johann Albert Fabricius, *Codex apocryphus Novi Testamenti, collectus, castigatus* (Hamburg: Benjamin Schiller, 1703).

16. J. Rendel Harris, *A Popular Account of the Newly-recovered Gospel of St. Peter* (London: Hodder and Stoughton, 1893), vi.

17. B. P. Grenfell and A.S. Hunt, *The Oxyrhynchus Papyri: Part I* (London: Egypt Exploration Fund, 1898), vi.

18. B. P. Grenfell and A.S. Hunt, *The Oxyrhynchus Papyri: Part IV* (London: Egypt Exploration Fund, 1904), 1.

19. For the scholarly analysis, see *New Testament Studies* issue 61.3 (July 2015): https://www.cambridge.org/core/journals/new-testament-studies; for the exposé of the forger, see Ariel Sabar, *Veritas: A Harvard Professor, A Con Man, and the Gospel of Jesus's Wife* (New York: Doubleday, 2020).

20. Ramsay MacMullen, *The Second Church: Popular Christianity A.D. 200–400* (Atlanta: Society of Biblical Literature, 2009).

Further Reading

On the Manuscript Discoveries

Marvin Meyer, *The Gnostic Discoveries* (New York: Harper-Collins, 2005).
An account of the Nag Hammadi manuscript finds.
Peter Parsons, *The City of the Sharp-Nosed Fish: Greek Lives in Roman Egypt* (London: Weidenfeld and Nicolson, 2007).
A highly informative and brilliantly written account of the Oxyrhynchus discoveries.

Scholarly Introductions

Markus Bockmuehl, *Ancient Apocryphal Gospels* (Louisville, KY: Westminster/ John Knox, 2017).

Hans-Joachim Klauck, *The Apocryphal Gospels: An Introduction* (London: Bloomsbury, 2003).
Both very helpful handbooks to non-canonical Gospel literature. Bockmuehl's is slightly clearer and more up to date, with lengthy discussion and very helpful bibliography for each individual work.

Translations of Other Apocryphal Literature

J. Keith Elliott, *The Apocryphal New Testament: A Collection of Apocryphal Christian Literature in an English Translation* (Oxford: Oxford University Press, 2005).
Covers a wide range of apocryphal material, including

non-canonical epistles and apocalypses as well as a selection of Gospels.

J. Keith Elliott, *Synopsis of the Apocryphal Nativity and Infancy Narratives. Second Edition, Revised and Expanded* (Leiden: Brill, 2016).
A particularly helpful English translation of all the infancy material.

Marvin Meyer, ed., *The Nag Hammadi Scriptures* (San Francisco: HarperSanFrancisco, 2007).
The most useful translation of the Nag Hammadi material, containing very helpful introductions, as well as including the Gospel of Judas and the Gospel of Mary.

Original-Language Texts

Bart D. Ehrman and Zlatko Pleše, *The Apocryphal Gospels: Texts and Translations* (Oxford: Oxford University Press, 2012).
Especially useful for its inclusion of the original language with facing translations, although it has a preference for narrative and sayings material similar in form to the canonical Jesus tradition, excluding works such as the Gospel of Truth.

Lance Jenott, ed., *The Gospel of Judas: Coptic Text, Translation, and Historical Interpretation of 'the Betrayer's Gospel'* (STAC 64; Tübingen: Mohr Siebeck, 2011).
The Coptic text of the Gospel of Judas, critically edited, with notes.

James M. Robinson, ed., *The Coptic Gnostic Library* (Leiden: Brill, 2002).
Contains the apocryphal literature from Nag Hammadi (as well as the Gospel of Mary) in both Coptic and English.

Constantin von Tischendorf, ed., *Evangelia Apocrypha* (Leipzig: Mendelssohn,[2] 1876).
Editions of many of the legendary texts, freely available at www.archive.org

Symbols

[. . .]   Indicates a lacuna in the manuscript

[Jesus]   Indicates the probable lost text of a lacuna

[p. 1]   Original manuscript page number

*   Indicates an accompanying comment in 'Notes'

†   Indicates a term explained in 'Times, Measurements and Currencies' (pp. 419–420)

I

INFANCY GOSPELS

Jesus enlivens clay birds
St Martin's, Zillis, c. 1120

1 The Protevangelium of James

(late second century CE*)*

INTRODUCTION

The Church of Santa Maria Maggiore in Rome contains an image of Mary receiving the announcement of Jesus' coming while she is spinning scarlet thread for the veil of the temple. This motif, not a feature of the canonical Gospels, comes from the *Protevangelium of James'* depiction of Mary (*Prot.* 10). The *Protevangelium* was an immensely popular work in early and medieval Christianity. It survives in a great number of manuscripts and was translated into Latin, Coptic, Syriac, Armenian, Georgian, Ethiopic, Slavonic and Arabic. The *Protevangelium*'s contents were also incorporated into other infancy legends, which indirectly extended its influence further.

The modern title 'Protevangelium', or 'first Gospel', alludes to the fact that this book's dramatic setting is earlier than any of the events in the four canonical Gospels. This work goes all the way back to before Mary's own birth, and so the births of Jesus and John the Baptist are the climax, rather than the beginning, of the story. The 'of James' in the title is derived from the end of the text, where there is a note on the circumstances in which James is purported to have composed the book: James, as the brother of Jesus, could be imagined to know the family history.

The *Protevangelium* is a work of some literary and theological sophistication, and its main doctrinal interest lies in Mary's *post partum* virginity. James and the other brothers and sisters of Jesus must therefore be his older step-siblings, children from Joseph's previous marriage. The reference to Joseph's son pulling along the pregnant Mary's donkey (*Prot.* 17) is probably a reference to James. Its literary points of interest include a vivid narrative, with variation of form: besides the narration there are extended poetic sections (e.g. chs. 3, 6) and Joseph's peculiar vision (ch. 18). The *Protevangelium*'s account of Jesus' birth runs counter to our traditional ideas of Jesus' birth in a stable. Here in the *Protevangelium* Mary gives birth to Jesus in a cave (ch. 19), and places him in a manger there. Jesus was quite commonly believed in the early church to have been born in a cave: Justin Martyr, for example, in the middle of the second century also recounts a similar story. Nor does this picture contradict the New Testament, which mentions the manger but not a stable.

The *Protevangelium of James* can be divided roughly into four parts: (i) the birth and childhood of Mary (chs. 1–10); (ii) Mary's pregnancy and Joseph's crisis (chs. 11–16); (iii) the journey to Bethlehem and the birth of Jesus (chs. 17–21); and (iv) the concealment of John the Baptist and the murder of Zechariah (chs. 22–24). As noted, there is a coda at the end describing James' writing of the book (ch. 25). The *Protevangelium* probably dates to the latter part of the second century.

DRAMATIS PERSONAE

MARY *The mother of Jesus*
JOACHIM *Mary's father*
ANNA *Mary's mother*
JUTHINE *Anna's maidservant*
JAMES *Joseph's son, Mary's stepson*
JESUS
TWO MIDWIVES
SALOME *An acquaintance of the midwife*
ZECHARIAH *A priest*
ELIZABETH *Zechariah's wife, and a relative of Mary*
JOHN *John the Baptist, son of Zechariah and Elizabeth*
SAMUEL (I) *A priest*
HEROD *Herod the Great, King of the Jews*
SAMUEL (II) *Joseph's servant*

ANNAS *A scribe, a Jewish official*
MAGI *Astrologers from the east who come to see Jesus*
SCRIBES *Authoritative experts in Jewish Law*
ELDERS *The Sanhedrin, or Jewish ruling council*

TRANSLATION

The Birth of Mary. The Revelation of James.

1. Joachim's distress

In the *History of the Twelve Tribes*, there is mention of a very rich man named Joachim. He would offer his gifts twice over to the Lord, thinking, 'The gift of my surplus can go to all the people, and the forgiveness offering will go to the Lord to atone for my sins.'

The great day of the Lord's festival came, and the sons of Israel were offering their gifts. A man from the tribe of Reuben stood in front of Joachim. 'It is not lawful for you to be first to offer your gifts,' the man said, 'because you have not raised up any offspring in Israel.'

Joachim was deeply distressed, and consulted the accounts of the twelve tribes of the people, thinking, 'I will check the twelve tribes of Israel to see if I am the only one not to have raised up offspring in Israel.' So he searched, and he found that all the righteous had raised up offspring in Israel. (He also remembered that the Lord God gave the patriarch Abraham a son, Isaac, at the very end of his life.) Joachim was sorely grieved, and did not return to his wife. Instead, he took himself off into the wilderness, pitched his tent there and fasted for forty days and forty nights, thinking, 'I will not go back either for food or drink until the Lord my God visits me. Prayer will be my food and drink.'

2. Anna's grief

His wife Anna had been wailing twice over and lamenting twice over, thinking, 'One lamentation for my widowhood, and one lamentation for my childlessness.'

When the great day of the Lord's festival came, Juthine her maidservant spoke to her.

'How long must you demean yourself? The great day of the Lord has come, so you mustn't lament. Take this headband, which my mistress of work gave me. I cannot wear it, because I am your maidservant and it bears the royal seal.'

'Get away from me!' Anna said. 'I have not brought this on myself! It is the Lord God who has humbled me so deeply. Perhaps some shady character has given you this, and you have come to embroil me in your sin.'

'Why should I pray for you,' Juthine the maidservant said, 'since you haven't listened to what I've said? The Lord God has closed up your womb, so you cannot produce any fruit in Israel.'

Anna was sorely grieved. She took off her mourning clothes, washed her face and put on her bridal garments. And around the ninth hour,† she went down to her garden for a walk. Seeing a laurel-tree, she sat down under it, and after she had rested, she entreated the Lord.

'O God of my fathers, bless me and hear my prayer, just as you blessed Sarah's womb and gave her a son, Isaac.'

3. Anna's lamentation

Then Anna looked up to the sky and saw a sparrow's nest in the laurel-tree.

'Woe is me!' she thought to herself, lamenting within. 'Who gave birth to me? What kind of womb produced me? I was born to be a curse in the eyes of everyone and in the eyes of the sons of Israel! I have been insulted! I have been mocked! I have been excluded from the temple of the Lord my God!

'Woe is me! What do I resemble? Not the birds of heaven, because even the birds of heaven are fruitful in your sight, O Lord.

'Woe is me! What do I resemble? Not the brute beasts, because even the brute beasts are fruitful in your sight, O Lord.

'Woe is me! What do I resemble? Not the livestock of the soil, because even the livestock of the soil are fruitful in your sight, O Lord.

'Woe is me! What do I resemble? Not these waters, because even these placid waters ripple, and their fish bless you, O Lord.

'Woe is me! What do I resemble? Not this soil, because even this soil produces its fruit in season and blesses you, O Lord.'

4. The angels' promise to Anna and Joachim

Then an angel of the Lord came and stood next to her.

'Anna, Anna,' he said, 'the Lord God has listened to your prayer. You will be with child and will give birth, and your child will be spoken of the whole world over.'

'As surely as the Lord God lives,' Anna said, 'if I do indeed give birth to a boy or girl, I will offer the babe as a gift to the Lord my God, to be a servant to him all the days of the child's life.'

Just then, two angels came. 'Behold, Joachim your husband is coming with his flocks,' they said. For an angel of the Lord had come down to Joachim, saying, 'Joachim, Joachim, the Lord God has listened to your prayer. Come down from there. Behold, your wife Anna has conceived!'

Immediately Joachim went down and called his shepherds.

'Bring me ten ewes, spotless and without blemish. Those ten ewes will be for the Lord. And bring me twelve tender calves. Those twelve calves will be for the priests and the council of elders. And bring a hundred goats, and those one hundred goats will be for the whole people.'

When Joachim arrived with his flocks, Anna was standing by the gate. When she saw Joachim coming with his flocks, she immediately ran to him and threw her arms around him.

'Now I know that the Lord God has blessed me greatly!' she said, 'For the widow is no more a widow, the barren has conceived!' On that first day, Joachim refreshed himself at his house.

5. The birth of Mary

On the following day Joachim brought his gifts, thinking, 'If the Lord God forgives me, may the high priest's crown* make it known to me.'

As Joachim was offering his gifts, he gazed upon the high

priest's crown on his way to the altar of the Lord. When he saw
no sin in himself, he said, 'Now I know that the Lord has been
merciful to me, and that he has forgiven all my sins.' So he went
down from the temple of the Lord justified, and came home.

After about six full months, Anna gave birth in the seventh
month.

'Is it a boy or a girl?' Anna called out to the midwife.

'It's a girl!' said the midwife.

'My soul is magnified today!' Anna declared, and laid the
baby down.

When the time came, Anna cleaned herself up from her dis-
charges, put the baby to her breast and called her 'Mary'.

6. Mary's first year

Day by day, the child grew stronger. When she was six months
old, her mother laid her down on the ground to see if she could
stand up. She took seven steps on her way to her mother's breast,
and Anna gathered her up into her arms.

'As surely as the Lord my God lives,' she said, 'you will not
walk on this ground again until I have taken you to the temple
of the Lord.' Anna made Mary a sanctuary in her bedchamber,
and did not let her eat anything impure or unclean. Then she
called the undefiled daughters of the Hebrews, and they enter-
tained her.

On Mary's first birthday, Joachim organized a great banquet and invited the chief-priests, priests, scribes, the council
of elders and all the people of Israel.

Joachim presented the child to the priests, and they blessed
her.

'O God of our fathers,' they said, 'bless this child and grant
her a name of everlasting fame for all generations.'

And all the people said, 'Indeed! Amen!'

They then presented her to the chief-priests, and they blessed
her.

'O God of the high heavens,' they said, 'look kindly upon
this child and bless her with a supreme blessing that can never
be surpassed.'

Her mother gathered her up in the sanctuary of her bed-chamber, and put her to her breast. She then composed a hymn to the Lord God:

> I will sing a sacred song to the Lord my God,
> for he has visited me
> and removed my enemies' insults from me.
> The Lord my God has given me
> the fruit of his righteousness
> unique yet manifold before him.
> Who is to declare to the sons of Reuben
> that Anna is nursing a child?
> Hear, hear, O twelve tribes of Israel –
> that Anna is nursing a child!

Then she laid Mary down to rest in the sanctuary of her bed-chamber, and went out again and waited on the guests. When the dinner was over, the guests went home rejoicing, and glorified the God of Israel.

7. Mary taken to the temple

The girl grew over the ensuing months. When she was two, Joachim said, 'Let's take her up to the temple of the Lord, and fulfil the promise which we made, in case the Lord sends disaster upon us and our offering is not acceptable to him.'

'Let's wait for her third birthday,' Anna said, 'in case she misses her father or mother.'

'Fine,' said Joachim. 'Let's wait.'

When the child was three, Joachim said, 'Let's invite the undefiled daughters of the Hebrews and they can each have a lamp and stand with the lamps burning, in case Mary turns back and her heart is enticed away from the temple of the Lord.'

This they did until they arrived at the temple of the Lord. The priest welcomed her and kissed her. Then he blessed her. 'The Lord God has magnified your name for all generations. Through you in these last days, the Lord will reveal his redemption to the sons of Israel.'

Then he sat her down on the third step of the altar, and the

Lord God cast his grace upon her. She did a little dance, and the whole house of Israel adored her.

8. Mary reaches the age for marriage

Her parents went home amazed, praising and glorifying the Lord God, because the child had not turned back to them.

Now Mary lived in the temple of the Lord, and was cared for there like a dove. She received her food from an angel.

When she was twelve years old, the council of the priests met.

'Mary is now twelve years old, and is still living in the temple of the Lord,' they said. 'We must do something about her, or the sanctuary of the Lord our God may be defiled.'

The other priests said to the priest on duty, 'You stand at the Lord's altar. Go in and pray for her. We will do whatever the Lord God reveals to you.'

The high priest then went in and took the twelfth bell into the Holy of Holies* and prayed for her.

Then an angel of the Lord appeared.

'Zechariah, Zechariah,' he said. 'Go and assemble the widowers among the people and tell each of them to bring a staff. Then whichever of them receives a sign from the Lord will marry her.'

The criers went out all over the Judaean countryside, and the trumpet of the Lord sounded, and the widowers all rushed to rally round.

9. Joseph is selected to marry Mary

Joseph put his axe aside and went out to meet them. When all the widowers were assembled, they went off with their staffs to the priest. The priest took the staffs from them and went in to the temple and prayed. When he had finished praying, he took the staffs, went out and distributed them. But there was no sign on any of them. Joseph received the last staff, and just then a dove flew out of the staff and perched on Joseph's head.

'Joseph, Joseph,' the priest declared, 'you have drawn the lot to take the Lord's virgin into your care.'

'But I am an old man and have sons already,' Joseph objected. 'She's a young girl. I'll be the laughing-stock of the sons of Israel!'

'Joseph, fear the Lord your God, and remember what the Lord did to Dathan, Abiram and Korah, when the earth split in two and everyone there was swallowed up because of their defiance. So now, be afraid, Joseph! Otherwise this might happen in your house!'

Joseph was afraid, and took her into his care. 'Mary, I have taken you from the Lord's temple,' he said to her. 'I am leaving you now in my house, because I must go away to do some building work, and then I'll come back to you. May the Lord protect you.'

10. Mary's weaving for the temple curtain

It so happened that a council of the priests was taking place.

'Let us have a curtain made for the Lord's temple,' they said.

'Summon for me the undefiled virgins from the tribe of David,' ordered the high priest. The temple-servants therefore went off looking for them and found seven. The high priest also remembered that the girl Mary was from the tribe of David and undefiled before God. The temple-servants went off and brought her.

Then they took all the virgins into the Lord's temple.

'Draw lots here before me now,' the high priest said. 'This will decide who is to spin the gold, the amiantus, the flax, the silk and the blue, scarlet and deep-purple fabrics.' Now the lot for the deep purple and scarlet work fell to Mary, so she took the thread and went home. (At that time Zechariah had lost his speech, and so Samuel was acting in his place until Zechariah could talk again.) Mary took the scarlet thread and spun it.

11. The angel's annunciation to Mary

Later, as she was taking a jar outside to fill it with water, a voice addressed her.

'Greetings, you who are highly favoured! The Lord be with you. Blessed are you among women!'

Mary looked around on both sides to see from where the voice had come. Terrified, she went back into her house and put the jar down. She took up the purple thread, sat down on her chair and drew in the thread.

Just then, the angel stood before her.

'Do not be afraid, Mary! For you have found favour before the Lord of all. You will conceive by his Word.'

When she heard this, Mary was confused. 'Will I conceive through the Lord, the living God, in the same way that all women do?'

The angel stood by. 'No, Mary,' he said. 'For the power of God will overshadow you, and so the holy one conceived in you will be called the son of the Most High. You are to call him Jesus, for he will save his people from their sins.'

'I am the Lord's maidservant,' Mary said. 'May this happen to me just as you have said.'

12. Mary's visit to Elizabeth

When she had worked the purple and scarlet thread, she took them up to the high priest. Taking them from her, he blessed her.

'Mary,' he said, 'the Lord God has magnified your name, and you will be blessed in all the generations of the earth.'

Mary was delighted and went away to her relative Elizabeth. She knocked at the door, and when Elizabeth heard she put aside her scarlet thread, ran to the door and opened it for Mary and blessed her.

'How can it be that the mother of my Lord should come to me!' Elizabeth exclaimed. 'Just now the baby in me leaped up, and blessed you!'

Mary had forgotten the mysteries of which the angel Gabriel had spoken. She looked up into heaven.

'Who am I that all the women of the earth should bless me?' she asked.

She stayed with Elizabeth for three months, and day by day her belly grew.

Now Mary went back home, and, afraid, hid away from the

sons of Israel. She was sixteen years old when these mysterious things happened to her.

13. Joseph returns to find Mary pregnant

It happened that in her sixth month Joseph came back from his building work. He went into the house and discovered her obviously heavily pregnant. He struck his face, threw himself on to the sacking on the ground and wept bitterly.

'How can I bear to look towards the Lord God,' he said, 'and how can I pray for her? I received a virgin from the temple of the Lord God but have not looked after her. Who has ensnared me? Who has done this wicked thing in my house? Who has enticed this virgin away from me and defiled her? Is the story of Adam being repeated in my life? Adam was in worship at the hour for glorifying God when the serpent came and found Eve alone and deceived her and defiled her. And now the same thing has happened to me!'

Then Joseph got up from the sacking and called Mary.

'And you – when God has taken such trouble over you!' he complained. 'Why have you done this? Have you forgotten the Lord your God? Why have you degraded your soul so – you who were brought up at the Holy of Holies and fed by an angel?'

She wept bitterly. 'I am pure and haven't known a man.'

'Then where does this thing in your belly come from?'

'As surely as the Lord my God lives, I don't know how it got there.'

14. The angel's appearance to Joseph

Joseph was very much afraid. He left her alone, and wondered what he would do with her.

'If I cover up her sin,' he said to himself, 'I'll turn out to have opposed the Law of the Lord, but if I expose her before the sons of Israel, I am afraid that she may be carrying some kind of angelic child, and I'll end up handing over innocent blood to be executed. What shall I do with her? I know: I'll divorce her secretly.' Then he was overcome by sleep.

Just then, an angel of the Lord appeared to him in a dream.

'Do not be alarmed at this girl,' the angel said, 'for what is in her is from the Holy Spirit. She will bear you a son and you are to call him Jesus, for he will save his people from their sins.'

Joseph got up, and glorified the God of Israel who had shown such favour to him. He looked after the girl.

15. The high priest's accusation of Joseph and Mary

Then Annas the scribe visited him.

'Joseph, why have you not appeared in our assembly?'

'I am tired from travelling and have taken a day to rest.'

Annas turned aside and saw Mary, obviously pregnant. He rushed away to the high priest.

'That Joseph to whom you testified has committed a terrible sin.'

'What has he done?' asked the high priest.

'Joseph has defiled that virgin he received from the Lord's temple, cheated her out of her wedding celebrations and has not turned up among the sons of Israel.'

'Joseph?' the high priest asked. 'Has he really done this?'

'Send some temple-servants along, and you'll find the "virgin" obviously heavily pregnant.'

So off the temple-servants went, and found her just as Annas had said. They took her away to the temple, and stood her in the courtroom.

'Mary, what have you done?' the high priest asked her. 'Why have you degraded your soul like this? Have you forgotten the Lord your God? You, who were brought up at the Holy of Holies and fed by angels! You, who heard their hymns and danced before them! What have you done?'

She wept bitterly. 'As surely as the Lord God lives, I am pure in his sight and have not known a man.'

'Joseph, what have you done?' the high priest asked.

'As surely as the Lord my God lives, and his Messiah lives, and the Witness of the Truth lives,* I am innocent of doing anything with her,' Joseph replied.

'Do not bear false witness!' the high priest said. 'Tell the truth! You have cheated yourself out of your wedding celebrations and have not turned up to the assembly of the sons of Israel. You have not bowed your head before God's mighty hand for him to bless your descendants.'

Joseph fell silent.

16. The test of adultery

'Put away the virgin you received from the Lord's temple,' the high priest instructed.

Joseph was overcome with tears [. . .]

'I will give you both the water of the Lord's judgement to drink,'* the high priest said. 'Then he will reveal your sin before your very eyes.'

The high priest took them away. He gave Joseph the drink, and sent him off into the wilderness. He came back safe and sound. Then he gave the drink to the girl, and sent her off into the wilderness. She too came back safe and sound. All the people were astonished that no sin had been uncovered.

'If the Lord God has not revealed any sin of yours,' the high priest determined, 'then neither do I condemn you.' So he sent them away. Joseph took Mary back and went off home rejoicing, glorifying the God of Israel.

17. The family sets out for Bethlehem

Now an order came from the emperor Augustus to register everyone who was in Bethlehem in Judaea.

'Now I must register my sons,' Joseph considered. 'What shall I do with the girl? How do I register her? As my wife? No, I'd be too ashamed. As my daughter? No, the sons of Israel know she is not my daughter. Today, the Lord will do as he wills.'

Joseph saddled his donkey, and sat Mary down on it. His son pulled it along, and Samuel followed behind. When they were nearly at the third milestone,† Joseph turned and saw Mary looking grim-faced. 'Perhaps the baby is distressing her,' he thought.

Then again he turned round and saw her laughing.

'Mary,' he asked, 'what's going on? One minute I see you grim-faced and the next minute you're laughing!'

'Joseph,' she replied, 'it is because I see in my mind's eye two peoples, one weeping and beating its breast, and another laughing with joy.'

They came to the mid-point of their journey.

'Joseph,' Mary said to him, 'get me down off this donkey! The baby is pushing on me to come out!' So he got her down.

'Where can I take you and shelter you from indignity?' Joseph responded to her. 'We're in the middle of nowhere.'

18. Joseph's vision

He found a cave there and took her inside. He settled her with his sons, and went out to look for a Hebrew midwife in the country of Bethlehem.

'I, Joseph, have been walking without walking.
I looked up into the summit of heaven and saw it
    standing still,
and into the air and I saw it startled,
and the birds of the air quietened.
I looked out upon the earth and saw a bowl set down,
and workers reclining, their hands in the bowl.
Those who were eating were not eating,
and those who were lifting did not carry,
and those who were eating put nothing in their
    mouths.
All their faces were looking upward.
I saw sheep being herded about,
and then the sheep stood still.
The shepherd raised his hand to strike them,
but his hand stayed upraised.
And I looked upon the torrent of the river
and I saw kid-goats, their mouths to the water, but not
    drinking.

'Then suddenly everything was set back on its course.'

19. The birth of Jesus

'I saw a woman coming down from the hill country,' Joseph continued. ' "Where are you going?" she asked me.

' "I am looking for a Hebrew midwife," I replied.

' "Are you an Israelite?"

' "Yes."

' "And who is the woman giving birth in the cave?"

' "She is my betrothed."

' "Not your wife?"

' "Mary was brought up in the Lord's temple," I told her. "I drew her as a wife by lot. She is not my wife, but is pregnant by the Holy Spirit."

' "Really?" the midwife said.

' "Come and see." '

So she went with him. They were standing by the cave when a dark cloud enveloped it.

'My soul is magnified today,' the midwife said, 'because my eyes have seen wondrous things! Salvation has come to Israel!' Immediately the cloud withdrew from the cave, and a great light, unbearable to look at, shone inside the cave. Then the light softened little by little, until a baby appeared! He took the breast of his mother, Mary. The midwife gave a great shout.

'What a wonder today,' she said, 'that I have seen this extraordinary sight!'

The midwife went out of the cave and Salome met her.

'Salome, Salome,' the midwife said, 'I must tell you about this extraordinary thing that I have seen! A virgin has given birth – something impossible for her to do!'

'As surely as the Lord my God lives,' Salome swore, 'unless I insert my finger and examine her hymen, I will not believe that the virgin has given birth.'

20. The test of Mary's virginity

So the midwife went in and said, 'Mary, get dressed. A great argument has arisen about you.'

When Mary heard this, she got dressed. Salome came and placed her finger in Mary's hymen. Then Salome cried out.

'Woe to me for my sin and unbelief! I have tested the living God! And now my hand has been burned off me!'

Then Salome kneeled before the Lord.

'O God of my fathers,' she prayed, 'remember me, for I am a descendant of Abraham, Isaac and Jacob. Do not expose me to disgrace before the sons of Israel, but place me back among the poor labourers. For you know, O Lord, that I have accomplished healings in your name and have received my wages from you.'

Just then, the angel of the Lord stood by.

'Salome, Salome, the Lord of all has heard your prayer. Present your hand to the child and lift him up. Then he will bring you healing and joy.'

Now joyful, Salome approached the child and lifted him up.

'I will worship him because he is born king of Israel,' she declared. Immediately, Salome was healed and left the cave justified. Just then a voice sounded.

'Salome, Salome, do not announce these extraordinary things you have seen until the boy has gone to Jerusalem.'

21. The visit of the Magi

Then Joseph prepared to leave Judaea, and there was a great uproar in Bethlehem in Judaea. Some Magi had come. 'Where is the king of the Jews?' they inquired. 'We saw his star in the east and so have come to worship him.'

When Herod heard this, he was deeply disturbed and sent his servants to the Magi. He also sent for the chief-priests and questioned them in the Praetorium.*

'What is written in Scripture about the Christ? Where is he supposed to be born?' Herod asked.

'In Bethlehem in Judaea – that is what is written.'

Then he let them go. He also questioned the Magi. 'What sign of this new-born king did you see?'

'We saw a gigantic star shining among the other stars,' they replied. 'In fact, it made the other stars so dim that they did not shine at all. Hence, we knew that a king must have been born for Israel, so we have come to worship him.'

'Go and look for him,' said Herod, 'and if you find him do come and tell me, so that I can go and worship him as well.'

So off the Magi went. Just then the star which they had seen in the east led them into the cave, and then rested over the child's head. When the Magi saw the boy next to Mary his mother, they took out gifts of gold, frankincense and myrrh from their bags. Having been warned by an angel not to go into Judaea, however, they went back to their own country by a different route.

22. Herod's slaughter of the innocents

When Herod realized that he had been tricked by the Magi, he was furious, and dispatched his assassins with instructions to kill all children of two years of age and below. When Mary heard that children were being murdered, she was terrified, and so took her son, swaddled him and put him in a cows' manger. Elizabeth also heard that John was being searched for, so she took him and went up into the hill country. She looked around for somewhere to hide him, but there was no concealed spot. Elizabeth was very upset.

'Mountain of God,' she pleaded, 'receive this mother and her child!' (Elizabeth was too frightened to climb up the mountain.) Immediately, the mountain split in two and received her. It also appeared translucent to her, for the angel of the Lord was with them, protecting them.

23. The murder of Zechariah

Herod continued looking for John, however, and dispatched those who served at the altar to inquire of Zechariah.

'Where have you hidden your son?' they asked.

'I am a servant of God and attend his altar!' Zechariah replied. 'How should I know where my son is!'

The altar-servants went off, then, and reported all this to Herod, who was furious.

'To think that his son could be king of Israel!' he exclaimed.

Herod sent the altar-servants back again with the message: 'Tell me the truth. Where is your son? You know that your life is in my hands.' They went off and reported the message to Zechariah.

'I am a martyr for God,' Zechariah replied. 'Take my life. The Lord will receive my spirit because you are to shed innocent blood by the entrance to the Lord's temple.' So Zechariah was killed at daybreak, but the sons of Israel did not know that he had been killed.

24. The lament for Zechariah

At the hour for salutation, the priests went out but were not greeted with Zechariah's customary blessing. The priests therefore stood waiting for Zechariah to greet them with a prayer and to glorify the Most High God.

Because of his delay, the priests were all afraid. One of them ventured to go into the sanctuary. He saw blood congealed by the altar of the Lord, and heard a voice.

'Zechariah has been murdered, and his blood will not be wiped away until his avenger comes.'

When the priest heard this, he was terrified, and went out and reported to the other priests what he had seen and heard. Then they all ventured in and saw what had happened. The ceilings of the temple cried out, and the priests tore their clothes from top to bottom. They did not find Zechariah's body, but discovered his blood frozen solid. Terrified, they left and announced that Zechariah had been murdered. When all the tribes of Israel heard this, they lamented him and mourned for three days and three nights. After three days, the priests took counsel about who would take Zechariah's place. The lot fell to Simeon, for he it was who had received an oracle from the Holy Spirit that he would not see death until he had seen the Messiah in the flesh.

25. Author's note

I, James, wrote down this account in Jerusalem, when the great tumult occurred at the death of Herod. I took myself off into the wilderness until the tumult in Jerusalem had died down. I will glorify the Lord who has given me the wisdom to write down this account. Grace be to all who fear the Lord. Amen.

The Birth of Mary. The Revelation of James

2 The Birth of Mary

(c. third century CE*)*

INTRODUCTION

The Gnostics were a group of related sects who, amongst other practices, frequently rewrote passages of the Bible to bring them into line with their own thinking. In this Gnostic text about Mary's birth (or, possibly, Mary's act of childbearing) the figure in the Jerusalem temple, who was worshipped by the Israelites, is described as a human figure with the form of a donkey. Moses (the 'lawgiver') had according to the Bible seen part of God, and hence according to the Gnostics knew the true identity of the deity in the temple. Moses therefore made provision for priests to carry bells into the temple so that the divine donkey would be warned and would be able to hide so that his identity would not be revealed. In contrast to the *Protevangelium of James*, then, this text shows how some groups developed apocryphal tales which were intended to contradict, rather than complement, conventional Gospel narratives.

This fragment is quoted – or paraphrased – by Epiphanius, bishop of Salamis in Cyprus in the late fourth century CE. Along with the Greek *Gospel of Philip*, the *Gospel of Eve* and the *Greater Questions of Mary* (see pp. 172–177 below), Epiphanius cites this work in his discussion of the Gnostics who produced these books. The snippet cited here does not actually deal with the birth of Mary itself, but is a story about the death of Zechariah, the father of John the Baptist, as he was officiating in the temple. The tale is probably based in part on the accounts of the temple service of Zechariah (John the Baptist's father) in Luke's Gospel, and the description of his murder in the

Protevangelium of James (see pp. 19–20 above). Additionally, however, it has a pronounced anti-Jewish slant. The text picks up the common pagan taunt against Jews (and Christians) that their god was a donkey and they were ass-worshippers; this is therefore an example of a Gnostic text incorporating established anti-Christian motifs. This text also gives an explanation, albeit a strange one, of the prescription in Jewish law (Exodus 28:35) that the priest must wear bells when he goes in and out of the sanctuary. Gnostics existed from the second century up to when Epiphanius was writing (the 370s CE), and so the *Childbearing of Mary* could have originated at any point in this time frame. It probably postdates the account of Zechariah's death in the *Protevangelium of James* in the late second century.

TRANSLATION

Zechariah was killed in the temple, since he saw a vision. He wanted to describe the vision, but his mouth was stopped out of fear. For at the hour of incense, as he was burning the incense, he saw a man standing there who had the form of a donkey. When Zechariah came out, he wanted to say, 'Woe to you! What are you worshipping!' But the figure who had appeared to him inside the temple stopped Zechariah's mouth so he could not speak. When his mouth opened again and he could speak, he disclosed the vision to them and they killed him. That is how Zechariah died. The reason the priest was commanded by the lawgiver himself to wear bells was so that, when the priest went inside to officiate, the object of the worship would hear the ringing and hide. Then the visible appearance of his form would not be discovered.

3 Cairo Papyrus 10735

(second or third century CE?)

INTRODUCTION

Most of the 'Gospel fragments' translated in this book contain sayings or actions of Jesus from his adult ministry, so it is unusual to find a manuscript leaf about Jesus' infancy. The present fragment is a single papyrus scrap of about 5cm × 6cm kept in the Museum of Egyptian Antiquities in Cairo, and preserves references to the flight of Joseph, Mary and Jesus to Egypt, and to the conception of John the Baptist. These two episodes come from Matthew's and Luke's Gospels respectively. Fragments such as this Cairo papyrus illustrate how difficult it can be to identify where a small piece of text like this might have originally belonged: it may have come from a homily or commentary or early Christian treatise. Alternatively, it may derive from either a free-standing apocryphal Gospel or a kind of harmony of the canonical Gospels. The fragment of this copy dates from around the sixth century CE, but it is difficult to tell when the original work might have been composed.

TRANSLATION

The conception of John the Baptist

[p. 1] [. . .] 'Let him interpret it for you.' The [. . .] said to the virgin, 'Behold [Elizabeth] your relative [has also conceived] and it is her [. . .] month [. . .].' In the sixth month, that is, [. . .], she conceived John. [. . .] the chief of the angelic host [. . .] 'servant, who is to go ahead of the coming of [the Lord . . .]'.

The flight to Egypt

[p. 2] [. . .] The angel of the Lord said, 'Joseph, [get up], take Mary [your] wife and flee to Egypt [. . .] every gift and if [. . .] his friends [. . .] of the king.' [. . .]

4 The Apocryphal Book of Seth on the Magi

(originally third century CE*?)*

INTRODUCTION

The account of the book of Seth translated below is a Latin summary of a legend which survives in a fuller version in Syriac (too long to be translated here). The summary is contained in the so-called *Incomplete Commentary on the Gospel of Matthew*, and the author of that commentary already implies that he is paraphrasing the story as part of his interpretation of the Magi episode in Matthew's Gospel. This is confirmed by the fact that some details do not really make sense without the larger narrative. There is no explanation of authorship by Seth, one of the sons of Adam; in the longer version we discover that Adam revealed the truth about the coming of the star to Seth, who undertook to preserve it for the Magi in the future. Similarly, the abbreviated form below implies that the cave in the mountain is significant, but it is only in the longer version that we find that the cave contained the secret book written by Seth, as well as the ancient treasures which the Magi were to take to Christ.

There are various surprising details in this summary, which well illustrates the way in which a brief reference in a canonical Gospel narrative can be elaborately expanded into a tale in its own right. There are twelve Magi, rather than the traditional three. (This is still consistent with the account in Matthew, however, which has the three gifts of gold, frankincense and myrrh, but no statement that there were only three wise men.) The Magi also come not just from the east, but from the extreme far east, on the edge of the world (called the land of 'Shir', according to the full version). This motif has parallels elsewhere in Christian literature from late antiquity. One apocalypse recounts the legend of Noah's fourth son Yonton, who goes to the east by the sea and receives revelations of astronomical lore; he then instructs the biblical figure of Nimrod in this knowledge. In another book, *The Cave of Treasures*, the revelation entrusted to Nimrod is what eventually led the Magi to Bethlehem.

The full version of the story is preserved in a Syriac chronicle from the eighth century, but that longer story probably goes back in substantially the same form to an earlier period, perhaps the third century. The commentary on Matthew noted earlier, in which this summary appears, was written in the fifth century.

TRANSLATION

The Apocryphal Book of Seth: The Victorious Mountain

I have heard some refer to a book which, even if not verified, is far from destructive of faith but actually delightful.

There was once a tribe which lived right on the boundary of the east next to the Great Ocean. Among them circulated a book attributed in its title to Seth, which was held to have been passed down from father to son through generations of scholarly men. It dealt with the star which was to appear, and the kinds of gifts which were to be offered to it. They chose from their own number twelve of the most learned scholars, devotees of the heavenly mysteries, and appointed them to wait for that star. If any of the twelve died, his son or another of his relatives who was found to be equally willing was appointed in the place of the deceased. They were called in their own language 'Magi', because they would worship God in silence, saying nothing at all. Year by year, after the month of the harvest and threshing, therefore, they would go up onto a mountain there which in their language was called 'Victorious Mountain', which contained a cave in the rock and was most delightfully furnished with fountains and choicest trees. When they had gone up onto the mountain and purified themselves, they prayed and praised God in silence for three days, and this they did generation after generation, always on the lookout in case it was perhaps in their own generation that that star of blessing should arise. When it did at last appear to them, it descended atop that Victorious Mountain, containing within it a form of a little boy and above it the likeness of a cross. It spoke to them, teaching and commanding them to set out for Judaea. The star went ahead of them on their journey for two years, and their bags were never empty of either food or drink. The other events described by them are briefly covered in the Gospel. However, when they returned, they continued to worship and glorify God even more zealously than before, and they preached to everyone of their own race, instructing a good many of them. Finally, after the resurrection of the Lord, the apostle Thomas went to their region. They joined him, were baptized by him and became supporters of his preaching.

5 The Infancy Gospel of Thomas

(second century CE)

INTRODUCTION

Rather than being a long-lost apocryphal work only rediscovered in modern times, the *Infancy Gospel of Thomas* has been known more or less continuously through church history, and has been widely distributed in a number of languages. It therefore provides evidence for the category of books which were not canonical, but appreciatively regarded as supplementary to Scripture. It survives in a host of manuscripts copied up to the advent of printing and beyond, both in its original Greek and in translation in Latin, Syriac, Slavonic, Arabic, Georgian and Ethiopic. One of its most famous episodes, in which the five-year-old Jesus makes live birds out of clay, also survives in the Qur'an (*IGT* 2/ Qur'an 3.49; 5.110).

The contents are easily described: as the headings added to the translation indicate, the scenes are often located when Jesus is a particular age (five, seven, eight and twelve). The action is primarily miraculous: Jesus makes live sparrows out of clay, strikes people dead with a curse, as well as healing and raising boys back to life again. There are also controversies with Jewish authorities, and charming scenes of Jesus at school. (He fails to fit in.) The work ends with Jesus in the temple aged twelve. This final scene overlaps with an almost identically described scene near the beginning of Luke's Gospel (Lk. 2:41–52), and the implication is that the *finale* leads the reader into Luke, which picks up the story where the *Infancy Gospel* has left off. Unlike some apocryphal Gospels which seek to supplant the canonical Gospels (such as the *Gospel of Judas*), the *Infancy*

Gospel was almost certainly intended to complement conventional accounts such as Luke.

Despite its straightforward contents and lack of complex theology, what has often puzzled scholars is *why* the work was written. Like a number of apocryphal texts, it fills in gaps left open in the canonical accounts of Jesus. But why simply focus on scenes of Jesus aged five, seven, eight and twelve? There may be a theological agenda in arguing that Jesus had his divine power in childhood, given that some heretics on the fringes of the early church argued that Jesus was only given the Holy Spirit or adopted as the Son of God at his adult baptism. There is little evidence of polemic in the book, however. Some have even argued that the *Infancy Gospel* was written to provide edifying and entertaining reading material for Christian children.

The *Infancy Gospel* does not have an extensive description of the nature of Jesus, but there are hints. In addition to Jesus' miraculous powers, there is a strong emphasis on his sublime wisdom, which he uses to confound his teachers. His analysis of the Greek letter 'A' (which looks the same as an English capital A) is one example. Here Jesus invites the teacher to 'notice here how it has diagonal lines and a stroke in the middle, and then you can see the *alpha*'s lines pointing and straddling, joining together and parting, leading off and going up, circling and darting, tripartite and double-edged, of similar shape and thickness and kind, rectilinear, equilibrious, isometric and isomeric' (*IGT* 6)! The other characters wonder who he is: when he is expelled from his first school, his teacher ponders whether Jesus is 'a god or an angel or, well, I have no idea what' (*IGT* 7). Jesus himself declares the truth that he existed before the creation of the world (*IGT* 6).

The early references to scenes of the *Infancy Gospel* in ancient Christian literature, and the text's knowledge of Luke's Gospel, point to a date in the second century.

DRAMATIS PERSONAE

JESUS
THOMAS *A disciple of Jesus*
JOSEPH *Jesus' father*
MARY *Jesus' mother*
JAMES *Jesus' brother*
ANNAS *The Jewish high priest*
ANNAS' SON
ZACCHAEUS *Jesus' first schoolteacher*
ZENO *A friend of Jesus*
SCRIBES *Authoritative experts in Jewish Law*
PHARISEES *An influential, elite Jewish movement*

TRANSLATION

1. Prologue

I, Thomas the Israelite, have considered it my duty to recount to all the gentile brethren the deeds of our Lord Jesus Christ who was born in our land of Bethlehem in the village of Nazareth. This is how it all began.

2. Jesus as a five-year-old

On one occasion when Jesus was a five-year-old child, he was playing at a ford across a fast-flowing stream after it had been raining. He stirred up the dirty water, collected it together into pools and made them clear and pure – by the simple expedient of a word: he exerted no force on the water. He then took some soft clay out of the mud and from it made twelve model sparrows. It was the Sabbath when he did these things, and a number of other children were with him. Now a Jew had seen Jesus doing all this with the other children, and went to Joseph, Jesus' father. He accused the child Jesus of making clay and moulding the twelve sparrows on the Sabbath, actions which were not lawful.

So Joseph went to him and reprimanded him. 'Why are you doing this when it's the Sabbath?'

Jesus clapped his hands, and the birds flew up in front of everyone. 'Go and take flight like real birds!' he shouted. Then the sparrows, flying away, went off with a squawk. The Pharisee saw this and was amazed, and told all his associates about it.

3. Jesus curses the high priest's son

The son of Annas the high priest asked Jesus, 'Why are you doing this on the Sabbath?' The boy took a branch of a willow tree and emptied out the pools. Draining the water which Jesus had collected together, he made the puddles dry.

When Jesus saw what he had done, he said, 'Rootless shall your fruit be, and dry shall be your shoots, like a branch scorched by a violent wind.' And immediately the boy was paralysed.

4. Jesus strikes a boy dead

From there he went off with his father Joseph. [Suddenly a boy came] running, and bumped into Jesus' shoulder.

'Cursed be the soul that guides you,' Jesus said. And immediately the boy died.

As soon as the people saw that the boy had died, they shouted, 'Where has this boy whose words perform miracles come from?'

When the dead child's parents saw what had happened, they complained to Joseph, Jesus' father.

'Wherever you got this child, you can't live in this village with us any more. Or if you do want to stay, teach him to pronounce blessings rather than curses! We have lost our son!'

5. Jesus and true wisdom

'Why do you say these terrible things?' Joseph demanded of Jesus. 'These people are suffering, and they hate us!'

'If you knew where wise speech came from,' the boy replied to Joseph, 'you wouldn't be ignorant in what you say. [. . .] Their words will not amount to anything, and these people will receive

their just deserts.' Immediately those who had hurled accusations against him were blinded. Joseph grabbed Jesus by the ear,
and pulled tufts of his hair out.

'May you be satisfied with looking for me and finding me,'
Jesus told him. 'Don't go too far by grabbing me and injuring
me – in your brute ignorance. You don't see clearly how I am
yours. You know you shouldn't harm me, because I belong to
you and have been delivered over to you.'

6. Jesus goes to school

Now a teacher named Zacchaeus was standing by and heard
Jesus saying this to his father Joseph. Dumbfounded, he said to
Joseph, 'Look here, brother – entrust him to me so he can be
taught to read and write, and study all the fields of knowledge.
And he'll also learn to rub along with other boys, to give honour to old age, and to respect his elders. Then he'll come to
have affection for the boys and in turn teach them.'

'But who can keep him under control, and actually teach the
boy?' Joseph said to the teacher. 'You mustn't just think of him
as some sweet little chap.'

'Entrust him to me, brother,' the teacher said, 'and don't
worry yourself over him.'

Jesus looked at them and said to Zacchaeus, 'You were born
good-natured, as a teacher, but you are really a stranger to that
title. I am from beyond where you all are, and from within you
because of my fleshly dignity. You may be a teacher of the Law
but you don't know the Law.' And to Joseph, he said, 'When
you were born, I already existed. I was standing by you so that
as a father you could be taught by me with the learning that
no-one else knows and no-one else can teach. Then you would
bear the saving name!'

At this, the Jews shouted out. 'What a novel, extraordinary
sight!' they exclaimed. 'This child is only about five years old,
and what amazing declarations he makes! We've never known
anyone to come up with such proclamations as this boy does,
not even a teacher of the Law or a Pharisee.'

In reply, the child said to them, 'Why are you so amazed?

Why can't you believe what I say to you? The truth is that when you were born – and the same goes for your parents and grandparents – why, I knew all about what already existed before the creation of the world!'

When they all heard this, they were silenced, and could not think of anything else to say to him. He went up to them and skipped. 'I was having a joke at your expense because I know how small-minded and impressed with trivialities you are!'

When therefore they appeared to be consoled by this reassurance from the child, the teacher said to the boy's father, 'Come on – bring the boy to school, and I'll teach him how to read and write.' Joseph duly seized the boy by the hand and took him off to school. The teacher jollied him along and took him into the classroom. Zacchaeus wrote down the alphabet for him, and started him on his elementary education. He said the same letter a number of times, but Jesus would not give any response. The teacher was peeved, and clipped him round the ear.

The boy was irritated at this. 'I should be teaching you, rather than being taught by you! After all, I know the letters you're teaching much better than you do. What you're giving me is like sounding brass and a clanging cymbal, producing neither sound nor thought nor any possible understanding!' When the child's anger abated, he spoke by himself all the letters, from *alpha* to *omega*, perfectly. He looked the teacher square in the eye.

'If you don't know the essence of the *alpha*,' Jesus said, 'how can you teach *beta* after it? You hypocrite! If you're so clever, first teach me *alpha*, and then I'll believe you when you talk about *beta*.' Then he started questioning his teacher about the letter *alpha*, but the man did not know what to say in reply.

A number of people were there listening in. 'Pay attention, sir,' Jesus explained to the teacher, 'and understand the arrangement of the first letter. Notice here how it has diagonal lines and a stroke in the middle, and then you can see the *alpha*'s lines pointing and straddling, joining together and parting, leading off and going up, circling and darting, tripartite and double-edged, of similar shape and thickness and kind, rectilinear, equilibrious, isometric and isomeric.'

7. Jesus' teacher put to shame

When the teacher heard this description from Jesus of the particular lines of the first letter, he was bamboozled by such teaching and explanation.

'Oh my goodness, my goodness,' the teacher said, 'I am a befuddled wreck of a man! I've brought nothing but shame on myself in taking on this pupil! Brother Joseph, get him away from me. I can't bear that gimlet eye of his or his pellucid speech. This child is simply not of this world! He can even control fire. Perhaps the boy really did exist before the creation of the world! What belly could have conceived him or what sort of womb could have brought him to birth I have no idea. My goodness, brother, he makes no sense to me. I can't follow it in my mind. I have been fooling myself, thrice-wretched that I am! I thought I had a pupil but have discovered I have a teacher!

'My friends, the shame of it! To think that I, an old man, should be beaten by a child! I must now retire and die, or leave this village – and all because of this child! I can't face the world any more, especially those who saw me defeated by this shrimp of a boy. How could I explain to anyone what he passed on to me about the lines of the first letter? I really am ignorant, my friends. I don't know the beginning or the end.

'So, brother Joseph, take him back home safe and sound. The child is some sort of great prodigy – a god or an angel or, well, I have no idea what.'

8. The salvation of those cursed by Jesus

The boy Jesus laughed. 'Now then, it is time for the barren to bear fruit, for the blind to see and for you who are stupid to think straight. For I have come from above to rescue those below and summon them upwards, just as the one who sent me to you instructed me.'

Immediately all those who had fallen under Jesus' curse were cured. No one dared to provoke him after that.

9. Jesus and Zeno

On another occasion, some time afterwards, Jesus was playing with some other boys up on a high roof. One of the boys fell off the roof and died. When they saw this, the other children went back to their houses and left Jesus behind on his own. Then the parents of the dead child came and accused Jesus.

'You pushed our son off the roof!'

'I did no such thing,' Jesus said.

While they were ranting and raving, Jesus climbed down off the roof and stood by the corpse. With a great shout, he cried out, 'Zeno, Zeno' – that was the dead boy's name – 'stand up and tell everyone whether I pushed you off.'

Zeno got up. 'No, you didn't, Lord.' When they saw this, they were astounded.

Then Jesus spoke to him again. 'Now go back to sleep.' The child's parents glorified God and worshipped the boy Jesus.

10. Jesus as a seven-year-old

When Jesus was about seven years old, he was sent off by Mary his mother to fetch water. A great crowd was by the water-hole, and Jesus' jar was knocked over and broke. He unfolded the cloak he was wearing, filled it with water and took it to his mother. When Mary saw this miracle that he had performed, she kissed him.

'O Lord, my God,' she said, 'bless this child of ours.' (They were afraid that someone might cast a spell on him.)

11. Jesus and the miraculous harvest

In the sowing season, while Joseph was sowing, Jesus joined him and sowed a *kor*† of wheat. When it came to harvest time, his father reaped 100 *kors*! Most of it Joseph gave to the poor and the orphans, and only took a portion from what Jesus had sown.

12. Jesus as an eight-year-old

When Jesus was about eight years old, his father, who was a carpenter, was working on some ploughs and yokes. He took a pallet from a rich man to extend it considerably and make it serviceable. One side was shorter than the other, and not the right length. Joseph was worried and did not know what to do, when the child came up to him. 'Put down the two planks of wood,' Jesus said, 'and square them up on your side.'

Joseph did as Jesus had told him. The boy stood on the other side and held the short plank. He stretched it, making it make it the same length as the other plank!

'Don't worry, now you can make it the way you want it,' he said to his father.

Joseph hugged him and kissed him. 'I am so blessed to have been given such a child by God!' he said.

13. Jesus goes to another school

When Joseph saw the wisdom and intelligence of the boy, he decided he did not want him to be illiterate, so he passed him on to another teacher. The teacher wrote down the alphabet for him and said, 'Say *"alpha"*.'

'You tell me first what *beta* is,' the boy said, 'and then I'll tell you what *alpha* is.' The teacher, irritated, beat him. Then Jesus put a curse on him, and the teacher fell down dead. The boy went off home to his parents. Joseph called the boy's mother and instructed her not to let him out of the house in case people who provoked him ended up dead.

14. Jesus at yet another school

A few days later, still another teacher said to Jesus' father Joseph, 'Come now, brother, entrust him to me at my school and I'll be able to sweet-talk him into learning how to read and write.'

'If you're up to it, brother,' Joseph said, 'by all means take him.'

The teacher therefore took the boy from him and went off, though with some fear and trepidation. The boy went along

happily. When he came into the classroom, he found a scroll rest-
ing on the reading desk. He took it but did not read what was
written in it because it was not from the Law of God. Instead, he
opened his mouth and made such awe-inspiring statements that
the teacher sitting opposite him listened to him with pure delight,
and urged him on to say more, while the crowd standing by was
staggered by the holy matters of which Jesus spoke.

Joseph quickly ran along to the classroom, suspecting that
the teacher was now well aware of Jesus, and struggling. 'Please
be aware, brother,' the teacher said to Joseph, 'that though I
took on your son as a pupil, he is full of great charm and wisdom. Go in peace, brother, and take him home.'

Jesus said to the teacher, 'Since you have spoken well and
testified accurately, because of you the teacher who was struck
down will be cured.' Immediately that other teacher was cured.
Joseph took the child home.

15. Jesus in the forest

James went off to a wood so he could tie up some firewood for
baking bread. Jesus went with him. While they were collecting
the sticks, a vicious viper bit James on the hand. As he was
stretched out on the ground and lay dying, the boy Jesus ran
over to James and blew down onto the bite, and it was immediately healed. The creature was killed, and James was cured.

16. Jesus heals a boy's foot

Again, on another occasion, while a young boy was chopping
logs into equal lengths, he chopped the bottom of his foot, lost
a lot of blood and died. There was a great commotion and
Jesus ran to the scene. Fighting his way through the crowd, he
grasped the injured foot and it was immediately healed.

'Now get back to your wood-chopping!' Jesus said to the
other boy.

When the crowd saw this, they were astonished. 'He has
saved a number of souls from death and can save people every
day of his life!'

17. Jesus as a twelve-year-old

When Jesus was twelve years old, his parents travelled to Jerusalem for the Passover* festival, as was their custom. While they were on their way back, Jesus stayed behind in Jerusalem without his parents realizing. Thinking that he was with them in the travelling party, they journeyed for a day and then looked for him among their friends and relatives. When they could not find him, they went back to Jerusalem to look for him. After three days they found him in the temple sitting amongst the teachers, listening to them and asking them questions. People listening to him were astonished at the way he was questioning the elders and explaining the main points of the Law and the difficult passages and parables in the Prophets.

His mother, though, said to him, 'Boy, how can you treat us this way? We have been worried to death looking for you!'

'Why have you been looking for me?' Jesus asked. 'Don't you realize that I had to be about my Father's business?'

The scribes and the Pharisees asked Mary, 'Are you the mother of this boy?'

'Yes.'

'Blessed are you,' they said to her, 'for the Lord God has blessed the fruit of your womb. We have never seen or heard such praiseworthy wisdom or virtuous thinking!'

Jesus got up from where he was and followed his mother, and was submissive to his parents. Mary kept all this stored up in her mind, and Jesus grew in wisdom, stature and grace before God and men.

To him be the glory!

6 Justin's Account of Baruch's Appearance to Jesus

(C. 150–200 CE)

INTRODUCTION

The extract below is cited by an anonymous church father in his attack on a second-century Gnostic teacher called Justin. The passage begins when Jesus is twelve years old. This is the point in time where the *Infancy Gospel of Thomas* breaks off (see p. 39 above), as well as where the account of Jesus as a child in Luke's Gospel stops. Justin's story is very different from these more conventional versions, however, and is cast in the form of mythic allegory rather than as biography.

In Justin's Gnostic philosophical system, there are three principles: the Good, 'Elohim' the Father, and the girl 'Eden'. Here, Justin is engaging in a kind of allegorical and mythological interpretation of Genesis. 'Elohim' is the word for 'God' in the Hebrew Bible, with 'Eden' obviously being a personification of the Garden. As in Plato, the supreme principle is 'the Good'; then comes Elohim, which is a lower but still positive spiritual principle; last of all is 'Eden', representing matter, which in Gnostic systems is invariably negative. Elohim and the girl Eden unite, but Elohim then ascends upwards and abandons her; since she contains the world, the ascent of Elohim means that he thereby abandons the world and deprives it of goodness. This ascent, therefore, explains the origin of evil, through Eden being left alone. Eden, distraught, gives the serpent-demon Nahash the authority to punish the spirit of Elohim, which has been left in human beings.

Elohim then embarks on a plan to save this spirit, by sending his angel Baruch in a series of different forms. Baruch first appears in Paradise in the guise of the tree of life, but Nahash seduces Eve so she cannot be saved. Baruch then comes to Moses, but Nahash also deceives Moses, and the same happens again with all the Israelite prophets – as well as with Hercules, who is co-opted into the story. Finally, Elohim sends Jesus, who is able to save the spirit through his crucifixion. Justin's presentation of Jesus illustrates a striking freedom from the established story. Here Jesus is not an artisan but a shepherd. Justin knows the canonical Gospels, but freely allegorizes them. Originally, in Jesus' words to Mary from the cross, 'Woman, behold your son', he was entrusting John to Mary (Jn 19:26); Justin interprets the verse philosophically, as Jesus giving back his material body to the female material principle, Eden. In doing this, he parallels an intellectual tradition in which Greek philosophers interpreted Homer's epics, the *Iliad* and the *Odyssey*, in allegorical terms. Justin probably wrote the *Book of Baruch*, from which this extract comes, between around 150 and 200 CE.

TRANSLATION

Finally, in the days of King Herod, Baruch was sent, dispatched again by Elohim. He came to Nazareth and found Jesus, the son of Joseph and Mary, a twelve-year-old boy, grazing his sheep. Baruch declared to Jesus everything that had happened since the beginning, from Eden and Elohim and thereafter.

'All the prophets before you were seduced,' Baruch said. 'Endeavour not to be seduced, then, Jesus son of man. Preach this word to people and declare to them the truth about the Father and about the Good. Then ascend to the Good, and be seated there with Elohim, the Father of us all.'

Jesus obeyed the angel. 'Lord, I will do this,' he replied. He therefore went about preaching. Nahash wanted to seduce him as well, but he could not, for Jesus remained faithful to Baruch. Furious, then, that he could not seduce Jesus, Nahash had him crucified. But Jesus left his body from Eden on the cross, and ascended to the Good. 'Woman, receive your son back,' he said to Eden, referring to his ensouled and material humanity, while his spirit he committed to the care of his Father. So he ascended to the Good.

II

MINISTRY GOSPELS

Christ the Good Shepherd (*c.* 200)
St Callistus Catacomb, Rome

7 The Gospel of Thomas

(c. 140–180 CE)

INTRODUCTION

On 21 July 1897, the London *Daily Graphic* published a sketch of an eight-year-old boy, Sabr' Said, with the accompanying legend, 'The boy who found the Logia'. These 'logia', or sayings of Jesus, were later recognized as part of the *Gospel of Thomas*. Not to be confused with the *Infancy Gospel of Thomas*, which is an account of Jesus' childhood (see pp. 29–39 above), this other *Gospel of Thomas* is more like a database of material from Jesus' adult ministry. Much of its content consists of individual, pithy sayings, with very little activity of Jesus. As is obvious from a brief glance at the text, the work is structured by the formula 'Jesus said . . . Jesus said . . . Jesus said . . .' which punctuates the whole. In addition to single logia, some of the sections are parables, and others consist of dialogues. About half the contents are familiar from the canonical Gospels, especially Matthew, Mark and Luke: *Thomas* does not really display much knowledge of John's Gospel. The other half of the collection, woven in amongst the familiar New Testament sayings, consists of more esoteric aphorisms and parables. The most striking of them is perhaps the *finale*, in which Jesus promises to make Mary Magdalene male so that she can enter the kingdom of heaven.

There has been knowledge of a 'Gospel of Thomas' throughout church history in the written attacks on it by church fathers beginning in the third century (an anonymous Roman theologian and Origen of Alexandria are the first to mention it). In these early ecclesiastical references, however, it is mostly a mere name, sufficient by virtue of being apocryphal to carry the whiff of heresy. The first fragment of the text discovered in 1897 among the 'Oxyrhynchus' hoard, a rubbish dump of ancient papyrus, was not yet identified as part of the *Gospel of Thomas* mentioned by the church fathers because there was nothing in that particular fragment to suggest any connection with the apostle Thomas. Then, a few years later in 1904, other fragments of similar 'logia' were published, one of which mentioned the disciple Thomas as Jesus' scribe (see Prologue below). There was then growing suspicion that all these Greek fragments might be part of a *Gospel of Thomas*. The connection met with some resistance, however, because the *Infancy Gospel of Thomas* had been well known for such a long time, and so scholars had assumed that mentions of a Thomas Gospel in the early centuries of the church referred to this infancy text. Finally, in the 1950s, scholars identified one of the Coptic Nag Hammadi codices as containing a complete work in the midst of which was all the material in these Greek fragments, and which was accompanied by a title at the end – 'The Gospel according to Thomas'.

The principal theme of the *Gospel of Thomas* is the unique revelation of the divine which Jesus unveils. Jesus is not said in the *Gospel of Thomas* to save through his death and resurrection, but through his disclosure of previously hidden truth (prologue; logion 17). This revelation from Jesus is not to be understood against the backdrop of the Old Testament, but is completely new and free-standing. The role of the disciple, therefore, is to master the content of this revealed truth, and understand its hidden meaning. This is the true path to salvation and immortality (logion 1). Consistent with this is the strong emphasis in the text not on 'faith' but on 'knowledge': there are thirty-two references to 'knowledge' or 'understanding' in *Thomas*, which is an extraordinary density, given how short the text is. (*Thomas* is roughly a quarter of the length of John's Gospel, and only a fifth as long as Luke.) This knowledge is not merely cerebral, since it leads to a transformation which unifies the previously fragmented person, and unites the disciple with the Jesus from whom he had been estranged. This unification is a spiritual reality which is achieved through transcending the body and the material world, and finding the kingdom. In fact, *re*-unification would be nearer the mark, because the spiritual soul is said to hail from the divine realm of light in Jesus' Paradise in the first place (logia 49–50). The marked difference in its message from more conventional Christianity is made clear in the polemics against Matthew's Gospel (logion 13) as well as against the Old Testament (logion 52) and standard practices such as prayer and fasting (logion 14). In addition to some clear fixed points which emerge from the *Gospel of Thomas*, a great deal of the sayings of Jesus there are deliberately enigmatic and require extensive labour to be interpreted correctly. The formula 'He who has ears to hear, let him hear' occurs six times in *Thomas*, emphasizing the importance of attentiveness and correct interpretation.

The fact that the *Gospel of Thomas* takes the form which it does – as a sequence largely of individual sayings of Jesus – shows how a group's understanding of salvation shaped the way in which they wrote down its message. If more conventional Christians understood salvation to be rooted in Jesus' *activity*, especially his death and resurrection, that comported with the canonical Gospels being composed as narratives. Similarly with the *Gospel of Thomas*, the medium is the message. Salvation is not based on believing in Jesus' death and resurrection, but in coming to a realization of the essence of his words. Hence the genre of the *Gospel of Thomas* is that of a sayings collection.

The earliest manuscripts of *Thomas*, the Greek fragments, come from the third century, as do the first references to the Gospel in early church history. Because *Thomas* is familiar with a number of New Testament books, as well as ideas from the second century, it was probably composed (in Greek) sometime between 140 and 180 CE.

DRAMATIS PERSONAE

JESUS
THOMAS *A disciple of Jesus*
SIMON PETER *A disciple of Jesus, a leader among the twelve*
MATTHEW *A disciple of Jesus*
MARY *Mary Magdalene, a female disciple*
SALOME *A female disciple of Jesus*

TRANSLATION

Prologue

These are the secret sayings which the living Jesus spoke, and
Didymus Judas Thomas wrote them down.

Logion 1

Jesus said, 'Whoever finds the interpretation of these sayings
will not taste death.'

Logion 2

Jesus said, 'He who seeks should not stop seeking until he
finds. When he finds, he will be troubled, and when he is
troubled, he will be astonished, and will reign over the All.'*

Logion 3

Jesus said, 'If those who lead you say to you, "Behold, the
kingdom is in heaven," then the birds of heaven would precede
you! If they say to you, "It is in the sea," then the fish would
precede you! No, the kingdom is inside you and outside you.
When you know yourselves, you will be known and will understand that you are sons of the living Father. But if you do not
know yourselves, you live in poverty and you are poverty.'

Logion 4

Jesus said, 'An old man will not hesitate to ask a seven-day-old baby about the place of life, and the man will live. For many who are first will be last. And they will become one.'

Logion 5

Jesus said, 'Know the one in front of you, and what is hidden from you will be revealed to you. For there is nothing hidden which will not be revealed.'

Logion 6

'Do you want us to fast?' Jesus' disciples asked him. 'And how should we pray? Should we give alms? And what diet should we observe?'

Jesus said, 'Do not lie, and do not do to others what you hate, because all things are visible in the presence of the truth. For there is nothing hidden which will not be revealed, and nothing covered which will not be uncovered.'

Logion 7

Jesus said, 'Blessed is the lion which the man eats, and the lion becomes a man. And cursed is the man whom the lion eats, and the man becomes a lion!'

Logion 8

Jesus said, 'Man is like a wise fisherman, who cast his net into the sea. He pulled it up from the sea full of small fish. Among them the wise fisherman found a good, large fish. He cast all the little fish back into the sea, and was content to choose the large fish. He who has ears to hear, let him hear.'

Logion 9

Jesus said, 'Now a sower went forth, filled his hand with seed and sowed. Some fell onto the path, and the birds came and gleaned them. Other seeds fell onto rock, and did not take root in the ground and produce ears of grain. Others still fell onto thorns, which choked the seed, and worms ate them. Others, however, fell onto the good soil, and yielded good fruit, bringing sixty or one hundred and twenty per measure.'

Logion 10

Jesus said, 'I have cast fire upon the world, and I am now guarding it until it burns.'

Logion 11

Jesus said, 'This heaven will pass away, as will the heaven above it. But the dead will not live, and the living will not die. When you ate what is dead you made it live. When you come into the light, what will you do? On the day when you were one, you became two. But when you become two, what will you do?'

Logion 12

'We know that you are going to leave us,' Jesus' disciples said to him. 'Who will be leader over us then?'

Jesus said to them, 'Wherever you have come from, go to James the Just, for the sake of whom heaven and earth came into being.'

Logion 13

Jesus said to his disciples, 'Compare me and tell me whom I resemble.'

'You are like a righteous angel,' Simon Peter said.

'You are like a wise philosopher,' Matthew said to him.

'Master,' replied Thomas, 'my mouth is completely unable to say whom you are like.'

Jesus said, 'I am not your master, Thomas. When you drank, you became drunk with the bubbling spring which I have dug.' Jesus took him and withdrew, and spoke three words to him.

When Thomas returned to his companions, they asked him, 'What did Jesus say to you?'

'If I told you one of the words which he spoke to me,' Thomas said, 'you would pick up stones and throw them at me. But fire would come forth from the stones, and burn you up.'

Logion 14

Jesus said to them, 'If you fast, you will bring forth sin within yourselves. If you pray, you will be condemned. If you give alms, you will harm your spirits. If you go into any region where you travel around in its districts, and are received there, eat what is set before you. (And heal whoever is sick there.) For whatever goes into your mouth will not defile you. Rather, it is what comes out of your mouth that defiles you.'

Logion 15

Jesus said, 'When you see the one not born of woman, prostrate yourselves on your faces and worship him. That one is your Father.'

Logion 16

Jesus said, 'Some may think that I have come to bring peace to the world. They do not know that I have come to bring division – fire, sword, war – to the earth. For when there are five in a house, three will be against two, and two against three; father against son, and son against father. And they will stand as solitary.'

Logion 17

Jesus said, 'I will give you what eye has not seen, what ear has not heard, what hand has not touched, and what has never occurred to the human mind.'

Logion 18

'Tell us how our end will be,' the disciples asked Jesus.

'Have you uncovered the beginning, such that you seek the end?' he said. 'For where the beginning is, there the end shall come to be. Blessed is he who stands in the beginning: he will know the end and will not taste death.'

Logion 19

Jesus said, 'Blessed is he who came into being before he came into being. If you become disciples of mine and heed my words, these stones will serve you. For there are five trees for you in Paradise, which do not sway in summer or winter, and whose leaves do not fall. Whoever knows them will not taste death.'

Logion 20

'Tell us what the kingdom of heaven is like,' the disciples inquired.

'It is like a grain of mustard,' Jesus said. 'It is the smallest of all seeds. But when it falls on worked soil, that soil produces a great branch which becomes a shelter for birds of the air.'

Logion 21

'What are your disciples like?' Mary asked Jesus.

'They are like children sojourning in a field which does not belong to them,' he said. 'When the owners of the field come and say, "Let us have our field," the children strip naked in their presence and let them have their field back.

'This is why I say that if the owner of the house knows that the thief is coming, he will be on guard until he comes, and will not let him dig into the house of his domain and carry off his possessions. As for you, be on guard against the world. Prepare yourself with great power in case the brigands find a way to come to you, since the crisis which you expect will come about. You will need a prudent man among you. When the fruit ripened, he came quickly with his sickle in hand and harvested it. He who has ears to hear, let him hear.'

Logion 22

Jesus saw some little ones being suckled.

'These little ones being suckled are like those who enter the kingdom,' he said to his disciples.

'Shall we, then, enter the kingdom like little ones?' they asked.

'When you make the two one,' Jesus replied, 'and when you make the inside like the outside, and the outside like the inside, and the above like the below, in order to make the male and the female one and the same, so the male is not male and the female is not female; when you make eyes in the place of an eye, a hand in place of a hand, a foot in place of a foot, and an image in place of an image – it is then that you will enter the kingdom.'

Logion 23

Jesus said, 'I will choose you, one out of a thousand, and two out of ten thousand. And they shall stand as a single one.'

Logion 24

'Show us the place where you exist,' his disciples said, 'since we must seek after it.'

'He who has ears, let him hear,' Jesus said. 'There is light within a person of light, and he gives light to the whole world. If he does not give light, he is darkness.'

Logion 25

Jesus said, 'Love your brother as your own soul; guard him like the pupil of your eye.'

Logion 26

Jesus said, 'You see the speck in your brother's eye, but not the beam in your own eye. When you remove the beam from your eye, then you will be able to see how to remove the speck from your brother's eye.'

Logion 27

Jesus said, 'Unless you fast from the world, you will not find the kingdom. Unless you observe the Sabbath, you will not see the Father.'

Logion 28

Jesus said, 'I stood in the midst of the world and appeared to them in flesh. I found them all drunk; none of them was thirsty. My soul is in anguish over the sons of men, because their hearts are blind and they cannot see. For they came into the world empty, and their intention is also to come out of the world empty. Now they are drunk, but when they put their wine away, they will repent.'

Logion 29

Jesus said, 'If the flesh has come into being because of the spirit, it is a marvel! And if the spirit exists because of the body, it is a wonder indeed! But I do marvel at how this great wealth has come to dwell in this poverty!'

Logion 30

Jesus said, 'Where there are three gods, they are gods. Where there are two or one, I am with them.'

Logion 31

Jesus said, 'A prophet is not acceptable in his own village. A doctor does not treat those who know him.'

Logion 32

Jesus says, 'A fortified city built upon a high mountain cannot fall, but nor can it be hidden.'

Logion 33

Jesus said, 'Whatever you hear in one ear, in the other ear proclaim from your rooftops. For no one lights a lamp and places it under a bushel measure,† nor would anyone hide it somewhere secret. No, a person places it upon its lampstand so that everyone who enters and goes out sees its light.'

Logion 34

Jesus said, 'If a blind man leads a blind man, they will both fall into a ditch.'

Logion 35

Jesus said, 'It is impossible for a person to enter the house of a strong man and subdue him before tying up his hands. Then the person will be able to steal from the strong man's house.'

Logion 36

Jesus said, 'Do not worry from morning to evening and from evening to morning about what you will wear.'

Logion 37

'When will you be revealed to us, and when will we see you?' his disciples asked.

'When you undress and are not ashamed,' Jesus said, 'and take your clothes and trample them under your feet like little children, then you will see the Son of the Living One and will not be afraid.'

Logion 38

Jesus said, 'Many times you have desired to hear these words which I am speaking to you, and you have no one else from whom to hear them. Days are coming when you will seek after me but not find me.'

Logion 39

Jesus said, 'The Pharisees and the scribes have taken the keys of knowledge and have hidden them. They have not entered, and have not allowed those who want to enter to do so. But you, be as clever as serpents, and as innocent as doves.'

Logion 40

Jesus said, 'A vine has been planted outside the Father, but it is not established. It will be pulled up by its root and perish.'

Logion 41

Jesus said, 'Whoever has something will receive more, but who-ever does not have, even the little which he has will be taken from him.'

Logion 42

Jesus said, 'Be passers-by!'

Logion 43

'Who are you to say these things to us?' his disciples asked.

'You do not understand who I am from what I say to you,'

Jesus said to them, 'but you have become like the Jews, for they love the tree but hate its fruit, or love the fruit but hate the tree.'

Logion 44

Jesus said, 'Whoever blasphemes the Father will be forgiven. Whoever blasphemes the Son will be forgiven. But whoever blasphemes the Holy Spirit will not be forgiven either on earth or in heaven.'

Logion 45

Jesus said, 'Grapes are not harvested from thorn bushes, nor are figs picked from thistles, for they do not produce fruit. A good man brings out good from his store; an evil man brings out wickedness from the store of evil in his heart, and speaks wickedness. For from the overflow of his heart he brings out wicked things.'

Logion 46

Jesus said, 'From Adam to John the Baptist, there has been no one born of woman higher than John the Baptist to make John distressed. But I say to you, whoever among you becomes a little one will know the kingdom and will be higher than John.'

Logion 47

Jesus said, 'It is impossible for a person to mount two horses or stretch two bows. It is impossible for a servant to serve two masters; otherwise, he will honour one and insult the other. No one drinks old wine and then wants to drink new wine. Nor is new wine put into old wineskins, in case they tear. Nor is old wine put into a new wineskin, in case the skin ruins the wine. An old patch is not stitched onto a new garment, since then there would be a tear.'

Logion 48

Jesus said, 'If two make peace with one another in this one house, they can say to a mountain, "Move away," and it will move.'

Logion 49

Jesus said, 'Blessed are the solitary and elect, for you will find the kingdom. For you are from it, and you will return there again.'

Logion 50

Jesus said, 'If they say to you, "From where have you come?" say to them, "We have come from the light, where the light came into being of its own accord and [stood] and appeared in their images."

'If they say to you, "Who are you?" say, "We are its children and we are the elect of the living Father."

'If they ask you, "What is the sign of your Father in you?" say to them, "It is motion and rest." '

Logion 51

'When will the rest for the dead come, and when is the new world coming?' his disciples asked.

'That rest which you are seeking has come,' Jesus said, 'but you do not know it.'

Logion 52

'Twenty-four prophets spoke in Israel. Did all of them speak about you?' his disciples asked.

'You have neglected the living one in front of you,' Jesus said, 'and spoken of the dead.'

Logion 53

'Is circumcision an advantage or not?' his disciples asked.

'If it were an advantage,' Jesus said, 'fathers would acquire children by their mothers already circumcised. No, it is true circumcision in the Spirit which is entirely profitable.'

Logion 54

Jesus said, 'Blessed are the poor, for yours is the kingdom of heaven.'

Logion 55

Jesus said, 'Whoever does not hate his father and mother cannot be a disciple of mine. And whoever does not hate his brothers and sisters, and take up his cross like me, will not be worthy of me.'

Logion 56

Jesus said, 'Whoever comes to know the world discovers a corpse. And whoever has discovered that corpse is one of whom the world is not worthy.'

Logion 57

Jesus said, 'The kingdom of the Father is like a man who had good seed. His enemy came in the night and sowed weeds over the good seed. The man did not allow his workers to pull up the weeds. He said to them, "It is in case you go to pull up the weeds and pull up the wheat along with them." For on the day of the harvest, the weeds will be revealed. They will be pulled up and burned.'

Logion 58

Jesus said, 'Blessed is the man who has laboured and found life.'

Logion 59

Jesus said, 'Look at the living one while you are alive, in case you die and then seek to see him, but cannot.'

Logion 60

Jesus saw a Samaritan carrying a lamb as he went into Judaea.
   'He is around the lamb,' he said to his disciples.
   'So that he might kill it and eat it,' they said to him.
   'While it is alive, he will not consume it,' Jesus stated. 'But if he kills it, it will become a corpse.'
   'Otherwise, he would not be able to eat it.'
   'As for you,' Jesus urged, 'seek for yourselves a place inside "rest", so that you do not become a corpse and become consumed.'

Logion 61

Jesus said, 'Two will rest on a couch; one will die, the other will live.'
   'Who are you, man,' asked Salome, 'to come up as from One on to my couch and eat from my table?'
   'I am he who is from the Equal,' Jesus replied. 'I have been given some of what belongs to my Father.'
   'I am your disciple,' Salome said.
   'This is why I say, "When he becomes equal, he will be filled with light. But when he becomes divided, he will be filled with darkness."'

Logion 62

Jesus said, 'I speak my mysteries to those who are worthy of my mysteries. Do not let your left hand know what your right hand is doing.'

Logion 63

Jesus said, 'There was a rich man who had a great deal of money. He said, "I shall make use of my money, and sow, reap, plant and fill my store with produce, so that I lack nothing." That is what he thought, but that same night he died. He who has ears, let him hear.'

Logion 64

Jesus said, 'A man was having some guests to his house. When he had prepared the dinner, he sent his servant to summon the guests.

'The servant went to the first and said to him, "My master summons you."

'The guest replied, "I have some claims against some merchants who are coming to see me this evening. I am going to give them orders. Please excuse me from the dinner."

'The servant went to another and said to him, "My master summons you."

'That one replied, "I have bought a house and am required today. I shall not have the spare time."

'The servant went to another and said to him, "My master summons you."

'This third one replied, "A friend of mine is getting married, and I am to arrange the dinner. I shall not be able to come. Please excuse me from the dinner."

'The servant went to another and said to him, "My master summons you."

'This one replied, "I have bought a village and am going to collect the rent. I shall not be able to come. Please excuse me."

'The servant returned and said to his master, "Those whom you invited to the dinner have asked to be excused."

'The master said to his servant, "Go outside to the streets and bring whomever you find, so that they may dine."'

Jesus said, 'Businessmen and merchants will not enter the places of my Father.'

Logion 65

He said, 'A [. . .] man had a vineyard. He leased it to farmers so that they would work it, and he would receive its produce from them. He sent his servant so that the farmers might give him the produce of the vineyard. They seized his servant and struck him, nearly killing him. The servant went and told his master. The master said, "Perhaps they did not recognize him." He sent another servant. The tenants struck this one too. Then the owner sent his son and said, "Perhaps they will respect my son." Since those tenants knew that he was the heir to the vineyard, they seized him and killed him. He who has ears, let him hear.'

Logion 66

Jesus said, 'Show me the stone which the builders rejected – that is the cornerstone.'

Logion 67

Jesus said, 'Whoever knows all, but is deficient in one thing, is deficient completely.'

Logion 68

Jesus said, 'Blessed are you when people hate you and persecute you. They will not find a place where they have persecuted you.'

Logion 69

Jesus said, 'Blessed are those who have been persecuted in their hearts. It is they who have truly known the Father. Blessed are those who hunger so that they may fill the belly of someone in need.'

Logion 70

Jesus said, 'When you bring out what is in you, what you have will save you. If you do not have that in you, what you do not have in you will kill you.'

Logion 71

Jesus said, 'I will dest[roy thi]s house, and no one will be able to build it [. . .].'

Logion 72

'Tell my brothers to divide my father's property with me,' a man said to him.

'Who has made me a divider?' Jesus said. He turned to his disciples and said to them, 'I am certainly no divider!'

Logion 73

Jesus said, 'The harvest is great, but the workers are few. Ask the Lord to send out workers to that harvest.'

Logion 74

He said, 'Lord, there are many around the well, but there is no one in the well.'

Logion 75

Jesus said, 'Many are standing at the door, but only the solitary will enter the bridal chamber.'

Logion 76

Jesus said, 'The kingdom of the Father is like a merchant who had a cargo of merchandise and found a pearl. That merchant was shrewd. He sold his merchandise and bought this one pearl for himself. As for you, seek his unfailing and enduring treasure, where no moth comes near to eat and no worm destroys.'

Logion 77

Jesus said, 'I am the light who is above all things. I am the All. From me the All came forth, and the All reaches to me. Split a piece of wood – I am there. Lift the stone and you will find me there.'

Logion 78

Jesus said, 'Why have you come out to the countryside? To see a reed shaken by the wind? Or to see a man who is wearing a soft garment like your kings and your nobles? They have soft garments on, but they are unable to know the truth.'

Logion 79

A woman in the crowd said to him, 'Blessed are the womb which bore you and the breasts which nursed you.'

'Blessed are those who have heard the word of the Father and have truly kept it,' he said. 'For days are coming when you will say, "Blessed are the womb which has not conceived and the breasts which have not given milk."'

Logion 80

Jesus said, 'Whoever has come to know the world has found the body. The world is not worthy of whoever has found that body.'

Logion 81

Jesus said, 'Whoever has become rich should reign; and whoever has power should renounce it.'

Logion 82

Jesus said, 'He who is near me is near the fire; and he who is far from me is far from the kingdom.'

Logion 83

Jesus said, 'The images are visible to man, but the light within them is hidden. In the image of the light of the Father it will be revealed, but his image is hidden by his light.'

Logion 84

Jesus said, 'When you see your likenesses, you rejoice! But when you see your images which came into being before you, which neither die nor are revealed, how much will you bear!'

Logion 85

Jesus said, 'Adam came into being from a great power and a great wealth, but he did not become worthy of you. For if he had been worthy, he would not have tasted death.'

Logion 86

Jesus said, 'Foxes have holes, and birds have their nests, but the son of man has no place to lay his head and rest himself.'

Logion 87

Jesus said, 'Wretched is the body which depends on a body, and wretched is the soul which depends on these two.'

Logion 88

Jesus said, 'Messengers and prophets will come to you, and will offer you what you already have. And you for your part, give them what you have, and say to yourselves, "When will they come and take what belongs to them?" '

Logion 89

Jesus said, 'Why do you cleanse the outside of the cup? Do you not realize that he who made the inside also made the outside?'

Logion 90

Jesus said, 'Come to me, because my yoke is kind and my dominion is mild, and you will find rest for yourselves.'

Logion 91

'Tell us who you are, so that we might believe in you,' Jesus was asked.

'You inquire into the appearance of the sky and the earth,' he said, 'but you do not know who is in front of you, nor do you know this season and inquire into it.'

Logion 92

Jesus said, 'Seek and you shall find. I now desire to tell you what I did not tell you before when you asked me. Only now you are not seeking it.'

Logion 93

Jesus said, 'Do not give what is holy to dogs, in case they throw it into the dung. Do not throw pearls to pigs, in case they make them [. . .] .'

Logion 94

Jesus said, 'He who seeks will find. To him who knocks, it will be opened.'

Logion 95

Jesus said, 'If you have money, do not lend it at interest; give it instead to someone from whom you will not receive it back.'

Logion 96

Jesus said, 'The kingdom of the Father is like a woman. She took a little leaven, hid it in some dough and made it into large loaves. He who has ears, let him hear.'

Logion 97

Jesus said, 'The kingdom of the Father is like a woman who was carrying a jar full of meal. While she was away on a long journey, the handle of the jar broke and the meal emptied out behind her on the road. She did not realize it. She did not feel tired. When she reached her house, she put the jar down and found it empty.'

Logion 98

Jesus said, 'The kingdom of the Father is like a man who wanted to kill a nobleman. He drew his sword at home and drove it into the wall, to find out whether his hand would be strong enough. Then he killed the nobleman.'

Logion 99

'Your mother and brothers are standing outside,' Jesus' disciples told him.

'Those who are here and do the will of my Father are my mother and brothers,' he said to them. 'It is they who will enter the kingdom of my Father.'

Logion 100

Jesus was shown a gold coin. 'Caesar's men demand taxes from us,' he was told.

'Give Caesar's property to Caesar; give God's property to God; and what is mine, give to me,' he said.

Logion 101

Jesus said, 'Whoever does not hate his father and his mother as I do cannot be a disciple of mine. And whoever does not love his Father and his Mother as I do cannot be a disciple of mine. For my mother who [. . .]; but my true Mother has given me life.'

Logion 102

Jesus said, 'Woe to those Pharisees, for they are like a dog sleeping in the manger of some cattle. For it does not eat anything itself, nor does it let the cattle feed.'

Logion 103

Jesus said, 'Blessed is the man who knows at what point the brigands will enter. Then he will arise and muster his kingdom and prepare himself before they come in.'

Logion 104

'Come, let us pray and fast today,' some said to Jesus.

'What sin have I committed, or how have I been defeated?' he said. 'But when the bridegroom comes out of the bridal chamber, then people should fast and pray.'

Logion 105

Jesus said, 'Whoever knows the Father and the Mother will be called "son of a prostitute".'

Logion 106

Jesus said, 'When you make the two one, you will become sons of man. And when you say, "Mountain, move away!" it will move.'

Logion 107

Jesus said, 'The kingdom is like a shepherd who had a hundred sheep. One of them, the largest, wandered off. The shepherd left the ninety-nine, and searched for this one until he found it. After his labour, he said to that sheep, "I love you more than the ninety-nine."'

Logion 108

Jesus said, 'Whoever drinks from my mouth will become like me. I myself will become him, and what is hidden will be revealed to him.'

Logion 109

Jesus said, 'The kingdom is like a man who had hidden treasure in his field without knowing it. After he died, he left the field to his son. The son did not know of the treasure either. He took that field and sold it. The person who bought it went ploughing it, found the treasure and began to lend money at interest to whomever he wished.'

Logion 110

Jesus said, 'Whoever has found the world and become rich should renounce the world.'

Logion 111

Jesus said, 'The heavens and the earth will roll up in your presence; and he who lives from the living one will not see death.' It is not that Jesus said, 'The world is not worthy of the person who has found only himself!'

Logion 112

Jesus said, 'Woe to the flesh which depends on the soul. Woe to the soul which depends on the flesh.'

Logion 113

'When will the kingdom come?' Jesus' disciples asked him.

'It will not come by looking for it,' Jesus said. 'People will not say, "Look! Here it is!", or "Look! There it is!" Rather, the kingdom of the Father is spread out upon the earth, and people do not see it.'

Logion 114

'Mary should leave us,' Simon Peter said, 'because women are not worthy of life.'

'Now I will draw her to me to make her male,' Jesus said, 'to make her a living spirit resembling you males. For every woman who makes herself male will enter the kingdom of heaven.'

The Gospel according to Thomas

8 Tatian's 'Diatessaron'

(165–180 CE)

INTRODUCTION

An anecdote from the church father Theodoret (*c.* 393–460 CE) illustrates both the popularity and unpopularity of Tatian's *Diatessaron*: 'This Tatian composed a Gospel called the "Diatessaron", cutting out the genealogies and whatever else shows that the Lord was born, physically speaking, from the line of David. It was not only those of Tatian's own sect who made use of this Gospel, but also people who otherwise followed the apostolic teachings. They did not recognize the wickedness of the composition but treated it naively as a compendium of the Gospels. I managed to find more than two hundred copies of the book revered in our own churches, so I collected them all and removed them, replacing them with the Gospels of the four evangelists.' As Theodoret's statement implies, Tatian's work combines all four canonical Gospels into one very long narrative – a 'Gospel harmony': the word *dia-tessarōn* is Greek for 'through four', i.e. one book combining four. It was perhaps initially composed as a study tool for Tatian's intellectual circle, but eventually became widely influential through its use in church settings. (Theodoret apparently discovered 200 copies of the *Diatessaron* in his diocese of Cyrrhus alone.) The *Diatessaron* is therefore the most prominent example of a new composition which could combine existing Gospels.

Tatian was a convert from pagan parents, and probably was an orator or philosopher before becoming a Christian. He was born around 115 CE in Assyria, and active between roughly 150 and 180 CE. It was probably towards the end of this period that Tatian assembled the *Diatessaron*. The other work of his which survives is the *Oration to the Greeks*, in which Tatian contests the exclusive claims to culture and true philosophy made by Greeks and explains Christian teaching in critical dialogue with Greek thought.

Although the *Oration to the Greeks* was quite frequently quoted by church fathers, his most influential work was the *Diatessaron*. As it was very common in antiquity for works to have multiple titles, Tatian's work was sometimes called the *Diatessaron*, while other authors refer to it simply as 'the Gospel'. It is called 'the Gospel' and even occasionally 'the New Testament' in Syriac Christianity, where it was especially influential. Unfortunately, no manuscripts of the original survive, and indeed scholars are not even sure what the original language was. (Probably the majority now favour Greek over Syriac.) The main manuscripts of the *Diatessaron* which survive are in Arabic translation, and there is also an inferior Latin version. Because the texts of the *Diatessaron* that we have today are at some remove from the original, it is clearly not possible to capture the original wording. What can more realistically be reconstructed is the sequence in which Tatian placed the different Gospel episodes.

It is only practicable here to list this sequence of episodes; providing a translation of the entirety of the *Diatessaron* would take a Penguin Classic of its own. The outline below lists the order of the episodes in the surviving Arabic version of Tatian's harmony.

OUTLINE

1. The eternal Word (Jn 1:1–5)
    The birth of John the Baptist foretold (Lk. 1:5–25)
    The birth of Jesus foretold (Lk. 1:26–38)
    Mary visits Elizabeth (Lk. 1:39–45)
    The *Magnificat* (Mary's Song) (Lk. 1:46–56)
    The birth of John the Baptist (Lk. 1:57–66)
    The *Benedictus* (Zechariah's Song) (Lk. 1:67–80)

2. The birth of Jesus (Mt. 1:18–25)
   Jesus in the manger (Lk. 2:1–7)
   The visit of the shepherds (Lk. 2:8–20)
   The circumcision and presentation of Jesus (Lk. 2:21–39)

3. The visit of the Magi (Mt. 2:1–12)
   The flight to Egypt and slaughter of the innocents (Mt. 2:13–18)
   The holy family returns to Nazareth (Mt. 2:19–23)
   The twelve-year-old Jesus in the temple (Lk. 2:41–52)
   John's ministry begins (Mt. 3:1–3; Mk 1:1–4; Lk. 3:1–6)
   The testimony of John about Jesus (Jn 1:7–17)

4. Further testimony of John about Jesus (Jn 1:18–28)
   The preaching of John (Mt. 3:4–10; Lk. 3:10–18)
   Jesus' baptism (Mt. 3:13–17; Mk 1:9–11; Lk. 3:21–22; Jn 1:29–34)
   The temptation of Jesus (Mt. 4:1–7; Mk 1:12–13; Lk. 4:1–12)

5. Conclusion to the temptation (Mt. 4:10–11; Lk. 4:13)
   The call of Andrew, Simon, Philip and Nathanael (Jn 1:35–51)
   The wedding at Cana (Jn 2:1–11)
   Jesus' Nazareth sermon (Lk. 4:14–22)
   The call of the first disciples (Mt. 4:17–22; Mk 1:14–20)
   The miraculous catch of fish (Lk. 5:1–7)

6. The calling of the first disciples (Lk. 5:8–11)
   Jesus and John baptize in Judaea (Jn 3:22–4:3)
   Herod imprisons John the Baptist (Lk. 3:19–20)
   Jesus heals the boy at Cana (Mt. 4:12; Lk. 4:44; Jn 4:46–54)
   Jesus' stay in Capernaum (Mt. 4:13–16)
   Jesus' exorcism in Capernaum (Mk 1:21–28; Lk. 4:31–37)
   The call of Matthew (Mt. 9:9)
   Simon's mother-in-law cured (Mt. 8:14–17; Mk 1:29–34; Lk. 4:38–41)

7. Healings in Galilee (Mt. 9:35; Mk 1:35–39; Lk. 4:42–44)
   The call of Levi (Mk 2:14)

The paralysed man forgiven (Mt. 9:2–8; Mk 2:1–12; Lk. 5:17–26)
New wine and old wineskins (Mk 2:21–22)
Jesus calls Levi and eats with sinners (Lk. 5:27–32)
Jesus questioned about fasting (Lk. 5:33–39)
Gleaning in the cornfields (Mt. 12:1–8; Mk 2:23–28; Lk. 6:1–5)
A man's withered hand healed (Mt. 12:9–13; Mk 3:1–6; Lk. 6:6–11)

8. Jesus heals many (Mt. 12:14–21)
   The call of the disciples (Lk. 6:12–13)
   Healings by the lake (Mk 3:7–12; Lk. 6:17–19)
   Sermon on the Mount (Mt. 5:1–32; Mk 4:21–23; Lk. 6:13–27)

9. Sermon on the Mount (cont.) (Mt. 5:33–48; Lk. 6:33–36)
   Sermon on the Mount (cont.) (Mt. 6:1–18; Lk. 11:1–2)
   Sermon on the Mount (cont.) (Mt. 6:19–23; Lk. 12:32–33; 11:35–36)

10. Sermon on the Mount (cont.) (Mt. 6:24–34; Lk. 12:26, 29)
    Sermon on the Mount (cont.) (Mt. 7:1–6; Mk 4:24–25; Lk. 6:37–42)
    Sermon on the Mount (cont.) (Mt. 7:12; Lk. 11:5–13)
    Sermon on the Mount (cont.) (Mt. 7:13–27; Lk. 6:44–48)

11. The healing of the centurion's servant (Mt. 7:28–8:13; Lk. 7:1–10)
    The raising of the widow's son at Nain (Lk. 7:11–17)
    A scribe and others offer to follow Jesus (Mt. 8:18–20; Lk. 9:57–62)
    The calming of the storm (Mt. 8:23–27; Mk 4:35–41; Lk. 8:22–25)
    The Gerasene demoniac (Mt. 8:28–34; Mk 5:1–16; Lk. 8:26–36)

12. Jesus returns across the lake (Mt. 9:1; Mk 5:21; Lk. 8:37–40)

Jairus' request for his daughter (Mt. 9:18; Mk 5:21–24; Lk. 8:41–42)

Healing of the bleeding woman (Mk 5:25–34; Lk. 8:43–48)

The raising of Jairus' daughter (Mt. 9:25; Mk 5:38–42; Lk. 8:49–56)

Two blind men healed (Mt. 9:27–31)

Jesus cures the dumb spirit and tours Galilee (Mt. 9:32–36)

Instructions to the twelve (Mt. 10:1–15; Mk 6:7–11; Lk. 9:1–3)

13. Further instructions (Mt. 10:16–11:1; Lk. 12:3–5, 51–53)

Jesus at the house of Mary and Martha (Lk. 10:38–42)

The apostles preach and heal (Mk 6:12–13; Lk. 9:6)

John the Baptist sends emissaries to Jesus (Mt. 11:2; Lk. 7:18–27)

14. John the Baptist, the Law and the prophets (Mt. 11:11–15; Lk. 7:29–30; 16:16–17)

Jesus' and John's differences (Mt. 11:18–19; Mk 2:19–20; Lk. 7:31–35)

The Beelzebul controversy (Mt. 12:24–37; Mk 3:22–30; Lk. 11:14–23)

Discerning the signs of the times (Mt. 16:2–4; Lk. 12:54–56)

Jesus cures the mute and blind demoniac (Mt. 12:22–23)

The return of the twelve (Mk 6:30–31)

A woman washes Jesus' feet (Lk. 7:36–39)

15. The woman's sins are forgiven (Lk. 7:40–50)

Many believe but Jesus does not trust them (Jn 2:23–25)

The mission of the seventy (Lk. 10:1–12)

Jesus rebukes Bethsaida and Capernaum (Mt. 11:20–24)

The return of the seventy (Mt. 11:25–27; Lk. 10:16–22)

The easy yoke (Mt. 11:28–30)

Counting the cost (Mt. 10:34–39; Lk. 14:25–33)

16. Seeking a sign (Mt. 12:38–45; Lk. 11:29–32)

The return of the unclean spirit (Mt. 12:45; Lk. 11: 24–26)

Jesus' mother and brothers (Mt. 12:46–50; Mk 3:31–35; Lk. 8:19–21)

Travel through Galilee supported by women (Lk. 8:1–3)

The parable of the sower (Mt. 13:1–9; Mk 4:1–9; Lk. 8: 4–8)

The reason for parables (Mt. 13:10–17; Mk 4:10–12; Lk. 8:9–10)

The sower parable explained (Mt. 13:18–23; Mk 4:13–20; Lk. 8:11–15)

The parable of the seed growing secretly (Mk 4:26–29)

17. The parable of the tares (Mt. 13:24–30)

The parable of the mustard seed (Mt. 13:31–32; Mk 4: 30–32; Lk. 13:18–19)

The parable of the leaven (Mt. 13:33; Mk 4:33; Lk. 13:20–21)

Explanation of the parable of the tares (Mt. 13:36–43)

The parable of the hidden treasure (Mt. 13:44)

The parable of the pearl (Mt. 13:45–46)

The parable of the dragnet (Mt. 13:47–53)

Jesus visits and preaches in Nazareth (Mk 6:1–6; Lk. 4: 16–30)

18. Herod executes John (Mt. 14:1–12; Mk 6:14–29; Lk. 9: 7–9)

Five thousand fed (Mt. 14:13–21; Mk 6:32–44; Lk. 9:12–17; Jn 6:1–13)

The disciples sent to Bethsaida (Mt. 14:22–24; Mk 6:45–47; Jn 6:14–18)

19. Jesus walks on the water (Mt. 14:25–33; Jn 6:19–21)

Jesus heals the sick (Mk 6:54–56)

Jesus the bread from heaven (Jn 6:22–59)

20. Many desert Jesus (Jn 6:60–71)

Jesus eats with unwashed hands (Lk. 11:37–41)

Debate with the Pharisees (Mt. 15:1–20; Mk 7:1–23)

Jesus visits Tyre and Sidon (Mt. 15:21–28; Mk 7:24–30)

21. Jesus cures a deaf and dumb man (Mk 7:32–37)
    Discussion with the Samaritan woman (Jn 4:7–42)

22. Cure of a man with leprosy (Mt. 8:2–4; Mk 1:40–45; Lk. 5:12–16)
    Cure of a man on the Sabbath (Jn 5:1–18)
    The Father and Son at work (Jn 5:19–47)

23. Healing in Galilee (Mt. 15:29–31)
    The feeding of the four thousand (Mt. 15:32–39)
    Jesus refuses the Pharisees a sign (Mt. 16:1, 4–12; Mk 8: 11–21)
    Jesus heals the blind man at Bethsaida (Mk 8:22–26)
    Jesus asks who people say he is (Mt. 16:13–23; Mk 8: 27–33)
    Self-denial (Mt. 16:24–28; Mk 8:34–38; Lk. 9:23–27)

24. The transfiguration (Mt. 17:1–13; Mk 9:2–13; Lk. 9:28–36)
    Herod seeks to kill Jesus (Mk 8:14–15; Lk. 13:31–33)
    Jesus heals a possessed boy (Mt. 17:14–21; Mk 9:14–29; Lk. 9:38–43)
    Jesus' death predicted again (Mt. 17:22–23; Mk 9:30–32; Lk. 9:43–45)

25. Debate about the disciples' greatness (Mk 9:33–34; Lk. 9:46)
    Payment of the temple tax (Mt. 17:24–27)
    The disciples' greatness (cont.) (Mt. 18:1–6; Mk 9:36–37; Lk. 9:47–48)
    Causes of stumbling (Mt. 18:7–11, 14; Mk 9:38–50; Lk. 9:49–50; 14:34–35)
    Adultery and divorce (Mt. 19:3–12; Mk 10:2–12)
    Children are brought to Jesus (Mt. 19:13–15; Mk 10:13–16)

26. The parable of the lost sheep (Mt. 18:13–14; Lk. 15:1–7)
    The parable of the lost coin (Lk. 15:8–10)
    The parable of the prodigal son (Lk. 15:11–32)
    The parable of the unjust steward (Lk. 16:1–12)

27. Forgiving a fellow believer (Mt. 18:23–35; Lk. 17:3–4; 12: 47–48)

Jesus comes to bring fire and a sword (Mt. 18:10–11; Lk. 12:49–50)

The Galileans and the tower of Siloam (Lk. 13:1–9)

The healing of the disabled woman (Lk. 13:10–17)

28. The Feast of Tabernacles (Mt. 19:1–2; Jn 7:2–31)

Life and the abundance of possessions (Lk. 12:13–15)

The parable of the rich fool (Lk. 12:16–21)

The rich young ruler (Mt. 19:16–22; Mk 10:17–23; Lk. 18:18–24)

29. The eye of the needle (Mt. 19:23–24; Mk 10:24–31; Lk. 18:25–30)

The parable of the rich man and Lazarus (Lk. 16:14–15, 19–31)

Jesus heals a man on the Sabbath (Lk. 14:1–6)

The parable of the labourers in the vineyard (Mt. 20:1–16)

30. Places at the feast (Lk. 14:7–15)

The parable of the great banquet (Mt. 22:1–14; Lk. 14:16–24)

Jesus heals ten men with leprosy (Lk. 17:11–19)

Jesus' death predicted again (Mt. 20:17–19; Mk 10:32–34; Lk. 18:31–34)

Request from the mother of James and John (Mt. 20:20–21; Mk 10:35–40)

31. The indignation of the other disciples (Mk 10:41–44)

The son of man's service (Mt. 20:28)

The few who are saved (Lk. 13:22–30)

Jesus and Zacchaeus (Lk. 19:1–10)

Jesus heals Bartimaeus (Mt. 20:29–34; Mk 10:46–52; Lk. 18:35–43)

The parable of the minas† (Lk. 19:11–27)

32. The temple purged (Mt. 21:12–13; Mk 11:15–18; Lk. 19:45–46; Jn 2:13–22)

The widow's mite (Mk 12:41–44; Lk. 21:1–4)

The parable of the Pharisee and the tax collector (Lk. 18:9–14)

Jesus curses the fig tree (Mt. 21:17–19; Mk 11:12–15; Lk. 9:11)

Jesus and Nicodemus (Jn 3:1–21)

33. The fig tree withers (Mt. 21:19–22; Mk 11:19–26; Lk. 17:5–10)

The parable of the unjust judge (Lk. 18:1–8)

Jesus' authority (Mt. 21:23–27; Mk 11:27–33; Lk. 20:1–8)

The parable of the two sons (Mt. 21:28–32)

The parable of the wicked tenants (Mt. 21:33–46; Mk 12:1–12; Lk. 20:9–19)

34. Render unto Caesar (Mt. 22:15–22; Mk 12:13–17; Lk. 20:20–26)

Marriage at the resurrection (Mt. 22:23–33; Mk 12:18–27; Lk. 20:27–39)

The most important commandment (Mt. 22:34–40; Mk 12:28–34)

The parable of the good Samaritan (Lk. 10:28–37)

Soldiers sent to take Jesus (Lk. 19:47–48; Jn 7:31–36)

35. The last day of the Feast (Jn 7:37–52)

Whose son is the Messiah? (Mt. 22:41–46; Mk 12:35–37; Lk. 20:41–44)

Jesus teaches in the treasury (Jn 8:12–50)

36. 'Before Abraham was, I am!' (Jn 8:51–59)

The cure of the man born blind (Jn 9:1–38)

37. Judgement and blindness (Jn 9:39–41)

The good shepherd (Jn 10:1–21)

The Feast of Dedication (Jn 10:22–42)

The death of Lazarus (Jn 11:1–16)

38. The raising of Lazarus (Jn 11:17–45)

Jesus retreats to Ephraem (Jn 11:46–54)

The approach of the Passover (Jn 11:55–57)

Jesus rejected by a Samaritan village (Lk. 9:51–56)

39. Mary anoints Jesus (Mt. 26:6–13; Mk 14:3–9; Jn 12:1–11)

The triumphal entry (Mt. 21:1–11; Mk 11:1–11; Lk. 19: 28–44; Jn 12:12–19)

40. Jesus in the temple (Mt. 21:14–16)
The Greeks desire to see Jesus (Jn 12:20–36)
The kingdom of God (Lk. 17:20–21; 21:31–38)
Woes on the scribes and Pharisees (Mt. 23:1–33; Mk 12: 38–40; Lk. 11:42–48)

41. The lament over Jerusalem (Mt. 23:34–39)
The reception of Jesus' teaching (Jn 12:36–50; Lk. 11: 53–12:3)
Discourse about the end (Mt. 24:1–14; Mk 13:1–13; 14: 1–2; Lk. 21:5–19)

42. Discourse about the end (cont.) (Mt. 24:15–44; Mk 13: 14–37; Lk. 21:20–37)

43. The parable of servants left in charge (Mt. 24:45–51; Lk. 12:41–48)
The parable of the ten virgins (Mt. 25:1–13)
The parable of the talents† (Mt. 25:14–30)
Warning to keep alert (Lk. 12:35–38)
The parable of the sheep and the goats (Mt. 25:31–46)

44. The plot to execute Jesus (Mt. 26:1–5, 14–16; Mk 14: 10–12; Lk. 22:1–6)
Jesus washes the disciples' feet (Jn 13:1–20; Lk. 22:24–30)
Passover begins (Mt. 26:17–24; Mk 14:12–21; Lk. 22: 7–23; Jn 13:21–22)

45. Judas goes out into the night (Mt. 26:25; Jn 13:23–30)
The Last Supper (Mt. 26:26–29; Mk 14:22–25; Lk. 22: 17–20; Jn 13:31–32)
Peter's denial (Mt. 26:30–35; Mk 14:26–31; Lk. 22:31– 34; Jn 13:33–38)
Farewell discourse (Jn 14:1–20)

46. Farewell discourse (cont.) (Jn 14:21–30)
Journey to the Mount of Olives (Jn 14:31; Lk. 22:35–39)
Farewell discourse (cont.) (Jn 15:1–16:15)

47. Farewell discourse (cont.) (Jn 16:16–17:26)

48. Jesus in the garden (Mt. 26:36–56; Mk 14:32–50; Lk. 22:
    40–53; Jn 18:1–11)
    Jesus and Annas (Mt. 26:57–58; Mk 14:51–54; Lk. 22:
    54–57; Jn 18:12–18)

49. Jesus' trial (Mt. 26:59–75; Mk 14:55–72; Lk. 22:58–65; Jn
    18:19–27)
    Jesus before Pilate (Mt. 27:1–2, 11; Mk 15:1–2; Lk. 23:
    1–3; Jn 18:28–38)

50. Jesus sent to Herod (Lk. 23:4–12)
    Return to Pilate (Mt. 27:12–30; Mk 15:3–20; Lk. 23:
    13–25; Jn 19:1–12)

51. Jesus at the judgement seat (Mt. 27:24–25; Jn 19:13–16)
    Judas returns the thirty pieces of silver (Mt. 27:3–10)
    Walk to Calvary (Mt. 27:31–33; Mk 15:21–22; Lk. 23:
    26–32; Jn 19:16–17)
    The crucifixion (Mt. 27:34–47; Mk 15:23–34; Lk. 23:
    33–45; Jn 19:18–27)

52. Crucifixion (cont.) (Mt. 27:48–54; Mk 15:36–39; Lk. 23:
    34–48; Jn 19:28–30)
    Jesus' bones not broken (Jn 19:31–37)
    The burial of Jesus (Mt. 27:55–66; Mk 15:40–47; Lk. 23:
    49–56; Jn 19:38–42)
    The empty tomb (Mt. 28:1–6; Mk 16:1–6; Lk. 24:1–3)

53. Commission to the women (Mt. 28:7–8; Mk 16:7–8; Lk.
    24:4–9; Jn 20:1–2)
    Two disciples visit the tomb (Lk. 24:12; Jn 20:3–10)
    Jesus appears to Mary Magdalene (Mk 16:9–11; Jn 20:
    11–17)
    The guards are bribed (Mt. 28:11–15)
    Jesus appears to the other women (Mt. 28:9–10; Lk. 24:
    9–11; Jn 20:18)
    Jesus on the road to Emmaus (Mk 16:12–13; Lk. 24:
    13–35)

54. Jesus appears to the disciples without Thomas (Lk. 24:
     36–49; Jn 20:19–23)
     Jesus appears to the disciples with Thomas (Jn 20:24–31)
     The second miraculous catch of fish (Jn 21:1–24)

55. The great commission (Mt. 28:16–20; Mk 16:14–18; Lk.
     24:49)
     The ascension (Mk 16:19–20; Lk. 24:40–53; Jn 21:25)

As an appendix in some manuscripts: Jesus' genealogies (Mt.
1:1–17; Lk. 3:23–38)

9 Dura Parchment 24

(second century CE)

INTRODUCTION

This parchment fragment has interested scholars because it is often seen as a fragment of Tatian's *Diatessaron*, summarized above. Recent research has cast considerable doubt on this connection, however. Nevertheless, this fragment was clearly also part of a Gospel harmony, combining material from Matthew, Luke, John and probably Mark: the text here merges Mt. 27:55–58, Mk 15:40–43, Lk. 23:49–54 and Jn 19:38. The manuscript was discovered during the excavation of Dura-Europus on the Euphrates, measures 9.5cm × 10cm, and is housed in the Beinecke Library at Yale University. The parchment dates from the early third century at the latest, in this case quite certainly, because of the fragment's discovery in a dateable archaeological layer. Many of the manuscripts translated in this volume are dated by their handwriting, the analysis of which is a rather inexact science. The Dura parchment's date makes it therefore a very early witness to multiple canonical Gospels in combination.

TRANSLATION

. . . of Zebedee, and Salome, and the women from among those who had followed him from Galilee, seeing him crucified. It was the Day of Preparation,[†] and the Sabbath was approaching. When it was evening on the Day of Preparation, that is, Sabbath Eve, there came a man whose name was Joseph. He was

from the Judaean town of Erinmathaea,* and was a member of
the council. He was also a good, righteous man and a disciple
of Jesus, though he kept this secret because he was afraid of the
Jews. He was awaiting the kingdom of God. He had not consented to the decision of the council.

10 Marcion's Gospel

(c. 150 CE)

INTRODUCTION

Marcion, like Tatian (see pp. 71–82), is a rare example of a known author of an apocryphal Gospel. Marcion was active in the middle of the second century and was quickly regarded as a heretic. What made his reputation was the idea that there was not just one God of the Bible, but two: a creator God of the Old Testament who meted out justice, and a merciful God of goodness who was revealed in Jesus. This particular view led him to reimagine Jesus not as a figure predicted in the Old Testament and who therefore fulfilled it, but as a revelation who came out of a clear blue sky.

Nevertheless, far from being completely disconnected from the Old Testament deity, Jesus was in fact the Jewish God's nemesis. This led Marcion to compose a book called the 'Antitheses', in which Old Testament and New Testament episodes were contrasted. This follows what Jesus to an extent already had done in the Sermon on the Mount, in contrasting 'an eye for an eye' with the expectation that disciples should turn the other cheek. An example which appears in Marcion's Gospel below is his reordering of Luke 4:27 in the middle of Luke 17:11–19, to highlight the point that Jesus' curing of ten lepers is far more impressive than the Old Testament prophet Elisha only curing one.

Marcion also produced an edition of Paul's epistles, in which some of the apostle's letters are substantially abbreviated. A section of Paul's letter to the Romans (2:3–11) dealing with God's judgement, for example, is excluded probably because for

Marcion the God of Jesus Christ is only a God of love and mercy. Large chunks of Romans 9–11 are cut from Marcion's text because they cover God's dealings with Israel (which is really the *creator God*'s domain) or Old Testament prophecy of Christ.

Some of the same concerns appear in Marcion's Gospel, which has a method of composition different from those seen previously: as he did with Paul's epistles, he took a Gospel text and applied his blue pencil to deleting what he considered later accretions. His base text from which he worked was something very close to our Gospel of Luke, which had been written sixty to seventy years earlier, and from this text of Luke he made substantial excisions. As with the case of Paul's letter to the Romans above, many of these omissions from Luke are of passages in which God is depicted as a judge, or in which Jesus fulfils Scripture. One especially large omission is of the beginning of Luke: most of the first four chapters are excised, and Marcion's Gospel probably began with the words 'In the fifteenth year of the emperor Tiberius, in the time of Pontius Pilate [from Lk. 3:1], Jesus came down to Capernaum, a town in Galilee [from 4:31]'. At this point in Luke, Jesus 'came down' from Nazareth, but, standing at the beginning of Marcion's Gospel, the same phrase refers to his descent from heaven. He therefore appears on earth fully grown, and in line with this Marcion displays some ambiguity about whether Jesus is truly a human being.

Marcion's Gospel does not survive in manuscript form, and can only be partially (and hypothetically) reconstructed on the basis of reports especially by the Christian authors Tertullian in the third century and Epiphanius in the fourth. These church fathers, in their zeal to expose Marcion as a false teacher, explain extensively what Marcion omitted from the Gospel narrative. Marcion continued long after his death to be perhaps the most iconic example of a heretic.

Because Marcion's Gospel is an abridged version of Luke's Gospel, the following translation uses the chapters and versification used in the Bible for Luke. The sections in plain text below are those which were likely to have been part of Marcion's Gospel; italicized sections are those which may have been but are not certainly part of it; scenes which Marcion almost certainly deleted from Luke's Gospel are noted in square brackets. (Square brackets in this section, therefore, do not indicate lacunae in a manuscript as they do elsewhere in this book.) Occasionally individual words, phrases or sentences which are uncertain or deleted by Marcion are noted below as well. The differences between Marcion and the canonical Gospels lie not only in the content, however, but also in how that content was understood. Some passages, like the parable of the rich man being tormented in hell (16:19–31), Marcion understood to describe the activity of the Old Testament creator God, who was harsh and just, unlike the God and Father of Jesus, who was merciful.

SELECT DRAMATIS PERSONAE

JESUS

THE TWELVE DISCIPLES

MARY MAGDALENE, JOANNA, SUSANNA, LEVI, CLEOPAS *Other disciples not among the twelve*

JOHN THE BAPTIST *The forerunner of Jesus*

MARTHA AND MARY, OF BETHANY *Friends of Jesus*

MARY, JAMES, JOSES, JUDAS AND SIMON *Jesus' (for Marcion, alleged) mother and brothers*

SIMON PETER'S MOTHER-IN-LAW, MARY THE MOTHER OF JAMES *Relations of the disciples*

PHARISEES *An influential, elite Jewish movement*

SIMON *A Pharisee*

SADDUCEES *Another influential Jewish movement*

SCRIBES *Authoritative experts in Jewish Law*

CHIEF PRIESTS *The ruling temple authorities*

ELDERS *Authorities over civic and synagogue affairs*

PILATE *The Roman governor of Judaea*

HEROD THE TETRARCH *A Jewish client-king, ruler of Galilee and Peraea*

JOSEPH *A member of the council*

SIMON OF CYRENE *A passer-by who carried Jesus' cross*

LEGION *Demonic name of a possessed man*

JAIRUS *A synagogue leader*
JAIRUS' DAUGHTER *Twelve-year-old girl healed by Jesus*
ZACCHAEUS *A tax collector*

TRANSLATION

1:1–2:52: Jesus' birth – omitted

3:1–20: John the Baptist prepares the way – omitted except for 3.1a

3:21–38: Jesus' baptism and genealogy – omitted

4:1–13: The temptation of Jesus – omitted

4:14–28: Jesus visits Nazareth – moved later or omitted

3:1a, with parts of 4:31–39 and 4:16–30: Jesus in Capernaum and Nazareth

In the fifteenth year of the principate of Tiberius Caesar, in the time of Pontius Pilate, Jesus came down to Capernaum, a town in Galilee, and taught there in the synagogue. The people were amazed at his teaching, because his word had such authority. In the synagogue there was a man with the spirit of an unclean demon.

'Leave me alone!' he shrieked. 'What do you want with us, Jesus of Nazareth? Have you come to destroy us? I know who you are – the Holy One of God!'

'Be quiet!' Jesus rebuked him. 'Come out of him!' The demon threw the man down in their midst, and came out leaving him unharmed.

He then came to Nazareth, and went to the synagogue as was the custom on the Sabbath.

'Perhaps you will tell me the proverb, "Physician, heal yourself!"' he said.

The people rose up and threw him out of the town. They forced him to the brow of the hill on which the town was built, so they could hurl him down. But he passed through the middle of the crowd and went on his way.

4:40–44: Jesus' healings

As the sun was setting, all who had people sick with various afflictions brought them to him. He laid hands on each of them and healed them. He also cast out demons from many people, which shrieked, 'You are the Son of God!' But he rebuked the demons and would not let them speak, because they knew he was the Christ.

When day came, Jesus went off to a solitary place. The crowds were looking for him, and when they found him, they tried to prevent him from leaving.

'I must proclaim the kingdom of God to the other towns as well,' Jesus responded. 'For that is the reason I was sent.' He then continued to preach in the Judaean synagogues.

5:1–11: The miraculous catch of fish

It happened that the people were pressing in on Jesus and listening to the word of God. He was standing by the Lake of Gennesaret, and saw two boats by the lake's edge; the fishermen had left them there and were washing their nets. Jesus got into one of the boats and asked Simon, whose boat it was, to put out a little from the shore. Then he sat down and taught the crowds from the boat. When he had finished speaking, he spoke to Simon.

'Put out into deep water, and let your nets down for a catch,' he said.

'Master, we've been toiling away all night and haven't caught anything,' Simon answered. 'But because you say so, I will let the nets down.'

When they had done this, they caught such a huge number of fish that their nets began to burst. They signalled for their partners in the other boat to come and help them, and they came. They all filled both the boats with so many fish that the boats sat very low in the water.

When Simon Peter saw this, he fell at Jesus' knees.

'Get away from me, Lord,' he exclaimed. 'I am a sinful man!'

Peter and all those in the boat with him were astounded at the catch of fish they had made, and so were James and John, the sons of Zebedee, Simon's partners.

'Don't be afraid,' Jesus said to Simon. 'From now on you will be fishers of men.'

They pulled their boats up on shore, left everything and followed him.

5:12–16: The cure of a man with leprosy

It happened that while Jesus was in one town, there was a man there with terrible leprosy. When he saw Jesus, he fell on his face.

'Lord,' he pleaded with Jesus, 'if you are willing, you can make me clean.'

Jesus stretched out his hand and touched him.

'I am willing!' Jesus said. 'Be clean!' Immediately the leprosy left him. But Jesus urged the man, 'Don't mention this to anyone. Go and show yourself to the priest and offer the sacrifice that Moses commanded for your cleansing, as a testimony for you all.'

The news about Jesus nevertheless spread all the more, so that great crowds came to hear him and to be healed from their sicknesses. Jesus, however, would often withdraw to solitary places and pray.

5:17–26: The paralysed man forgiven

It happened one day that Jesus was teaching, and some Pharisees and scribes who had come from every village of Galilee and from Judaea and Jerusalem were sitting there. The healing power of the Lord was with Jesus. Just then, some people came carrying on a mat a man who was paralysed, and they tried to take him into the house and set him down in front of Jesus.

Unable to find a way in because of the crowd, they went up onto the roof, and lowered him on his mat through the tiles into the middle of the crowd in front of Jesus.

Seeing their faith, Jesus said, 'Your sins are forgiven!'

The scribes and the Pharisees began wondering, 'Who is this man who speaks blasphemy? Who can forgive sins but God alone?' Jesus knew that this was what they were thinking.

'Why are you thinking this?' he asked. 'Which is easier to say: "Your sins are forgiven," or, "Get up and walk"? But so that you all may know that the Son of Man has authority on earth to forgive sins, I tell you,' he said to the paralysed man, 'get up, take your mat and go home.' Immediately he got up in front of them, took the mat on which he had been lying and went home giving glory to God. Everyone there was dumbfounded and also gave glory to God. Awestruck, they declared, 'We have seen remarkable things today.'

5:27–32: Jesus calls Levi and eats with sinners

After this, Jesus went off, and he saw a tax collector called Levi sitting at his tax office.

'Follow me,' Jesus said to him. Levi got up, left everything and followed him.

Levi then held a great banquet for Jesus at his house, and with them was a large group of tax collectors and others dining. The Pharisees and the scribes, however, complained to Jesus' disciples, 'Why do you eat and drink with tax collectors and sinners?'

'It is not the healthy who need a doctor, but the sick,' Jesus answered them. 'I have not come to call the just to repentance, but sinners.'

5:33–39: Jesus questioned about fasting

The Pharisees and scribes continued, 'John's disciples often fast and pray, as do those who follow the Pharisees, but yours continue to eat and drink.'

'Can you make the friends of the bridegroom fast while the

bridegroom is with them?' Jesus answered. 'But days are coming when the bridegroom will be taken from them. Then they will fast.'

Then he told them a parable. 'No one puts new wine into old wineskins. If they do, the wine will burst the wineskin and be spilt, and the wineskin will be ruined as well. No, new wine goes in new wineskins. No one tears a piece of unshrunk cloth from a new garment and sews it onto an old one. If they do, the new garment will be torn, and the patch from the new will not match the old.'

6:1–5: Gleaning in the cornfields

One Sabbath, Jesus was walking through fields, and his disciples began to pick some ears of grain and rub them in their hands.

'Why are you doing what is not lawful on the Sabbath?' some Pharisees asked.

'Have you not read what David did when he and his companions were hungry?' Jesus answered them. 'He entered the house of God, and took the shewbread.* He shared it with his companions and they ate what is lawful only for priests to eat.' Jesus continued, 'The Son of Man is Lord even of the Sabbath.'

6:6–11: A man's withered hand healed

On another Sabbath Jesus went into a synagogue and was teaching, and there was a man there whose right hand was deformed. The scribes and the Pharisees were watching Jesus closely to see if he would heal on the Sabbath, looking for a means of accusing him. Jesus knew what they were thinking, and spoke to the man with the shrivelled hand.

'Get up and stand in front of everyone,' Jesus instructed him. The man stood up there.

'Let me ask you all,' Jesus said to them, 'what is lawful on the Sabbath? To do good or evil, to save life or to kill?'

He looked around at them all, and then said to the man, 'Stretch out your hand.' This he did, and his hand was restored. *The scribes and the Pharisees were irate, however, and discussed with one another what to do about Jesus.*

6:12–16: The call of the disciples

One day Jesus went out onto a mountainside to pray, and stayed there all night in prayer to God. When morning came, Jesus summoned his disciples, and chose twelve of them to be designated apostles: Simon (whom he called 'Peter'), his brother Andrew, James, John, Philip, Bartholomew, Matthew, Thomas, James the son of Alphaeus, Simon (called 'the Zealot'), Judas the son of James and Judas Iscariot (who became the traitor).

6:17–26: Blessings and woes

He went down with them and stood on a plain. A great crowd of his disciples and a huge throng of people were there from all over Judaea, Jerusalem and the coast around Tyre and Sidon. They had come to hear him and to be healed of their diseases. Those disturbed by impure spirits were cured, and all the people tried to touch him, because power was radiating from him and healing them all. Looking up at his disciples, he said:

> Blessed are the poor,
> for theirs is the kingdom of God.
> Blessed are those who hunger now,
> for they will be filled.
> Blessed are those who weep now,
> for they will laugh.
> Blessed are you when people hate you,
> when they exclude you and insult you and consider you
>   wicked because of the Son of Man.

'Rejoice on that day and leap for joy, because great is your reward in heaven. For in the same way their ancestors treated the prophets.' He continued:

> But woe to you who are rich,
> for you have received your comfort.
> Woe to you who are full,
> for you will be hungry.
> Woe to you who laugh now,

for you will weep and wail.
Woe to you when everyone speaks well of you,
for their ancestors treated the false prophets
in the same way.'

6:27–35: Love for one's enemies

'I declare to those of you listening,' Jesus said, 'love your enemies, do good to those who hate you, bless those who curse you, pray for those who mistreat you. If someone strikes you on one cheek, offer them the other one as well. If someone takes your tunic, do not stop them taking your cloak. Give to everyone who asks of you, and if anyone takes what is yours, do not ask for it back.

'Do to others as you would want them to do to you. If you love those who love you, what credit is that to you? Even sinners love those who love them. And if you treat well those who treat you well, what credit is that to you? Even sinners do that. And if you lend money to those from whom you expect to receive it back, what credit is that to you? Even sinners lend to sinners, so they can be repaid in full. But love your enemies, and treat them well. Lend to them expecting nothing in return. Then your reward will be great, and you will be sons of God, because he is kind to those who are ungrateful and wicked.'

6:36–42: Not judging others

'Be merciful, just as your Father has shown mercy to you,' Jesus continued. 'Do not judge, and you will not be judged. Do not condemn, and you will not be condemned. Forgive, and you will be forgiven. Give, and it will be given to you – a good measure, pressed down and shaken together will run over onto your lap. For the measure you use will be used for you in return.'

He also told them this parable: 'Can the blind lead the blind? Will they not both fall into the ditch? The student is not above the teacher, but everyone who is fully trained will be like their teacher.

'How can you look at the speck in your brother's eye but ignore the plank in your own eye? How can you say to your brother, "Brother, let me remove that speck from your eye," when you cannot see the plank in your own eye? You hypocrite! First take the plank out of your eye, and then you will be able to see clearly enough to remove the speck from your brother's eye.'

6:43–45: The tree and their fruit

'No good tree can bear rotten fruit, nor can a rotten tree bear good fruit. Each tree is recognized from its particular fruit. Figs cannot be picked from thorn bushes, nor grapes from brambles. A good man brings out good from the good stored up in his heart, and an evil man brings out evil from the evil stored up in his heart. For out of the overflow of the heart, the mouth speaks.'

6:46–49: The wise and foolish builders

'Why do you call me, "Lord, Lord" but do not do what I say?' Jesus asked. *'As for everyone who comes to me and hears my words and puts them into practice, I will show you what they are like. They are like a person who built a house, dug down deep and laid the foundations on rock. When a flood came, the waters crashed against that house but could not shake it, because it was well built. But the person who hears my words and does not put them into practice is like a person who builds a house on the ground without a foundation. When the waters crash against that house, it will collapse and its destruction will be complete.'*

7:1–10: The healing of the centurion's servant

When Jesus had finished saying all this to the people listening, he went into Capernaum. A centurion there had a servant whom he valued. The servant was sick and on the point of death, so when the centurion heard about Jesus he sent some

elders of the Jews to him to ask him to come and heal the servant. When the elders reached Jesus, they pleaded with him.

'This centurion is worthy. He loves our nation and has built
a synagogue for us.'

Jesus went with them. While he was still not far from the
house, the centurion sent a message through some of his men.

'Lord, don't trouble yourself, for I am not worthy to have
you under my roof. That is why I did not consider myself
worthy to come to you. But only say the word, and my servant
will be healed. For I myself am a man under authority and I
have soldiers under me. I order one to go, and he goes, and
another to come, and he comes. I order a servant, "Do this,"
and he does it.'

When Jesus heard this, he was amazed at him, and turned to
the crowd trailing behind him.

'I tell you, I have not found faith as great as this in Israel.'
When the centurion's companions who had been dispatched
returned to his house, they found the servant healthy.

7:11–17: The raising of the widow's son in Nain

It happened shortly afterward that Jesus went to a town called
Nain, and his disciples as well as a great crowd accompanied
him. As he was approaching the town gate, the dead body of a
young man – the only son of his widowed mother – was being
carried out. A great crowd from the town was with her, and
when the Lord saw her, he felt pity for her.

'Don't cry,' he said. He then approached the bier and touched
it, and the pall-bearers stopped.

'Young man, I say to you, get up!' Jesus said. The dead man
sat up and began to talk, and Jesus presented him to his mother.
The people were all dumbstruck and gave glory to God.

'A great prophet has arisen among us,' they said. 'God has
come to rescue his people!' The news about Jesus spread
throughout Judaea and the surrounding countryside.

7:18–28: John the Baptist sends emissaries to Jesus

John's disciples reported all this to him. Calling two of them, John sent them to the Lord to ask him if he was the coming one or whether they should wait for another. When the men reached Jesus, they said, 'John the Baptist sent us to ask you: "Are you the coming one, or should we wait for another?" '

At that time Jesus had cured many people of their diseases, afflictions and evil spirits, and given sight to many who were blind. He gave the messengers this reply.

'Go back and report to John what you have seen and heard:
'"The blind receive sight,
 the lame walk,
those with leprosy are cleansed,
the deaf hear,
the dead are raised,
and the poor are told the good news."
'Blessed is the man who does not stumble because of me.'

When John's envoys had left, Jesus began to speak to the crowds about John.

'What did you go out into the wilderness to see? A reed blown about by the wind? Or did you go out to see something else? A man dressed in fine clothes, perhaps? Well, those who wear glorious apparel and live in luxury are inside their palaces. But what did you go out to see? A prophet? Yes, I say to you, and more than a prophet, because he is the one about whom the prophet writes:
'"I will send my messenger ahead of you,
who will prepare your way before you."
'I tell you, among those born of women there is none greater than John, but the least in the kingdom of God is greater than he.'

7:29–35: Jesus' and John's differences

Now all the people, including the tax collectors, who had been baptized by John and had heard Jesus' words, declared God to be in the right. But the Pharisees and teachers of the

Law, however, refused to be baptized by John and rejected God's purpose for them.

'To what, then, can I compare the people of this generation?' Jesus asked. 'What do they resemble? They are like the children who sit in the marketplace and call to one another:

' "We played the flute for you,
but you did not dance;
we sang a lament,
but you did not weep."

'For John the Baptist did not come eating bread or drinking wine, and you say, "He is demon-possessed." But when the Son of Man comes eating and drinking, you say, "Here is a glutton and a drunkard, a friend of tax collectors and sinners." But wisdom is proved right by all her children.'

7:36–50: A sinful woman is forgiven

One of the Pharisees invited Jesus to dine with him, so he went to the Pharisee's house and reclined at the table. Now a sinful woman of that town learned that Jesus was dining at the Pharisee's house, so she went there and took a jar of perfume. She stood behind the end of Jesus' dining couch weeping, and began to wet his feet with her tears. Then she wiped his feet with her hair, kissed them and anointed them with the perfume.

When the Pharisee who had invited Jesus saw this, he thought, 'If this man were a prophet, he would know what sort of woman was touching him – a sinner.'

'Simon,' Jesus said in response, 'I have something to tell you.'

'Tell me, teacher,' he said.

'Two people were in debt to a moneylender. One owed him five hundred *denarii*,[†] the other owed fifty. When neither of them was able to pay him back, he released them both from their debts. So then, which of them will love him more?'

'I expect it is the one released from the larger debt,' Simon replied.

'You are right,' Jesus said. He turned to the woman, but continued to address Simon.

'You see this woman? When I came into your house, you did not give me water for my feet. But she has wet my feet with her tears and wiped them with her hair. You did not give me a kiss, but ever since I entered the house this woman has not stopped kissing my feet. You did not anoint my head with oil, but she has anointed my feet with perfume. Because of all this, I tell you, it is clear that her many sins have been forgiven, because she loves much. But whoever is forgiven little loves little.'

'Your sins are forgiven,' Jesus declared to her.

'Who is this who even forgives sins?' the guests began to say to one another.

'Your faith has saved you,' Jesus said to her. 'Go in peace.'

8:1–8: The parable of the sower

It happened after this that Jesus travelled through various towns and villages, proclaiming the good news of the kingdom of God with his twelve disciples. Also with him were some women who had been cured of evil spirits and sicknesses: Mary (called Magdalene) from whom he had cast out seven demons, Joanna the wife of Herod's steward Chuza, Susanna and many others who were supporting Jesus and the twelve out of their own means.

As a large crowd was gathering and people were coming to Jesus from the towns, he told them a parable.

'A farmer went out to sow his seed. As he was sowing the seed, some fell on the path and was trampled on, and the birds ate it up. Some seed fell on rocky ground, and it came up but quickly withered because it had no moisture. Other seed fell among thorns, which grew up with it and choked it. Still other seed fell on good soil. When it came up it yielded a crop a hundred times what was sown.'

After this, he called out, 'Whoever has ears to hear, let them hear.'

8:9–15: Explanation of the parable of the sower

His disciples asked him what this parable meant.

'The knowledge of the secrets of the kingdom of God has

been given to you,' he said, 'but to the rest I speak in parables,
so that,

' "though seeing, they may not see,
and though hearing, they may not understand."

'This is what the parable means. The seed is the word of
God. The seed on the path stands for those who hear, but
whom the devil approaches and deprives of the word, so that
they cannot believe and be saved. Those on the rocky ground
are those who hear and accept the word joyfully, but have no
root. They believe for a while, but fall away as soon as they
are tested. The seed that fell among thorns represents those
who hear, but as they go on their way they are choked by
worries, wealth and life's pleasures, and so do not grow. But
the seed on good soil stands for those with fine and good
hearts. They hear the word, hold on to it and bear fruit as
they persevere.'

8:16–18: What is hidden will be revealed

'No one lights a lamp and then covers it with a jar or puts it
under the bed. No, they put it on a lamp stand, so that whoever comes in can see its light. For there is nothing hidden that
will not be made manifest, and nothing concealed that will not
be made known and come to light. Consider how you listen,
then. Whoever has will be given more, but whoever does not
have will be deprived even of what they think they have.'

8:19: Jesus' mother and brothers introduced – omitted

8:20–21: Jesus' true mother and brothers

Jesus was told, 'Your mother and brothers are standing outside
and want to see you.'

'Who are my mother and brothers?' Jesus replied. 'It is only
those who listen to my words and obey them.'

8:22–25: The calming of the storm

It happened one day that Jesus got into a boat with his disciples.

'Let us go over to the other side of the lake,' he said to them. They therefore set off. As they were sailing, he fell asleep. A mighty gale came down on the lake; the boat was being engulfed, and they were in great danger.

The disciples went and woke Jesus, saying, 'Master, master, we are drowning!'

Jesus got up and rebuked the wind and the torrent of water. The storm subsided, and all was calm again.

'Where is your faith?' he asked his disciples.

Terrified and amazed, they said to one another, 'Who is this? He even gives orders to winds and water, and they obey him!'

8:26–32: The healing of the Gerasene demoniac

They sailed to the region of the Gerasenes, which is across the lake from Galilee. When Jesus disembarked, a demon-possessed man from the town came up to him. Now, for a long time this man had not worn any clothes; he lived not in a house but among the tombs. When he saw Jesus, he cried out and fell down in front of him.

'What do you want with me, Jesus, Son of God?' he screamed. 'I beg you, do not torture me!' For Jesus had commanded the unclean spirit to come out of the man. Many times that spirit had seized him, and though he was chained hand and foot, he would often break through his chains and was driven by the demon into the wilderness.

'What is your name?' Jesus asked him.

'Legion,' he replied, because many demons were within him. They begged Jesus not to order them into the Abyss. A large sounder of pigs was feeding there on the mountain, and the demons begged Jesus to let them go into the pigs. Jesus gave them permission.

8:33–39: The demons enter the pigs and fall off a cliff

When the demons came out of the man, they went into the pigs, which all rushed down the cliff into the lake and were drowned.

Seeing what had taken place, those tending the pigs ran to the town and the fields and reported it to others. When they heard, these others also went out to see what had happened. When they came to Jesus, they found sitting at his feet the man from whom the demons had gone out, clothed and in his right mind. They were terrified. Those who had seen how the demon-possessed man had been cured told the people of it. Then the whole population of the Gerasene region, overcome with fear as they were, requested Jesus to leave them. So Jesus got into the boat and left. The man from whom the demons had come out begged to be able to stay with him, but Jesus sent him away.

'Go home, and recount everything that God has done for you.' The man went away, reporting all over the town everything that Jesus had done for him.

8:40–41: Jesus raises a dead girl

Now when Jesus returned to the other side of the lake, a crowd welcomed him. (They had all been waiting for him.) There came a man named Jairus, a leader of the synagogue. He fell at Jesus' feet and begged him to come to his house because his only daughter, who was about twelve years old, was dying.

8:42–48: Jesus heals a sick woman

While they were on their way, the crowds were pressing in on Jesus. There was a woman there, who had had a flow of blood for twelve years. She had spent all she had on doctors, but none of them made her any better. She came up behind Jesus and touched the corner of his garment, and immediately her bleeding stopped.

'Who touched me?' Jesus asked.

When they all denied it, Peter said, 'Master, the whole crowd is enveloping you and bearing down on you!'

But Jesus said, 'Someone touched me. I know that power has radiated out from me.'

The woman realized that she would not be able to go unnoticed, and came to Jesus shaking. She fell at his feet, and in front of everyone she said why she had touched him and that she had been instantly healed.

'Daughter, your faith has saved you,' Jesus said to her. 'Go in peace.'

8:49–56: Jesus raises a dead girl
(continued from 8:40–41)

While Jesus was still speaking, a messenger came from the leader of the synagogue's household.

'Your daughter has died,' the messenger said to Jairus. 'Don't trouble the teacher any more.'

'Don't be afraid!' Jesus said when he heard this. 'Only believe, and she will be restored.'

When he came to Jairus' house, Jesus only allowed Peter, John, James and the child's parents in with him. All the others remained outside, lamenting and mourning the girl.

'Stop crying,' Jesus said. 'She is not dead but asleep.'

Knowing that she was dead, they laughed at him. But he took her hand and spoke.

'Child, get up!' he said.

Her spirit returned to her, and she immediately stood up. Jesus ordered her to be given something to eat. Her parents were astounded, but Jesus instructed them not to tell anyone what had happened.

9:1–9: Jesus sends out the twelve

Jesus had called the twelve together and gave them power and authority to drive out every kind of demon and to cure diseases. He also sent them out to preach the kingdom of God and to heal the sick.

'On the journey,' he instructed them, 'take nothing – no staff, no bag, no food, no money, no spare tunic. Whenever you enter a house, stay there until you depart from that town. Wherever you are not welcomed, leave the town shaking the dust off your feet as a testimony against them.'

So they set out and went from town to town and village to village, preaching the good news and healing people everywhere.

Now Herod the tetrarch heard about all this, and he was perplexed because some were saying that John had risen from the dead. Others were saying that Elijah had appeared, and still others that one of the prophets of old had returned.

'I cut off John's head,' Herod said. 'So who is this I am hearing about?' He therefore tried to see Jesus.

9:10–17: The feeding of the five thousand

The apostles returned and reported to Jesus what they had done. He took them with him when he withdrew privately to a town called Bethsaida. Yet crowds found him out and followed him. He welcomed them and spoke to them about the kingdom of God, and cured those in need of healing.

As the day drew on, the twelve came to him.

'Send the crowd away,' they advised, 'so they can go into the surrounding villages and countryside, and lodge and find food there. This is a barren area.'

'Give them something to eat yourselves,' Jesus replied.

'We have no more than five loaves and two fish – unless you want us to go and buy food for all this crowd!' (About five thousand men were there.)

'Get them to sit down in groups of about fifty,' Jesus instructed his disciples.

This they did, and everyone sat down. Taking the five loaves and the two fish, Jesus looked up to heaven, gave a blessing over them and broke them. Then he gave them to the disciples to distribute to the crowd. They all ate and were satisfied, and the left-overs amounted to twelve basketfuls of broken pieces.

9:18–20: Peter confesses Jesus as Messiah

On one occasion Jesus was praying in private with his disciples.

'Who do the people say I, the Son of Man, am?' he asked them.

'Some say John the Baptist,' they replied, 'others say Elijah, and still others that one of the prophets of old has returned.'

'But who do you say I am?' he asked.

'The Christ of God,' Peter replied.

9:21–25: Jesus predicts his death

Now Jesus warned them sternly not to say this to anyone, but stated that the Son of Man must suffer greatly and be rejected by the elders, the chief priests and the scribes, and be killed but raised again on the third day.

'If anyone wants to be a disciple of mine,' he said to them all, 'he must deny himself, take up his cross daily and follow me. For whoever wants to save his life will lose it, but whoever loses his life for me will save it. What good is it for someone who has gained the whole world if he loses or forfeits himself?'

9:26–27: Future judgement and the kingdom of God

'The Son of Man will be ashamed of whoever is ashamed of me and my words,' Jesus continued, *when he comes in his glory with the glory of the Father and of the holy angels. Truly I tell you, there are some standing here who will not taste death before they see the kingdom of God.'*

9:28–36: The transfiguration

About eight days later, after this teaching, Jesus took Peter, John and James and went up onto a mountain to pray. As he was praying, the appearance of his face changed, and his clothes flashed white. Just then, two men, Moses and Elijah, appeared in glory and began to converse with him. [*Reference to Jesus 'fulfilling his departure' then omitted.*] Peter and the other two were feeling very sleepy, but when they revived, they saw his glory as well as the two men standing with him. The men then distanced themselves from Jesus.

'Master,' Peter said to him, 'it is good for us to be here. Let us make three shelters – one for you, one for Moses and one for Elijah.' (He did not know what he was saying.)

While Peter was speaking, a cloud appeared and enveloped them. They were afraid as they went into the cloud. Then a voice came from heaven.

'This is my Son, whom I have chosen. Listen to him!'

After the voice had gone, Jesus was then alone. The disciples were silent, and did not tell anyone of what they had seen at that time.

9:37–43: Jesus heals a possessed boy

The next day, after they had come down from the mountain, a great crowd met Jesus. Just then, a man called out from the crowd:

'Teacher, I beg you to look at my son, for he is my only child. A spirit seizes him and he will suddenly scream. It convulses him and he foams at the mouth. It scarcely ever leaves him, and is killing him. I asked your disciples to cast it out, but they were not able.'

'O unbelieving generation,' Jesus replied, 'how long must I stay with you and put up with you? *Bring your son here.*'

While he was on his way, the demon threw the boy down and convulsed him. Jesus rebuked the impure spirit, healed the boy and returned him to his father. And they were all amazed at the greatness of God.

9:43–48: Jesus' death predicted again

As they were all marvelling at everything which Jesus did, he instructed his disciples.

'Listen carefully to this,' he said. 'The Son of Man is going to be delivered to his enemies.'

They did not understand what he meant, however. It was hidden from them, and they were afraid to ask him about it.

A dispute arose among them as to which of them might be the greatest. Jesus knew their hearts, and so took a child and placed him beside him.

'Whoever welcomes this little child in my name welcomes me,' he said to them, 'and whoever welcomes me welcomes the one who sent me. It is the least among you all that is great.'

9:49–50: Whoever is not against you is for you

'Master,' said the apostle John, 'we saw someone driving out demons in your name, so we tried to stop him because he was not one of us.'

'Do not stop him,' Jesus said, 'for whoever is not against you is for you.'

9:51–56: Opposition in a Samaritan village

It happened that as the time for him to be taken up was approaching, Jesus set his face towards Jerusalem. He sent messengers on ahead, who went to a Samaritan village to make preparations for him. The people there did not welcome him, however, because he was on his way to Jerusalem. When the disciples James and John found this out, they asked, 'Lord, shall we call down fire from heaven to destroy them?' Turning to them, Jesus rebuked them, and they all set off for another village.

9:57–62: The cost of following Jesus

As they were travelling along the road, a man addressed him.

'I will follow you wherever you go.'

'Foxes have holes and birds of the air have nests,' Jesus replied, 'but the Son of Man has nowhere to lay his head.'

He said to another, 'Follow me.'

'Lord, let me first go and bury my father,' the man replied.

'Let the dead bury their own dead,' Jesus said to him. 'As for you, go and proclaim the kingdom of God.'

Still another said, 'I will follow you, Lord; but first let me go back and say goodbye to those in my household.'

'No one who sets his hand to the plough but looks back is fit for the kingdom of God,' Jesus replied.

10:1–11: Jesus sends out the seventy-two

After this, the Lord appointed seventy-two others and sent them out ahead two by two, to every town and place where he was planning to go.

'The harvest is plentiful, but the workers are few,' he told them, 'Pray to the Lord of the harvest, therefore, to send out workers to the harvest. Go! I am sending you out now like lambs among wolves. Do not take a purse or a bag or sandals, and do not greet anyone on the way.

'Whenever you enter a house, first say to the household, "Peace be upon this house." If there is a son of peace there, your peace will rest on it. If not, it will return to you. Stay at that house, eating and drinking whatever they give you, for the labourer is worthy of his hire. Do not go about from house to house.

'Wherever you enter a town and are welcomed, eat what is set before you. Heal the sick there and tell them, "The kingdom of God has come near you!" But if you enter a town which does not welcome you, go out into its streets and declare, "Even the dust of your town on us we wipe off our feet. Be warned! The kingdom of God has come near."'

10:12–15: Jesus pronounces judgement upon Galilean towns

'On that day, I tell you, it will be more bearable for Sodom than for that town,' Jesus said. 'Woe to you, Chorazin! Woe to you, Bethsaida! For if the wonders performed in you had occurred in Tyre and Sidon, they would have repented in sackcloth and ashes long ago. But it will be more bearable for Tyre and Sidon on the day of judgement than it will be for you. And you, Capernaum, will you be lifted to the heavens? No, you will go down to Hell.'

10:16–24: The sending of the seventy-two (continued)

'Whoever listens to you listens to me, but whoever rejects you rejects me. And whoever rejects me rejects him who sent me.'

The seventy-two returned, overjoyed.

'Lord, even the demons submit to us in your name,' they said.

'I saw Satan fall like lightning from heaven,' Jesus replied. 'I have given you authority to trample on serpents and scorpions, and authority over all the power of the enemy. Nothing will harm you! Do not rejoice that the spirits submit to you, however, but rejoice that your names are written in heaven.'

At that time Jesus was full of joy through the Holy Spirit.

'I thank and praise you, Lord of heaven,' he exclaimed, 'because you have concealed these things from the wise and clever, but revealed them to little children. Yes, Father, for this is your will in your presence. All things have been committed to me by my Father. No one knows who the Father is except the Son and no one knows who the Son is except the Father and those to whom the Son chooses to reveal him.'

Jesus turned to his disciples and spoke privately to them.

'Blessed are the eyes that see what you see. For I tell you, the prophets did not see what you see, and did not hear what you hear.'

10:25–28: Discussion with a teacher of the Law

A teacher of the Law stood up to test Jesus.

'Teacher,' he asked, 'what must I do to inherit eternal life?'

'What is written in the Law?' Jesus replied to him. 'How do you understand it?'

'"Love the Lord your God with all your heart, soul, strength and mind,"' he replied, 'and "love your neighbour as yourself."'

'You have answered correctly,' Jesus replied. 'Do this and you will live.'

10:29-37: The Parable of the Good Samaritan

Wanting to justify himself, however, he asked Jesus, 'And who is my neighbour?'

'A man was going down from Jerusalem to Jericho when he fell among thieves. They stripped him of his clothes, beat him and went away, leaving him half dead. A priest chanced to be going down that way, but when he saw the man, he passed by on the other side. Similarly, a Levite, when he came to the place and saw him, also passed by on the other side. But a Samaritan travelling there came upon the man, and when he saw him, he took pity on him. He went over to him, bound up his wounds and poured oil and wine on them. He set the man on his own pack animal and took him to an inn. There he took care of him. On the following day, he gave the inn-keeper two denarii.† *"Take care of him," he said, "and if you incur any additional expense, I will repay you when I come back."*

'So then,' Jesus asked, 'which of the three was a neighbour to the man who fell among thieves, do you think?'

'The man who had mercy on him,' the teacher replied.

'Go, then,' Jesus said, 'and do the same yourself.'

10:38–42: At the home of Martha and Mary

In the course of their journey, they entered a village. A woman there named Martha welcomed Jesus into her house. She had a sister named Mary, who sat at Jesus' feet, listening to him speaking, while Martha was occupied with doing things for them. She went over to Jesus.

'Lord,' she said, 'don't you care that my sister has left me to do all the work on my own? Tell her to help me!'

'Martha, Martha!' Jesus replied. 'You are anxiously running around doing many things, but only one is necessary. Mary has chosen what is better, and it will not be taken away from her.'

11:1–13: Prayer

It happened that Jesus was praying in a certain place. When he finished, one of his disciples said to him, 'Lord, teach us to pray, just as John taught his disciples.'

He said to them, 'When you pray, say:

' "Father,
grant us the Holy Spirit,
your kingdom come.
Give us each day our daily bread.
Forgive us our sins,
for we also forgive everyone who sins against us.
And do not let us be brought into temptation." '

'Suppose you have a friend,' Jesus continued, 'and you go to him in the middle of the night and say, "My friend, lend me three loaves of bread because an acquaintance of mine has visited me on a journey, and I have nothing to offer him." Then the man inside answers, "Don't bother me. My door is already locked, and my children and I are in bed. I can't get up and give you anything." I tell you, even though he will not get up and give you anything out of friendship, if you are shameless enough to persist he certainly will get up and give you whatever you need.

'So I say this to you. Ask and it will be given to you. Seek and you will find. Knock and the door will be opened to you. For everyone who asks receives, whoever seeks finds, and whoever knocks will have the door opened to him.

'You fathers – if your son asked for a fish, would you give him a snake instead? Or if he asked for an egg, would you give him a scorpion? If you then, though you are evil, understand about giving good gifts to your children, how much more will your Father give the Holy Spirit to those who ask him!'

11:14–22: The Beelzebul controversy

Jesus was driving out a demon that was mute. It happened that when the demon left, the man who had been mute spoke, and the crowd was amazed. Some of them, however, said, 'He is driving out demons by the power of Beelzebul, the prince of demons.' Others tested him by asking him for a sign from heaven.

Jesus knew their thoughts.

'Any kingdom divided against itself will be destroyed, and a house divided against itself will fall,' he said. 'If Satan is divided against himself, how can his kingdom stand? I say this because you claim that I am driving out demons by the power of Beelzebul. Now if it is by Beelzebul that I am driving out demons, by whom do your followers drive them out? So then, they will be your judges. But if I am driving out demons by the finger of God, then the kingdom of God has come upon you.

'When a strong man, fully armed, is guarding his house, his possessions are secure. But when someone even stronger attacks and overpowers him, the stronger man will take away the armour in which the man had been confident, and divide up the spoils.

11:23: Indifferent opponents

'Whoever is not with me is against me, and whoever does not gather with me scatters.'

11:24–26: Migrations of unclean spirits

'When an unclean spirit comes out of someone, it goes through arid places looking for somewhere to rest but cannot find it. Then it says, "I will return to the place from where I came." When it arrives, it finds the house swept clean and set in order. Then it goes and fetches seven other spirits more wicked than itself, and they go in and take up residence there. As a result, the person ends up worse than he had been at first.'

11:27–29c: Physical birth vs obedience to God

As Jesus was saying this, a woman in the crowd called out, 'Blessed is the womb which bore you, and the breasts which nursed you.'

'Blessed rather are those who hear the word of God and

obey it,' Jesus replied. As the crowds gathered, Jesus said, 'This is a wicked generation. It seeks a sign but will receive none.'

11:29d–32: Comparison of Jesus with Jonah and Solomon – omitted

11:33–36: The Lamp of the Body

'No one lights a lamp and puts it somewhere hidden, or under a bushel† measure. No, they set it on a lamp stand, so that whoever goes in may see the light. Your eye is the lamp of your body. When your eyes are healthy, your whole body is also full of light. But if they are evil, your body is also full of darkness. See to it, then, that the light within you does not grow dark. If your whole body is full of light, then, and no part of it is dark, it will be as full of light as when a lamp shines its light on you.'

11:37–48: Woes against the Pharisees and teachers of the Law

As Jesus was speaking, a Pharisee invited him to dine with him. So Jesus went in and reclined. The Pharisee was surprised, however, when he saw that Jesus did not first wash before the meal.

'You Pharisees!' the Lord said to him. 'You clean the outside of the cup and dish, but inside you are grasping and wicked. Fools! Are the maker of the outside and the maker of the inside not one and the same? As for what is inside you, give alms to the poor. Then you will be entirely clean.

'Woe to you Pharisees! You tithe your mint, rue and every other herb, but neglect the calling and the love of God. You should have practised the latter without neglecting the rest.

'Woe to you Pharisees! You love the most important seats in the synagogues, and greetings in the marketplaces.

'Woe to you! You are like unmarked graves which people trample over unawares.'

'Sir,' a teacher of the Law objected, 'when you say these things, you insult us as well.'

'Woe to you, too, you teachers!' Jesus replied. 'You load people down with intolerable burdens, but don't lift a finger to ease their loads.

'Woe to you! You build tombs for the prophets, though it was your ancestors who killed them. So then, you testify that you do not approve of what your ancestors did. They killed the prophets, but you build tombs for them.'

11:49–51: Judgement on this generation – omitted

11:52–54: Woes on the Pharisees and teachers of the Law (continued from 11:37–48)

'Woe to you teachers of the Law! You have taken away the key to knowledge. You have not gone through the door yourselves, but you have prevented others from entering.'

Jesus went outside, and the Pharisees and the scribes began to attack him viciously, continually interrogating him, waiting to catch him out in something he said.

12:1–5: Warnings of judgement

At that time, an enormous crowd had gathered, so many that they were trampling on one another. Jesus began to speak first to his disciples.

'Be on your guard against the yeast of the Pharisees, which is hypocrisy,' he said. 'There is nothing concealed that will not be revealed, or hidden that will not be made known. What you say in the dark will be heard in the daylight, and what you whisper indoors will be shouted from the rooftops.

'I tell you, my friends, do not be afraid of those who can kill the body but can do no more after that. Let me tell you whom you should fear. Fear him who has the authority to throw you into hell after your body has been killed. Yes, I tell you, fear him.'

12:6–7: Comparison with sparrows – omitted

12:8–12: Confessing Jesus publicly

'I tell you, whoever publicly confesses me before others, I will also confess before God. But whoever denies me before others will be denied before God. Whoever speaks a word against the Son of Man will be forgiven, but whoever blasphemes against the Holy Spirit will not be forgiven. When you are brought before synagogues, rulers and authorities, do not worry about how or what to speak in your defence, for the Holy Spirit will teach you at that time what to say.'

12:13–21: The parable of the rich fool

Someone from the crowd said to Jesus, 'Teacher, tell my brother to share our inheritance with me.'

'Who appointed me an arbiter between you?' Jesus replied. 'Watch out! Guard yourself against any kind of greed, because a person's life is not derived from the abundance of his possessions.'

He told them this parable.

'There was once a rich man whose land yielded abundant harvests. He thought to himself, "What shall I do? I have nowhere to store my produce." Then he said, "I know what I'll do. I will pull down my barns and build bigger ones, then I can store all my grain and produce. I'll be able to say to myself, 'My soul, you have plenty of produce laid up for many years. Relax, eat, drink and be merry.'" But God said to him, "You fool! This very night your soul will be demanded from you. Then who will get what you have prepared for yourself?" This is how it will be for whoever stores up treasure for himself but is not rich toward God.'

12:22–32: Do not worry about food or clothes

'Therefore I tell you,' Jesus said to his disciples, 'do not worry your soul about food, or your body about clothing. For the soul is more than food, and the body more than clothes. Consider how the ravens do not sow or harvest. They do not collect food in barns. And how much more valuable you are than birds. Which of you by worrying can add a moment to your life? If you cannot even do this, why worry about the other matters?

'Consider how the lilies grow. They do not labour or spin. Yet I say to you, not even Solomon in all his glory was dressed like one of them. [*Reference to 'God clothing the grass' then probably omitted.*] Do not look out for what you will eat or drink – do not be anxious about that. For the nations of the world chase after all these things, but the Father knows that you need them. Now seek his kingdom, and you will receive these things in addition. Do not be afraid, my little flock, for the Father has resolved to give you the kingdom.'

12:33–34: Instruction to sell possessions

'Sell your possessions and give alms to the poor. Make purses for yourselves that do not wear out, an unfading treasure in heaven, where thief does not come near and moth does not destroy. For where your treasure is, there your heart will also be.'

12:35–48: Warning to keep alert

'Be ready, with your lamps kindled. You should be like servants who wait for their master to return from a wedding, so that when he arrives and knocks they will be able immediately to open the door for him. Blessed are those servants whose master finds them awake when he returns. Truly I say to you, they will be dressed to wait on his table. Blessed are those servants, even if their master comes back at the evening watch. Be warned! If the owner of the house knew when the thief was coming, he would not have let his house be robbed. You too must be ready, because the Son of Man will come at an unexpected hour.'

'Lord,' Peter asked, 'are you addressing this parable to us, or to everyone?'

'Who, then, is the faithful and wise manager,' the Lord

replied, 'whom the master has appointed over his body of servants to give them their regular allocation of food? Blessed is that servant whom the master finds doing this when he comes. Truly I tell you, he will appoint him over all his property. But if that servant thinks, "My master must have been delayed," and then begins to beat the other male and female servants, and to eat, drink and get drunk, that servant's master will come back unexpectedly. He will cut him to pieces and assign him a place with the unbelievers.

'The servant who knows his master's will and does not prepare or do what the master wants will be punished severely. The one who does not know, however, and does things deserving punishment will be treated less severely. From everyone who has received much, much will be required; and from everyone entrusted with much, more will be asked.'

12:49–53: Jesus brings not peace but division

'I have come to cast fire on the earth, and how I wish it were already kindled!' Jesus continued. 'I have a baptism to undergo, and how burdened I am until it is completed! Do you think I have come to bring peace to the earth? No, I tell you – to bring division. Henceforth there will be five divided in one household, three against two and two against three. Father will be divided against son and son against father, mother against daughter and daughter against mother, mother-in-law against daughter-in-law and daughter-in-law against mother-in-law.'

12:54–59: Signs of the times

Jesus then addressed the crowds:

'When you see a cloud rising in the west, you immediately conclude, "It is going to rain," and that is what happens. When you see a south wind blowing, you deduce, "It is going to be hot," and it is. You hypocrites! You can evaluate how the earth and the sky look. Why is it that you do not know how to evaluate this present moment?

'Why can you not judge for yourselves what is right? When

you are on your way to face your adversary before the magistrate, take pains to be reconciled on the way. Otherwise your adversary may take you before the judge, and the judge hand you over to the sergeant, and the sergeant throw you into prison. I say to you, you will then not get out until you have paid the last *quadrans*.'†

13:1–5: The Galileans and the tower of Siloam – omitted

13:6–9: The parable of the fig tree – omitted

13:10–17: The healing of the disabled woman

One Sabbath, Jesus was teaching in a synagogue. A woman there had been afflicted by a spirit for eighteen years. She had a stoop and was unable stand up properly. When Jesus saw her, he called out to her, 'Woman, be free from your affliction!' He placed his hands on her, and immediately she stood up straight and glorified God.

The synagogue leader objected, vexed because Jesus had healed on the Sabbath.

'There are six days to work,' the synagogue leader said to the people. 'Come and be healed on those days, but not on the Sabbath.'

'You hypocrites!' the Lord replied. 'Would any of you refuse to release your ox or donkey from the stall to water it on the Sabbath? This is a daughter of Abraham, whom Satan has kept bound for eighteen long years – should she not be released from her shackles on the Sabbath?'

When he had said this, all those who had opposed him were humiliated, and the congregation was delighted with all the wonderful things he was doing.

13:18–21: The parables of the mustard seed and the leaven

'What is the kingdom of God like?' Jesus said. 'To what shall I compare it? It is like a mustard seed, which a man took and sowed in his garden. It grew and became a tree, and the birds of the air nested in its branches.'

Again he asked, 'To what shall I compare the kingdom of God? It is like yeast which a woman mixed with three *seahs*† of flour until all the dough was leavened.'

13:22–24: The few who are saved

Jesus made his way to Jerusalem through the towns and villages, teaching as he went.

Someone asked him, 'Lord, is it only a few who will be saved?'

'Make every effort to enter through the narrow gate,' Jesus replied, 'for many, I tell you, will try to enter but will not be able.'

13:25–28: The parable of the householder

'As soon as the owner of the house gets up and closes the door,' Jesus continued, 'you may be standing outside, knocking and pleading, "Sir, open the door for us." But he will reply, "I don't know where you have come from." Well might you say, "We ate and drank with you, and you taught in our town." But he will reply, "I don't know where you have come from. Away from me, all you unrighteous!" There will be weeping and gnashing of teeth there, when you see the righteous in the kingdom of God, but you are kept outside.'

13:29–30: The feast in the kingdom of God – omitted

13:31–35: Jesus' sorrow for Jerusalem – omitted

14:1–11: Jesus at a Pharisee's house

It happened that Jesus visited the house of one of the leading Pharisees, to dine there on the Sabbath. Those present were keeping a close eye on him. There was also a man there whose body was swollen with fluid.

'Is it lawful to heal on the Sabbath or not?' Jesus asked the Pharisees and the teachers of the Law. They said nothing. Jesus took hold of the man, healed him and sent him on his way. Jesus then addressed the others;

'Which of you who has a child or an ox that falls into a well would not immediately pull it out on the Sabbath?' They were not able to give an answer.

Jesus addressed a parable to those who had been invited, when he saw how they would select the best-placed dining couches.

'When you are invited to a wedding banquet, do not recline on the best-placed dining couch, in case someone more distinguished than you has been invited. If that happens, the host will come and say to you, "Give your place up for him." Then out of shame you will have to take the least important place. But when you are invited, take the least important place, so that when the host comes, he will say to you, "My friend, move up to a better place." Then you will receive honour in front of all the other guests. For everyone who exalts himself will be humbled, and whoever humbles himself will be exalted.'

14:12–14: Teaching about the rewards of hospitality

Jesus said to his host, 'When you give a lunch party or dinner, do not invite your friends, family and other relatives, or your rich neighbours. If you do, they may invite you back and that will be your recompense. But when you host a dinner, invite those who are poor, crippled, lame or blind. Then you will be blessed, because although they cannot repay you, you will be repaid at the resurrection.'

14:15–24: The parable of the great banquet

When one of the guests dining there heard all this, he said to Jesus, 'Blessed is he who eats in the kingdom of God.'

'There was a man holding a great banquet who had invited a great number of guests,' Jesus replied. 'When the time for the banquet came, he sent his servant out to tell those who had been invited to come, because everything was now ready.

'But they all made similar excuses. The first said, "I have just bought a field, and I must go and see it. Please excuse me."

'Another said, "I have just bought five yoke of oxen, and I am going to try them out. Please excuse me."

'Still another said, "I have just got married, and so am not able to come."

'The servant came back and told all this to his master. The owner of the house was angry, and told his servant, "Go out straight away into the highways and byways of town and bring in those who are poor, crippled, blind and lame."

' "Master," the servant said, "I have done what you ordered, but there is still space."

'Then the master told his servant, "Go out into the paths and lanes and make them come, so that my house is full. For I say to you, not one of those others who were invited will taste anything of my banquet." '

14:25–35: The cost of being a disciple

Large crowds were travelling with Jesus, and he turned to address them:

'*If anyone comes to me and does not despise his father and mother, his wife and children, his brothers and sisters – and even his very life, he will not be able to be my disciple. Nor can whoever does not carry their cross and follow me be my disciple.*

'*Suppose one of you wants to build a tower. Would you not first sit down and count the cost to see if you could carry it through? Otherwise, you might lay the foundation and not be able to finish it. Then everyone who sees it will laugh at you and say, "This person began a building but was not able to finish it."*

'*Or imagine a king planning to go to war against another king. Won't he sit down first and plan whether he can oppose with ten thousand men an enemy coming against him with twenty thousand? If he cannot, he will send a delegation to the enemy while he is still far off and will sue for peace. Similarly, any of you who does not give up all he has cannot be my disciple.*

'Salt is fine, but if it loses its saltiness, how can it be made savoury again? It is useful neither for the soil nor for the dungheap, and must be thrown away. Whoever has ears to hear, let them hear.'

15:1–7: The parable of the lost sheep

Now tax collectors and sinners were all drawing near to Jesus to hear him. The Pharisees and scribes complained at Jesus welcoming sinners and eating with them, however. Then Jesus told them this parable.

'Which of you who has a hundred sheep and loses one of them does not leave the ninety-nine out in the open and go after the lost one until he finds it? When he finds it, he carries it on his shoulders joyfully and goes home. Then he calls his friends and neighbours together and says to them, "Rejoice with me, because I have found my lost sheep!" I tell you that in the same way there will be more joy in heaven over one sinner who repents than over ninety-nine righteous people who have no need to repent.'

15:8–10: The parable of the lost coin

'Or imagine that a woman has ten *drachmas*.† If she lost one of them, would she not light a lamp, sweep the house and look carefully until she found it? When she finds it, she calls her friends and neighbours together and says to them, "Rejoice with me, because I have found the *drachma* which I lost." In the same way, I tell you, there is joy in the presence of God over one sinner who repents.'

15:11–32: The parable of the prodigal son – omitted

16:1–15: The parable of the unjust steward

Jesus told his disciples, 'There was a certain rich man. He had a steward who was accused of wasting his possessions. "What is this I hear about you?", his master questioned him. "Prepare the accounts of your stewardship, because you cannot be manager any longer."

' "What shall I do now?" the steward wondered. "My master is taking my job away. I am too weak to dig, but too ashamed to beg ... I know what I'll do to be welcomed into other people's houses when I lose my job here."

'He summoned each of his master's debtors. "How much do you owe my master?" he asked the first.

' "One hundred *baths*† of olive oil," he replied.

'The steward told him, "Take your receipt, sit down quickly and make it fifty."

'He then asked another, "How much do you owe?"

' "A hundred *kors*† of wheat," he replied.

'He told him, "Take your receipt and make it eighty."

'The master praised the unrighteous steward because he had acted shrewdly. For the people of this age are cleverer with their contemporaries than are the people of the light. I say to you, make friends through unrighteous mammon, so that when it is gone, they will welcome you into everlasting dwellings.

'Whoever is trustworthy in very little can be trusted with much, and whoever is unjust in very little will be unjust in much. If therefore you have not been trustworthy with unrighteous mammon, who will entrust you with true riches? And if you have not been trustworthy with someone else's property, who will give you mine?

'No servant can serve two masters. If he does, he will hate one and love the other, or be devoted to one and despise the other. You cannot serve both God and mammon.'

Now the Pharisees, who loved money, heard all this and were disapproving.

'You may justify yourselves in the eyes of others,' Jesus said to them, 'but God knows your hearts. What people prize is abominable in God's sight.'

16:16–18: John the Baptist and the Law and the Prophets

'The Law and the Prophets lasted until John. Since then, the kingdom of God has been proclaimed, and everyone is forcing their way into it. It is easier for heaven and earth to pass away than for a single serif of my words to pass away.

'Anyone who divorces his wife and marries another woman commits adultery, and whoever marries a divorced woman is like an adulterer.'

16:19–31: The parable of the rich man and Lazarus

'There was once a rich man. He would dress in finest purple and linen, and do himself well every day. A poor man, called Lazarus, was covered in sores and lay at the rich man's gate, longing to eat what fell from the rich man's table. Even the dogs came and licked his sores.

'When the poor man died, angels carried him off to Abraham's side. The rich man died, and he was buried. In Hades, he looked up in his torment, and saw Abraham far away, with Lazarus by his side. "Father Abraham," he called out, "have pity on me! Please send Lazarus to dip a fingertip in water and cool down my tongue, because I am in agony in this fire."

'"Son," Abraham replied, "remember that you had your good things during your lifetime, while Lazarus received bad. Now he is comforted here and you are in agony. Because of this, a great chasm has been fixed between us and you, so that however much someone might want to cross from here to you they cannot, nor can anyone cross from there to us."

'"Then may I ask you, father," he answered, "to send Lazarus to my father's household? I have five brothers. Have him warn them, so they do not end up in this place of torment as well."

'"They have Moses and the Prophets," Abraham replied. "They should listen to them."

'"No, father Abraham," he said, "but if someone from the dead went to them, they would repent."

' "If they do not listen to Moses and the Prophets," Abraham said to him, "they would not be persuaded even if someone rose from the dead." '

17:1–9: Faith and Duty

Jesus continued to teach his disciples.

'Stumbling blocks are bound to come,' Jesus warned, 'but woe to anyone through whom they come! It would be better for him not to have been born or to have a millstone tied around his neck and be thrown into the sea than to cause one of these little ones to stumble. Watch yourselves!

'If your brother sins, rebuke him. Then if he repents, forgive him. Even if he sins against you seven times in a day and comes back to you seven times and says, "I repent," you must forgive him.'

'Increase our faith!' the apostles said.

'If you have faith as small as a mustard seed,' the Lord replied, 'you can say to this sycamore tree, "Pull yourself up and plant yourself in the sea," and it will obey you.

'If someone has a servant ploughing or tending sheep, would he say to the servant coming in from the fields, "Come along now and sit down to eat"? No – wouldn't he say instead, "Prepare my dinner, and dress yourself to wait on me while I eat and drink. Then you can eat and drink"? And would he thank the servant simply for carrying out his orders?'

17:10: The duty of unworthy servants – omitted

17:11–19 (incl. 4:27): Jesus heals ten men with leprosy

It happened that on his way to Jerusalem, Jesus passed between Samaria and Galilee. As he came into one village, ten men with leprosy hailed him from a distance. He sent them away.

'There were many in Israel with leprosy in the time of the prophet Elisha, yet none of them was cleansed except Naaman the Syrian,' he said. 'But all of you – go and show yourselves to the priests.' And as they went away, they were cleansed.

One of them, seeing that he had been healed, came back shouting praise to God. He fell on his face at Jesus' feet thanking him. He was a Samaritan.

'Was it not ten who were cleansed?' Jesus asked. 'Where are the other nine? Why have they not returned to give praise to God, and only this foreigner has? Rise and go,' Jesus said to him. 'Your faith has saved you.'

17:20–37: The coming of the kingdom of God

On one occasion, Jesus was asked by the Pharisees when the kingdom of God would come.

'The kingdom of God will not come according to observation,' Jesus replied. 'Nor will people say, "Here it is!" or "There it is!" For the kingdom of God is in your midst.'

To his disciples, Jesus said, 'Days are coming when you will long to see one of the days of the Son of Man, but you will not be able. *People will tell you, "There he is!" or "Here he is!" Do not go chasing after them. For just as lightning flashes across the sky from one end to the other, so it will be with the Son of Man on his day.* [*These italicized sentences perhaps omitted.*] But first he must suffer greatly and be rejected by this generation.

'Just as it was in the days of Noah, so it will also be in the days of the Son of Man. People were eating, drinking, marrying and being given in marriage right up to the day Noah entered the ark. Then the flood came and killed them all.

'Similarly, in the days of Lot, people were eating and drinking, buying and selling, planting and building. *But the day Lot left Sodom, fire and sulphur rained down from heaven and killed them all. So it will be on the day the Son of Man is revealed. On that day no one on his roof, who has his possessions inside the house, should go down to get them. In the same way, no one in his field should go back for anything.* [*These italicized sentences perhaps omitted.*] Remember Lot's wife!'

17:33–37: Selective judgement in the future – probably omitted

18:1–8: The parable of the unjust judge

Jesus told them a parable about the need to pray at all times and never give up.

'In one city there was a judge who neither feared God nor paid any attention to people. There was a widow in that city who would come pleading with him, "Get me justice against my adversary."

'For a time he kept refusing, but in the end he thought, "Even though I don't fear God or pay people any attention, I will get justice for this widow because of the bother she is causing me. Otherwise she may eventually come and attack me!"

'Listen to the unjust judge,' the Lord said. 'Will God not bring justice for his chosen ones who cry out to him day and night? Will he continue to delay them? I say to you, he will see that they get justice, and quickly. But when the Son of Man comes, will he find faith on the earth?'

18:9–14: The parable of the Pharisee and the tax collector

Jesus spoke a parable to some who were confident of their own righteousness and looked down on everyone else.

'Two men went up to the temple to pray, one a Pharisee and the other a tax collector. The Pharisee stood on his own and prayed. "God, I thank you that I am not like other people such as robbers, evildoers, adulterers, or the likes of this tax collector. I fast twice a week and give a tenth of everything I earn."

'The tax collector stood at a distance. He would not even lift his eyes to heaven, but beat his breast and said, "God, have mercy on me, a sinner."

'I tell you that this man, rather than the other, went home justified. For everyone who exalts himself will be humbled, and everyone who humbles himself will be exalted.'

18:15–17: Jesus and the little children

People presented little children to Jesus for him to lay hands on them. When the disciples saw this, they rebuked them, but Jesus called for the children.

'Let the little children come to me,' he said. 'Do not hinder them, for the kingdom of heaven belongs to such as these. Truly I say to you, whoever does not receive the kingdom of God like a little child will certainly not enter it.'

18:18–23: The rich and the kingdom of God

A leader among the Jews asked him, 'Good teacher, what must I do to inherit eternal life?'

'Why do you call me good?' Jesus replied to him. 'No one is good except the one God, the Father. Do you know the commandments? "You shall not commit adultery, you shall not murder, you shall not steal, you shall not bear false witness, honour your father and mother." '

'All these I have kept since I was a boy,' he said.

'You lack one thing,' said Jesus on hearing this. 'Sell everything you have and distribute it to the poor. Then you will have treasure in heaven. And come and follow me!' When the man heard this, he was distraught, because he was very rich.

18:24–30: The rich and the kingdom of God

Jesus looked at him and said, 'How difficult it is for the rich to enter the kingdom of God. It is easier for a camel to go through the eye of a needle than for a rich person to enter the kingdom of God.'

Those who heard this asked, 'So who can be saved?'

'What is impossible with man is possible with God,' Jesus replied.

'But we have left everything behind to follow you!' Peter objected.

'Truly I say to you,' Jesus responded, 'no one who has left home, wife, brothers, parents or children for the sake of the

*kingdom of God will fail to receive many times more in this
age, as well as everlasting life in the age to come.'*

18:31–34: Jesus' death predicted again – omitted

18:35–43: Jesus heals a blind beggar

It happened that as Jesus was approaching Jericho, a blind beg-
gar was sitting by the road. When he heard the crowd going by,
he asked what was happening. People told him, 'Jesus is passing by.'

'Jesus, son of David,' he shouted, 'have mercy on me!'

Those at the front ordered him to be quiet. Then he shouted
more loudly, 'Son of David, have mercy on me!'

Jesus stopped, and ordered the man to be brought to him.
As he came near, Jesus asked him, 'What do you want me to
do for you?'

'Lord,' he replied, 'I want to see.'

'See again!' Jesus told him. 'Your faith has saved you.' Immediately he could see again, and, glorifying God, began to follow
Jesus. When all the people saw this, they also praised God.

19:1–10: Jesus and Zacchaeus

Jesus entered Jericho and was passing through. Now there was
a man called Zacchaeus, who was a chief tax collector, and
was wealthy. He tried to see who Jesus was, but because he
was short he was unable to see because of the crowd. He therefore ran ahead and climbed a sycamore tree to see Jesus as he
was passing through that way.

When Jesus came to the place, he looked up.

'Zacchaeus, hurry down from there,' Jesus told him. 'Today
I am to stay at your house.' So Zacchaeus rushed down at once
and welcomed Jesus gladly.

All the people saw this and complained, 'He has gone to be
the guest of a sinner.'

Now Zacchaeus, in his house, stood up and said to the Lord,
'I am now going to give half my possessions to the poor, Lord,

and if I have cheated anybody out of anything, I will repay him fourfold.'

'Today salvation has come to this house,' Jesus declared to him, 'since this man is a son of Abraham. For the Son of Man has come to seek and to save what was lost.'

19:11–27: The parable of the *minas*

As they were listening to him, Jesus added a parable, because he was near Jerusalem, and the people believed that the kingdom of God was going to appear immediately.

'A nobleman travelled to a far country to be granted his kingdom and then return. He summoned ten of his servants and gave them ten *minas*.† "Invest this money," he said, "until I come back."

'Now his citizens hated him and sent an embassy after him to say that they did not want him to be their king. It happened that he was granted the kingdom, however, and returned home. He had the servants to whom he had given the money summoned, to find out how they had invested it.

' "Master, your *mina* has made a further ten," the first told him.

' "Well done, my good servant!" ' his master replied. "Because you have been trustworthy in very little, take charge of ten cities."

' "Master, your *mina* has earned five more," the second said.

' "Then take charge of five cities," his master answered.

'Then another servant came and said, "Master, here is your *mina*. I wrapped it in a piece of cloth and put it away, for I was afraid of you because of your severity. You take what you have not given, and reap what you have not sown."

' "I will convict you out of your own mouth, you wicked servant!" his master replied. "You knew that I am severe, taking what I have not given, and reaping what I have not sown. Why then did you not put my money in a bank, so that when I came back, I could have had it back with interest?"

' "Take his *mina* away from him and give it to the one with ten," he said to those standing by.

' "But master," they said, "he already has ten!"

' "I say to you that to all who have, more will be given, but from the person who has nothing, even what he thinks he possesses will be taken away. And as for those enemies of mine who did not want me to be their king – bring them here and slaughter them in front of me." '

19:28–44: The triumphal entry – omitted

19:45–46: God's house a robbers' cave – omitted

19:47–48: The authorities seek to kill Jesus

Jesus was teaching each day in the temple, but the chief priests, the scribes and the leaders among the people were trying to kill him. Yet they did not find any opportunity to do it, because the people all hung on his every word.

20:1–8: Jesus' authority

It happened that one day when Jesus was teaching the people in the temple and proclaiming the good news, the chief priests, scribes and the elders stood by.

'Tell us by what authority you are doing these things,' they said. 'Or, who is it that gave you authority?'

'Let me ask you a question,' Jesus replied. 'Tell me – was John's baptism from heaven, or of human origin?'

After discussing the question among themselves they thought, 'If we say, "From heaven," he will ask, "Then why did you not believe him?" But if we say, "Of human origin," all the people will stone us to death, because they were convinced that John was a prophet.' So they answered, 'We don't know where it was from.'

'Then neither will I tell you by what authority I am doing these things,' Jesus replied.

20:9–18: The parable of the wicked tenants – omitted

20:19–26: Render unto Caesar

Now the scribes and the chief priests were trying to seize him at that time, but they were afraid of the people. After watching Jesus, they sent spies, who pretended to be righteous, to catch him in something he said so they could hand him over to the authority of the governor.

'Teacher,' they asked him, 'we know that you speak and teach correctly, and do not show favouritism. You teach the way of God truly. Tell us, is it right for us to pay tax to Caesar, or not?'

Jesus realized their trickery.

'Show me a *denarius*,'[†] he said. 'Whose face and name are on it?'

'Caesar's,' they replied.

'Then render to Caesar what is Caesar's,' he said to them, 'and to God what is God's.'

They were unable to catch him out in what he had said among the people. Nonplussed by his answer, they fell silent.

20:27–40: Marriage at the resurrection

Some of the Sadducees, who deny that there is any resurrection, came to Jesus.

'Teacher,' they asked, 'Moses commanded us that if a man's brother dies having married but having had no children, the man must marry the widow and raise up offspring for his brother. Now there were seven brothers. The first married but died childless. The second and then the third married her, and in the same way all seven died childless. Finally, the woman died too. At the resurrection, therefore, whose wife will she be? For all seven had been married to her.'

'The children of this age marry and are given in marriage,' Jesus replied. 'But those whom the God of the age to come has counted worthy of a share in the resurrection from the dead neither marry nor are given in marriage. For they can no longer die, because as children of God and of the resurrection, they are like angels.' [*Quotation from the book of Exodus and its explanation then omitted.*]

'Well said, teacher!' some of the scribes interjected. No one dared thereafter to ask him anything else.

20:41–44: Whose son is the Messiah?

Then Jesus turned to them:

'Why is it said that the Messiah is the son of David?' he asked. 'For David himself states in the Book of Psalms:

' "The Lord said to my Lord:

'Sit at my right hand

until I make your enemies

a footstool for your feet.' " *

Therefore if David calls him "Lord", how can he be his son?'

20:45–47: Warning against the scribes

While all the people were listening, Jesus addressed his disciples:

'Watch out for those scribes! They like to prance around in long robes, and delight in greetings in the marketplaces. They take the most important seats in the synagogues and the most distinguished dining couches at banquets. They eat widows out of their houses and pray at great length for appearances' sake. They will be judged most severely.'

21:1–4: The widow's mite

Jesus looked up and saw the rich putting their gifts into the temple treasury. He also saw one destitute widow put in two lepta.†

'Truly I say to you,' he said, 'this poor widow has put in more than all the others. All these people contribute gifts out of their surplus, but she out of her penury contributed her whole livelihood.'

21:5–38: Discourse on the end times

Some were commenting on how beautifully adorned the temple was with stones and with offerings.

'Days are coming,' Jesus said in reply, 'when not one of these stones you see will be left on another. They will all be cast down.'

'Teacher,' they asked him, 'when will this happen? What sign will there be that it is about to take place?'

'Watch out that you are not deceived,' Jesus replied. 'For many will come in my name announcing, "I am the Christ," and, "The time is near." Do not follow them. When you hear of wars and crises, do not be alarmed. These must come first, but the end will not come straight away.

'Nation will rise up against nation, and kingdom against kingdom,' Jesus continued. 'There will be great earthquakes, and famines and pestilences all over, accompanied by terrors, and great signs from heaven.

'But before all this, you will be seized and persecuted by those who turn you over to the synagogues or put you in prison. You will be brought before kings and governors on account of my name. You will bear testimony to me. Therefore, be determined not to worry beforehand about how you will offer a defence. For I will give you wisdom which none of your adversaries will be able to counter or gainsay. You will be betrayed even by parents, brothers, relatives and friends, and they will put some of you to death. Everyone will hate you because of me. [*Statement, 'Not a hair on your heads will be harmed,' then omitted.*] Persevere, however, and you will save yourselves.

'When you see Jerusalem surrounded by armies, you will know that its desolation is near. [*Reference to scriptural fulfilment of the days of vengeance then omitted.*] Woe to those women who are pregnant or nursing mothers in those days. There will be a great emergency in the land and wrath against this people. They will fall by the sword and will be taken captive to every nation. Jerusalem will be trampled by gentiles until the times of the gentiles are fulfilled.

'There will be signs among the sun, moon and stars, and on

the earth, distress and confusion among the nations at the wild crashing of the sea. People will faint from the fearful expectation of what is to come upon the world, for the powers of heaven will be shaken. Then people will see the Son of Man coming from heaven with great power. When these things begin to take place, look up, because your redemption is near.

'Consider the fig tree and all the other trees,' he said, speaking in a parable. 'As soon as they have sprouted, you know from what you have seen that summer is near. In the same way, when you see these things taking place, you know that the kingdom of God is near.

'Truly I say to you, heaven and earth will certainly not pass away until all these things have taken place. Heaven and earth will pass away, but my word endures forever.

'Watch out that your hearts are not weighed down with drunken revels and life's worries, or that day will close on you suddenly like a trap. *For it will come on everyone, all across the world. Stay awake continually, and pray that you may have the strength to escape everything that will take place and to stand before the Son of Man.*'

Jesus taught every day in the temple, and in the evenings he would leave for his lodgings on the hill known as the Mount of Olives. All the people came early in the morning to hear him at the temple.

22:1–6: The plot to execute Jesus

The Feast of Unleavened Bread, called the Passover,[†] was approaching, and the chief priests and the scribes were looking for a way to kill Jesus, for they were afraid of the people. [*Reference to Satan entering Judas then omitted.*] Judas went and conferred with the officers about how he could hand Jesus over to them. They were delighted and were willing to pay him money. He agreed to their terms, and looked for an opportunity to hand Jesus over to them while no crowd was around.

22:7–22: The Last Supper

When the day of Unleavened Bread and of the sacrifice of the Passover lamb came, Jesus sent Peter and John off, telling them, 'Go and make preparations for us to eat the Passover.'

'Where do you want us to prepare for it?' they asked.

'When you enter the city,' he replied, 'a man carrying a jar of water will meet you. Follow him into the house he enters and say to the owner of the house, "The Teacher asks: Where is the guest room where I am to eat the Passover with my disciples?" He will show you a large upstairs room, richly furnished. Make preparations there.'

They left and everything happened as Jesus had said. So they prepared for the Passover. When the time came, Jesus and his apostles reclined to eat.

'I have very much wanted to eat this Passover with you before I suffer,' he told them. [*Reference to the fulfilment of feasting in God's kingdom then omitted.*]

He took the cup, gave thanks and said, 'Take this and share it among you.' [*Reference to the fulfilment of drinking in God's kingdom then omitted.*] He then took the bread, gave thanks and broke it. He gave it to them, saying, 'This is my body given for you. Do this in memory of me.'

In the same way, after dinner he took the cup, saying, 'This cup is the new covenant in my blood poured out for you. The hand of my betrayer, however, is with mine at the table. The Son of Man is going as it has been decreed for him, but woe to that man through whom he is betrayed!'

22:23–27: The disciples argue about their greatness

They began to ask one another which of them it might be who would do this, and a dispute arose among them as to which of them was thought the greatest.

'*The rulers of the Gentiles lord it over them,*' *Jesus said,* '*and those who exercise authority over them are called "benefactors". You are not to be like this. No, the greatest among you should be like the youngest, and the leader like a servant.*

For who is greater, the person reclining at the table or the server? Is it not the person reclining at the table? Yet I am in your midst serving.'

22:28–30: The promise of feasting in the kingdom

'You have remained with me through my trials,' Jesus said. 'Therefore I now grant you a kingdom, just as my Father granted one to me.' [Reference to eating and drinking in the kingdom of Christ then probably omitted.]

22:31–32: Jesus prays to protect Peter from Satan

'Simon, Simon, Satan has asked to sift you all like wheat, but I have prayed that your faith, Simon, will not fail. When you turn back, strengthen your brothers.'

22:33–34: The prediction of Peter's denials

'Lord,' Peter replied. 'I am ready to go to prison or to death with you.'

'I tell you, Peter,' Jesus declared, 'the cock will not crow today until you have denied knowing me three times.'

22:35–38: Jesus fulfils scripture and the disciples should buy swords – omitted

22:39–41: Jesus prays on the Mount of Olives

Jesus walked out on to the Mount of Olives, as was his custom, followed by his disciples. When they reached it, he said to them, 'Pray that you will not enter the tribulation.' He withdrew about a stone's throw from them, kneeled down and prayed.

22:42–44: Jesus' anguished prayer

'Father, if you are willing,' he pleaded, 'take this cup from me. Yet not my will, but yours be done.' An angel appeared to him

from heaven to strengthen him. In anguish, Jesus prayed even more assiduously, and his sweat was like drops of blood as it poured onto the ground.

22:45–46: Jesus rebukes the sleeping disciples

When he got up from prayer, he came to his disciples and found them asleep, exhausted by their distress.

'Why are you asleep?' he asked them. 'Get up and pray that you will not enter the tribulation.'

22:47–53: Jesus is arrested

While Jesus was still speaking a crowd appeared, and the man called Judas, one of the twelve, was leading them. He came to Jesus to kiss him, but Jesus asked him, 'Judas, are you going to betray the Son of Man with a kiss?'

[*Reference to cutting off and healing of the servant's ear then omitted.*]

To the chief priests, the temple guard and the elders, who had come for him, Jesus said, 'Have you come with swords and clubs to arrest a revolutionary? I have been with you every day in the temple courts, and you have not laid a hand on me. But now you have your moment in this hour of darkness – and its authority.'

22:54–62: Peter denies Jesus

Having arrested him, they led him away into the high priest's house. Peter was following at a distance. Some had kindled a fire in the middle of the courtyard, and were sitting together, so Peter sat down with them. A servant girl saw him sitting in the firelight, looked closely at him and said, 'This man was with him.'

'Woman, I don't know him,' Peter said, in denial.

Shortly afterwards someone else saw him and said, 'You are one of them too.'

'I am not!' Peter replied.

About an hour later someone else declared, 'He was definitely with him, because he is a Galilean.'

'I don't know what you mean!' Peter replied. Then immediately, while he was still speaking, the cock crowed. The Lord turned and looked at Peter. Peter then remembered what the Lord had said to him: 'Before the cock crows today, you will deny me three times.' Peter went outside and wept bitterly.

22:63–65: The guards mock Jesus

The men guarding Jesus were mocking and hitting him. They blindfolded him and then asked, 'Prophesy - who has hit you?' And they committed many other blasphemies against him.

22:66–71: Jesus before the council

When day dawned, the council of the elders convened, along with the chief priests and the scribes. Jesus was brought before them.

'If you are the Christ,' they said, 'tell us.'

'If I told you, you would not believe me,' he replied, 'and if I asked you, you would not respond. But from now on the Son of Man will be seated at the right hand of the power of God.'

'Are you then the Son of God?' they all asked.

'You say that I am,' he answered.

'Why do we need any further testimony?' they declared. 'We have heard it from his own lips!'

23:1–7: Jesus before Pilate

Then the whole assembly got up and took him to Pilate. They accused him with the report: 'We have found this man subverting our people, destroying the Law and the prophets, opposing payment of taxes to Caesar and sending away wives and children. He claims that he is the Christ, the king.'

'Are you the Christ?' Pilate asked Jesus.

'You have said so,' Jesus answered.

Pilate told the chief priests and the crowd, 'I find no basis for a charge against this man.'

'He is stirring up the people with his teaching all over Judaea,' they countered. 'He started in Galilee and has now come here.'

When Pilate heard this, he asked if Jesus was a Galilean. When he found out that Jesus was under Herod's jurisdiction, he sent him to Herod, who was also in Jerusalem at that time.

23:8–12: Jesus sent to Herod

When Herod saw Jesus, he was delighted, because he had been wanting for some time to see him. He had heard about Jesus and hoped to see him perform a sign. He questioned Jesus at length, but Jesus gave no reply. The chief priests and the scribes were standing there making stern accusations, while Herod along with his soldiers ridiculed and mocked Jesus, dressing him in a fine robe. Then they sent him back to Pilate. On that day Herod and Pilate became friends, though previously they had been enemies.

23:13–25: Return to Pilate

Pilate summoned the chief priests, the leaders and the people.

'You brought me this man on the charge that he was inciting revolution,' he told them. 'I have cross-examined him in your presence, however, and have found no basis for your accusations against him. Nor did Herod, for he has sent him back to us. So Jesus has obviously done nothing to deserve death. I will take disciplinary action against him, then, and release him.'

The whole crowd, however, cried out, 'Take him away and release Barabbas for us!' Now Barabbas was imprisoned for an insurrection in the city, and for murder. Pilate addressed them again, however, because he wanted to release Jesus, but the people continued to shout, 'Crucify him! Crucify him!'

He spoke to them again a third time. 'What crime has this man committed? I have found nothing from him to deserve the death penalty. I will take disciplinary action against him, then release him.'

They persisted in their shouting for Jesus be crucified, and their shouts prevailed. Pilate decided to grant them what they asked. He released the man imprisoned for insurrection and murder, the one they asked for, but Jesus he surrendered to their will.

23:26–31: The walk to Calvary

As the soldiers led him away, they seized Simon of Cyrene as he was coming in from his farm. They put the cross on him and forced him to carry it behind Jesus. A great crowd of the people was following him, including women who were mourning and wailing for him. Jesus turned to them.

'Daughters of Jerusalem, do not weep for me,' he said, 'but weep for yourselves and for your children. For the days are now coming when you will say, "Blessed are the women who are barren, the wombs that have not carried a child, and the breasts that have not nursed!" Then "they will say to the mountains, 'Fall on us!' and to the hills, 'Cover us!'"* For if people do these things when the tree is green, what will happen when it is dry?'

23:32–34: The crucifixion

Two other criminals were also led out with him to be executed. When they came to the place called 'the Skull', they crucified him there, along with the criminals, one on his right, and the other on his left. Jesus said, 'Father, forgive them, for they know not what they do.' *They then divided up his clothes by casting lots for them. [These words uncertain.]*

23:35–42: Mockery of Jesus as Messiah and king of the Jews

The people stood watching. The Jewish leaders jeered at him, saying, 'He saved others – he should save himself if he is God's chosen Messiah.'

The soldiers also mocked him as they came. They offered

*him wine vinegar and said, 'If you are the king of the Jews,
save yourself.' (Inscribed above him was the charge, 'This is
the king of the Jews.')*

*One of the criminals being crucified railed against him.
'Aren't you the Messiah? Save yourself and us!' he shouted.*

*But the other rebuked him. 'Have you no fear of God? You
are suffering the same penalty, only we are suffering it justly
because we're getting what our deeds deserve. But this man
has done nothing wrong.'*

*Then he said, 'Jesus, remember me when you come into
your kingdom.'*

23:43: 'Today you will be with me in Paradise' – omitted

23:44–49: The death of Jesus

It was now about the sixth hour,[†] yet darkness came over the
whole land until the ninth hour,[†] for the sun had stopped shining. The curtain of the temple split down the middle. Then
Jesus called out with a loud voice, 'Father, into your hands I
commit my spirit.' So saying, he gave up his breath.

The centurion who saw what had happened praised God.
'Surely this was a righteous man,' he said.

When all the crowds who had come to witness the spectacle
had seen what had happened, they beat their breasts and went
home. But all those who knew Jesus stood at a distance, and
the women who had followed him from Galilee were watching
it all.

23:50–56: The burial of Jesus

Now there was a good and upright man named Joseph, who
was a member of the council but had not consented to their
decision and action. He came from Arimathaea, a Judaean
town, and was waiting for the kingdom of God. He went to
Pilate and asked for Jesus' body. Then he took it down,
wrapped it in linen and placed it in a tomb carved out of the
rock, and in which no one had yet been buried. *It was the Day*

of Preparation,† *but the Sabbath was beginning.* [*This sentence uncertain.*]

The women who had accompanied Jesus from Galilee followed Joseph and saw the tomb when his body was laid in it. Then they went home and prepared the spices and perfumes, and afterwards rested on the Sabbath in accordance with the Law.

24:1–12: The empty tomb

Very early on the first day of the week,† the women went to the tomb with the spices they had prepared. They found the stone rolled away from the tomb, and when they went in, they did not find the body of the Lord Jesus. While they were wondering what had happened, two men suddenly stood beside them, dressed in shining clothes. Terrified, the women fell on their faces to the ground.

'Why do you look for the living among the dead?' the men said to them. 'He is not here – he has risen! Remember what he said to you while he was still in Galilee: "The Son of Man must be delivered over to the hands of sinners and be crucified, but on the third day rise again."' Then they remembered his words.

When they had returned from the tomb, they reported everything that had happened to the eleven and to all the others. But the apostles treated what Mary Magdalene, Joanna, Mary the mother of James and the others were saying as nonsense, and did not believe them. Peter, however, got up and ran to the tomb. Peering in, he saw only the strips of linen, and he went away wondering what had happened.

24:13–27: Jesus on the road to Emmaus

Now that day two other disciples were going to a village called Emmaus, about sixty stades† from Jerusalem. They were talking about everything that had taken place. As they were discussing and considering these things, Jesus himself came up and journeyed with them, but their eyes were kept from recognizing him.

'What are you discussing as you walk along?' Jesus asked. They stopped, looking gloomy. One of them called Cleopas replied.

'Are you the only visitor to Jerusalem who does not know what has happened there in the last few days?'

'What has happened?' he asked.

'Jesus of Nazareth was a prophet, powerful in word and deed before God and all the people,' they replied, 'but our chief priests and leaders handed him over to be sentenced to death, and they crucified him. We had believed that he was the one to redeem Israel. On top of all that, it is now the third day since all this took place, and some of our women astounded us, because they went to the tomb first thing this morning but couldn't find his body. They came and told us that they had also seen a vision of angels telling them that Jesus was alive. Some of us went off to the tomb and found it just as the women had described, but they did not find Jesus there.'

'How foolish you are,' Jesus said, 'and slow of heart to believe everything which I spoke to you! [*Jesus as subject of Old Testament scripture rephrased here.*] Did not the Christ have to suffer these things and then enter his glory?' [*Reference to Jesus as subject of Old Testament scripture then omitted.*]

As they approached the village where they had been heading, Jesus acted as if he were going on further. The other two remonstrated with him.

'Stay with us, because evening is approaching and the day is almost over.' So Jesus went in to stay with them.

While he was eating with them, he took some bread, said a blessing and broke it. Then he gave it to them – and their eyes were opened and they recognized him. And he vanished from them. [*Jesus' exposition of Old Testament scripture then probably omitted.*]

24:33–43: Jesus appears to the disciples

They got up and immediately returned to Jerusalem. They found the eleven and the others assembled together and saying that the Lord really had risen and had appeared to Simon. The other two explained what had happened on the road, and how they recognized Jesus when he broke bread. While the two were speaking, Jesus stood in their midst.

'Peace be with you!' he said to them.

Startled and terrified, they thought they had seen a phantasm.

'Why are you so alarmed?' he asked. 'Why are doubts arising in your minds? See from my hands and my feet that it is me! *Grasp me and see* [*these words uncertain*] – a spirit does not have *flesh and* [*these words uncertain*] bones, as you see I have.'

After saying this, he showed them his hands and feet, but in their joy and amazement they could still not believe it.

'Do you have any food here?' he asked them. They gave him a piece of broiled fish, and he took it and ate it in front of them.

24:44–46: Jesus' fulfilment of Old Testament scripture – probably omitted

24:47–49: Jesus commissions the disciples

'Repentance for the forgiveness of sins,' he said, 'will be preached in my name to all nations, beginning at Jerusalem. You are witnesses of these things. Now I will send upon you what my Father has promised, but stay in the city until you are clothed with power from on high.'

24:50–53: The ascension

When Jesus had led them out towards Bethany, he raised his hands and blessed them. And it happened that while he was blessing them, he left them and was taken up into heaven. They worshipped him and returned to Jerusalem overjoyed. During that time they remained in the temple, praising God.

11 Jesus' Correspondence with Abgar
(third century CE)

INTRODUCTION

This is a rather unusual example of a 'ministry Gospel' episode because it involves not Jesus' teaching or miraculous activity, but an exchange of letters. This legendary correspondence has Abgar, king of the Mesopotamian kingdom of Osrhoene, writing to Jesus during his earthly life, and requesting healing. It is preserved in Eusebius' *Ecclesiastical History* (*EH* 1.13.5–10). In his letter, Abgar Ukkama modestly describes himself as a 'toparch', or governor, although he was in fact a client-king of the Romans (just as Herod the Great was). He ruled from around 4 BCE to 40 CE, so the legend is at least chronologically accurate. Less plausible is the fact that it has Jesus almost quoting from John's Gospel. Compare the first half of Jesus' reply with, 'Because you have seen me, you have believed; blessed are those who have not seen and yet have believed' (Jn 20:29). There may also be an allusion to Jesus' charge 'you have seen me and still you do not believe' (Jn 6:36).

Eusebius further writes that, appended to his copy of the letters, there was an account written in Syriac of how Jesus fulfilled the promise made in his reply to Abgar (*EH* 1.13.11–22). Immediately after Jesus' ascension, the apostle Thomas (no longer doubting Thomas) sent the disciple Thaddaeus to heal Abgar. Abgar wanted to hear from Thaddaeus all about Jesus' ministry, but the disciple asked Abgar to summon all his citizens first. Thaddaeus then proclaims the good news of Jesus' teaching, death, descent to Hell, resurrection and ascension to a delighted audience. Abgar offers him gold plate as a reward, which Thaddaeus naturally refuses.

Eusebius wrote his history in the early fourth century, and the Abgar correspondence probably came into existence not long before that. The correspondence was perhaps fabricated to establish the idea that Christianity had existed in Abgar's 'small city' (Edessa) from the beginning, and had therefore pre-dated the heretical groups which were strong there in the third century.

TRANSLATION

A copy of the letter written by Abgar the Toparch, to Jesus, and taken to him in Jerusalem by Ananias the courier:

'Abgar Ukkama the Toparch, to Jesus the good saviour who has appeared in the district of Jerusalem: Greetings. I have heard about you and your acts of healing performed without medicines or herbs. I gather that you make the blind see, enable the lame to walk, cleanse those with leprosy, cast out unclean spirits and demons, and heal those tormented by chronic diseases – even raising the dead! When I heard all this about you, I reckoned that either you are doing these things because you are God and have come down from heaven, or you do them because you are the son of God. Therefore I am now writing to you and asking you to take the trouble to come to me and heal the affliction I have. For I have heard that the Jews complain about you and want to do you harm. I have a very small city, a place of sanctity, which has room enough for us both.'

The reply of Jesus to Abgar the Toparch, taken by Ananias the courier:

'You are blessed, because you have believed in me without seeing me. For it has been written of me that those who have seen me will not believe in me, while those who have not seen me will believe and live. On my coming to you, about which

you have written: I must fulfil everything for which I have been
sent here, and after everything has been thereby fulfilled, I
must ascend to him who sent me. When I ascend, however, I
will send one of my disciples to heal your affliction and to
bring life to you and your subjects.'

12 The 'Unknown Gospel', or Egerton-Cologne Papyrus

(second century CE)

INTRODUCTION

The Egerton fragments, first published in 1935, were the first major Gospel manuscript discovery after the Greek fragments of the *Gospel of Thomas*. In 1987 a second part of one of the Egerton pages, kept in the Institut für Altertumskunde in the University of Cologne, was published and immediately connected with its sister fragments. In all there are four fragmentary leaves of papyrus, making it a fairly substantial portion of a Gospel, although the fourth fragment contains only a single letter. How long the whole Gospel originally was is unknown, but the reference to Jesus' deeds bearing witness to him (frag. 2, p. 2) probably implies narratives of miracles, and the statement that the hour for Jesus to be handed over had not come (frag. 1, p. 2) suggests that there was an account of the arrest and crucifixion.

Part of the scholarly interest in this text has lain in the question of its literary relationship to the canonical Gospels. Some have even tried to argue that this text was a source for John's Gospel, but this is unlikely, as it would involve the author of John's Gospel carefully sifting out the material paralleled in Matthew, Mark and Luke. More probably this is a work, from the mid-second century, which harmonized the four Gospels. The Egerton-Cologne papyrus is also one of the earliest copies of a non-canonical Gospel, dating from sometime around 200 CE.

TRANSLATION

Fragment 1, page 1: Jesus and Moses

'[. . .] to the teachers of the Law [. . .] every transgressor [. . .] and not me [. . .] how he does what he does.'

Turning to the leaders of the people, Jesus spoke as follows: 'You search the Scriptures, by which you think you have life, but they are testimony to me. Do not think that I have come to accuse you to my Father. Your accuser is Moses, the very person on whom you set your hopes.'

'We know perfectly well that God spoke to Moses,' they said, 'but you we do not know [. . .].'

'Now your unbelief stands accused by what he [. . .],' Jesus responded. 'For if you had believed [Moses], you would have believed [me], because he [wrote] about me for your forefathers. [. . .]'

Fragment 1, page 2: Jesus escapes stoning and heals a leper

[. . .] stones so they together could stone him. The rulers tried to lay their hands upon him to seize him and hand him over to the mob. [They were unable] to seize him, however, because the hour for him to be handed over had not yet [come]. The Lord slipped through their fingers and stole away.

Just then a man with leprosy came up to him. 'Jesus, teacher, because I have been travelling with lepers and eating with [them] at an inn I have [contracted leprosy] myself. But if [you will] it, I can be clean.'

'I do will it!' the Lord said, 'Be clean!' Immediately the leprosy left him. 'Go and show yourself to the [priests],' Jesus said, 'and make the offering for purification, as [Moses] has commanded. Then sin no more [. . .].'

Fragment 2, page 1: The miracle at the River Jordan

[. . .] having shut up in the place [. . .] was secretly subjected [. . .] its weight unmeasured [. . .] While they were still puzzled at his unusual question, Jesus walked along and stood on the bank of the River Jordan. He stretched out his right hand [. . .] and sowed on the [. . .] and then [. . .] water onto the ground [. . .] and [. . .] he brought forth fruit [. . .].

Fragment 2, page 2: Dialogue about Caesar's rule

They gave him an exacting inquisition, and asked, 'Jesus, teacher, we know that you have come [from God], because what you do bears greater witness than any of the prophets. [Tell] us, then: is it right to give emperors what is appropriate to give to an authority?'

Jesus knew what they were thinking and grew angry. 'How can you call me "teacher" with your mouths, yet not do what I say? Isaiah was quite right when he prophesied about you: "This [people] honours me with its lips, but their hearts are [far from] me. [They worship me] in vain, and their regulations [. . .]." '

Fragment 3, page 1: Unidentifiable fragment

[. . .] if [. . .] his [. . .] knowing [. . .]

Fragment 3, page 2: Christ and the Father are one

'we are one [. . .]' kill [. . .], he says [. . .]

13 Oxyrhynchus Papyrus 210

(second century CE?*)*

INTRODUCTION

Much of this fragment, measuring 9.4cm wide by 17.2cm high, is impossible to decipher. The best that can be said of page 1 (the front side) is that it has an episode involving an angel. It is tolerably clear that page 2 has a version of Jesus' teaching about people being like good trees which bear good fruit or rotten trees which bear rotten fruit (Mt. 7:16; 12:34–35; Lk. 6:44–45; *Gos. Thom.* 45); this page then probably continues with words of Jesus in which he claims to be the image of the divine and to be in the form of God. Since what survives is so difficult to understand, the fragment may well not have come from a Gospel at all. Some scholars have thought it to be a part of the Greek *Gospel of the Egyptians*, but this is no more than a guess; other suggestions include that it is part of a sermon weaving together different biblical motifs. Whatever the original form of the surviving text, it certainly reflects a developed understanding of Jesus' self-presentation. The claim of Jesus himself to be the 'image' or 'form of God', probably evidenced here, is not found in the New Testament Gospels even though the canonical Jesus does make similar assertions. The manuscript, housed in the University Library in Cambridge, is probably from the third century CE, and the original composition dates to an indeterminate timeframe prior to that.

TRANSLATION

[p. 1] '[. . .] will have [. . .] is not able to [. . .] to endure [. . .] an angel commanded [. . .] said through the angel [. . .] to us [. . .] can [. . .] he [. . .] still will have [. . .]. [p. 2] [. . .] good [. . .] he said [. . .] Father's [. . .] good [. . .] good [. . .] Bring [. . .] God, who [. . .] but [. . .] Jesus and he will say [. . .] brings [. . .] the good [. . .] brings [. . .] good [. . .] fruit from a good tree [. . .] under the good. I am [. . .] I am the image of the [. . .] who is in the form of God [. . .] as an image [. . .] to God, to the God who [. . .] to be [. . .] visible things [. . .] of the [. . .] saw that [. . .] person [. . .].'

14 Oxyrhynchus Papyrus 840

(second or third century CE?*)*

INTRODUCTION

The most immediately striking feature of this single manuscript page is its small size, with the complete page measuring 7cm × 9cm. Despite this size, the scribe managed to cram in twenty-two to twenty-three lines of text on each side. The page has been classified as part of a 'miniature codex', and so was probably for private use; it would have been impractical to read a small book with such tiny writing in a church setting. The manuscript is housed, like many of the Oxyrhynchus manuscripts, in the University of Oxford's papyrology collection. The main subject of the text is purity, involving a controversy over the efficacy or necessity of ceremonial washing between Jesus and the high priest, each accusing the other of uncleanness. The significance of this fragment is that it probably reflects polemics between Jews and Christians in the author's environment when the text was written. Despite its label above, the text is written on parchment, rather than papyrus, and this – together with the style of handwriting – suggests that the manuscript dates to the fourth or fifth century, although the original composition is probably rather earlier.

TRANSLATION

[p. 1] [. . .] 'formerly doing wrong first, he deals with everything craftily. But pay attention, in case you also suffer the same things as they do. For people who do evil not only receive their recompense among the living; they will also endure a punishment of great torture.'

The Saviour took them and led them into the place of purification, and walked around in the temple. Then a Pharisee who was the high priest, named Levi, came along and met them.

'Who has permitted you to trample on this place of purification and to see [these] sacred vessels?' he said to the Saviour. 'You in your unwashed state, with your disciples not having washed their feet either! You have been walking about defiled in the holy [place], which is pure, where no one can go and [venture to see these] sacred vessels [without] washing and changing their clothes.'

[The Saviour stood by with his] disciples. [p. 2] 'Are you, standing as you are in this temple, really pure yourself?' he asked.

'Of course I am pure! I have washed in the pool of David. I went down by one flight of steps and came up by the other and put on pure white clothes. Only then did I come and look upon these sacred vessels.'

'Woe to those who are blind and cannot see!' the Saviour said to him. 'You have washed in this running water in which dogs and pigs are thrown night and day. You may have scrubbed and soaped yourself on your skin on the outside, just as prostitutes and flute-girls perfume and scrub and soap and prettify themselves to elicit the lust of men. But inside they are crammed with scorpions and [. . .] evil. But [my disciples] and I, whom you accuse of being unwashed – we have washed in living waters [. . .] which have come from [. . .]. But woe to the [. . .].'

15 Oxyrhynchus Papyrus 1224

(second or third century CE?)

INTRODUCTION

These portions of a manuscript from the fourth century preserve, unusually for such small fragments, some of the page numbers at the tops of the pages. These pages are all from the same codex (now housed in Oxford's Bodleian Library); it is possible, however, given the wide separation between pages 139–140 and 173–176 of the codex, that there is more than one composition included here. The language is mostly familiar from other Gospels, including the injunction from the Sermon on the Mount to pray for one's enemies. Indeed, the text is so similar to that of the canonical Gospels that it could easily have been a paraphrase or harmony not imagined as a separate Gospel *per se*.

TRANSLATION

[p. 139] '[. . .] in everything [. . .]. Amen [I say to you . . .].' [p. 140] '[. . .] will be. You [. . .].' . . . [p. 173]: '[. . .] 'burdened me, and' [. . .] Jesus [. . .] in a vision [. . .]. 'Why are you disheartened? For not [. . .] but rather [. . .].' . . . [p. 174] '[. . .] not replying [. . .] you denied [. . .] What kind of new teaching [. . .]? [. . .] new [. . .] and [. . .].' . . . [p. 175] The scribes, the [Pharisees] and the priests watched him, and were indignant [that he was dining] with sinners. Jesus heard them. 'It is not the healthy who need [a doctor,' he said . . .] . . .

[p. 176] '[. . .] and pray for your enemies. For whoever is not [against] you is for you [. . .] a long way tomorrow [. . .] will be, and in [. . .] opponent [. . .].'

16 Oxyrhynchus Papyrus 4009

(second century CE*)*

INTRODUCTION

This very fragmentary leaf of papyrus, now only 9cm high by 3cm wide, clearly has some reference to sayings of Jesus. Indeed, some have even been confident enough to assign the fragment to the *Gospel of Peter* (translated on pp. 205–211 below). This is probably over-optimistic, but as in the *Gospel of Peter* the narrator is – unusually – one of the apostles: the reply 'to *me*' in the text below shows that it is a rare example of an autobiographical Gospel. Only one side of the papyrus can be reconstructed at all, and even in the case of this page the reconstruction (on the basis of the canonical Gospels and another passage, in 2 *Clement*) is speculative. The text is too brief to allow a confident dating of the manuscript, although some manuscripts with comparable handwriting date from the second and third centuries CE.

TRANSLATION

'[...] harvest [... Be] innocent as [doves], but wise [as serpents]. You will be like [lambs] among wolves.'

'Then are [we to be torn apart?' I said to] him.

['When wolves] tear [apart a sheep, they can] no longer do it [any harm,' Jesus] replied to me. ['Therefore I say to you,] do not fear those [who may kill you but after killing you can] no longer [do you any harm ...].'

17 Oxyrhynchus Papyrus 5072

(second century CE)

INTRODUCTION

This small double-sided page (7cm × 7cm in size), first published in 2011, contains two fragments of incidents known from the canonical Gospels. The first page clearly refers to Jesus casting out the demons from 'Legion', the man possessed by demons who lives in the wild and cannot be restrained by any chains, but who is cured by Jesus and then comes to his senses and dresses normally (cf. Mk 5:1–20). Oddly enough, however, there does not seem to be room in the manuscript for the most graphic scene in the canonical account of the miracle, in which Jesus sends the demons into pigs which then plunge, lemming-like, over a cliff and into the Sea of Galilee. The second page contains Jesus' teaching about the priority of following him over everything else (cf. Mt. 10:32–33). This is one of the oldest copies of an apocryphal Gospel, probably dating from the late second, or early third century CE. The original therefore most probably comes from the second century.

TRANSLATION

[p. 1] Jesus casts out demons

[. . .] in the sight of [. . .] not [. . .] but he would shatter whatever [. . .] he shrieked, saying, 'Son of [. . .], have you come before due time to [. . .] us?' [. . .] He rebuked him, saying, '[. . .] Come out from the man!' [. . .] He came and he sat down

[. . .] their [. . .] about [. . .] Jesus [. . .] clothes [. . .]. One of them [. . .].

[p. 2] The priority of discipleship

'[. . .] with [. . .] does not confess [. . .] teacher. I will not deny you as my disciple. And you will be ashamed [. . .] last. Yes, I tell you, whoever [. . .] his [. . .] more than me is not [. . .] disciple. Therefore if a scribe [. . .] Jerusalem, and if a wise [. . .] The kingdom is [. . .] before you. [. . .] He has hidden from the clever [. . .] disciples [. . .].'

18 Merton Papyrus II 51

(second century CE?)

INTRODUCTION

This single papyrus fragment, only around 4cm × 5cm in size, helpfully (or perhaps unhelpfully) further illustrates the difficulty faced with a number of manuscripts of apocryphal Gospels. Clearly this text could easily come from an early Christian sermon or another commentary-like text, rather than necessarily being a witness to another non-canonical Gospel. Like some other non-canonical Gospel manuscripts, it has not left much of a footprint, and is a 'dead-end' as far as influence is concerned: texts such as these may have been produced for private use. It is fairly obvious that the first page recounts material like that in Luke 7:29–30, and the second, like Oxyrhynchus Papyrus 210 and *Gos. Thom.* 45 (see pp. 57, 153), parallels Luke 6:43–46/ Matthew 12:33–37. This manuscript copy, housed in the Chester Beatty Library in Dublin, probably dates from the third century, although when the work was originally composed is unknown.

TRANSLATION

[p. 1] [. . . the] people and the tax collectors [heard] this, and acknowledged God's justice, [confessing] their sins. [The Pharisees, however,] refused baptism [. . .] the will of God [. . .] rejected God's [. . .] rejects [. . .] with him [. . .].

[p. 2] '[. . .] brings forth [. . .] brings, as from [. . .]. And when [. . .] from the good treasure [. . .] it perishes. [. . .] Not, then [. . .] you do not do [. . .].'

19 Berlin Papyrus 11710

(third–fourth century CE)

INTRODUCTION

This text consists of two small papyrus fragments (about 7cm × 7cm in size), and is notable for containing both part of a Greek narrative and a Coptic coda, 'Jesus Christ, God.' It was probably an extract used as an amulet: one of the pages has a cord attached to it, and the two leaves were probably originally joined together. Some early Christians are known to have carried amulets: in the fourth century, St Augustine attacked those who sold them, and John Chrysostom denounced wearing them as idolatrous. The text here is loosely based on an episode in John's Gospel (1:45–51), and the final line probably employs the name of Jesus as an apotropaic device. The manuscript, now held in the Egyptian Museum in Berlin, was copied around the sixth century CE, but the fragment is too small to allow us to date the original composition. The presence of Coptic, if that was original to the work, suggests a later rather than an earlier date.

TRANSLATION

He said, 'Rabbi, Lord, you are the Son of God.'
   The Rabbi said, 'Nathanael, go into the sun.'
   'Rabbi, Lord,' Nathanael responded, 'you are the Lamb of God who takes away the sins of the world.'
   The Rabbi said, [. . .]
   Jesus Christ, God.

20 The Gospel According to the Hebrews

(second century CE*)*

INTRODUCTION

The *Gospel According to the Hebrews* caused a stir on occasion in the early church. One fourth-century sermon tells a story about a debate between a monk and Cyril, the archbishop of Alexandria. The monk appealed to a 'fifth Gospel', the *Gospel According to the Hebrews*, for the idea that the virgin Mary was the incarnation of the archangel Michael, but Cyril would not countenance either this teaching about Mary or the thought of a fifth Gospel. Origen in the third century had already taken issue with the idea that the Spirit is the mother of Jesus, a theme present in the fragments below. The *Gospel According to the Hebrews* is one of several apocryphal Gospels for which no manuscript survives. It is only preserved in quotations scattered amongst various church fathers. Because we only have a patchwork of quotations, the surviving fragments do not enable us to get much of a sense of the whole work. Whether, for example, it had a specifically 'Jewish-Christian' outlook – as its title might suggest – is hard to gauge.

What is clear is that it was probably a full-length Gospel, like those in the New Testament: at the beginning of the timeline of Jesus' ministry, we have an account of the baptism of Jesus, and at the end come references to Palm Sunday, the crucifixion and Jesus' resurrection appearances. In between, there is both teaching and miraculous activity. Overall, the surviving extracts suggest that the Gospel was an edited version of the Gospel of Matthew. Almost all the material paralleled in the New Testament can be found in Matthew, with the exceptions of Jesus' rescue of the woman condemned to stoning (preserved only in late manuscripts of John's Gospel), and the replacement of Judas which appears in the book of Acts.

Since we have an early quotation by Clement of Alexandria around 200 CE, the *Gospel According to the Hebrews* can be securely placed in the second century. It is more likely that the *Gospel According to the Hebrews* is dependent on Matthew than the other way around, because *Hebrews* also knows the book of Acts. Its original language is likely to have been Greek (the form in which it is known to Clement), but it was probably translated into Aramaic and/or Hebrew soon after its original composition.

Because what survives of the Gospel is fragmentary, the presentation below is unusual. Some of the quotations are substantial enough, but other references to the *Gospel According to the Hebrews* by the church fathers merely comment on where it differs from the canonical Gospels, or from Matthew's Gospel in particular. These references have been placed or explained in square brackets [. . .], and the variants in the *Gospel According to the Hebrews* underlined.

DRAMATIS PERSONAE

JESUS
JAMES *A brother of Jesus*
JOHN THE BAPTIST *The forerunner of Jesus*
SIMON PETER *Jesus' disciple*
JESUS BARABBAS *The prisoner released at the Passover*
MATTHIAS LEVI *A candidate for replacing Judas*

TRANSLATION

Fragment 1: Jesus questions his need for baptism

The Lord's mother and brothers said to him, 'John the Baptist is baptizing, for the forgiveness of sins. Let's go and get baptized by him.'

'What sin have I committed,' Jesus asked them, 'to have to go and be baptized by him? That is, unless perhaps what I have just said was an unintentional sin!'

Fragment 2: Jesus' baptism

Then it happened that when the Lord came up out of the water, the fount of the entirety of the Holy Spirit came down upon him and rested upon him.

'My Son,' the Spirit said, 'in all the prophets I have been waiting for you to come, so I could rest on you. For you are my rest, you are my first-born Son, who will reign for ever.'

Fragment 3: Jesus chooses his disciples

'I choose for myself the best, whom my Father in heaven gives to me.'

(Fragments 4–8: Jesus' teaching about discipleship)

Fragment 4: Amazement, reign and rest

'He who seeks should not stop seeking until he finds. Having found, he will be amazed! Struck with amazement, he will reign, and having reigned, will rest.'

Fragment 5: The Lord's Prayer

['When you pray, say:
Our Father in heaven, hallowed be your name,
your kingdom come,
your will be done,
on earth as it is in heaven.
Give us today our bread <u>for tomorrow</u> . . . ']

Fragment 6: True happiness

The Lord said to his disciples, 'You will never be happy except when you look upon your brother with love.'

Fragment 7: One of the greatest sins

(Jesus defines one of the greatest sins as that committed by) 'the one who saddens the spirit of his brother.'

Fragment 8: Forgiveness seventy-seven times

'If your brother has sinned in speech and makes restitution to you,' Jesus said, 'you should bear with him seven times a day.'
    'Seven times a day?' his disciple Simon said.
    'Yes,' the Lord answered, 'I say to you, as much as seventy-seven times. For sinful speech could even be found in the prophets after they had been anointed with the Holy Spirit.'

Fragment 9: The transfiguration

The Saviour said, 'Just now, my Mother, the Holy Spirit, grasped me by a strand of my hair and carried me away to the great Mount Tabor.'

Fragment 10: The woman condemned to stoning

A woman was condemned by the Jews for a sin, and she was sent away to be stoned at the place where that punishment usually took place. When the Saviour saw her, and realized that they were on the point of stoning her, he said to those who were about to pelt her with stones, 'Let him who has not sinned take up a stone and cast it. If anyone is secure in his conscience that he has not sinned, he can take up a stone and strike her.' No one dared to. They knew in their hearts that in certain respects they were guilty, and, realizing this, they did not dare to strike her.

Fragment 11: Jesus heals the mason's hand

'I was a mason, earning my bread with my hands. I beg you, Jesus, restore my health to me, or else I will have the shame of begging for food.'

'Stretch out your hand,' Jesus said to the man. He stretched it out, and it was restored to health just like the other.

Fragment 12: The eye of the needle

The other rich man said to him, 'Master, what good thing must I do to live?'

'Do what the Law and the Prophets say,' Jesus said.

'I have done that.'

'Go, then,' Jesus said, 'and sell everything you possess and distribute it to the poor. Then come and follow me.'

The rich man, not pleased, began to scratch his head.

'What do you mean by saying, "I have done the Law and the Prophets"?' the Lord inquired. 'It is written in the Law, "Love your neighbour as yourself", and look – you have many brothers, fellow sons of Abraham, who are clothed in dung, dying from hunger. Yet your house is full of abundant good things, while absolutely nothing goes out of it to those brothers of yours.'

Simon, Jesus' disciple, was sitting by him. Jesus turned to him.

'Simon, son of Jonah,' he said, 'it is easier for a camel to go in through the eye of a needle than for a rich man to enter the kingdom of heaven.'

Fragment 13: Jesus' lament over Jerusalem

['And so upon you will come all the righteous blood that has been shed on earth, from the blood of righteous Abel to the blood of Zechariah son of Jehoiadah, whom you murdered between the temple and the altar.' Compare Matthew's Gospel, which has 'Zechariah son of Berekiah' (Matthew 23:35).]

Fragment 14: The entry into Jerusalem on Palm Sunday

[The Gospel according to the Hebrews had an account of Jesus' entry into Jerusalem accompanied by shouts of 'Hosanna in heaven': compare Matthew 21:1–9/ Mark 11:1–10/ Luke 19: 28–38.]

Fragment 15: Barabbas

[At that time they had a well-known prisoner whose name was Jesus 'Barabbas', which means, 'son of their master'.]

Fragment 16: Breaking of the lintel

[The huge lintel of the temple broke, splitting in half.]

Fragment 17: The risen Jesus appears to James

When the Lord had given his shroud to the priest's servant, he went to James and appeared to him. (For James had sworn that he would not eat bread from that hour on which he had drunk from the Lord's cup until he had seen him arising from those who are asleep.) ... The Lord said, 'Bring a table with some bread.' Jesus took the bread, blessed it, and broke it, and gave it to James the Just. 'My brother,' he said to him, 'eat your bread, because the Son of Man has risen from those who are asleep!'

Fragment 18: The replacement of Judas

[The *Gospel of the Hebrews* explains that the Matthias who replaced Judas in the circle of the twelve disciples was also called Levi.]

21 The Gospel of the Ebionites

(late second or third century CE)

INTRODUCTION

The enigmatic sect known as the 'Ebionites' undoubtedly derived their name from the Hebrew word for 'poor' (*ebyon*), and so they perhaps styled themselves as the humble and down-trodden believers. Early sources, such as Irenaeus of Lyon (writing around 180 CE) and Origen in the third century, comment that at least some Ebionites denied the virgin birth and thought that Jesus was Joseph's biological son who was only later adopted as God's Son at his baptism. Other common features in reports about them are their rejection of Paul's letters and their observance of Jewish Law. The Ebionites are therefore often labelled by scholars as 'Jewish Christians'.

In the 370s CE Epiphanius of Salamis makes a number of quotations of their 'Gospel'. According to Epiphanius, the Ebionites simply referred to it as the Gospel of Matthew. Although it is not the Matthew either that he knew or that we know today, it is quite plausible that, like the *Gospel According to the Hebrews* (see pp. 162–167), it was a revision of Matthew's Gospel. Their Gospel was originally written in Greek, as is clear from what seems like an alteration of the canonical statement that the locust (*akris*) was part of John the Baptist's diet: the *Gospel of the Ebionites* says that what he ate was something like a cake (*egkris*). If this is a deliberate rather than an accidental change, it may fit with the final fragment translated, in which Jesus refuses to eat meat; John's avoidance of locusts and Jesus' abstinence from lamb probably implies the Ebionites' vegetarianism, which Epiphanius says they practised. Jesus' statement about sacrifice is consistent with this: 'I have come to abolish sacrifices, and unless you abandon sacrificing, God's wrath will not abandon you.' Some sacrifices – both in Jewish and pagan ritual – were, after all, eaten. The avoidance of meat may have been a conviction based on a particular view of animal flesh. Alternatively, it may (at least in origin) have arisen from a worry about buying meat which had previously been sacrificed to a pagan god – a scenario discussed in Paul's first letter to the Corinthians.

The *Gospel of the Ebionites* was probably written either in the late second or the third century. Only a few fragments survive, the first of which may be a Preface in which 'Matthew' narrated the commissioning of the apostles.

DRAMATIS PERSONAE

JESUS
HIS DISCIPLES
HIS MOTHER
HIS BROTHERS
HEROD *King of Judaea*
JOHN THE BAPTIST *The forerunner of Jesus*
ZECHARIAH *John's father*
ELIZABETH *John's mother*
PHARISEES *An influential, elite Jewish movement*

TRANSLATION

Fragment 1: Jesus calls his disciples

There was a man named Jesus, and when he was about thirty years old, he chose us. Coming to Capernaum, he went into the house of Simon, also called Peter. Opening his mouth, he said, 'As I went along by Lake Tiberias I chose John and James (Zebedee's sons), Simon and Andrew, [Philip and Bartholomew, Thomas and James the son of Alphaeus], Thaddaeus,

Simon the Zealot and Judas Iscariot. And I called you, Matthew, as you sat at your tax-office, and you followed me. I want you all, then, to be my twelve apostles as a testimony to Israel.'

Fragment 2: John the Baptist and his family

[The beginning of their Gospel]: It happened, in the days when Herod was king of Judaea, that John came baptizing in the River Jordan with a baptism for repentance. He was said to be a descendant of Aaron the priest, and the son of Zechariah and Elizabeth. And everyone went out to him.

Fragment 3: John's ministry

It happened that when John was baptizing, some Pharisees went out to him, and they were baptized and all Jerusalem with them. John had a garment made from camel-hair and a leather belt around his waist. And he had a diet of wild honey which tasted like manna, like a cake made with olive oil.

Fragment 4: The baptism of Jesus

When the people had been baptized, Jesus also came and was baptized by John. As he came up out of the water, the heavens opened, and he saw the Holy Spirit in the likeness of a dove descending and entering him. There was also a voice from heaven. 'You are my beloved Son! In you I am well pleased!' And then, 'Today I have begotten you!'

Immediately a great light illuminated the place. When John saw this light, he asked Jesus, 'Who are you, lord?' The voice from heaven came again.

'This is my beloved Son, in whom I am well pleased!'

Then John fell to the ground. 'I beg you, lord,' he said to Jesus, 'please baptize me!'

But Jesus refused. 'No,' he said, 'this is how it is right that everything should be fulfilled.'

Fragment 5: Jesus and his family

'Jesus, your mother and brothers are outside.'

'Who are my mother and brothers?' Jesus said. He stretched out his hand to his disciples. 'They are my brothers and mother and sisters – those who do what my Father wills.'

Fragment 6: Jesus' abolition of sacrifice

'I have come to abolish sacrifices, and unless you abandon sacrificing, God's wrath will not abandon you.'

Fragment 7: A meat-free Passover

'Where do you want us to make the preparations for you to eat the Passover?' his disciples asked.

'Would I really desire to eat meat with you on this Passover?' Jesus said.

22 The Gospel of Eve

(second or third century CE?)

INTRODUCTION

Epiphanius, bishop of Salamis in Cyprus in the late fourth century, composed a lengthy anti-heretical treatise, *The Medicine Chest*. Among the heresies for which he provides a diagnosis and a remedy are 'the Gnostics, or Borborites', and one of their works which he attacks is the *Gospel of Eve*. He introduces this work by saying, presumably on the basis of another passage in the book, that Eve obtained saving knowledge through a revelation to her by the serpent in the Garden of Eden. This is another example of a Gnostic writing, therefore, which deliberately subverts the biblical story – as, for example, in the *Birth of Mary* (see pp. 22–23). This extract cited by Epiphanius contains the common idea among Gnostic and other related groups that the soul or spirit of the true Gnostic disciple is a part of Christ (who is probably the speaker in the text below). Through either some cosmic fall or primordial event of salvation, the divine substance became scattered, and the full, final redemption is the regathering of these dispersed fragments. It is hard to say when this Gospel might have been written. Any time between the beginning of the Gnostic movements in the second century and Epiphanius' time of writing (in the 370s CE) is possible.

TRANSLATION

I stood upon a high mountain and saw a tall man, and a short man with him. I heard something like the sound of thunder,

and went nearer so I could hear it. Then the tall man spoke
to me:

> 'I am you and you are me;
> wherever you are, there am I.
> In all things am I sown –
> whence you wish, you may gather me;
> and gathering me, you gather yourself.'

23 The Greek Gospel of Philip

(second or third century CE*?)*

INTRODUCTION

This extract, like the *Gospel of Eve* (see above), is quoted and criticized by Epiphanius in his denunciation of the Gnostics and their writings. The proliferation of such texts by Gnostics suggests that they were not interested in having a 'closed' canon of scripture, but were liberal in their creation of new sacred texts. The *Gospel of Philip* resembles the *Gospel of Eve* in emphasizing the 'gathering' of soul-material. It also contains the motif, common in this kind of literature, of how to pass by the hostile powers blocking the way to the afterlife (see, for example, *Gos. Thomas* 50). This theme, already prominent for centuries in Egyptian *Book of the Dead* texts, became important in sectarian Christian literature as well. Presumably Philip the disciple of Jesus is the speaker in this extract. The text could have been written any time between the birth of the Gnostics in the second century and the time of Epiphanius in the late fourth.

TRANSLATION

'The Lord revealed to me what the soul must say when it ascends into heaven, and how to answer each of the powers above:

"I have recognized myself
and I have gathered myself from all about.

I have not sown children for the archon,*
but have uprooted his roots and gathered the scattered
members.
And I know who you are!
For I am one of those from above."

'And so the soul is released. But if the soul is found to have given birth to a son, it is kept down below, until it is able to take up its own children and draw them up into itself.'

24 The Greater Questions of Mary

(second or third century CE*?)*

INTRODUCTION

The *Greater Questions of Mary* is another book attributed by
Epiphanius of Salamis to the Gnostics. (Epiphanius also mentions the *Lesser Questions of Mary*, though he cites nothing
from it.) Here Jesus is said to have revealed to Mary the obscene
rituals which Epiphanius' pornographic account has attributed
to the Gnostics, rituals which Jesus himself allegedly initiated.
This is perhaps the most surprising of all apocryphal Gospel
fragments. The *Greater Questions* could date from any time
from the mid-second to the mid-fourth century.

TRANSLATION

Epiphanius' quotation from the Questions

Jesus took Mary aside onto the mountain and prayed. He produced a woman from his side and began to have sex with her.
Then he took some of his emission to show that 'this must be
done, so that we might live.' And when Mary, dumbstruck, fell
to the ground, he picked her up again and said to her, 'Why do
you doubt, you of little faith?'

Epiphanius' additional comment

They [i.e. the Gnostics] say that this is the meaning of what is
said in the Gospel: 'If I tell you earthly things and you do not

believe them, how will you believe heavenly things?' (Jn 3:12). And as for the saying, 'When you see the Son of Man going up to where he was before' (Jn 6:62) – according to them, that means: 'When the emission comes to partake of that from which it came.'

25 The Gospel Used by Apelles

(second century CE*)*

INTRODUCTION

Apelles was a successor of the arch-heretic Marcion in the second century, and there are some reports in antiquity of him having his own Gospel. This is questionable, and the more common view today is that Apelles modified Marcion's Gospel (see p. 85). However, in one place a saying is attributed to a Gospel at least used by Apelles. On the other hand, it is one of the most widely quoted non-canonical sayings of Jesus, and so was not original to any Gospel which Apelles might have written or used: one scholar has counted seventy quotations of it. Apelles introduces the saying: 'For thus Christ has said in the Gospel . . . ', and the saying encourages discernment, perhaps about false teachings or prophetic revelations.

TRANSLATION

'Be approved money-changers.'

26 The Greek Gospel of the Egyptians

(second century CE*)*

INTRODUCTION

All the surviving fragments of the Greek *Gospel of the Egyptians* are preserved in quotations from the church father Clement of Alexandria. He notes that some who read this Gospel despised this world and prized 'continence', that is, they abstained from sex and reproduction. At this time there was not yet a tradition of monastic celibacy, but towards the end of second century such ideas about the value of virginity were on the rise. The orthodox Tertullian around 200 CE understood St Paul's comparison 'it is better to marry than to burn' as damning marriage with faint praise: it was equivalent to the comparison of having one eye with having no eyes at all! He also ranked virgins, along with martyrs, as deserving of greater heavenly rewards than were ordinary Christians. The negativity towards sexual reproduction in the *Gospel of the Egyptians* is reflected in the dialogues between Jesus and Salome, one of his female disciples mentioned in passing in the Gospel of Mark. (Compare logion 61 of the *Gospel of Thomas*, which also contains a dialogue between Jesus and Salome: see p. 60.) Since Clement wrote the work containing these quotations in about 200 CE, the Gospel can be dated confidently to the second century. This Greek *Gospel of the Egyptians* is not to be confused with the Coptic text of the same name (see below, pp. 338–358), which is a different work entirely.

TRANSLATION

Fragment 1: Dialogue about childbirth

'How long will people go on dying?' Salome asked.
    'As long as women go on giving birth,' Jesus replied.
    'Have I done right, then, not to have children?' she continued.
    'Eat every plant except the bitter one,' Jesus answered.

Fragment 2: Dialogue about rejection of marriage

'When will what I have asked be known?' Salome asked.
    'When you trample on the garment of shame,' Jesus answered, 'and when the two become one, and the male with the female are neither male nor female.'

Fragment 3: Jesus' removal of spiritual weakness

Jesus said, 'I have come to destroy the works of the female.'

27 The Gospel, or Traditions, of Matthias

(second century CE)

INTRODUCTION

These disconnected extracts, cited by Clement of Alexandria, are attributed to the apostle Matthias, who, according to the book of Acts, replaced Judas Iscariot after the latter's death. Clement refers to the *Traditions of Matthias*, while others speak of a *Gospel of Matthias*, and the two titles might well refer to the same work. The first extract notably contains a fairly clear allusion to Greek thought, namely to the idea in Plato's *Theaetetus* that wonder is the beginning of philosophy (*Theaet.* 155d). This reflects an environment quite different from that of the New Testament, where there is little or no contact with the Greek intellectual tradition; in the second century, however, Christianity began to engage much more with its cultured despisers on their own terms. The other two sayings are similar to the rigorous ethical demands of certain Christian groups who strongly contrasted the soul with the flesh (see, for example, the *Gospel of Thomas*, pp. 45–70 above). Since Clement was writing in about 200 CE, the *Traditions of Matthias* quoted by him can safely be dated in the second century.

TRANSLATION

Fragment 1: Wonder as the beginning of wisdom

'Marvel at what is present! This is the first step to knowledge of the realm beyond.'

Fragment 2: The flesh and the soul

'Fight against the flesh, and ill-treat it; do not give an inch to it for unbridled pleasure. But to the soul give increase through faith and knowledge.'

Fragment 3: The effects of righteousness

'If a neighbour of an elect one sins, the elect one has sinned. For if that elect one had conducted himself as the Word dictates, the neighbour would be so ashamed of his behaviour that he too would not sin.'

28 The Jewish Anti-Gospel

(c. *mid-second century* CE)

INTRODUCTION

This 'Jewish anti-Gospel' is quoted in a Greek philosophical treatise, which is itself only preserved in quotations by one of the church fathers. The different works involved, then, are like a series of Russian dolls. The largest doll is Origen's great work *Against Celsus*, composed in around 250 CE, and one of the earliest defences of Christianity against paganism. This is a response to the work of the Platonist philosopher Celsus, an anti-Christian treatise called 'The True Word'. In the early parts of 'The True Word', Celsus makes extensive use of an anti-Christian Jewish source, which appears in two parts. The first part, which is translated below, is an attack on Jesus and the Gospels, and the second is an attack on Christians who have converted from Judaism to Christianity.

This second part also furnishes various comments of Celsus' quoted Jew on the Gospel events. He accuses Christians of having been tricked by Jesus, and is particularly sceptical of Jesus' forecasting of his betrayal by Judas, reckoning both the betrayal and the prophecy implausible. As he questions the evidence for Jesus' vision in the fragment about the baptism translated below, so in the second part he attacks the Christian view of Jesus' resurrection as reliant on the testimony of a 'hysterical female'. He also questions whether resurrection in the same body is conceivable. Overall, the disciples are accused of having falsified the Gospel records of Jesus, and Celsus' Jewish source recounts how Jesus ought to have acted if he really had been divine.

Celsus' Jew is certainly a cultured figure, so much so that

Origen thinks he is really an invention of Celsus himself. The Jewish source quotes from Homer's *Iliad* in its contrast between Jesus' blood and the 'ichor such as flows in the blessed gods'. The Jewish author takes the view that God's son is the Logos (Word, or Reason), a position known from the philosophical interpreter of Scripture Philo of Alexandria. The first speech, in its attack on Jesus' virgin birth, refers to Danaë, Melanippe, Auge and Antiope (though not with enough context to be translated adequately below). These are all women who in Greek mythology have intercourse with a god: Danaë and Antiope have children through Zeus, and Auge became pregnant by Hercules; the Melanippe mentioned here is probably the daughter of the centaur Chiron or the horse Pegasus.

Most of the first speech is a counter-narrative to what we find in the canonical Gospels, and follows the outline of the main events of Jesus' life narrated in the New Testament. Perhaps the whole was originally in the form of a speech addressed to Jesus himself, although Celsus preserves some of the narrative in the third person. The speech forms part of a wider Jewish tradition of anti-Christian polemic in antiquity, a tradition which in the Middle Ages was expanded into a very long, legendary account of Jesus called the 'Toledoth Yeshu', or 'Generation of Jesus'. The overlap between the Jewish source below and the wider Jewish tradition can be seen, for example, in the naming of Jesus' alleged father as 'Panthera'.

As noted, Origen's response to Celsus was written in about 250 CE. The original work by Celsus probably comes from some time in the late second century, and the Jewish source perhaps from the middle of the same century.

TRANSLATION

Fragment 1: The virgin birth

He invented his birth from a virgin . . . He came from a Judaean village, born of a poor country-girl who spins wool! She was thrown out by her husband, a carpenter by trade, and was convicted of adultery . . . When Jesus' mother was thrown out by her betrothed, a carpenter, she was convicted of adultery, and gave birth to a child by a soldier named Panthera . . . Having been thrown out by her husband, and while wandering about disgracefully, she secretly gave birth to Jesus . . . Neither the power of God nor persuasive speech rescued her when she was despised by the carpenter and thrown out. These things therefore have nothing to do with the kingdom of God.

Fragment 2: Visit of the Magi and the slaughter of the innocents

The story is told by Jesus that Chaldaeans were moved to visit his birth in order to worship him as a god while he was still a baby. They informed Herod the Tetrarch of this, so he sent men to kill those who had been born at the same time, thinking that he would kill Jesus along with them, in case when he, Jesus, had grown sufficiently older he should come to reign.

If Herod did this to prevent you from ruling instead of him when you had grown up, why did you not take the throne when you were grown up? Instead, you, 'the son of God', so ignobly go about begging, cowering in fear and wandering around and about in destitution!

Fragment 3: The flight to Egypt

Because of his poverty, he was forced to earn a wage in Egypt. While he was there he attempted various magical powers of which the Egyptians boast. He grew arrogant because of these powers, and because of them announced himself as a god.

But why was it necessary for you to be taken off to Egypt when you were still a child, in case you were murdered? It is hardly likely that a god would be afraid of death. But – ah, yes – an angel came from heaven, instructing you and your family to flee, and if you did not leave you would die. But would the great God not be able to preserve you, his own son, there? He had already sent two angels because of you!

Fragment 4: Jesus' baptism

When you were having a wash next to John, you say that an apparition of a bird fluttered down to you from the sky. But what credible witness saw this apparition? Or who heard the voice from heaven appointing you as a son to God? It is only your say-so, and of another of those punished with you, that you adduce.

Fragment 5: Prophecy of Jesus as Son of God

But a prophet of mine in Jerusalem once said, *A son of God will come, a judge for the holy ones and the punisher of the ungodly.* Why are these things prophecies of you, rather than of the countless others who have been born since that prophecy? Some frenzied individuals and others who are vagrants say that they are sons of God who have come from above . . . The prophecies applied to the life of this Jesus can also fit other events . . . If you say that every man born according to divine providence is a son of God, then how are you any different from anyone else? . . . There are thousands who will convict Jesus of falsehood, by claiming that the very prophecies apparently uttered about him were actually spoken about them.

Fragment 6: Jesus' ministry

You attached to yourself ten or eleven notorious men without even a primary education – tax collectors and sailors of the most degenerate kind. With them you ran in flight hither and yon, shamefully and rudely scavenging for food.

Fragment 7: The miracles and Jesus as Son of God

The various healings, a resurrection, feedings of multitudes with a few loaves (with lots of scraps left over), or whatever other stories the disciples may have wildly recounted – let us say for the sake of argument that you really did these things. They are still no better than the works of sorcerers who claim quite wonderful miracles, or like what the savants of Egypt do in the marketplaces for a few *obols*† – dishing out solemn lore, driving spirits out of people, blowing away diseases, and invoking the souls of heroes who display lavish dinners and tables with pastries and meals which are not real, and who make things move as though they were alive, although they are not really alive but just appear so to the imagination. Since they do these things, should we think that they are sons of God? Or should we say that these are the pursuits of wicked men possessed by an evil genius? . . . The ancient myths assigning divine birth to Perseus or Amphion or Aeacus or Minos – not that we believe them – nevertheless do demonstrate their great deeds and truly superhuman wonders. These men, then, do not seem untrustworthy. But as for you! – what have you done that is noble or noteworthy either in word or deed? You showed us nothing, even when people challenged you in the temple to provide some clear indication that you were the son of God.

Fragment 8: The death of Jesus

He was not helped by his Father, nor was he able to help himself . . . The blood which poured forth on the cross was not 'ichor such as flows in the blessed gods'* . . . Such a body as yours would not have belonged to God. A body born in the way you were born, Jesus, would not have been possessed by God . . . Nor would the body of God eat such food . . . Nor would the body of a god use such a voice, or that kind of persuasion.

Fragment 9: Conclusion

These were really the actions of someone hated by God, a sorcerous scoundrel.

III

ACCOUNTS OF JESUS' TRIAL AND DEATH

Jesus before Pontius Pilate
Athens Codex 93 (11th cent.)

29 Vienna Greek Papyrus 2325 (The 'Fayyum Gospel')

(second or third century CE)

INTRODUCTION

This tiny papyrus sheet (about 4cm × 4cm) is notable for having Peter's name written in red. This has led some scholars to see it as a fragment of the *Gospel of Peter* (see pp. 205–211 below), but a connection is unlikely, because there Peter narrates the story in the first person, whereas here he is named. The episode, consisting of a quotation by Jesus of the prophet Zechariah, and his own prophecy of Peter's denial, is well known from the canonical Gospels. This manuscript, now held in the Austrian National Library in Vienna, probably dates from the third century CE.

TRANSLATION

[. . .] going out, when [he said], 'Tonight, [you will all] fall away [in accordance with] what is written: "I will strike the [shepherd and the] sheep will be scattered." '*

'Even if everyone else does, [I won't!]' Peter [replied].

'[Before] the cock crows twice,' [Jesus said, '. . . you will] deny [me three times].'

30 The Gospel of Judas

(C. 150 CE)

INTRODUCTION

Having come to public attention only in 2006, the *Gospel of Judas* is one of the 'newest' of ancient apocryphal Gospels. It attracted interest when it was first published because of its apparent transformation of Judas from a betrayer into a positive character. The *Mail on Sunday*, not wanting to understate the text's importance, proclaimed the *Gospel of Judas* as the 'greatest archaeological discovery of all time' and a 'threat to 2000 years of Christian teaching'. Although the initial sensationalism has died down, it is still remarkable to have a Gospel casting Judas as a special recipient of Jesus' revelation (even if he is not necessarily a positive figure).

In fact, the subversive character of the *Gospel of Judas* does fit into a tendency we see in other literature like it. The related *Apocryphon of John* (also a Gnostic work) criticizes the work of Moses in the first five books of the Bible, pointing out his theological misunderstandings. The Coptic *Gospel of the Egyptians* (see below, p. 357) comments on how neither the Old Testament prophets nor the apostles of Jesus grasped the truth which is announced in the book. Like the *Gospel of Judas*, the authors of the *Gospel of Mary* and the *Gospel of Thomas* (the doubter) also chose unconventional patron saints for their works, criticizing the other apostles and their claims to authority.

The *Gospel of Judas*, like the *Gospel of the Egyptians*, is a product of the Gnostic school. This is a collection of groups which shared the view that both the creator and the world were evil, a position which attracted considerable opposition. They were not just regarded as heretics by the church fathers, but also condemned as 'heretical' philosophers by the Platonic thinkers of the school of Plotinus, who took the goodness of the world to be axiomatic. More detail on the Gnostics can be found in the Introduction.

The focus in the *Gospel of Judas* is on what Jesus secretly reveals during the last days before his crucifixion. In keeping with the work's subversive agenda, it presents Jesus as deriding the disciples' celebration of the eucharist; they are condemned as murderous and sexually deviant priests. In the course of Jesus' meeting with the disciples, he singles out Judas for special revelation. The focus of this revelation is twofold. First, the story is told of how the supreme, transcendent being (called 'the Great Invisible Spirit') spawns further spiritual beings in the upper echelons of the heavenly hierarchy. These additional beings are not so much creations as emanations, like rays of the sun or streams of a river delta. Eventually these beings are so far removed from the Great Invisible Spirit, however, that a corrupt heavenly 'Cosmos' comes about. Second, demonic forces construct a cosmos below as a copy of the 'Cosmos' above, and along with it generate Adam and Eve. As in some other apocryphal Gospels, the goal for true disciples (here called the 'holy' or 'great' generation) is to transcend material reality and gain knowledge about the soul. Having disclosed his revelation, Jesus instructs Judas to proceed with his betrayal. After all, Jesus remarks, in crucifying him, his opponents are not really doing him any harm: all that is affected, Jesus says, is 'the man who carries me around' (codex p. 56). The Gospel therefore ends with Judas making a bargain with the chief priests and scribes, and delivering Jesus to them. So the work stops before there is any account of the death and resurrection of Jesus. In the Gnostic system, after all, it is revelation and knowledge which have saving significance, not events in the earthly realm.

The text of the *Gospel of Judas* comes in a fourth-century manuscript now held in the Coptic Museum in Cairo. Since the *Gospel of Judas* shows knowledge of the New Testament, and is mentioned by Bishop Irenaeus in about 180 CE, most scholars date the Greek original of the work to the middle of the second century.

DRAMATIS PERSONAE

In the dialogue:

JESUS
JUDAS ISCARIOT
JESUS' OTHER DISCIPLES
CHIEF PRIESTS *Ruling temple authorities*
SCRIBES *Authoritative experts in Jewish Law*

In the myth:

THE GREAT INVISIBLE SPIRIT *The supreme spiritual being*
BARBELO *Female consort of the Invisible Spirit*
AUTOGENES *An emanation from the Invisible Spirit*
ADAMAS *An emanation from Autogenes*
SETH *Child of Adamas*
THE GENERATION OF SETH *Gnostic disciples*
MICHAEL AND GABRIEL *Archangels*
EL *An angel*
ARCHONS *Demonic authority figures*
NIMROD-YALDABAOTH *Creator with Saklas of earthly reality*
SAKLAS *Co-creator with Nimrod-Yaldabaoth*
CHRIST, HARMATHOTH,
GALILA, YOBEL, ADONAIOS *Minions of Nimrod and Saklas*
THE ALL *The spiritual realm; possibly the material universe*
ADAM *The earthly reflection of Adamas*
EVE *Adam's wife*

TRANSLATION

1. Prologue

[p. 33] The secret message of the revelation which Jesus spoke to Judas Iscariot in the week leading up to the third day before he celebrated Passover.

2. Jesus' public ministry

When he appeared upon the earth, Jesus performed signs and great wonders for the salvation of humanity. Since some were [walking] in the way of righteousness, and others were walking in their transgression, the twelve disciples were called. Jesus began to speak to them of the mysteries beyond this world, and about what would come to pass until the end. On some occasions, he did not reveal himself openly to his disciples, but was present as a child among them.

3. First day: Jesus mocks the disciples' piety

One day in Judaea, Jesus came to the disciples and found them sitting together practising their piety. When he [met] them [p. 34] sitting together and giving thanks over the bread, he laughed.

'Master,' the disciples asked, 'why are you laughing at [our] thanksgiving? Or is it right what we are doing?'

'I am not laughing at you,' Jesus answered. 'You are not doing this by your own will, but because your god [receives] praise from it.'

'Master,' they said, 'you [. . .] are the son of our god.'

'How do you know me?' Jesus asked them. 'Truly, [I] say to you, no generation of the people in your midst can know me.' When his disciples heard this, they were annoyed and angry, and blasphemed him in their hearts.

4. Judas comes to the fore

When Jesus saw their stupidity, [he said] to them, 'Why this angry agitation? Your god who is within you and [. . .] [p. 35] annoyed with your souls. If any of you is strong, bring forth the perfect man and stand before me.'

'We are strong enough,' they all replied. But none of their spirits was bold enough to stand in his presence, except that of Judas Iscariot. He was able to stand before Jesus, though not to look into his eyes, and so he turned his face away.

'I know who you are and from where you have come,' Judas

said to him. 'You have come from the immortal aeon of Barbelo!
But I am not worthy to utter the name of him who sent you.'

Jesus, knowing that Judas was also pondering another exalted
matter, said to him, 'Separate yourself from them. I will utter to
you the mysteries of the kingdom. Not so that you enter it, but
so that you grieve greatly. [p. 36] For another will take your
place, so that the twelve [. . .] will be complete in their god.'

'When will you tell me these things,' Judas inquired of him,
'and when will the great day of the light of the generation dawn
[. . .]?' But when he asked these things, Jesus left him.

5. Second day: Jesus speaks incomprehensible mysteries

When it was morning, Jesus appeared to his disciples.

'Master, where did you go?' they asked. 'What did you do
when you left us?'

'I went to another great generation, which is holy.'

'Lord,' his disciples asked, 'what is the great, holy generation which is more exalted than us and which is not in these
aeons?'

When Jesus heard them asking this, he laughed.

'Why are you thinking about that powerful and holy generation? [p. 37] Truly [I] say to you, [no] one born [of] this aeon
will see that [generation]. No army of star-angels will rule over
it, nor will anyone born of mortal man be able to join it. For
that generation is not from [. . .] which has come into being.
[. . .] the generation of men who are in their midst, but it is
from the great generation of humanity [. . .] the powerful
authorities who [. . .] nor any powers [. . .] by which you rule.'

When his disciples heard these things, they each were disturbed in their spirits and were not able to say anything.

6. Third day: The temple vision

Jesus came to them on another day.

'Master, we have seen you in a vision!' his disciples said.
'For last night we saw great dreams [. . .].'

'Why have [. . .] you hidden yourselves?' Jesus asked.

[p. 38] 'We have seen a great house with a great altar in it,' they [answered], 'and twelve men (who, we think, are priests), and a name. There was a crowd waiting at that altar for the priests [to come] out [and conduct] the service. We were also waiting.'

'What were [the priests] like?' Jesus inquired.

'Some fast for two weeks,' the disciples replied. 'Others sacrifice their own children. Others sacrifice their wives in "blessing" and "humility" with each other. Others sleep with men. Others do murderous deeds. Still others perform a multitude of sins and transgressions. But the men who stand at the altar call upon your [name] [p. 39] and are in the midst of all the slaughter which the sacrifices fill up [. . .].' When they had said these things, they fell silent, as they were troubled.

'Why are you troubled?' Jesus asked. 'Truly, I say to you, all the priests who were standing at that altar call upon my name. Again I say to you, my name has been written upon this [house] for the generations of stars by the generations of men. But they have shamefully planted fruitless trees in my name.

'You are the ones offering service at the altar which you saw,' Jesus continued. 'That is the god whom you serve, the twelve men whom you saw are you yourselves, and the animals offered as the sacrifices which you saw are the multitude which you deceive [p. 40] at that altar. [. . .] will arise and this is how he will treat my name. The generations of the "pious" will attend him. After this, another man will bring forward the adulterers. Another will bring forward those who murder children, and still another those who sleep with men, and those who fast, as well as the other impurities, iniquities and errors. Those who say "we are like angels" are stars which bring everything to fulfilment. For they have said to the generations of men, "Behold, God has accepted your sacrifices from the priest" – who is the minister of error. But the Lord who commands is the one who is Lord over the All. On the last day they will be found guilty.'

[p. 41] Jesus went on. 'Stop sacrificing animals [. . .] upon the altar,' he said, 'since they are above your stars and your angels which have already died out there. So let them be [. . .] before you and be visible.'

His disciples [said], '[. . .] cleanse us from the [. . .] which we have done through the deception of the angels.'

'It is impossible [. . .],' Jesus told them. 'Nor is it possible for a well to quench the fire of the whole inhabited world. Nor can a spring in [a city] satisfy all the generations except the great generation which is appointed. And a single lamp cannot illuminate all the aeons, except the second generation. Nor can a baker feed all creation [p. 42] under [heaven].'

And [when the disciples heard these things], they said to him, 'Lord, help us and [save us.]'

'Stop contending with me,' Jesus instructed them. 'Each one of you has his star and [. . .] of the stars will [. . .] what is his. [. . .] I was not sent to the corruptible generation, but to the strong and incorruptible generation. For that generation no enemy has ruled over, nor has any of the stars. Truly I say to you, the pillar of fire will fall suddenly, and that generation will not be moved by the stars.'

When Jesus had said these things, he withdrew and [took] Judas Iscariot with him. He said to him, 'The water on the lofty mountain is from [. . .] [p. 43] [. . .] it came not to [. . .] spring of the tree of [. . .] of this aeon [. . .] after time [. . .]. But it came to water the Paradise of God, and the generation which will endure, because [. . .] will not defile the [. . .] of that generation. But [. . .] is everlasting.'

7. Dialogue on the hereafter: The holy generation and the rest

Judas asked [him], '[. . .], what is the fruit which this generation has?'

'The souls of every generation of man will die,' Jesus replied. 'But in the case of the holy generation, when the time of the kingdom is fulfilled and the spirit separates from them, their bodies will die, but their souls will be made alive and will be raised up.'

'What then will become of the rest of the generations of men?' Judas inquired.

'It is impossible [p. 44] to plant on a rock and then reap fruit,' Jesus answered. 'This is how . . . [. . .] of the generation

[. . .] with corrupt Sophia [. . .] the hand which created mortal men whose souls go up to the higher aeons. Truly I say to you, [. . .] angel [. . .] power will be able to see those [. . .]. These who [. . .] the holy generation [. . .] them.'

When Jesus had said these things, he went away.

8. Judas' temple vision

Judas said, 'Master, just as you have listened to all the others, listen to me as well. For I have seen a great vision.'

When Jesus heard this, he laughed.

'Why do you struggle so, O thirteenth spirit?' he answered Judas. 'But speak, and I will be patient with you.'

'I saw myself in the vision,' Judas replied, 'and the twelve disciples were throwing stones at me. They were [p. 45] chasing [me] [. . .]. I also went to the place [. . .] after you. I saw [a house] [. . .] and its measurements my eyes were unable [to measure]. Some great men were surrounding it, and the house had a roof of lightning. In the middle of the house was [. . .]. Master, receive me in with these men.'

'Your star has deceived you, O Judas,' Jesus answered. 'No progeny of any mortal man is worthy to enter into the house which you saw, for that place, where the sun, the moon and the day will have no dominion, is kept for the holy ones. They will stand for all time in the aeon with the holy angels. Behold, I have spoken to you the mysteries of the kingdom, [p. 46] and I have taught you [about the] deception of the stars, and [. . .] sent [. . .] over the twelve aeons.'

9. Judas' destiny

Judas said, 'Master, surely my seed will never submit to the archons?'

'Come,' Jesus answered, 'and I will [. . .], but so that you grieve greatly as you see the kingdom with all its generation.'

When Judas had heard this, he asked, 'What is the benefit which I receive as a result of you setting me apart from that generation?'

'You will become the thirteenth,' Jesus answered. 'You will be cursed by the other generations, but you will rule over them. In the last days, they will [. . .] you, but you will not ascend to the [p. 47] holy generation.'

10. Jesus' account of the creations

Jesus said, '[Come], and I will teach you about [. . .] which [no] man can see. For a great, limitless aeon exists, whose measure no generation of angels has seen. In it is [the] Great Invisible Spirit, "whom no angel's eye has seen; nor has the thought of a mind received him; nor has he been called by any name." '

11. The clouds, Autogenes and his angels

'There appeared in that place a cloud of light.
' "Let there be an angel to attend me," the cloud asked. And there came forth from the cloud a great angel, Autogenes the god of light. Another four angels then came into being for his sake, from another cloud. And they came into being to attend Autogenes the angel.'

12. Creation of the aeons, luminaries and ministering angels

'And Autogenes said, [p. 48] "Let [. . .] come into being." And there came into being [. . .]. He then made the first luminary to rule over him. And he said, "Let some angels come into being to minister to him." And tens of thousands without number came into being.

'And he said, "Let an aeon of light come into being." And he came into being, and Autogenes created the second luminary to rule over him, with myriads of innumerable angels for his service.

'Thus he created the rest of the aeons of light. He appointed the luminaries to rule over them, and created for them myriads of innumerable angels for their service.'

13. Creation of the generation of Seth

'Adamas was in that first cloud of light which no angel among all those who are called gods has seen. And he [p. 49] [. . .] that [. . .] the image [. . .] and according to the likeness of [this] angel. He revealed the incorruptible [generation] of Seth [. . .] the twelve l[uminaries] [. . .].

'He revealed seventy-two luminaries in the incorruptible generation by the will of the Spirit.

'The seventy-two luminaries revealed 360 luminaries in the incorruptible generation by the will of the Spirit, so that there would be five for each of them.

'Their father is the twelve aeons of the twelve luminaries. And there are six heavens for each aeon so that there might be seventy-two heavens for the seventy-two luminaries, and for each one [p. 50] [of them, five] firmaments, [so that there might be] three hundred and sixty [firmaments.]'

14. The emergence of the cosmos

'[They] were given authority and a [great] host of [in]numerable angels, for glorification and service, as well as virgin spirits for the glorification and [service] of all the aeons and the heavens and their firmaments. The host of those immortals is called "Cosmos", that is, "corruption", by the Father and the seventy-two luminaries who are with Autogenes and his seventy-two aeons.

'In Cosmos, the first man appeared with his incorruptible powers. The aeon who appeared with his generation is that which contained the cloud of knowledge and the angel called [p. 51] El [. . .] with [. . .] aeon [. . .].'

15. Creation of the rulers of the underworld

'After these things, [. . .] said, "May twelve angels come into being, [to] rule over chaos and Hades." And behold, an [angel] appeared out of the cloud with his face pouring forth fire. His appearance was polluted with blood, and his name was

"Nimrod", which interpreted means "apostate"; others call him "Yaldabaoth". Again, another angel called Saklas came forth from the cloud. Nimrod created six angels for assistance, as did Saklas. And so they generated the twelve angels in the heavens, and took a portion in the heavens for each one.

'The twelve archons said to the twelve angels, "May each one of you [p. 52] [. . .] and they [. . .] generation [. . .] angel."

'The first is [. . .], who is called "Christ".

'The [second] is Harmathoth, who [. . .].

'The third is Galila.

'The fourth is Yobel.

'The fifth is Adonaios.

'These are the five who ruled over the underworld, and were pre-eminent over chaos.'

16. The creation of Adam and Eve

'Then Saklas said to his angels, "Let us make man according to the likeness and according to the image." And so they created Adam and his wife Eve, who in the cloud is called Zoë. For by his name, all the generations inquire about Adam, and everyone calls the woman by either of her two names. Saklas did not [p. 53] command [. . .] produced except [. . .] generations [. . .] which this [. . .].

'And the [ang]el said to him, "Your life and the lives of your children are for an allotted time."'

17. Dialogue on the future

Judas asked Jesus, 'How much longer will mankind live?'

'Why are you amazed,' Jesus replied, 'that Adam with his generation received his allotted time where he received his allotted kingdom with his archon?'

'Does the spirit of a man die?' Judas asked.

'The way God commanded Michael to give men's spirits to them, so that they might serve, was as a loan,' Jesus answered. 'But the Great One commanded Gabriel to give the spirits – the spirits and the souls – to the great kingless generation. For this

reason, the rest of the souls [p. 54] [. . .] mountain [. . .] light
[. . .] Chaos [. . .] to return [. . .] spirit within you all which you
have caused to dwell in this flesh in the generations of the
angels. But God had them bring knowledge to Adam and to
those with him, so that the rulers of Chaos and Hades might
not have dominion over them.'

18. The destiny of the cosmos

Judas asked Jesus, 'What, then, will become of those
generations?'

'Truly I say to you,' replied Jesus, 'when the stars over them
have all completed their courses, and when Saklas has completed the times which have been appointed for him, their
leading star will come with the generations, and what has been
spoken of will be fulfilled. Then they will commit sexual immorality in my name, and will kill their children [p. 55] and [. . .]
evil and [. . .] the aeons which bring their generations, presenting them to Saklas. After that, [. . .]rael will come bringing the
twelve tribes of Israel from [. . .] and all the generations which
sinned in my name will serve Saklas. And your star will ru[le]
over the thirteenth aeon.' After this, Jesus laughed.

'Master, wh[y are you laughing?]' asked Judas.

'I am not laughing at all of you,' he said, 'but at the error of
the stars, because these six stars were deceived with these five
warriors, and all these will perish with their creations.'

19. Judas' destiny

Judas inquired further, 'What will become of those who have
been baptized in your name?'

'Truly, I say [to you],' replied Jesus, 'this baptism [p. 56] [. . .]
my name [. . .] not [. . .] it will destroy the whole generation of
the earthly Adam. Tomorrow, the one who carries me about
will be tormented. Truly I say to you all, no human mortal
hand will sin against me. Truly, [I] say to you, Judas, [those
who] offer up sacrifice to Saklas [. . .] all, since [. . .] everything
which is evil. But you will be "greater" than them all. For you

will sacrifice the man who carries me around. Already your horn has become exalted, your anger has burned, your star has passed overhead and your mind has [. . .].

[p. 57] 'Truly [I say to you that] your final [. . .] of the aeon [. . .] the kings have become weak, and the generations of the angels have grieved and those who are evil [. . .] the archon who will be destroyed, [and] then the [image] of the great generation of Adam will be exalted, for that generation from the aeons exists before heaven and earth and the angels.

'Behold, everything has been told to you. Lift up your eyes and behold the cloud and the light which is in it, and the stars which surround it. The star which is the leader – that is your star.'

Judas lifted up his eyes and saw the cloud of light. Then Jesus entered it. Those who stood underneath heard a voice coming from the cloud, which said, [p. 58] '[. . .] great generation [. . .].' [. . .] and [. . .] and Judas stopped looking at Jesus.

20. Epilogue: The 'betrayal'

Just then there was a disturbance among the Jews [. . .]. Their chief priests were angry that Jesus had gone to his lodging place to pray. Some of the scribes were there looking to arrest him at prayer, for they feared the people, because the people all held him as a prophet. They approached Judas.

'Why are you here?' they asked him. 'You are Jesus' disciple.'

He answered them according to their wish. Judas received money, and handed Jesus over to them.

The Gospel of Judas

31 The Gospel of Peter (including Oxyrhynchus Papyrus 2949)

(mid- to late second century CE)

INTRODUCTION

The codex containing the long Greek fragment of the *Gospel of Peter* is a curious item, because it is a copy specifically designed to begin in the middle of a paragraph and end in the middle of a sentence. The elaborate decorative illustrations at the beginning and end of the text in the so-called Akhmim Codex show that the scribe has planned the manuscript this way. (Curiously, the Akhmim Codex has gone missing, although photographs survive.) What survives here of the *Gospel of Peter* is an account of the death and resurrection of Jesus, and a small Oxyrhynchus fragment also overlaps with this text. Probably the work was originally a full-length Gospel beginning with Jesus' birth or baptism: in addition to knowing that there must have been more of this spliced text just by looking at the manuscript, a longer narrative may well be suggested by a report by the third-century church father Origen. According to him, the *Gospel of Peter* expresses the view that Jesus' siblings, mentioned in the New Testament, were children of Joseph from a former marriage. Like the *Protevangelium of James* (see pp. 3–21 above), it upheld the perpetual virginity of Mary.

The *Gospel of Peter* is also noteworthy in that it is the only example of a Gospel we know to have been read out in a church, at least for a time, alongside the canonical Gospels. Bishop Serapion of Antioch, writing in about 180–200 CE, reports on the incident at the church in Rhossus in Syria: 'When I was with you, I assumed that you were on course in the right faith, and did not read the Gospel published by those others in the

name of Peter. I stated that, if this was the only thing provoking acrimony among you, let it be read. But now that I have
been informed that their minds were skulking in some heresy,
I will make haste to come back to you. Therefore, brothers and
sisters, expect me soon!' The *Gospel of Peter*'s (albeit short-
lived) use in church services is an exceptional case of canonical
and non-canonical Gospels being used together.

Two features of the surviving texts of the *Gospel of Peter*
particularly stand out to the reader familiar with the accounts
of Jesus' death in the New Testament. First, there is the depiction of the crucified and risen Jesus. During Jesus' execution,
he is entirely silent except for the words at the moment he
expires. When he rises, however, his resurrected body is gigantic, and as it comes out of the tomb it extends in height beyond
the heavens. Jesus is also accompanied by a talking cross,
which gives verbal confirmation that Jesus after his crucifixion
preached to the souls of the dead in Hell.

Second, there is a pronounced anti-Jewish tone in the *Gospel of Peter*. The actions of the Roman soldiers in the canonical
portrayal of the crucifixion of Jesus are, in the *Gospel of Peter*,
all transferred to Jews: the decision to execute him, the mockery, the presentation of the crown of thorns and of the vinegary
drink, and the crucifixion itself. (Surprisingly, the Jewish soldiers refuse to break the legs not of Jesus, as in the traditional
account, but of one of those crucified with him.) As a result, a
curse comes over Judaea and upon the Jewish people, with a
specific forecast of the destruction of Jerusalem. The resurrection scene is also filled with panic on the part of the Jews who
had taken part in Jesus' execution.

In terms of when the *Gospel of Peter* may have been written,
the reference to the Gospel by Serapion of Antioch shows that
Peter must have been written before about 200 CE. Serapion
was probably referring to substantially the same text as the
fragments which have survived. Even though neither the long
manuscript nor the brief Oxyrhynchus fragment is given a
title, Peter at the end of the text refers to himself in the first
person, and so the extract is likely to come from the *Gospel*

of Peter. Since the author of the text is well acquainted with probably all the canonical Gospels, a date of composition in the mid- to late second century is therefore likely.

The versification system for the *Gospel of Peter* is peculiar, because two ways of dividing up the text have developed. Hence in the translation below, there are numbers in Roman numerals as well as in Arabic numerals.

DRAMATIS PERSONAE

JESUS

HIS DISCIPLES

MARY MAGDALENE *A female disciple of Jesus*

SIMON PETER, ANDREW, LEVI *Disciples of Jesus*

THE TWO CRIMINALS *Those crucified either side of Jesus*

HEROD *The Jewish 'king', or tetrarch of Galilee and Peraea*

PILATE *The Roman Prefect of Judaea*

PILATE'S SOLDIERS *Those guarding the tomb*

PETRONIUS *A Roman centurion*

JOSEPH *Joseph of Arimathaea, a follower of Jesus*

ELDERS *Authorities over civic and synagogue affairs*

SCRIBES *Authoritative experts in Jewish Law*

PHARISEES *An influential, elite Jewish movement*

THE YOUNG MAN *An angel*

TRANSLATION

Jesus led out to crucifixion

I.*1* . . . Now none of the Jews, including Herod and his judges, washed his hands. Since they refused to wash their hands, Pilate stood up. *2* King Herod then ordered his men to take the Lord.

'Do what I have ordered you to do to him,' Herod commanded them.

II.*3* Standing by was Joseph, a friend of Pilate and of the

Lord. Knowing that they were about to crucify him, he went to Pilate and asked for the Lord's body so he could bury him. *4* So Pilate sent a message to Herod asking for the body.

5 'Brother Pilate,' Herod responded, 'even if nobody had asked for the body, we would have buried him, especially since the Sabbath is approaching. For it is written in the Law, "The sun must not set over a murdered man."' Herod handed the Lord over to the people on the day before the Feast of Unleavened Bread,† their festival.

III.*6* Those who were taking the Lord ran along pushing him.

'Let's drag this son of God along, since we're in charge of him!' they shouted. *7* They dressed him in purple and sat him on the seat of judgement.

'Judge righteously, O king of Israel!' they added. *8* One of them brought a crown of thorns and fastened it on the Lord's head. *9* Some standing by were spitting in his eyes, others slapped his cheeks, and still others were stabbing him with reeds. Some also whipped him and said, 'This is the way to honour the "son of God"!'

The crucifixion

IV.*10* They then brought two criminals, and crucified them, with the Lord between them. He was silent, as if he were not in any pain. *11* When they lifted up the cross, they inscribed on it, 'THIS IS THE KING OF ISRAEL.' *12* Laying out his clothes in front of him they divided them up and cast lots for them. *13* One of the criminals reproached them, 'We are suffering like this because of crimes we have committed, but he is the saviour of mankind! What harm has he done you?' *14* But the executioners got annoyed with him and ordered his legs not to be broken, so that he would die in agony.

V.*15* It was mid-day, but darkness engulfed the whole of Judaea. The people were in uproar, distressed at the thought that the sun had already set while he was alive. (It is written for them, 'The sun must not set over a murdered man.')

16 'Give him a drink of gall with vinegar,' one of them said. They mixed it and gave it to him to drink. *17* And so they brought everything to fulfilment, heaping upon themselves the full measure of their sins. *18* Many people, thinking it was night, were stumbling around with lamps.

19 Then the Lord cried out, 'My power, O power, you have abandoned me.' After he said this, he was taken up. 20. And at the same hour the curtain of the temple in Jerusalem was torn in two.

The burial of Jesus and reactions to his death

VI.*21* They then removed the nails from the hands of the Lord and placed him on the ground. The whole land shook, and terror gripped them. *22* Then the sun shone again, and it was discovered to be the ninth hour.† *23* The Jews rejoiced and gave the body to Joseph so that he could bury it, since he had been watching all the good things which Jesus had done. *24* Taking the Lord, he washed him and wrapped him in a linen cloth, and placed him in a tomb he owned, called 'Joseph's Garden'.

VII.*25* Then the Jews, with their elders and priests, realized what sort of evil they had brought upon themselves, and began to mourn.

'Woe to us for our sins! The judgement and end of Jerusalem is looming!'

26 I grieved along with my companions and, our minds distraught, we hid because we were being hunted down by the Jews as criminals who wanted to burn down the temple. *27* In addition, we fasted and sat mourning and weeping all day and all night until the Sabbath.

VIII.*28* The scribes, Pharisees and elders met together because they had heard that all the people were grumbling, beating their breasts and saying, 'If these awesome signs have appeared at his death, what a righteous man he must have been!' *29* The elders were afraid, and went to Pilate.

30 'Give us soldiers to guard his tomb for three days,' they petitioned, 'in case his disciples come and steal the body. Otherwise the people might imagine he has risen from the dead, and bring disaster on us.'

31 So Pilate granted them the centurion Petronius with his men to guard the tomb. The elders and scribes went there with them. *32* Everyone there – with the centurion and his men – together rolled a great stone along and placed it at the entrance to the tomb. *33* They then placed seven seals on it, pitched a tent there and stood guard.

Jesus' resurrection

IX.*34* Early the next morning, as the Sabbath dawned, a crowd came from Jerusalem and the surrounding countryside to see the sealed tomb.

35 During the following night in which the Lord's day[†] dawned, as the soldiers were guarding two by two on duty, there was a great voice in the sky. *36* The soldiers saw the heavens opened and two men coming down from there, in brilliant light, approaching the tomb. *37* The stone which had been placed at the entrance rolled away of its own accord and made some space for them to enter. Since, then, the tomb was open, both the young men went in.

X.*38* When the soldiers saw this, they woke up the centurion and the elders. (They were also on guard there.) *39* As they were explaining what they had seen, they saw three men coming out from the tomb, two of them holding the other one aloft, and a cross following behind them. *40* The heads of the two reached up to heaven, but the head of the one carried along by them went up beyond the heavens. *41* Then those present heard a voice from the heavens.

'Have you preached to those who are asleep?'

42 'Yes!' came the answer from the cross.

XI.*43* The soldiers were considering whether to go off and report this to Pilate. *44* While they were still pondering this, again the heavens looked as though they were open, and a man came down and went into the tomb. *45* When the centurion's men saw this, they hurried to Pilate, even though it was night. They left the grave they were guarding to report on everything they had seen. They were in turmoil.

'Truly this man was the son of God!' they told him.

46 'I am innocent of this son of God's blood,' Pilate replied.

'This was your doing.' 47 Then they all came to petition him, imploring him to order the centurion and his men not to say anything of what they had seen.

48 'It is better for us,' they said, 'to be liable for a very great sin before God than to fall into the hands of the Jewish people and be stoned.' 49 So Pilate ordered the centurion and his men not to say anything.

XII.50 Now at dawn on the Lord's Day, Mary Magdalene, a disciple of the Lord, was afraid of the Jews because they were inflamed with anger. As a result, she had not carried out at the tomb of the Lord what is customary for women to do for their dead loved ones. 51 Now she took her friends with her and went to the tomb where he had been placed, 52 though they were afraid that the Jews would see them.

'Even if we were not able to weep and mourn on the day on which he was crucified,' they said, 'let's now do those things at his tomb. 53 But who will roll away for us the stone which has been put at the entrance to the tomb, so we can go in and sit beside him and do what we should do? 54 The stone was big, and someone might see us. But even if we can't do it, let's put what we're taking in his memory at the entrance. Then we can weep and mourn on our way back home.'

XIII.55 So off they went. But they found the tomb opened. They went up to it, peered in, and saw sitting in the middle of the tomb there a beautiful young man wearing a dazzling robe.

56 'Why have you come?' he asked them. 'Who are you looking for? Not the man who was crucified, surely? He has risen and gone! If you don't believe me, peer in and see that he is not in the place where he was laid. He has risen and gone to the place from where he was sent.' 57 Then the women fled in terror.

XIV.58 Now it was the last day of the Feast of Unleavened Bread, and many people were leaving, going back home now that the feast was over. 59 The twelve of us, the disciples of the Lord, were weeping and grieving. Each of us went back home, lamenting what had happened. 60 I, Simon Peter, and Andrew my brother took our nets and went off to the sea, and with us was Levi the son of Alphaeus whom the Lord . . .

32 The Gospel of Nicodemus

(fifth century CE*)*

INTRODUCTION

The ancient Rabbis preserved a number of stories about a fabulously wealthy dynasty of men with the names Gurion and Nicodemus, whose family line can be traced back to the first century CE. This is the time-frame for the Gospel of John's Nicodemus, who is the inspiration for the *Gospel of Nicodemus* here. According to the Gospel of John, he is a member of the Jewish ruling elite and extremely rich, as is evident from his provision of about 70 pounds of myrrh and aloes for Jesus' tomb. The Rabbis mention similar wealth: it was said of one Nicodemus ben Gurion that he could provide wheat and barley for the whole population of Jerusalem for several years, and that his daughter's perfume allowance was 400 gold coins a day.

The *Gospel of Nicodemus* belongs to the genre of 'pseudo-archive', and purports to be a Jewish record, composed by the Jewish councillor Nicodemus while Pontius Pilate was prefect of Judaea. A certain Ananias (who himself may be fictional) claims to have rediscovered it and translated it from Hebrew into Greek (see Prologue). The narrative begins with the Jews accusing Jesus to Pilate, and Pilate showing incredulity that they are condemning Jesus for healing on the Sabbath. Jesus is also accused of sorcery and blasphemy. This being Nicodemus' account (ch. 5), he himself plays a significant role in Jesus' defence, as do various beneficiaries of Jesus' healing (chs. 6–8). Pilate vacillates, however, because the majority of Jews in this work oppose Jesus, while others maintain his innocence and goodness. Eventually Jesus is crucified, and the disciples go into hiding – all except for Nicodemus. When Joseph of Arimathaea appears (along with Nicodemus) in the Jewish assembly, he is promptly arrested and locked in a windowless room, with one guarded door; miraculously, however, he disappears (ch. 12). We learn later (ch. 15) that the risen Jesus raised the prison building off its foundations, enabling Joseph to walk out. Other Jewish authorities also claim to have seen the risen Jesus: Phinehas, Adas and Haggai witnessed some appearances of Jesus in Galilee (chs. 14–16). Some nice traditional legends are included in the *Gospel of Nicodemus*, such as the images of the emperor on Roman soldiers' standards bowing down to Jesus. In another late legend, when Jesus goes to Egypt as a child, various Egyptian statues crash down before him.

Although the claim that the text comes from the Jewish archives is a fiction, it is possible that the author has some direct acquaintance with Judaism. The phraseology that 'Rabbi Levi said, testifying to the words from Rabbi Simeon' sounds very like the Rabbinic language of one teacher transmitting a statement from another teacher (ch. 16). The *Gospel of Nicodemus* also notes at the beginning of the archival record that the proper name of the high priest, Caiaphas (a nickname), was actually Joseph. This is a detail which cannot be derived from the New Testament, but only from the historian Flavius Josephus or some other Jewish source. On the other hand, the Jews in the story are generally presented in a very negative light. For most of the narrative they resemble pantomime villains; Pilate, on the other hand, is exonerated, and even becomes a kind of honorary Christian, 'circumcised in heart' (ch. 12). This is just one example of a development seen elsewhere, in which some Christian literature becomes pro-Roman at the expense of being anti-Jewish. Surprisingly, however, the majority of the Jewish authorities seem convinced by the end of the *Gospel of Nicodemus* that Jesus really has risen from the dead.

This text, also known as the *Acts of Pilate*, might be possible to date fairly precisely if one goes by the dates of the emperors mentioned in the Prologue. Theodosius II succeeded his father in 408; hence his seventeenth year is 424–5. Valentinian III was born in 419, hence his sixth year of age is the same as Theodosius' seventeenth regnal year. However, that date might also be part of the authorial fiction. Nevertheless, the work probably does not originate much later than the early fifth century, and some of the component parts go back considerably earlier. In some versions, the *Gospel of Nicodemus* text is followed by an account of Christ's descent into Hell rather like the account in the *Questions of Bartholomew* (see pp. 285–301).

DRAMATIS PERSONAE

JESUS

NICODEMUS   *A leading figure among the Jews*

JOSEPH CAIAPHAS   *The high priest*

ANNAS   *A chief priest, father-in-law of Caiaphas*

PILATE   *The prefect, or governor of Judaea*

PILATE'S WIFE

PILATE'S COURIER

JOSEPH OF ARIMATHAEA   *A member of the Jewish ruling council*

LAZARUS, ASTERIUS, ANTONIUS, JAMES, AMNES, ZERAS, SAMUEL, ISAAC, PHINEHAS, CRISPUS, AGRIPPA AND JUDAH   *The twelve men who insist on Jesus' legitimate birth*

PHINEHAS, ADAS, HAGGAI   *A priest, teacher and Levite who report on Jesus*

JAIRUS, BOUTHAM, RABBI ISAAC, RABBI LEVI   *Jewish teachers*

LEVI'S FATHER

SHEMESH, DATHAES, GAMALIEL, JUDAS, NAPHTHALI AND ALEXANDER   *Other Jewish leaders*

CHIEF PRIESTS   *Senior temple authorities*

SCRIBES   *Authoritative experts in Jewish Law*

ELDERS   *Authorities over civic and synagogue affairs*

LEVITES   *Descendants of the patriarch Levi, or, teachers of the Law*

SANHEDRIN   *The Jewish ruling council*

SYNAGOGUE LEADERS *Those in authority over local assemblies*
BERNICE *A woman healed of a flow of blood by Jesus*
DYSMAS *A criminal crucified with Jesus*
LONGINUS *The soldier who stabbed Jesus with a spear*

TRANSLATION

Prologue

I, Ananias, a member of the governor's bodyguard, being learned in the Law, recognized from the divine scriptures our Lord Jesus Christ, approached him by faith and was counted worthy of holy baptism. I searched the records which had been compiled at that time, in the days of our Master Jesus Christ, records which the Jews had deposited in the time of Pontius Pilate. I found these records in Hebrew, and with God's approval translated them into Greek for the information of all who call on the name of our Lord Jesus Christ now that our master Flavius Theodosius is emperor, in his seventeenth year, which is the sixth year of Flavius Valentinianus, in the ninth indiction.*

All you who read and copy this into other volumes, then, remember me and pray that God would be merciful to me and forgive the sins which I have committed against him.

Peace be to the readers and hearers of this book, and to their households. Amen.

Preface to the record

These things took place in the fifteenth year of the principate* of Tiberius Caesar, the emperor of the Romans, in the nineteenth year of the reign of Herod king of Galilee, on the eighth day before the Kalends of April [that is, 25 March], in the consulship of Rufus and Rubellio, in the fourth year of the 202nd Olympiad, when Joseph Caiaphas was high priest of the Jews. Nicodemus recounted what took place after the Lord's crucifixion and suffering, and passed it on to the chief priests and the other Jews. Nicodemus composed this in Hebrew.

1. Jesus is summoned to Pontius Pilate

Now when the chief priests and the scribes (Annas, Caiaphas, Shemesh, Dathaes, Gamaliel, Judas, Levi, Naphthali, Alexander, Jairus) along with the other Jews had held a council, they went to Pilate accusing Jesus of many crimes.

'We know that this man is the son of that carpenter Joseph and the offspring of Mary,' they asserted, 'yet he claims that he is king and Son of God! He also desecrates the Sabbath and wants to overthrow our ancestral Law.'

'What has he been doing and wanting to overthrow?' Pilate asked.

'We have a law against healing a person on the Sabbath,' the Jews replied, 'yet he has been healing the lame, the hunchbacked, the withered, the blind and the paralysed, as well as the dumb and the demon-possessed – he with his evil deeds!'

'What sort of evil deeds?' Pilate asked them.

'He is a sorcerer,' they replied, 'and by the power of Beelzebul the Prince of Demons he can cast out demons, and they all submit to him.'

'This is not casting out demons by some unclean spirit,' Pilate said to them, 'but by the divine Asclepius.'

'We request your excellency,' the Jews said to Pilate, 'to set him before your seat of judgement so he can stand trial.'

Pilate summoned them. 'Tell me,' he asked, 'how I, a mere governor, can cross-examine a king?'

'No, we are not saying he is king,' they replied. 'Only that he claims to be one.'

Pilate summoned his courier. 'Have Jesus brought to me – considerately, though.'

The courier went off and, when he had identified Jesus, bowed down to him. He took his handkerchief and spread it out on the ground.

'Sir, come and stand on this,' he said to Jesus. 'The governor has summoned you.'

When the Jews saw what the courier had done, they railed at Pilate.

'Why did you have him summoned by a mere courier and

not by a herald?' they thundered. 'The courier bowed down to him when he saw him, and spread out his handkerchief on the ground, letting him walk on it like a king!'

Pilate called the courier back. 'What were you doing spreading out your handkerchief on the ground and letting Jesus walk on it?' he asked.

'Lord governor,' the courier said, 'when you sent me to Jerusalem to deal with Alexander, I saw Jesus sitting on a donkey, and the children of the Hebrews were clutching branches in their hands and shouting, and others were spreading out their clothes for him and calling out, "Save us, ye in the heights! Blessed is he who comes in the name of the Lord!" '

The Jews railed at the courier. 'The children of the Hebrews shouted in Hebrew, so how did you know what it meant in Greek?'

'I asked one of the Jews to tell me the meaning of the Hebrew they were shouting,' the courier said to them, 'and he translated it for me.'

'What were they shouting in Hebrew?' Pilate asked.

'*Hosanna membromē barouchamma Adonai*,'* the Jews said to him.

'This *Hosanna* business – what does it mean?' Pilate inquired.

'*Save us, ye in the heights!*' they said, 'And, *Blessed is he who comes in the name of the Lord!*'

'If you agree that this is what the children were saying,' Pilate said, 'then what has the courier done wrong?' They had nothing to say.

'Go,' Pilate said to the courier, 'and bring him in whatever manner you wish.'

The courier went off and repeated what he had done before.

'Sir, come – the governor is summoning you,' he said to Jesus.

When Jesus came in, accompanied by the standard-bearers holding the ensigns, the emblems of the emperor on them bowed down and worshipped Jesus. When the Jews saw how the standards were bowing down and worshipping Jesus, they railed against the standard-bearers. Pilate then addressed the Jews.

'Aren't you struck by how the emblems of the emperor are bowing down and worshipping Jesus?' he said.

'We saw that it was the standard-bearers that bowed down and worshipped him,' they said. The governor called to the standard-bearers.

'Why did you do this?' he asked them.

'We are Greeks, and temple-servants,' they answered. 'How could we worship him? When we were holding the emblems, they bowed down and worshipped him all by themselves.'

Pilate addressed the synagogue leaders and the elders of the people.

'Choose for yourselves some mighty, strong men, to hold the standards,' he said. 'Then we will see if the emblems bow down by themselves.'

The Jewish elders therefore took twelve strong men, arranging them in groups of six to hold each standard. Then they stood before the governor's judgement seat.

'Fetch Jesus from the Praetorium,'* Pilate said to the courier, 'and bring him back in whatever manner you wish.'

Jesus came out of the Praetorium with the courier, and Pilate summoned those who had previously been holding the imperial emblems. 'I swear by the health of Caesar,' he said, 'that unless the standards bow down when Jesus comes in, I will cut off your heads.'

The governor ordered Jesus to come in again, and the courier did as before. He implored Jesus to stand on his handkerchief. Jesus stepped on it and went in. When he came in, the standards again bowed down and worshipped Jesus.

2. Debate over whether Jesus was conceived illegitimately

When Pilate saw this, he was terrified and tried to stand up from his judgement seat. While he was still struggling to stand up, his wife sent him a message saying, 'Have nothing to do with this righteous man, for I suffered terribly because of him last night.' Pilate summoned all the Jews and addressed them.

'You know that my wife is god-fearing and, indeed, even follows Jewish customs like you.'

'Yes,' they said, 'we know.'

'She has just sent me a message telling me not to have anything to do with this righteous man, because she suffered terribly in the night because of him.'

'Didn't we tell you he was a sorcerer?' the Jews replied. 'He has just sent your wife a bad dream.'

Pilate summoned Jesus. 'Why are these people making accusations against you?' he asked. 'Are you not going to say anything in response?'

'Unless they had authority,' Jesus said, 'they would not have said anything. For each person has authority over his mouth to speak good or evil. They will see.'

'What will we see?' the elders of the Jews asked. 'First, that you were illegitimately conceived? And then that your birth in Bethlehem led to the slaughter of babies? And then that your parents, Joseph and Mary, fled to Egypt because they were ashamed to show their faces in public in Israel?'

Some of those standing there were pious Jews.

'We do not say that he was conceived illegitimately,' they objected. 'We know that Joseph was betrothed to Mary, and so Jesus was not conceived illegitimately.'

Pilate said to the Jews who said that he was a bastard, 'This statement of yours is not true, because a betrothal had taken place, as these fellow countrymen of yours are saying.'

'Our whole assembly is declaring the facts, and yet you don't believe our declaration that he was conceived illegitimately!' said Annas and Caiaphas to Pilate. 'These others are only proselytes and disciples of Jesus.'

Pilate addressed Annas and Caiaphas. 'What are "proselytes"?' he asked.

'Those born gentiles but who have now become Jews,' they said.

Now those who had said that he was not conceived illegitimately were as follows: Lazarus, Asterius, Antonius, James, Amnes, Zeras, Samuel, Isaac, Phinehas, Crispus, Agrippa and Judah. 'We are not proselytes,' they said, 'but children of Jews.

We are speaking the truth, because we were present at the betrothal of Joseph and Mary.'

Pilate addressed these twelve men who had said that Jesus was not born illegitimately. 'I charge you by the health of Caesar: is what you say true about him not being conceived illegitimately?'

'Our Law forbids us from taking an oath because it is sinful,' they said to Pilate. 'Those others will, of course, swear by Caesar's health that what we say is not true and that we are guilty and deserve death.'

'Do you have anything to say to that?' Pilate asked Annas and Caiaphas.

'These dozen men believe that Jesus was not conceived illegitimately,' they both replied to Pilate, 'but our whole assembly declares he was – and that he is a sorcerer and claims to be a king and Son of God, but we are not believed.'

Pilate then ordered the whole crowd to leave, apart from the twelve men. He also gave the command for Jesus to be kept apart from them.

'For what possible reason do they want to put Jesus to death?' he asked the men.

'They are irritated because he heals on the Sabbath,' they replied.

'Do they really want to put him to death for doing something good?'

'Yes,' they said.

3. Jesus appears before Pilate

Pilate was furious and went out of the Praetorium.

'I have the sun as my witness that I find this man not guilty.'

'We would not have handed him over to you if he were not a criminal,' the Jews replied.

'You take him, then,' Pilate said. 'Judge him by your own law.'

'We do not have licence to execute someone.'

'Did God say, "Thou shalt not kill" to you, then, but not to me?'

Pilate went back in to the Praetorium and spoke to Jesus in private.

'Are you the king of the Jews?' he asked.

'Are you saying what you think, or have other people told you this about me?'

'I am not a Jew, am I?' Pilate said. 'Your people and their chief priests have handed you over to me. What have you done?'

'My kingdom is not from this world,' Jesus replied. 'If it were from this world, my servants would have struggled against my being handed over to the Jews. So then my kingdom is not from here.'

'So you are a king, then?'

'You say I am a king,' Jesus said. 'The reason I was born and have come is so that everyone who belongs to the truth should hear my voice.'

'What is truth?' Pilate asked.

'The truth is from heaven,' Jesus replied.

'Is there no truth on earth?'

'You can see how those who speak the truth are judged by those with earthly authority.'

4. The Jewish accusations against Jesus

Leaving Jesus inside the Praetorium, Pilate went out to the Jews and spoke to them.

'I find him not guilty,' Pilate declared.

'But Jesus said, "I can destroy this temple and rebuild it in three days!"' they objected.

'Which temple?' Pilate asked.

'The one Solomon took forty-six years to build. Jesus says he can destroy it and build it again in three days.'

'I am innocent of this righteous man's blood,' Pilate insisted. 'Sort this out yourselves.'

'May his blood be upon us and upon our children, then!' the Jews pledged.

Pilate called the elders, the priests and the Levites to a secret conference.

'Don't pursue this,' he said. 'Nothing of which you have accused him merits the death penalty. Your only charges against him are defiling the Sabbath, and healing.'

'If someone were to blaspheme Caesar,' the elders, priests and Levites pressed him, 'would he be worthy of death, or not?'

'He would indeed,' Pilate replied.

'Well then, whoever blasphemes Caesar merits the death penalty – and Jesus has blasphemed God!'

The governor ordered the Jews out of the Praetorium and called Jesus back in.

'What am I going to do with you?' Pilate asked.

'What you have been entrusted to do,' Jesus replied.

'What do you mean?' Pilate inquired.

'Moses and the Prophets proclaimed my death and resurrection in advance,' he replied.

When they had inquired about what Jesus had said, the Jews spoke to Pilate.

'What further blasphemy do you need to hear?' they asked him.

'If what he says is blasphemous, then arrest him yourselves for blasphemy and take him away to the synagogue,' Pilate said. 'Then you can judge him by your own Law.'

'Our Law is clear,' they replied. 'If a man sins against another man, he deserves thirty-nine lashes. But if he blasphemes against God, he is to be stoned to death.'

'Take him away and exact upon him whatever vengeance you want,' Pilate said.

'We want him crucified.'

'He doesn't merit crucifixion,' Pilate retorted.

Looking around at the crowds of Jews standing about him, he saw a number of them crying.

'You don't all want him put to death,' Pilate challenged them.

'Our whole assembly has come to see him die.'

'Why should he die?'

'Because he claimed to be king and Son of God.'

5. Nicodemus addresses Pilate

One man, a Jew named Nicodemus, stood before Pilate and spoke up.

'O venerable governor, may I be permitted to speak briefly?'

'Permission granted.'

'This is what I have said to the elders, the priests and the Levites – and indeed to the whole Jewish assembly in the synagogue: "What do you want with this man? He has performed many miracles and wonders – as no one has done before or could do in the future. Let him go and do not contrive any evil against him. If the miracles he performs are from God, they will stand the test of time, but if they are just human trickery, they will come to nothing. For Moses was sent from God to Egypt and performed many miracles which God had instructed him to do in front of Pharaoh king of Egypt. There Pharaoh had two servants, Jannes and Jambres, and they too performed a number of the miracles which Moses had done. Indeed, the Egyptians revered the two of them as gods. But since these miracles which they performed were not from God, Jannes and Jambres as well as those who believed in them perished. Therefore let this man go. He does not deserve to die." '

'You have become one of his disciples!' the Jews said to him. 'That's why you're defending him!'

'Has Pilate become a disciple of his as well?' Nicodemus asked. 'He also spoke up for Jesus. Didn't Caesar appoint him to his position?'

The Jews were furious, grinding their teeth at Nicodemus.

'Why are you grinding your teeth at him?' Pilate asked. 'You have only heard the truth from him.'

'Nicodemus, you can have the truth of that Jesus – and his destiny with it,' they said.

'Truly,' Nicodemus said. 'I will indeed have what you say.'

6. The testimony of those healed by Jesus

One of the Jews bounded up and asked the governor for permission to speak.

'If you wish to speak, do so,' Pilate said.

'I was laid up on a stretcher for thirty-eight years suffering terribly. But when Jesus came, he healed numbers of people possessed by demons and laid up with various diseases. Some young men took pity on me and lifted me up on my stretcher and took me to him. When Jesus saw me, he had compassion on me. "Pick up your stretcher and walk!" he said. And I picked up my stretcher and walked.'

'Ask him what day it was when he was healed,' the Jews said to Pilate.

'It was the Sabbath,' said the man who had been healed.

'Didn't we say that it was on the Sabbath he healed and cast out demons?' they remarked.

Another Jew bounded up and spoke.

'I was born blind – I could hear people speaking but couldn't see them,' he said. 'When Jesus came along I gave a loud shout: "Have mercy on me, son of David!" He took pity on me and placed his hands on my eyes, and straight away I was able to see again.'

Another Jew leaped up. 'I was hunchbacked,' he said, 'but Jesus straightened me up with a single word!'

And another: 'I was a leper, and he healed me with a word!'

7. The testimony of Bernice

One woman, named Bernice, called out from a distance.

'I had a flow of blood, and touched the edge of his cloak,' she said. 'Then the flow of blood, which had run for twelve years, was stemmed.'

'We have a law that a woman cannot testify in court,' the Jews declared.

8. Further testimony to Jesus' supernatural power

Some others, indeed a great number of men and women, shouted out as well.

'This man is a prophet, and demons submit to him.'

'Why do your teachers not submit to him then?' Pilate asked them.

'We don't know,' they said.

Others said that he had raised a dead man, Lazarus, who had been in a tomb for four days. The governor grew fearful, and said to the whole assembly of the Jews, 'Why do you want to shed innocent blood?'

9. Pilate pronounces judgement

Pilate called Nicodemus and the twelve men who had insisted that Jesus was not conceived illegitimately.

'What am I going to do?' he said to them. 'There is dissent among the people.'

'We don't know,' they said. 'That is their concern.'

Pilate again addressed the whole assembly of the Jews.

'You know that there is a custom at the Passover* of one of your prisoners being released,' Pilate said. 'I have a condemned criminal in the prison, a murderer called Barabbas, but this Jesus in front of you here I cannot find guilty of anything. Whom do you want me to release to you?'

'Barabbas!' they shouted.

'What shall I do with this Jesus who is called the "Christ"?' Pilate said.

'Crucify him!' said the Jews to the governor. 'You are no friend of Caesar if you release this man,' some of the Jews added, 'because he claims to be a king and a son of God. If you let him go, you would be choosing him as king rather than Caesar.'

Pilate was furious with the Jews. 'You lot are always seditious, even attacking those who do you good.'

'Which do-gooders?' they said.

'From what I hear,' said Pilate, 'your god brought you out of gruelling slavery in Egypt, rescuing you through the sea as if it were dry ground, and feeding you manna and quail in the desert, providing you with water to drink from rock and giving you a law. Yet in response to all this you aggravated your god and looked to a calf cast in metal instead. You provoked your god and he sought to do away with you. It was only because Moses prayed for you that you were not put to death. And now you're telling me that I hate Caesar!'

Pilate got up from his judgement seat and tried to make his way out. The Jews shrieked, however.

'We know that Caesar, not Jesus, is king. Certainly those

Magi brought him gifts from the east as if he were a king. But when Herod heard from these Magi that a king had been born, he tried to kill Jesus. When Joseph, his father, found out, he took Jesus and the child's mother and escaped to Egypt. Hearing this, Herod killed the children of the Hebrews who had been born in Bethlehem.'

When Pilate heard this, he was afraid. He silenced the crowds who were baying, and spoke.

'So this is the one Herod pursued!'

'Yes,' the Jews said, 'this is the one.'

Pilate then took some water and washed his hands before the sun, saying, 'I am innocent of the blood of this righteous man. This is your concern.'

Again the Jews cried out, 'May his blood be upon us and upon our children!' Pilate then ordered that the curtain be drawn before the judgement seat where he was presiding.

'Your people have convicted you of being a king,' he said to Jesus. 'That is why I make my judgement: you are first to be flogged according to the decree of the pious emperors, and then hanged on a cross in the garden where you were arrested, with the criminals Dysmas and Gestas crucified alongside you.'

10. The crucifixion of Jesus and the two criminals

Jesus therefore went out of the Praetorium, along with the two criminals. When they had come out to the place, they stripped him of his clothes and put a cloth around him, and placed a crown of thorns around his head. They also hanged the two criminals.

'Father forgive them,' Jesus said, 'for they do not know what they are doing.' The soldiers then divided up his garments while the people stood by watching. The chief priests mocked him, and the rulers joined in.

'He saved others – he should save himself!' they said. 'If he really is the Son of God, he should get down off the cross!' The soldiers also joked at him, and went and offered him vinegar with gall. 'You're the king of the Jews, so save yourself!' they said.

After pronouncing judgement, Pilate ordered that the charge that he was 'king of the Jews' (as the Jews had said) should be inscribed in Greek, Latin and Hebrew.

One of the crucified criminals spoke to Jesus.

'If you are the Messiah, save yourself – and us!'

'Do you have no fear of God?' the other, Dysmas, rebuked him. 'You're paying the same penalty as he is, but we are paying it justly. We are getting our just deserts, but he has done nothing wrong.' Then he said to Jesus, 'Remember me, Lord, in your kingdom.'

'Truly, truly, I say to you, today you will be with me in Paradise,' Jesus said to him.

11. Jesus' death and burial

It was about the sixth hour, and darkness came over the earth until the ninth hour.† When the sun had darkened, the curtain of the temple split down the middle. Jesus cried out in a loud voice, 'Father, *baddach ephkid rouel*,'* which means, 'Into your hands I commit my spirit.' After he had said this, he gave up his spirit. The centurion saw what had happened, and glorified God, saying, 'This was a righteous man!' When all the crowd present at the spectacle saw what had taken place, they beat their breasts and returned home.

The centurion reported to the governor what had happened. When Pilate and his wife heard the news, they were very distressed, and neither ate nor drank that day. Pilate sent for the Jews.

'Did you see what happened?' he asked.

'There was an eclipse of the sun, as sometimes occurs,' they replied.

Jesus' companions had been standing far off, and the women who had accompanied him from Galilee saw it all. A man named Joseph, a council member from the town of Arimathaea who was waiting for the kingdom of God, approached Pilate and requested Jesus' body. Taking it down, Joseph wrapped it in a clean linen shroud and placed it in a tomb cut out of rock, in which no one had yet been buried.

12. Joseph of Arimathaea is imprisoned

When the Jews heard that Joseph had requested Jesus' body, they looked for him and the twelve men (those who had denied that Jesus was conceived illegitimately), as well as for Nicodemus and the many others who had stood up in front of Pilate and revealed Jesus' good deeds. But they had all hidden, except for Nicodemus who went about openly, because he was one of the leaders of the Jews.

'How did you get into the synagogue?' Nicodemus said to them.

'How did *you* get into the synagogue?' they asked him. 'You are one of his accomplices, and will receive in the age to come what is coming to him.'

'Indeed, indeed,' said Nicodemus.

Just then Joseph interrupted and spoke. 'Why are you agitated with me because I asked for Jesus' body? I have just laid him in a fresh tomb after wrapping him in a clean linen shroud and rolled a stone over the opening of the hollow. You did not treat this righteous man properly and are showing no regret at crucifying him; you even stabbed him with a spear.'

The Jews seized Joseph and ordered him to be secured until the first day of the week.[†]

'You should know that time prevents us from acting against you now,' they said, 'because the Sabbath is approaching. But be warned that you will not be deemed worthy of burial. We will leave your body for the birds.'

'This is what Goliath in his arrogance claimed,' Joseph said to them, 'when he insulted the living God and his holy one, David. For God said through his prophet, "Vengeance is mine, and I will repay, says the Lord."[*] Now the person who is uncircumcised in his flesh but circumcised in heart has washed his hands before the sun and said, "I am innocent of the blood of this righteous man. You deal with this." So you said to Pilate, "May his blood be upon us and upon our children." Now I am afraid that the wrath of God will indeed come on you and your children, just as you have said.'

When the Jews heard this, they were deeply embittered. They seized Joseph, arrested him and shut him up in a windowless building, with warders attending the door. They also sealed the door where Joseph was imprisoned.

On the Sabbath, the synagogue leaders, the priests and the Levites made a determination that everybody should be in the synagogue on the first day of the week. The whole assembly arrived at the synagogue first thing in the morning to decide how they would put Joseph to death. When the Sanhedrin had come to a decision, they ordered him to be brought in total disgrace. But when they opened the prison door, they could not find him. All the people were beside themselves, and were terrified that they had found the seals all intact, and that Caiaphas had the key. No one dared any longer to lay hands on those who had spoken to Pilate in Jesus' defence.

13. The guards report Jesus' resurrection

While they were still seated in the synagogue, and amazed at what had become of Joseph, there came some members of the guard which the Jews had requested from Pilate to watch Jesus' tomb in case his disciples came and stole the body. They reported to the synagogue leaders, the priests and the Levites what had happened.

'There was a great earthquake, and we saw an angel coming down from heaven, rolling away the stone from the opening of the hollow, and sitting on top of the stone! The angel gleamed like snow, or like lightning, and we were absolutely terrified, and collapsed to the ground like corpses. We heard the angel's voice speaking to the women who were visiting the grave, saying to them, "Do not be afraid! I know you are looking for Jesus who was crucified. He is not here. He has risen, just as he said he would. Come and see the place where the Lord lay. Now go quickly and tell his disciples that he has risen from the dead and is in Galilee." '

'Which women was he speaking to?' the Jews asked.

'We don't know,' the guards said.

'What time was it?'

'The middle of the night.'

'Then why did you not arrest the women?' the Jews continued.

'We were scared to death, not expecting to live till morning, so how could we arrest them?'

'As surely as the Lord lives, we do not believe you.'

'You saw such great signs done by that man and didn't believe him, so how could you believe us? And well might you swear "as surely as the Lord lives" – because he is alive! We have heard,' the guards continued, 'that you have locked up the man who asked for Jesus' body, and sealed up the door, but didn't find him when you opened it. Give us Joseph and we'll give you Jesus!'

'Joseph has gone away to his home town,' the Jews said.

'Jesus has risen,' the guards said, 'as we heard the angel say, and he is in Galilee.' When the Jews heard all this, they were terrified.

'If this gets out, everyone will turn to Jesus!' they said. The Jews therefore took counsel and paid the guards plenty of money and instructed them: 'Say that you were asleep when Jesus' disciples came in the night and stole his body. If the governor gets to hear about it, we will talk to him and make sure that you have nothing to worry about.' The guards took the money and said what they had been told to say.

14. The report of the risen Jesus by Phinehas, Adas and Haggai

One of the priests called Phinehas, a teacher named Adas, and Haggai the Levite went down from Galilee into Jerusalem and reported to the synagogue leaders, priests and Levites.

'We have seen Jesus and his disciples sitting on Mount Mamilch, and he said to his disciples, "Go into all the world and preach to all creation. Whoever believes and is baptized will be saved, but whoever does not believe will be condemned. These things will accompany believers as signs: they will cast out demons in my name, they will speak in novel tongues, they will pick up snakes, they may drink deadly poison and it will not harm them, they will lay hands on the sick and make them well."* While Jesus was still speaking to his disciples, we saw him being taken up into heaven.'

The elders, the priests and the Levites then spoke.

'Swear by the glory and praise of the God of Israel,' they said, 'if you have really heard and seen these things which you have recounted.'

'As surely as the Lord, the God of our fathers Abraham, Isaac and Jacob, lives, we heard these things and saw him being taken up into heaven.'

'Have you come to preach to us, or to pray to God?' the elders, priests and Levites asked.

'To pray to God,' they said.

'If you have come to pray, then why are you spouting this nonsense in front of all the people?'

'If these things which we have spoken of and seen are sinful, then we are in your hands. Do with us as you see fit,' said Phinehas, Adas and Haggai. The elders and the priests therefore took a scroll of the Law, and made Phinehas, Adas and Haggai swear that they would say nothing more of these matters to anyone. Then they gave them food and drink, and got them out of the city, giving them money and sending three men with them. They sent them back to Galilee, and Phinehas, Adas and Haggai went in peace.

When the men had set off for Galilee, the chief priests, synagogue leaders and elders gathered in the synagogue, closed the gate and bemoaned the situation terribly.

'Could this have happened as a sign to Israel?' they wondered.

'Why are you fretting and crying?' objected Annas and Caiaphas. 'Don't you realize that his disciples gave plenty of money to the men guarding the tomb and instructed them to say that an angel came down and rolled away the stone from the entrance to the tomb?'

'Let's grant that his disciples stole the body. But in that case how did his soul re-enter his body, so he could go about in Galilee?' asked the priests and the elders. Annas and Caiaphas were not able to give an answer. All they could say was: 'We shouldn't trust gentiles.'*

15. Nicodemus' defence of the Galilean teachers

Nicodemus got up and stood before the Sanhedrin.

'Speak the truth,' he said. 'You who are the Lord's people know full well that the men who came down from Galilee were God-fearing people, upstanding men who hate greed and love peace. They recounted on oath that they had seen Jesus on Mount Mamilch with his disciples, and that he had indeed taught what you heard them report, and that they saw him being taken up to heaven. Yet no one asked them about the manner of his ascension. For, as the scroll of the holy scriptures teaches us, Elijah too was taken up into heaven, upon which Elisha cried out with a great shout. Elijah threw his sheepskin cloak over Elisha, and Elisha threw his cloak over the Jordan and reached the other side and came to Jericho. Then the children of the prophets met him. "Elisha," they said, "where is your master Elijah?" He told them that he had been taken up to heaven. They said to Elisha, "A spirit didn't snatch him away and throw him onto one of the mountains, did it? Let's take our servants with us and go and look for him." And they persuaded Elisha and he went off with them. They searched for him for three days but could not find him. Then they realized that he had indeed been taken up. Now listen to me: let us send people to every district in Israel and see if Christ may have been taken up by a spirit and cast upon one of the mountains.'

They all thought this was a good idea. They therefore sent people into every district in Israel to look for Jesus, but they could not find him. They found Joseph in Arimathaea, but no one dared lay a finger on him.

So they reported back to the elders, the priests and the Levites.

'We have travelled the length and breadth of Israel but have not found Jesus. We did find Joseph in Arimathaea, though.'

When they heard about Joseph, they rejoiced and gave glory to the God of Israel. The synagogue leaders, the priests and the Levites held a council about how to deal with Joseph. Then they cut some papyrus and wrote to Joseph as follows:

Peace be upon you.

We know that we have sinned against God and against you, and we pray to the God of Israel that you would deign to come to your fathers and your children, for we are all distraught. For when we opened the door we did not find you. We know that we plotted evil against you, but the Lord came to your aid and the Lord himself also confounded our plot against you, O esteemed father Joseph.

They then chose from all the Israelites seven friends of Joseph, whom Joseph himself would acknowledge. The synagogue leaders, the priests and the Levites said to them, 'Observe him. If he takes our letter and reads it, you know that he will come back with you to us. If he does not read it, then you know that he is still angry with us; in that case, greet him in peace and return to us.' They pronounced a blessing on the men and sent them off.

When the men came to Joseph, they bowed down before him and said, 'Peace be with you.'

'Peace be with you and all the people of Israel,' Joseph said. They presented him with the letter on the scroll. Joseph took it and read it, rolled up the scroll of the letter and blessed God. 'Blessed be the Lord, the God who has rescued Israel from shedding innocent blood,' he said. 'Blessed be the Lord who has sent out his angel and sheltered me under its wings.' He then set a table for them, and they ate and drank. The men also slept there.

Early in the morning, they prayed. Joseph saddled his donkey and set off with the men, and they came to the holy city of Jerusalem. Then all the people met Joseph and called out, 'Peace be upon your entry to the city!'

In reply, he said to all the people, 'Peace to you.'

Everyone kissed him. Then the people prayed with Joseph, astonished as they were at the sight of him. Nicodemus welcomed him into his house and gave a great banquet for him. He invited Annas and Caiaphas, as well as the elders, the priests and the Levites to the house. There was great cheer as they ate and drank with Joseph. After they had sung hymns of praise, each of them went on his way home except for Joseph, who stayed in Nicodemus' house.

First thing in the morning on the following day, which was the Day of Preparation,† the synagogue leaders, priests and Levites went to Nicodemus' house, and Nicodemus welcomed them.

'Peace be with you,' he said.

'Peace be with you,' they replied, 'and with all your household, and with Joseph and his household.'

Nicodemus invited them into the house. All the members of the Sanhedrin sat down, and Joseph sat between Annas and Caiaphas, but no one dared to say anything to him.

'Why have you invited me?' Joseph said. They nodded to Nicodemus to speak to Joseph. Nicodemus began to speak.

'Father,' he said, 'you know that the esteemed teachers, priests and Levites want to learn something from you.'

'Do ask,' Joseph said.

Annas and Caiaphas took the scroll of the Law and had Joseph take an oath.

'Swear by the glory and praise of the God of Israel. Achan took an oath from the prophet Joshua and did not break it; he told Joshua everything and kept nothing back. Now then, you should keep nothing at all from us.'

'I will not keep anything from you,' Joseph said.

'We were troubled that you asked for Jesus' body, rolled it up in a clean linen shroud and laid it in a tomb,' they said to him. 'This is why we secured you in that windowless building and placed locks and seals on the doors, and stationed warders to guard where you were locked up. Then on the first day of the week,† when we opened the door and you were not there, we were deeply disturbed. The whole people has been in a panic until yesterday. So then, tell us what happened.'

'It was the Day of Preparation at about the tenth hour† when you locked me away,' Joseph said. 'I remained there for the whole of the Sabbath. Then, in the middle of the night, while I was standing up and praying, the building in which you imprisoned me was picked up from its four corners, and I saw something like a flash of light in my eyes. Terrified, I collapsed to the ground. Then someone grasped my hand and pulled me out from the place where I had fallen, and a liquid ran from my head to my feet, and the scent of myrrh came to my nostrils. The person wiped my face, kissed me and said, "Do not be afraid, Joseph. Open your eyes and see who is speaking to you." I opened my eyes and saw Jesus there. Terrified, I thought it was a ghost, so I began reciting the commandments, and he joined in with me. (As you well know, if a ghost meets someone and hears the commandments, it runs away.) Seeing that he was joining in with me, I said to him, "Rabbi Elijah!"

' "I am not Elijah," he said to me.

' "Who are you, lord?" I said.

' "I am Jesus, whose body you requested from Pilate. You wrapped me in a clean linen shroud and put a towel on my face, and placed me in a new tomb, and rolled a great stone across the entrance to the tomb."

' "Show me where I buried you," I said to the figure speaking to me. He then took me off and showed me where I had placed him. The shroud lay there in it, along with the towel which had been on his face. Then I knew that it was Jesus. He led me by the hand and stood me up in the middle of my house though the doors were still closed. Then he took me away to my own bed and said to me, "Peace be upon you!" He then kissed me and said, "Do not come out of your house for forty days. I am going now to Galilee to my brothers." '

16. The account of the Galilean teachers confirmed

When the synagogue leaders, the priests and the Levites heard all this from Joseph, they fell to the ground as if they were dead. They fasted until the ninth hour.† Nicodemus and Joseph comforted Annas, Caiaphas, the priests and the Levites.

'Get up on your feet! Have something to eat and refresh your hearts, because tomorrow it is the Lord's Sabbath.'

They got up and prayed to God, ate and drank, and then all went home.

On the Sabbath, our teachers, priests and Levites conferred with one another, wondering, 'What is this judgement which has come upon us? We know his father and mother.'

'I know that his parents are God-fearing,' said Levi, a teacher, 'not missing their prayers, and paying their tithes three times a year. When Jesus was born, his parents brought him up to this place, and offered sacrifices and whole burnt offerings to God. When the great teacher Simeon placed him on his shoulders, he said:

> "Now dismiss your servant in peace, Master,
> according to your word,
> for my eyes have seen the salvation
> which you have prepared before all peoples,
> a light as revelation for the nations,
> and the glory of your people Israel."

'Simeon blessed them,' Levi continued, 'and said to Mary, Jesus' mother, "I bring good news to you about this child of yours." And Mary asked, "Good, my lord?" "Good indeed!" said Simeon:

> He is set for the falling and rising of many in Israel,
> and as a sign to be rejected.
> A sword will also pierce your soul,
> so the thoughts of many hearts will be laid bare.'*

'How do you know this?' they asked the teacher, Levi.

'Did you not know that it was from Simeon that I learned the Law?' Levi said.

'We want to see your father,' the Sanhedrin said to him. So they sent for his father, and questioned him.

'Why do you not believe my son?' he replied. 'The blessed and righteous Simeon himself taught him the Law.'

'Rabbi Levi, is what you say true?' the Sanhedrin asked him. 'It is true.'

The synagogue leaders, the priests and the Levites then said to him, 'Now then, let us send a message to Galilee to those three men who came and reported to us Jesus' teaching and ascension, so they can tell us how they saw him taken up.' All agreed to this proposal. So they sent the three men, who had previously gone off to Galilee with the others, with these instructions:

'Tell Rabbi Adas, Rabbi Phinehas and Rabbi Haggai, "Peace be upon you and all those with you. Because an important investigation is under way in the Sanhedrin, we have been sent to you to invite you to this holy place, Jerusalem."'

So the men set off for Galilee, and found Adas, Phinehas and Haggai sitting down and studying the Law. They greeted them with the peace. Then the Galileans spoke to the envoys.

'Peace be upon all Israel.'

'Peace be upon you,' the men from Jerusalem said.

'Why have you come?'

'The Sanhedrin invites you to the holy city of Jerusalem,' the envoys said. When the Galileans heard that they were being sought by the Sanhedrin, they prayed to God and reclined with the envoys and ate and drank. Then they got up and made their way in peace to Jerusalem.

The following day, the Sanhedrin convened in the synagogue, and they questioned the Galileans.

'Did you really see Jesus seated on Mount Mamilch, teaching his eleven disciples? And did you see him being taken up?'

'We did see him being taken up,' the men replied, 'just as we said.'

'Separate them from one another,' Annas said, 'so we can see if their stories agree.' They moved them away from one another. First, they called Adas.

'How did you see Jesus being taken up?' they asked him.

'While he was still sitting on Mount Mamilch and teaching his disciples, we saw a cloud overshadow him and his disciples. Then the cloud took him up to heaven, and his disciples lay face down on the ground.'

Then they called Phinehas the priest, and asked him, 'How did you see Jesus being taken up?' He gave the same reply. They finally asked Haggai, and he gave the same reply.

'The Law of Moses states, *On the word of two or three any matter rests*,'* the Sanhedrin concluded.

'It is written in the Law, *And Enoch walked with God, and he was not, because God took him*,'* the teacher Boutham said.

'We have heard of the death of holy Moses,' the teacher

Jairus said, 'but we have not seen the place. For it is written in the Law of the Lord, *And Moses died by the command of the Lord, but to this day no man knows where he is buried.'*

'What is it that Rabbi Simeon said when he saw Jesus?' Rabbi Levi said. *'He is set for the falling and rising of many in Israel, and as a sign to be rejected.'*

'It is written in the Law, *Behold I send my messenger ahead of you who will go before you to protect you on every good path, because my name is invoked in it,'* said Rabbi Isaac. Then Annas and Caiaphas spoke:

'You rightly say that these things are written in the Law of Moses: that no one saw the death of Enoch, and no one has described the death of Moses. But Jesus gave testimony to Pilate, and we saw him receiving beatings, and spitting in his face; we saw that the soldiers crowned him with a wreath of thorns, that he was flogged, and received sentence from Pilate; that he was crucified on Golgotha along with two bandits; that they gave him vinegar mixed with gall; that Longinus the soldier pierced his side with a spear; that Joseph our esteemed father requested his body, and – as he says – Jesus rose again; that, as the three teachers have testified, they saw him being taken up to heaven, and that Rabbi Levi said testifying to the words from Rabbi Simeon: *He is set for the falling and rising of many in Israel, and as a sign to be rejected.'*

All the teachers addressed the Lord's people.

'If this is from the Lord and it is marvellous in our eyes, then know this, house of Jacob, that it is written: *Cursed is everyone who hangs on a tree.* And another passage of scripture teaches: *The gods who did not make heaven and earth will perish.'*

The priests and the Levites then said to one another, 'If the memory of this incident lasts until the harvest season of the year called Jubilee,* then know that it will prevail forever, and that God is raising up a new people for himself.'

The synagogue leaders, the priests and Levites then made an announcement to all Israel:

'Cursed is the man who worships a creation of human hands,

and cursed is the man who worships created things rather than
the creator.'

And all the people said, 'Amen! Amen!'

All the people therefore sang a hymn of praise to the Lord:

> Blessed is the Lord, who has granted rest to his people
>   Israel,
> in accordance with everything he had said.
> No word has ever failed, of all his good words
>   which he spoke to his servant Moses.
> May the Lord be with us, just as he was with our fathers.
>   May he not destroy us, may he not destroy us,
>   but turn our hearts to him,
>   to lead us in all his ways,
>   to keep his commandments and the judgements
>   which he commanded to our fathers.
> And the Lord will be king over all the earth on that day.
>   And there will be one Lord, with one name,
>   the Lord our king – he will save us!
>
> There is no one like you, O Lord;
>   great are you, O Lord, and great is your name.
> By your power heal us, O Lord, and we shall be healed;
>   save us, O Lord, and we shall be saved,
>   for we are your portion and your inheritance.
> The Lord will not abandon his people, for the sake of his
>   great name,
>   for the Lord has begun to make us his people!

When they had all sung the hymn, each of them went home,
glorifying God, because his glory is for ever and ever. Amen!

33 The Narrative of Joseph of Arimathaea

(fifth–sixth century CE*)*

INTRODUCTION

This is a legendary account of the death of Jesus told from the perspective of Joseph of Arimathaea, reported in the canonical Gospels as a wealthy member of the Jewish ruling council who provided a tomb for Jesus' burial. In addition to Jesus being centre stage, part of the significance of this work lies in the evidence it provides for a developing interest in the two criminals crucified alongside Jesus, Demas the penitent criminal, and Gestas, who persists in wickedness until his death. The introductory section of the narrative provides a backstory for them, they make full-blown speeches while being crucified, and Demas enters into Paradise in fulfilment of Jesus' promise that he would be with him there 'today'. Joseph of Arimathaea is also a notable figure, who, as in the *Gospel of Nicodemus*, is arrested and imprisoned but miraculously rescued. One new character is Caiaphas' daughter, who along with Judas – now Caiaphas' nephew! – accuses Jesus of stealing the Torah scroll, a charge which in this text is one of the grounds for Jesus' execution.

Notably, there seems to be some contact with Jewish tradition about Jesus. In some versions of the *Toledoth Yeshu*, a medieval Jewish anti-Gospel, Jesus is alleged to have acquired his magical powers by stealing the ineffable name of God from the temple, writing it down and inserting the inscribed copy under his flesh so that he could later learn it. In Joseph's account, Jesus is accused of stealing the Torah scroll from the assembly in Jerusalem, though there is some confusion in the fact that the scroll is described as stolen by Demas, while Caiaphas' daughter – who seems to be the guardian of the scroll – maintains that it has been found. If there is response here to Jewish counter-narratives about Jesus, that could provide the context for the vitriolic accusations against the 'the murderous and God-battling Jews' at the beginning of the text.

There are only occasional flashes of theology. The reference to Jesus coming from the Father 'inseparably' is one example of a technical term used in the trinitarian discussions of the early church. More striking are the letters embedded in the narrative. While on the cross, Christ somehow writes a letter to the angelic powers in charge of Paradise, and, when he rises from the dead, receives their reply, brought to him by the also-resurrected Demas.

The Joseph narrative here seems to be reliant upon the *Gospel of Nicodemus*, which probably dates to the fifth century. The *Narrative of Joseph of Arimathaea* probably comes from sometime in the couple of centuries following that.

DRAMATIS PERSONAE

JESUS

JOSEPH OF ARIMATHAEA *Jewish councillor and friend of Jesus*

NICODEMUS *With Joseph, a dissenter against the verdict on Jesus*

JOHN *A disciple of Jesus*

GESTAS *A criminal crucified with Jesus*

DEMAS *A criminal, who repents, crucified with Jesus*

ANNAS AND CAIAPHAS *Priests*

SARAH *Caiaphas' daughter, a priestess*

JUDAS ISCARIOT *Here Caiaphas' nephew, and a secret disciple of Jesus*

TRANSLATION

The Account of Joseph

The Account of Joseph of Arimathaea, who had requested the body of the Lord. Containing within it the charges against the two thieves.

1. The charges against Gestas, Demas and Jesus

I, Joseph of Arimathaea, am he who requested from Pilate the body of the Lord Jesus to bury him, and for this reason was imprisoned by the murderous and God-battling Jews. They cling to the Law, but have become a cause of grief to Moses himself, provoking him, the legislator. They also failed to acknowledge God, and so crucified him, making it quite clear to those who knew him that it was the Son of God who was crucified. Seven days before Christ's passion, two brigands from Jericho were condemned and sent for by Pilate. These are the charges against them.

The first, whose name was Gestas, would murder travellers by putting them to the sword, and others he stripped naked. He hung women upside down by their ankles and cut off their breasts, drank blood from the limbs of children, never acknowledged God or followed the Law and was violent from his earliest days in activities like these.

The charge against the other was this. He was an innkeeper named Demas, a Galilean by birth. He would rob the rich with gangs of pirates but treat the poor well. He was a 'thief' like Tobit and would provide burial for the poor. He tried to rob the Jewish assembly, stealing the very scroll of the Law kept in Jerusalem, stripping naked Caiaphas' daughter, who was a priestess of the sanctuary, and removing the mystical deposit left in that place by Solomon. Such were his deeds.

Jesus was arrested three days before Passover,† in the evening. Caiaphas and the Jewish assembly were not yet celebrating Passover, but were lamenting sorely that a brigand could commit such a robbery in the sanctuary. They summoned Judas

Iscariot, the nephew of Caiaphas the priest. He was not a disciple of Jesus openly: the whole Jewish assembly had persuaded him to follow Jesus by stealth, not so that Judas would give credence to the signs Jesus performed or would confess him, but so he would hand Jesus over to them. Wanting to catch Jesus saying something false, they paid Judas two gold *drachmas*[†] a day for such a brave operation as this. He carried this out in Jesus' company for two years, as one of the disciples called John relates.

On the third day before Jesus was arrested, Judas spoke to the Jews.

'Come, let us hold council,' he said, 'because it was not the brigand who stole the scroll of the Law, but Jesus, and I can convict him.'

After Judas had said this, Nicodemus, the keeper of the sanctuary keys, went in with them.

'Do not carry out such a deed,' Nicodemus said to them all. For he was more honest than all the rest of the Jewish assembly.

'But he has said all kinds of things against this holy temple!' cried out Caiaphas' daughter, named Sarah. 'He has said, "I can destroy this temple and rebuild it again in three days."'

'You are more trustworthy than any of us,' the Jews said to her. Indeed, they reckoned her a prophetess. After the council had met, then, Jesus was arrested.

2. Jesus' arrest

On the following day, the fourth day of the week, they brought him at the ninth hour[†] to Caiaphas' courtyard.

'Tell us,' Annas and Caiaphas said to him, 'for whom did you steal our scroll of the Law? Have you sold the testimonies of Moses and the prophets?'

Jesus gave no answer. With the assembly also present, they asked him a second time.

'This is a sanctuary which Solomon took forty-six years to construct. What makes you want to destroy it in a moment?'

Jesus gave no answer to the accusation, because the sanctuary of the synagogue had been robbed by the brigand.

At the end of the evening on that fourth day of the week, the whole assembly was looking for Caiaphas' daughter, to condemn her to be burned for losing the scroll of the Law, without which they would not know how to celebrate Passover.

'Wait, my children,' she said to them. 'Let us kill this Jesus. The scroll has been found and the holy festival will certainly take place.'

Annas and Caiaphas had secretly given Judas Iscariot plenty of money.

'Tell us, as you told us before,' they instructed him, 'that you know that the scroll of the Law was stolen by Jesus. Then the accusation will fall on him and not on this blameless girl.' Judas agreed to this.

'The assembly must not know,' he said, 'that I was instructed by you to do this against Jesus. Release Jesus, and I will persuade the assembly that this is true.' So they released him secretly.

Judas went into the sanctuary as the fifth day of the week[†] was beginning.

'What are you willing to give me,' he asked the people, 'if I hand over the destroyer of the Law and the thief of the Prophets to you?'

'If you hand him over to us,' the Jews said to him, 'we will give you thirty gold pieces.' The people did not realize that Judas was speaking about Jesus, for many of them had confessed him as Son of God. Judas took the thirty gold pieces.

He went off at the fourth hour,[†] and at the fifth hour[†] he found Jesus walking in the street. Just before the evening, Judas addressed the Jews:

'Give me a band of soldiers armed with swords and clubs,' Judas said. 'Then I will hand him over to you.' They therefore sent him servants to arrest Jesus.

As they were on their way, Judas instructed them.

'Seize the one whom I kiss,' he said. 'For he is the one who has stolen the Law and the Prophets.'

He then approached Jesus and kissed him, saying, 'Greetings, Rabbi.'

It was now evening on the fifth day, and they seized Jesus and handed him over to Caiaphas and the chief priests.

'He is the one who has stolen the Law and the Prophets,' Judas said. The Jews then subjected Jesus to an unlawful cross-examination.

'Why did you do this?' they asked. But he gave no answer.

Nicodemus and I, Joseph, witnessing this pestilential session, got up from them, not wanting to join in the destruction with this council of the ungodly.

3. Jesus' crucifixion and promise to Demas

They did many other terrible things to Jesus that night, and as the Day of Preparation[†] was dawning they handed him over to the governor, Pilate, to crucify him. They all gathered for this. When the investigation was complete Pilate the governor ordered him to be nailed to the cross, as he did with the two brigands. These two, then, were crucified together with Jesus – Gestas on his left, and Demas on his right.

Gestas, on the left, began to shout out to Jesus:

'What terrible things I have done on the earth,' he wailed. 'If I had known that you were the king, I would have tried to kill you. Why do you say that you are the Son of God, but aren't able to help yourself in a crisis? Or how can you help another person when they pray? If you are the Messiah, come down from the cross, and then I'll believe in you! As far as I can see, you're not even a man; you're just a wild animal dying just as I am.' He started saying many other things against Jesus, blaspheming and grinding his teeth at him. For the brigand had been caught in the devil's trap.

The brigand on his right, named Demas, saw the divine grace of Jesus and also shouted out.

'I know, Jesus Christ,' he said, 'that you are the Son of God. I can see you, O Christ, being worshipped by myriads of myriads of angels. Forgive me the sins which I have committed! While I am assessed when you come to judge all the world, do not bring the stars or the moon as witnesses against me, for I have plotted many evils during the night. Do not call the sun, which is currently darkened because of you, to recount the evils of my heart. For I cannot provide you with any gift for the forgiveness of my sins. Already death is overtaking me for my sins. May your atonement deliver me, Master of all, from your fearful judgement. Do not grant the Enemy authority to consume me, and to inherit my soul as he has done with him hanging on your left. For I can see the devil rejoicing at capturing his soul, just as his flesh is withering away. Do not consign me to the lot of the Jews, because I can see Moses and the Patriarchs* lamenting bitterly, and the devil gleefully gloating over them. Therefore, Master, before my spirit departs, grant that my sins be washed away, and remember me – though a sinner – in your kingdom, when you sit on your great and highly exalted throne and come to judge the twelve tribes of Israel. For you have prepared abundant punishment for your world on its own account.'

When the brigand had said these things, Jesus addressed him.

'Amen, amen, I say to you, Demas,' he said, 'today you will be with me in Paradise. The sons of the kingdom, the children of Abraham, Isaac, Jacob and Moses, will be cast into the outer darkness. There will be weeping and gnashing of teeth there. You alone will dwell in Paradise until my second coming, when I come to judge those who have not confessed my name. Go to the Cherubim and the powers who turn the flaming sword,' Jesus continued, 'and who have guarded Paradise ever since Adam the first-formed was there when he transgressed and did not keep my commandments, and they expelled him. Tell them that none of the earlier pious ones will see Paradise until I come a second time to judge the living and the dead. This is what I have written:

Jesus Christ the Son of God, who came down from the heights of heaven, who came from the side of the invisible Father inseparably, and came down to the world to be incarnate and nailed to the cross in order to save Adam whom I fashioned.

To my Archangelic Powers, guardians of the gates of Paradise, servants of my Father.

My will and command is that the man crucified with me is to be allowed admission. He is to receive for my sake forgiveness

of sins, be clothed in an incorruptible body, and enter Paradise,
to dwell where no one has yet dwelt.

Just as he said these words, Jesus handed over his spirit. It was
the ninth hour on the Day of Preparation.[†] Darkness covered
the whole earth, and because of a great earthquake the sanctuary and the pinnacle of the temple collapsed.

4. Jesus' burial and resurrection

I, Joseph, requested the body of Jesus, and laid it in a fresh
tomb where no one had yet been buried. The body of the thief
crucified on Jesus' right-hand side had disappeared; the appearance of the thief on his left was like a serpent, so contorted was
his body.

When I requested Jesus' body to bury him, the Jews were
carried away with a furious zeal and locked me in prison,
where those who committed crimes were tortured. This was
my fate on the evening of the beginning of the Sabbath, which
our nation was breaking. Yet now this very nation of ours has
endured terrible sufferings on the Sabbath.

When evening came on the first day of the week, in the fifth
hour of the night, Jesus came to me in prison with the brigand
who had been crucified next to him on his right, whom he had
sent to Paradise. There was a great light in the building, which
was suspended from its four corners, detached from the
ground. I then went out of the building. I recognized Jesus
first, and then the brigand carrying a letter to Jesus. While we
were travelling in Galilee, a great light shone, so great that
creation could not bear it. It was the brigand's great fragrance,
which had come forth from Paradise.

When Jesus was sitting down in a certain place, he read the
letter brought by the brigand.

We, the Cherubim and the Six-winged angels commanded
by your divinity to guard the garden of Paradise, declare
in this letter delivered by the brigand providentially cru-
cified with you as follows:

When we saw the impression of the nails of the brigand crucified with you, and the beam of the letters of your divinity, fire burned but it was not able to bear the brightness of the scar, and we were completely terrified. For we heard the maker of heaven and earth and all creation coming from on high to visit the lower regions of the earth because of the first-formed Adam. When we saw the undefiled cross flashing like lightning through the brigand, its lustre seven times that of the brightness of the sun, fear overcame us as we struggled to keep our grip on the subterranean regions as they shook. The servants of Hades called out with us in a loud voice: 'Holy, holy, holy is the one who was in the highest in the beginning!' And the powers sent up the cry, 'Lord, you have appeared in heaven and on earth, bringing everlasting joy to the world and rescuing your own creation from death.'

5. The transfiguration of Jesus and Demas

After I saw this, and was travelling into Galilee with Jesus and the brigand, Jesus was transfigured. He was not as he was before he was crucified, but appeared completely as light. Angels constantly ministered to him, and Jesus was conversing with them. I spent three days with him, and none of the other disciples was with him – only the brigand.

It was the middle of the Feast of the Passover[†] when Jesus' disciple John came, and we no longer saw the brigand and did not know what had become of him.

'Who is this?' John asked Jesus. 'You have not introduced me to him.'

Jesus made no reply, and John fell at his feet.

'Lord, I know that you have loved me from the beginning,' he said. 'Why have you not revealed that man to me?'

'Why are you inquiring into what is hidden?' Jesus asked him. 'Are you still ignorant? Can you not see the fragrance of Paradise filling this place? Do you not know who he was? The brigand on the cross has become the heir of Paradise. Truly,

truly, I say to you that it belongs to him alone until the great day comes.'

'Make me worthy so that I can see him,' John replied.

While John was still speaking the brigand suddenly appeared. Then John, dumbfounded, fell to the ground. The brigand was not in the same form as he had been before John came, but was like a king in all his strength, wearing the cross. A voice of a great multitude came forth:

'You have come to Paradise, the place prepared for you! We have been appointed to serve you by the one who sent you until the great day.'

When that voice came, the brigand as well as I, Joseph, disappeared. I found myself back at home, and could no longer see Jesus.

Epilogue

After seeing these things, I have composed this account so all can believe in Jesus Christ crucified, our Lord, and no longer serve the Law of Moses but believe the signs and wonders which came through Jesus, and so that by believing we can inherit everlasting life and come into the kingdom of heaven. For to him belong glory, power, praise and greatness for ever and ever, Amen!

IV

DIALOGUES WITH
THE RISEN JESUS

Fragment of the *Gospel of Mary*
(P. Oxy. 3525, 3rd cent.)

34 The Gospel of Mary

(second century CE*)*

INTRODUCTION

The *Gospel of Mary* has attracted considerable interest in current scholarship, no doubt partly because of its purported female author. Moreover, Peter in the Gospel states that Jesus loved Mary more than any other woman and revealed to her truths to which the male disciples did not have access. Peter then seems to change his mind, however, and with his brother Andrew doubts whether Jesus would really have taught a woman what he had not taught the male disciples. Mary is upset by this, but Levi jumps to her defence and criticizes Peter's misogyny. In the end, Levi and Mary prevail and the disciples go forth as a united front to preach the good news.

The main theological theme of the surviving text, which comes in Mary's vision, is how to pass hostile powers and arrive at a vision of the supreme God (compare, for example, *Gos. Thomas* 50 (p. 58) and the Greek *Gospel of Philip*: see pp. 58, 174–175). Here, however, the powers are not so much external demonic forces which need to be thwarted as apparently personifications of a person's sinful tendencies. Hence the powers named 'Desire' and 'Ignorance' (pages 15 and 16 of the Coptic text) become later 'my desire' and 'my ignorance' at the end of Mary's vision. Another motif is that Jesus (who is never actually named) is apparently an incarnation of 'the Good', the supreme Platonic form or idea.

The *Gospel of Mary* survives in three fragments, two of which are very small Greek manuscripts, and one a more substantial stretch of text (in two parts) in Coptic. The Greek fragments, however, date to the third century (two hundred years earlier than the Coptic), and so enable us to date the original – which is dependent on the canonical Gospels – to the second century. In the translation below, the pages of the numbered Greek manuscript appear in Roman numerals, with the Coptic page numbers printed in Arabic numerals.

DRAMATIS PERSONAE

JESUS *Called here 'the Saviour', 'Lord' or 'the Blessed One'*
MARY *Probably Mary Magdalene*
PETER *Simon Peter, the disciple, one of the twelve apostles*
ANDREW *Peter's brother, also one of the twelve apostles*
LEVI *Also a disciple*
DESIRE AND IGNORANCE *Adversaries blocking the soul's ascent*

TRANSLATION

1. Jesus' teaching about matter and sin

[p. 7] 'Will matter, then, [be destroyed] or not?'

'Each nature, each form and each created thing exists in and with one another,' the Saviour said, 'but will be dissolved into its root. For the nature of matter dissolves into what is proper to its own nature. Whoever has ears to hear, let him hear!'

'Since you have told us about everything, tell us one more thing,' Peter said to him. 'What is the world's sin?'

'Sin does not exist. No, you are what brings sin about when you do what resembles the nature of the adultery which is called sin. The reason that the Good has come into your midst, to what is proper to every nature, is to restore it to its root.'

Again, the Saviour added, 'The reason why you get sick and die is that [. . .] [p. 8] of the one who has [. . .]. He who reflects, let him reflect upon this. Matter generated passion, which has no image because it has come from what is unnatural. Then a disturbance came about in each body. This is why I said to you, "Be content, and if you are discontented, be content in the presence of each of nature's forms." Whoever has ears to hear, let him hear!'

When the Blessed One had said this, he greeted them all. 'Peace be upon you! Receive my peace! Watch out, or someone may deceive you by telling you, "Here he is – look!" or "There he is – look!" The Son of Man is within you. Follow him! Those who seek him will find him. Go, then, and preach the gospel of the Kingdom. Do not [p. 9] set up any restrictions beyond what I have fixed for you. Nor should you give any law of the kind that the lawgiver* did, in case you are caught by it.'

When he had finished speaking, he went away. The disciples were distraught and wept bitterly.

2. Mary's reassurance of the disciples

'How can we go to the nations and preach the gospel of the kingdom of the Son of Man?' the disciples wondered. 'If he was not spared, how will we be?'

Then Mary stood up and kissed them all.

'Don't cry or be upset,' she said to her brethren. 'Nor should you doubt, for his grace will be with you in all its fullness, and it will protect you. No, let us praise his greatness, because he has made us ready and made us human.'

When Mary had finished, she turned their intellects towards the Good, and they began to study the utterances of the Saviour.

3. Mary's vision of Jesus

[p. 10] 'Sister,' Peter said to Mary, 'we know that the Saviour loved you more than any other woman. Tell us the Saviour's words as you remember them – those which you know but we don't and didn't hear.'

'What you missed but which I remember,' Mary replied, 'I will declare to you.' So she began telling them the words.

'Once I saw the Lord in a vision and I spoke to him:

' "Lord, this very day I have seen you in a vision!"

' "You are blessed," he answered me, "because you did not waver when you saw me! For where the intellect is, there the treasure is."

' "O Lord," I said, "does the person who now sees a vision see himself with the soul or the spirit?"

' "He does not see by the soul or by the spirit," the Saviour replied. "It is the intellect which is between them which sees the vision, and [. . .]." '

[pages 11–14 are missing]

4. Mary's vision of the soul ascending

[p. 15] ' "[. . .] it."

'And Desire said, "I did not see you descending, but now I can see you ascending! How can you lie to me when you belong to me?"

' "I saw you," the soul answered, "though you did not see me or recognize me. To you I was only a garment and you did not know me."

'When it had finished speaking, the soul went on with much rejoicing.

'Then it reached the third power, called "Ignorance". It too interrogated the soul.

' "Where are you trying so wickedly to go? You are under arrest! You are under arrest to face judgement!"

' "Why do you judge me, when I have not judged?" the soul said. "And why am I under arrest when I have arrested no one? I have not been recognized, but I recognize the dissolution of the All,* both its earthly [p. 16] and its heavenly parts."

'After the soul had defeated the third power, it ascended. Then it saw the fourth power. It had seven forms:

> The first form was Darkness,
> the second Desire,
> the third Ignorance,

> *the fourth Death's Jealousy,*
> *the fifth Flesh's Kingdom,*
> *the sixth Flesh's Foolish "Understanding",*
> *the seventh Angry Wisdom.*

'These were the seven wrathful powers which interrogate the soul.

' "From where have you come, you murderer?" they asked. "And where are you going, you world-destroyer?"

' "What arrested me has been slain," the soul replied, "and what surrounded me has been defeated. My desire has come to an end and my ignorance has perished. By a [world] I have been released [p. 17] from a world, and by a heavenly form from a form and from the temporary fetter of oblivion. From now [p. xxi] on, I can receive the silent rest that belongs to the course of the Aeon's time." '

When Mary had finished speaking, she fell silent, since that was all that the Saviour had spoken.

5. Dialogue about Mary's vision

'Brethren,' Andrew replied, 'what do you think about what she has said? I for one don't believe that the Saviour said all that! After all, it is in quite a different vein from his thinking.'

Having thought carefully about the question, Peter said, 'Would he really have talked in secret with a woman rather than out in the open for us all to hear? Are we all supposed to turn to listen to her? Did he think her more worthy than us?'

[p. 18] On this, Mary wept. 'My brother Peter,' she said, 'what do you think, then? Do you think that I have invented this myself? Would I lie about [p. xxii] the Saviour?'

'Peter, you are always bad-tempered!' Levi put in. 'Now you are arguing with this woman as the Adversaries do! If the Saviour counted her worthy, then who are you to despise her? He certainly knew and truly loved her. We should be ashamed of ourselves! Let us put on the perfect man and do what he commanded us. Let us preach the gospel without setting up any other restrictions or making any laws, just as the Saviour instructed us.'

When he said this, Levi [p. 19] [. . .] and they began to go and to proclaim and preach.

The Gospel according to Mary

35 The Epistle of the Apostles

(C. 170 CE)

INTRODUCTION

This work is part epistle, part Gospel, part polemical treatise, and part apocalypse, showing the flexibility of genre in early Christian literature. It is an epistle, insofar as it is sent by the apostles to churches across the world, with the customary greetings found in a letter. It is a Gospel, because much of what it seeks to achieve is done through recounting episodes in Jesus' ministry: it contains, at various points, accounts of the incarnation (chs. 13–14), Jesus' miracles (4–6), his resurrection (9–12), his descent to Hell (27–28), and a forecast of his future coming (15–17). Much of this material is put together with a polemical intent, whose target is the teaching of the notorious heretics Cerinthus and Simon (chs. 1, 7–8). Their false teaching is not spelled out here in the *Epistle*, but they are known from other early Christian writings. According to Irenaeus around 180 CE, for example, Cerinthus had been notorious for the belief that 'Christ' was an entirely spiritual being, who came upon the human being 'Jesus' at his baptism. (Simon is a rather more shadowy figure.) Such teaching of Cerinthus about a bodily Jesus distinct from a spiritual Christ might account for the emphasis in the *Epistle of the Apostles* on the 'flesh', mentioned about twenty times in the book: it was the Son of God, the eternal Word who 'became flesh of Mary' (ch. 3; cf. 14, 19), he 'became flesh and suffered' (ch. 39) and he truly rose from the dead 'in flesh' (ch. 12). Cerinthus and Simon themselves were no longer alive at the time of the *Epistle*'s composition, but were presumably chosen because they were rough contemporaries of

Jesus and the apostles, and because the *Epistle*'s author assumed that the heresies which worried him originated and overlapped with the teachings of Simon and Cerinthus.

There is also material, however, which is not necessarily of a polemical nature. Surprisingly for a Gospel-like narrative, the ministry of Paul – who received from the apostles everything which Jesus had taught – is a focus (31). There is also a strong emphasis on divine justice (39–40), and on how to deal with sin in the church (46–50). One major concern is plague (34–36), which may refer to an epidemic that afflicted the Roman Empire between 165 and 180 CE. The work begins by describing itself as 'what Jesus Christ revealed to his disciples and to all', hence the *Epistle* is, among its other genres, also an apocalypse like the biblical Book of Revelation.

The *Epistle* has connections with a number of other Gospels. It appears to know all four canonical Gospels, with John's Gospel being a particularly prominent source. The miracle of the water into wine at the Cana wedding is derived from John, while the miracle of the coin appearing in the fish's mouth comes from Matthew (*Epistle*, ch. 5). The *Epistle* also reproduces an abbreviated version of the story, found in the *Infancy Gospel of Thomas* (see pp. 34–35, 37), of Jesus going to school (ch. 4). Jesus also descends to Hell to preach to, and save, those who believed before he came (ch. 27), a theme mentioned also in the *Gospel of Peter*, and developed at length in the *Questions of Bartholomew* (see pp. 287–288).

The original Greek text of the *Epistle* is unfortunately lost. A small Latin fragment survives, and a more extensive Coptic text. The whole work is preserved only in Ethiopic manuscripts from about the fifteenth century to as late as the nineteenth century; the number of copies is a result of its canonical status in the broader canon of the Ethiopian church. Because of this, the *Epistle* has had some longitudinal influence in at least one wing of the church. Fortunately, although they are late, the best Ethiopic texts usually agree with the Coptic, so where the Coptic does not survive, the Ethiopic can generally be assumed to be reliable.

The *Epistle of the Apostles* probably originated in Asia Minor shortly before 180 CE: the second coming of Jesus is forecast to occur in the 150th year after Jesus' ministry (ch. 17) which took place in about 30 CE. Hence a date of approximately 170 CE is the most likely, although a variant reading in the manuscripts refers to the 120th year, and so an earlier date is possible.

The translation has been kindly provided by Professor Francis Watson, with minor stylistic changes made.

DRAMATIS PERSONAE

JESUS CHRIST *Most often referred to as 'Lord'*

JOHN, THOMAS, PETER, ANDREW, JAMES, PHILIP, BARTHOLOMEW, MATTHEW, NATHANAEL, JUDAS THE ZEALOT AND CEPHAS *Jesus' disciples*

JOSEPH AND MARY *Jesus' parents*

MARY AND MARTHA OF BETHANY, AND MARY MAGDALENE *Witnesses to the risen Jesus*

SAUL *Paul the apostle*

PONTIUS PILATE *Prefect of Judaea*

ARCHELAUS *Ethnarch of Judaea*

SIMON AND CERINTHUS *False apostles*

MICHAEL, GABRIEL, URIEL AND RAPHAEL *Angels*

LEGION *A demon*

TRANSLATION

Introduction

1. This is what Jesus Christ revealed to his disciples and to all. It has been written on account of Simon and Cerinthus, the false apostles, so that no one should associate with them, for there is in them a venom by which they kill people – and so that you may be strong and not waver or be disturbed or depart from what you have heard, the word of the gospel. What we have heard and

remembered and written for the whole world we entrust to you, our sons and daughters, with joy. In the name of God, ruler of the whole world, and of Jesus Christ, grace be multiplied to you.

2. John, Thomas, Peter, Andrew, James, Philip, Bartholomew, Matthew, Nathanael, Judas the Zealot and Cephas:

To the churches of the east and the west, and to those in the north and the south. As we heard, so have we written, proclaiming and declaring to you our Lord Jesus Christ, and we touched him after he rose from the dead, when he revealed to us what is great and wonderful and true.

Confession of Faith

3. This we declare: that our Lord and Saviour Jesus Christ is God, the Son of God,

who was sent from God, ruler of the whole world, maker of every name that is named;

who is above all authorities, Lord of lords and King of kings, Power of the heavenly powers;

who sits above the cherubim at the right hand of the throne of the Father;

who by his word commanded the heavens and founded the earth and what is in it, and established the sea so that it did not cross its boundary, and the depths and springs to gush forth and flow into the earth day and night;

who established the sun, moon and stars in heaven;

who separated light and darkness;

who summoned Gehenna, and summons rain in the twinkling of an eye for the winter time, and mist and frost and hail, and the days each in its time;

who shakes and makes firm;

who made humankind in his image and likeness;

who spoke with the forefathers and prophets in parables and in truth,

whom the apostles preached and the disciples touched.

We confess God the Son of God, the Word who became flesh of Mary, carried in her womb through the Holy Spirit. He was born not by the desire of the flesh but by the will of God, and he was swaddled in Bethlehem and manifested and nourished, and he grew up, as we saw.

Jesus taken to school

4. This is what our Lord Jesus Christ did when he was taken by Joseph and Mary his mother to where he was to be taught to read and write. As the teacher was teaching, he said to Jesus, 'Say, "Alpha."'

'You tell me first what beta is, and then I will trust you and say alpha!' Jesus replied.

The miracles of Jesus

5. Then there was a wedding in Cana in Galilee, and he was invited with his mother and his brothers. He turned water into wine. He also raised the dead, made those who were paralysed walk, and restored the man whose hand was withered.

A woman who suffered in her periods for twelve years touched the hem of his garment and was immediately well. As we pondered and wondered at the glorious things he had done, he said to us, 'Who touched me?'

'Lord, the press of the crowd touched you!' we said.

'I felt power coming forth from me,' he said to us.

Immediately the woman came before him and said to him, 'Lord, I touched you.'

'Go, your faith has made you well,' Jesus said in response. Then he made the deaf hear, the blind see, and he exorcized those with demons and cleansed those with leprosy.

The demon Legion, who dwelt in a man, met Jesus and cried out.

'Have you come to drive us out before the day of our destruction?' he said.

Jesus rebuked him. 'Go out of this man and do nothing to him!' he said. And Legion went into the pigs, plunged them into the sea and they were drowned.

After that, Jesus walked on the sea, and when the winds blew he rebuked them, and the waves of the sea he stilled.

When we his disciples had no *denarii*,[†] we said to him, 'Teacher, what shall we do about the tax collector?'

'One of you should cast a hook into the deep and draw out a fish,' he answered, 'and he will find *denarii* in it. Give them to the tax collector for myself and for you.'

On another occasion, when we had no food except five loaves and two fishes, he commanded the men to lie down. Their number was found to be five thousand, besides women and children. We brought pieces of bread to them, and they were satisfied. There was some left over, and we collected twelve basketfuls of pieces. If we ask, 'What do these five loaves mean?', they are an image of our faith as true Christians; that is, in the Father, ruler of the whole world, and in Jesus Christ, and in the Holy Spirit, and in the holy church, and in the forgiveness of sins.

The apostles' purpose in writing

6. These things our Lord and Saviour revealed to us and showed us, as we are doing for you, so that you may be partakers in the grace of the Lord and in our ministry and our praise, as you think of eternal life. Be strong and do not waver in the knowledge and certainty of our Lord Jesus Christ, and he will be merciful and gracious, and save for ever, to the end of the age.

7. Cerinthus and Simon have gone forth, and are going around the world, but they are enemies of our Lord Jesus Christ, for they pervert the words and the work, that is, Jesus Christ. Beware of them! For in them there is death and a great corrupt defilement. [Their] end will be judgement and eternal perdition.

8. This is why we have not hesitated to write to you about the testimony of Christ our Saviour, and about the things he did as we watched him, and which are still in thoughts and deeds.

The dawning of Easter faith

9. This we confess, that the Lord was crucified by Pontius Pilate and Archelaus between the two thieves, and was buried

in a place called 'The Skull'. There came to that place three women, Mary, Martha and Mary Magdalene. They took ointment to pour over his body, weeping and grieving over what had happened. But when they reached the tomb and looked inside they did not find the body.

10. As they were grieving and weeping, the Lord appeared to them and said to them, 'For whom are you weeping? Weep no longer! I am the one you are seeking. But one of you should go to your brothers and say, "Come, the Teacher has risen from the dead!" ' Martha then came and told us.

'What do you want with us, woman?', we asked her. 'Can someone who has died and has been buried live?' We did not believe her statement that the Saviour had risen from the dead.

Then she returned to the Lord. 'None of them believed me that you are alive,' she reported to him.

'Another of you should go to them and tell them again,' he said.

Mary came, and she also spoke to us, but we did not believe her either. She returned to the Lord, and reported the same thing to him.

11. Then the Lord said to Mary and her sisters, 'Let us go to them.' And he came and found us indoors. He called us out, but we thought it was a phantasm and did not believe that it was the Lord.

'Come, fear not,' he said to us. 'I am your teacher, whom you denied three times, Peter. Are you now denying me again?' We went to him, doubting in our hearts whether it was Jesus.

'Why do you still doubt, you unbelievers?' he said to us. 'I am he who spoke to you about my flesh, my death and my resurrection. So you may know that it is I, Peter, put your fingers into the nail-marks on my hands; and you, Thomas, put your fingers into the spear wounds in my side; and you, Andrew, look at my feet and see if they are not in contact with the ground. For it is written in the prophet, "As for an appearance of a demon, its foot is not in contact with the ground." '*

12. Then we touched him, to know that he had truly risen in flesh. We fell on our faces, confessing our sins, because we had not believed.

Then the Lord our Saviour said to us, 'Arise, and I will reveal to you what is above the heavens, what is in the heavens, and your rest in the kingdom of the heavens. For my Father gave me authority to take you up along with those who believe in me.'

Jesus' descent through the heavens

13. This is what he revealed to us.

'It happened that when I came from the Father of all and travelled through the heavens,' he recounted, 'I put on the wisdom of the Father and clothed myself in the power of his might. I was in the heavens, and archangels and angels I passed in their likeness as though I were one of them. Among the powers and rulers and authorities I passed, with the wisdom of the one who sent me. The commander of the angels is Michael, with Gabriel, Uriel and Raphael, and they followed me down to the fifth firmament, for they thought that I was one of them – such was the power given me by the Father. On that day I prepared the archangels with a voice of wonder to go in to the altar of the Father and serve and fulfil the ministry until I returned to him. This is what I did in the wisdom of the likeness, for I became all in all so that I might fulfil the will of the Father of glory who sent me, and return to him.'

14. 'You know that the angel Gabriel brought the good news to Mary?' Jesus continued.

'Yes, Lord,' we answered.

'Do you not remember that I told you a moment ago that I became an angel among angels and all in all?' he asked again.

'Yes, Lord,' we replied.

'When I took the form of the angel Gabriel,' Jesus continued, 'I appeared to Mary and spoke with her. Her heart received me, she believed, she [moulded] me; I entered into her, and became flesh. For I became my own servant in the appearance of the likeness of an angel. I will do the same again after I have returned to the Father.'

Jesus' teaching about Passover

15. 'And as for you, celebrate the memorial of my death when the Passover Feast† comes,' Jesus continued. 'At that time, one of you will be thrown into prison for the sake of my name. He will be grieved and distressed that you celebrate the Passover while he is in prison and away from you, for he will be grieved that he cannot celebrate the Passover with you. Then I will send my power in the form of the angel Gabriel, and the doors of the prison will open, and he will go out and come to you. He will keep watch with you, and stay with you until the cock crows. And when you have completed my Memorial and my Agape,* he will again be thrown into prison as a testimony, until he comes out from there and preaches what I have given you.'

'Lord, is it again necessary for us to take the cup and drink?' we asked.

'Yes, it is necessary,' Jesus replied, 'until the day when I come with those who were put to death for my sake.'

Jesus' return

16. 'Lord, great indeed are the things you have now revealed to us! But in what power or likeness will you come?'

'Truly I say to you,' he answered, 'I shall surely come like the rising sun, shining seven times more than it in my glory. On the wings of clouds I shall be borne in glory, with the sign of the cross before me. And I will come down to the earth and judge the living and the dead.'

17. 'Lord, after how many years will these things be?' we said to him.

'When the hundred and fiftieth year is completed, between Pentecost† and the Feast of Unleavened Bread,† the coming of my Father will take place.'

'Did you not say to us just now, "I will come"?' we asked. 'So how can you say to us, "The one who sent me will come"?'

'I am wholly in my Father and my Father is in me,' he told us.

Then we said to him, 'Will you really leave us until your coming? Where will we find a teacher?'

'Do you not know that I am already both here and there,' he answered, 'with the one who sent me?'

'Lord, is it possible that you can be both here and there?' we asked.

'I am wholly in the Father and the Father is in me, by likeness of form and power and fullness and light and the full measure and the voice.

18. 'I am the Word. I became a reality to him – that is, [I am the] thought fulfilled in the type. I came into being on the eighth day, which is the Lord's Day. The fulfilment of all fulfilment you will see through the redemption which has come to pass in me. You will see me go to heaven, to my Father who is in heaven. But behold, I give you a new commandment: love one another, and may there be continual peace among you. Love your enemies, and what you do not wish them to do to you, may you not do to another, or that one to you.'

19. 'Preach and teach those who believe in me, and preach about the kingdom of my Father. As he has given me authority, I have given it to you so that you may bring his children near to my heavenly Father. You who are to bring the children to the kingdom of heaven – preach, and they will believe.'

'Lord, you can do what you have told us,' we said. 'But how is it possible for us?'

'Truly I say to you, preach and proclaim, as I will be with you,' he said to us. 'For I am pleased to be with you. You will be heirs of the heavenly kingdom which belongs to him who sent me. Truly I say to you, you will be brothers and companions, for my Father is pleased with you and with those who believe in me through you. Truly I say to you, my Father has prepared such great joy that the angels and authorities longed to see it, but they will not be permitted.'

'Lord, what do you mean?' we asked him.

'You will surely see a light from shining light,' he replied, 'the perfect perfected [in the] perfect. (And the Son will be perfected by the Father, the light – for the Father who perfects is perfect [. . .] death and resurrection, and the perfection will surpass perfection.) I am entirely the right hand of the Father, in the one who is the fullness.'

'Lord in everything you have become to us salvation and life,' we said, 'proclaiming such a hope to us!'

'Have confidence and be content!' he said. 'Truly I say to you, such will be your rest, where there is no eating or drinking, no anxiety or grief, and no corruption for those who are above. For you will participate not in the lower creation but in that which is incorruptible, that of my Father. You yourselves will be incorruptible. As I am always in him, so are you in me.'

The resurrection of the flesh

We continued, asking him, 'In what form? That of angels or flesh?'

'Behold, I have taken on your flesh,' he answered, 'in which I was born and in which I was crucified and raised by my heavenly father, so that the prophecy of David the prophet about what was proclaimed about me and my death and my resurrection might be fulfilled:

> Lord, many are those who afflict me,
> and many have risen against me!
> Many there are who say of my soul,
> 'There is no salvation for you with God.'
> But you, Lord, are my support,
> my glory and the lifter of my head.
> With my voice I cried to the Lord,
> and he heard me.
> I lay down and slept,
> I was raised, for you, Lord, are my support.
> I will not be afraid of tens of thousands
> who oppose me round about.
> Rise, Lord,
> save me, my God,
> for you have struck all those who without cause are my
>   enemies,
> the teeth of sinners you have broken.
> Salvation is the Lord's,
> and his love is upon his people.

'And if all the words spoken by the prophets are fulfilled in me (because I was in them) then how much more will what I say to you certainly be fulfilled! Truly, what I say to you will come to pass, so that he who sent me will be glorified by you and by those who believe in me!'

20. When he had said these things to us, we asked, 'Lord, in everything you have been merciful to us. You have saved us and have revealed everything to us. Once again we wish to inquire of you, if you permit us.'

'I know indeed that you will bear it and that your heart is pleased to hear me,' he answered. 'Therefore ask what you want, and I will gladly speak with you.

21. 'Truly I say to you, as my Father raised me from the dead, so you too will rise and you will be taken up above the heavens to the place of which I spoke to you in the beginning, to the place prepared for you by him who sent me. This is how I will fulfil every dispensation, by being unborn – yet born among humans; and without flesh – yet I have borne flesh. For I came so that you who were born in flesh might be raised in your flesh as in a second birth, in a garment that will not perish, with all who hope and believe in him who sent me. For my Father's will is that I give life, the hope of the kingdom, to you and to those I desire.'

'Great is the hope you give, of which you speak!' we said to him.

'Do you believe that everything I say to you will come to pass?' he asked.

'Yes, Lord!' we answered.

'Truly I say to you, I have received all authority from my Father so that I may turn those in darkness to light, and those in corruption to incorruptibility, and those in error to truth, and those in death to life, so that those in prison should be released. For what is impossible for humans is possible for the Father. I am the hope of the despairing, and the helper of those who have no helper, the wealth of the needy, the physician of the sick, the resurrection of the dead.'

22. After he said this to us, we said to him, 'Lord, is the flesh really to be judged with the soul and the spirit? And will some

find rest in the kingdom of heaven and others be condemned forever while living?'

'How long will you question and seek?' he asked.

23. 'Lord, because you command us to preach,' we replied, 'we need to question you, to know with certainty through you, and be useful preachers, and so those who are taught by us may believe in you. That is why we question you so much!'

24. 'Truly I say to you,' he answered, 'the resurrection of the flesh will occur with the soul and spirit within it.'

'Lord, is it possible for what is dissolved and destroyed to be saved?' we said to him. 'We are not asking you out of unbelief, or as if it were impossible for you. We do truly believe that what you say will come to pass.'

Then he was angry with us. 'O you of little faith, how long will you question?' he said. 'But ask me what you want, and I will tell you unreservedly. Only keep my commandments and do what I tell you, and do not turn your face from anyone in case I turn my face from you. Without delay or shame or partiality, serve in the way that is straight and narrow and difficult. This is the way of my Father himself, and he will rejoice over you.'

25. 'Lord, we are now ashamed that we are questioning you so much and are wearying you,' we continued.

'I do know that you are asking wholeheartedly and in faith,' he replied, 'and so I rejoice over you! Truly I say to you, I am glad, as is my Father who is in me, that you ask me, for your shamelessness brings me joy and gives you life.' When he said this to us, we were glad that we were questioning him.

'Lord, in everything you grant us life and show mercy,' we went on. 'For you will tell us what we ask!'

'Which is it that perishes,' he asked, 'the flesh or the spirit?'

'It is the flesh that perishes!' we said.

'Indeed,' he said, 'what has fallen will rise, what is lost will be found and what is weak will recover, so that in this the glory of my Father may be revealed. As he has done for me, so I will do for all of you who believe. 26. Truly I say to you that the flesh will rise alive with the soul alive, so that they may both be judged on that day for what they have done, whether good or evil, so that there may be a selection of believers who have performed the commandments of my Father who sent me. The judgement will therefore be strict. For my Father said to me, "My Son, on the day of judgement you shall neither be ashamed before the rich nor pity the poor, but according to the sin of each you shall deliver them to eternal punishment." But to my beloved, who have performed the commandments of my Father who sent me, I will give rest and life in the kingdom of my Father in heaven. Then they will see what he has granted me: he has given me authority to do as I will, and to give what I promised and what I wanted to give them.'

Jesus' descent into Hell

27. 'The reason I descended to the place of Lazarus and preached to your fathers and the prophets is so that they would go forth from the rest below and ascend to that which is in heaven. With my right hand I poured over them the baptism of life and forgiveness and deliverance from all evil, as I have done for you and for those who believe in me. But if anyone believes in me and does not do my commandments after confessing my name, he receives no benefit at all but has run his course in vain. Such people will incur loss and punishment, because they have transgressed my commandments.

28. 'But I have granted you to be children of life, and have delivered [you] from all evil and from the power of the rulers, with everyone who believes in me through you. For what I have promised to you I shall also give them, so that they may come forth from the prison, the chains of the rulers and the terrible fire.'

'Lord,' we [replied], 'you have surely given us rest [and life], and you have given us joy with signs to [confirm] faith. Will you now preach to us what you preached to our fathers and the prophets?'

'Truly I say to you,' he said, 'everyone who believes in me and who believes in him who sent me I will lead up to heaven, the place which my Father prepared for the elect. I will give you the appointed kingdom in rest and eternal life.'

Heretical teachings

29. 'But as for those who transgress my commandments, who teach doctrines other than what is written, and add to them their own, and establish their own glory: if they teach differently those who correctly believe in me but who then fall away through them, those teachers will receive an everlasting punishment.'

'Lord, will there come teachings other than what you have told us?' we said to him.

'It is indeed necessary for them to come,' he said to us, 'so that those who do evil and those who do good may be revealed. This is how the judgement will reveal those who do these works, and according to their works they will be judged and delivered to death.'

The mission of the disciples

Again we said to him, 'Lord, blessed are we that we see you and hear you as you say such things, for our eyes have seen these great signs that you have done.'

'Blessed rather are those who have not seen and yet believed.' he replied, 'They will be called sons of the kingdom, and will be perfect in the perfect one. I will be life to them in the kingdom of my Father.'

'Lord, how will people believe, when you go and leave us behind?' we asked. 'For you have told us, "A day and an hour are coming when I shall ascend to my Father."'

30. 'Go and preach to the twelve tribes,' he said, 'and preach to the gentiles and to the whole land of Israel from east to west and from south to north. Then many will believe in the Son of God.'

'Lord, who will believe us, or who will listen to us, or who will then teach the mighty works and signs you have done, and the wonders?'

'Go and preach the mercy of my Father,' he answered, 'and what he has done through me I will do through you, since I will be in you. And I will give you my peace, and by my Spirit

I will give you power, and you will prophesy to them their eternal life. To others I will also give my power, and they will teach the rest of the gentiles.'

Paul the persecutor and confessor

31. 'Behold, you will meet a man whose name is Saul (which, translated, means "Paul"). He is a Jew, circumcised according to the commandment of the Law. He will hear my voice from heaven in astonishment, fear and trembling. He will be blinded, and by your hand shall his eyes be sealed with saliva. Do everything for him that I have done for you, and convert him for others. Then this man's eyes will immediately be opened, and he will praise God my heavenly Father. He will be strong among the people, and will preach and teach many; they will be glad to hear him, and many will be saved. But he will be hated and delivered into the hand of his enemy, and he will confess me before transitory kings. Instead of persecuting me and hating me, he will confess me, and he will bring his confession of me to completion. He will preach and teach, and will be an elect vessel among my elect, and a wall that shall not fall. As the least of the least of the apostles, he shall be a preacher to the gentiles, perfected by the will of my Father. As you have learned from the scriptures that the prophets spoke about me and their true fulfilment is in me, so you must provide him with the guidance in them. Every word that I have spoken to you and that you write about me as the Word of the Father and about the Father being in me, you also must pass on to that man, as is fitting for you. Teach him and remind him what is said in the scriptures about me and is now fulfilled, and then he will be the salvation of the gentiles.'

32. 'O Master,' we said to him, 'do we have one hope of inheritance with them?'

'Are the fingers of the hand alike, or the ears of corn in the field? Or do fruit-bearing trees give the same fruit? Do they not bear fruit each according to its kind?'

'Lord,' we said, 'you are again speaking with us in parables!'

'Do not be troubled!' he said to us. 'Truly I say to you, you are my brothers, with a share in my Father's kingdom, for that is his will. Truly I say to you, I will give that hope to those whom you teach and who believe in me.'

33. Again we asked, 'Lord, when shall we meet that man? And when will you go to your Father and ours, our God and our Lord?'

'That man will go out from the land of Cilicia to Damascus in Syria,' he answered, 'in order to tear apart the church that you are to found. It is I who will speak through you, and it will happen soon. In this faith he will be strong, so that what the prophetic voice said might be fulfilled:

> Behold, from the land of Syria
> I will begin to call a new Jerusalem,
> and Zion I will subdue to myself
> and it will be captured.
> The barren woman who has no children
> will have a child,
> and she will be called the daughter of my Father.
> She will be my bride,
> for this is the will of him who sent me.*

'That man I will turn aside so that he cannot come and fulfil his evil intention, and his shall be the glory of my Father. For when I have gone and am with my Father, I will speak with him from heaven. All that I have predicted to you about him will take place.'

The time of trial

34. Again we said to him, 'Lord, what great things you have spoken to us, announcing and revealing to us things never yet spoken. In everything you have comforted us and been gracious to us! For after your resurrection you revealed all this to us, so that we might truly be saved. But you have told us only about the signs and wonders in heaven and on earth before the end of the world comes; therefore teach us about the end, so that we may know.'

'I will teach you,' he said to us, 'and it is not only to you that these things will happen but also to those whom you teach and who believe, and those who hear this man and believe in me. In those years and in those days it will happen.'

'Lord, what is it that will happen?' we asked.

'At that time believers and unbelievers will perceive
the sound of a trumpet from heaven
and the sight of great stars that appear during the day,
and a sign from heaven that reaches the earth,
and stars falling like fire,
and great hailstones like raging fire,
and sun and moon fighting together,
and constant terror of thunder and lightning and thunderbolt
and an earthquake following.
Cities shall fall and people shall die in their ruins,
and there will be constant drought from lack of rain,
and a great plague and widespread death and many trials,
so that funerals will cease for those who die.
The passing of child and parent will be on a single bed,
and parent will not turn to child nor child to parent,
and one person will not turn to another.
Those who are bereaved will rise up
and see their departed being carried out.
For there will be a plague everywhere,
hatred and suffering and jealousy,
and what one person has will be taken and given to another.
And what follows will be even worse than this.

35. 'Then my Father will be angry at people's evil, for many are their transgressions, and their unclean abomination is greatly against them in the corruption of their life.'

The fate of the elect

Then we said to him, 'Lord, what then of those who hope in you?'

'How long are you still going to be slow of heart?' he answered. 'Truly I say to you, as the prophet David spoke about me and about those who are mine, so God wills the same for those who believe in me. There will be deceivers and enemies of righteousness in the world, and there shall come to pass David's prophecy about them which says:

> *"Swift are their feet to shed blood,*
> *their tongues weave deceit,*
> *and the venom of snakes is under their lips.*
> *And I see you as you go about with a thief,*
> *and with an adulterer is your portion.*
> *And while you sit you slander your brother*
> *and set a stumbling-block for your mother's son.*
> *What do you think, that I am like you?"**

'See, then, how the prophet spoke about everything, so that everything that was said in advance may be fulfilled.'

36. We further asked him, 'Lord, will the gentiles not say, "Where is their God?"'

'By this the elect will be made known,' he answered, 'that they depart after enduring such torment.'

'Will their departure from the world be through the plague that torments them?'

'No,' he said, 'but when they are tormented the affliction will be to test them. If there is faith within them, and they remember these words of mine and obey my commandments, they will be raised. Their situation will last only a few days, so that he who sent me may be glorified and I with him, for he sent me to you. This I tell you, and you must tell it to Israel and to the gentiles, that they may hear, be saved and believe in me, and depart after the affliction of the plague. Whoever survives the affliction of death will be taken and kept in prison, punished like a thief.'

'Lord,' we said to him, 'will they be like those who do not believe? Will you punish those who survive the plague in the same way?'

'If they believe in my name but have acted as sinners,' he said, 'they have behaved like unbelievers.'

'Lord, is the fate of those who survive, then, that they fail to attain life?'

'Whoever glorifies my Father will dwell with my Father,' he answered.

37. Then we said to him, 'Lord, teach us what will happen after this.'

'In those years and days there will be war after war,' he said, 'and the four corners of the world will be shaken and will make war against one another. Then there will be a tumult of clouds, darkness and drought, and the persecution of those who believe in me and of the elect! After that, dissension, strife and evil conduct will come among them, and some of those who believe in my name will follow evil and teach vain doctrine. People will follow them and obey their wealth, their wickedness, their drunkenness and their bribery; and there will be partiality among them.'

38. 'Those who desire to see the face of God, who do not show partiality to rich sinners, and who are not ashamed before those who go astray but rebuke them – they will be crowned in the presence of the Father. So too, whoever rebukes his neighbour will be saved: he is a son of wisdom and faith. If he is not a son of wisdom, however, he will hate and persecute and not turn to his neighbour but will despise and reject him. Those who conduct themselves in truth and in the knowledge of faith, with love for me, endure abuse; they will be despised as they walk in poverty and endure those who hate them, mock them and torment them; destitute, since people sneered at them in their hunger and thirst. Yet because they have endured until the blessedness of heaven, they will be with me forever. But woe to those who walk in arrogance and boasting! For their end is perdition.'

Divine justice

39. 'Lord,' we said to him, 'it is in your power not to allow these things to befall them!'

'How will the judgement take place for either the righteous or the unrighteous?'

'Lord, on that day they will say to you, "You did not separate righteousness and unrighteousness, light and darkness, evil and good!"'

Then Jesus said, 'This is how I will answer them: "Adam was given the power to choose between two courses. He chose the light and stretched out his hand for it, but the darkness he rejected and cast it from him. All people therefore have the power to believe in the light, which is the life of the Father who sent me." Everyone who believes and does the works of light will live through them. But if there is someone who confesses that he belongs to the light while doing the works of darkness, such a person has no defence, nor will he lift his face to look at the Son of God, which is I myself. For I shall say to him, "As you sought you have found, and as you asked you have received! Why did you condemn me, O man? Why did you proclaim me and deny me? And why did you confess me and deny me?" Therefore every person has the power to live or to die, and so the one who keeps my commandments will become a son of light, that is, of the Father who is within me. Because of those who corrupt my words I have come down from heaven, I the Word who became flesh and suffered, to teach that those who are called will be saved and that those who are lost will be lost eternally, tormented alive and punished in their flesh and their souls.'

40. And we said to him, 'Lord, truly we are concerned for them!'

'You are right to be so,' he said, 'for the righteous are concerned for sinners and pray for them, interceding with my Father.'

'Lord, does no one then intercede with you yourself?' we continued.

'Yes, and I will hear the prayer the righteous make for them.'

The ministry of the disciples

When he had said this to us, we questioned him further.

'Lord, in everything you have taught us, pitied us and saved us so that we may preach to those who are worthy of salvation – and do we gain a reward with you?'

41. 'Go and preach,' he replied, 'and you will be workers and servants.'

'It is you who will preach through us.'

'Will you not all be fathers?' Jesus said. 'Will you not all be teachers?'

'Lord, you said to us, "Do not call anyone your father on earth, for there is one who is your Father who is in heaven, and your teacher." Why do you now say to us, "You will be fathers of many children, and servants and teachers"?'

'It is as you have said,' he answered. 'For truly I say to you, whoever hears you and believes in me will receive [from] you the light of the seal through [me]. You will be [fathers] and servants and teachers.'

42. 'Lord, how can each of us be these three?'

'Truly I say to you that you will indeed be called fathers, because with a willing heart and love you have revealed to them the things of the kingdom of heaven. You will be called servants because they will receive the baptism of life and the forgiveness of their sins – by my hand through you. And you will be called teachers because you have given them the word without envy. You admonished them, and when you rebuked them they separated themselves. You were unafraid of their wealth and their person, but you kept the commandments of my Father and did them. There will be a great reward for you with my Father who is in heaven, and for them there will be forgiveness of sins and eternal life, and they will share in the kingdom of heaven.'

'Lord,' we said to him, 'if each of us had ten thousand tongues for his speech, we would not be able to give thanks to you that you promise us such things!'

'Just do what I tell you, the things I myself have done,' the Lord said.

The parable of the virgins

43. He continued: 'You will be like the wise virgins who stayed awake, and did not go to sleep but went out to meet the Lord and entered with him into the wedding chamber. The foolish ones, however, were unable to stay awake and fell asleep.'

'Lord,' we asked, 'who are the wise and who are the foolish?'

'There are five wise. Of them the prophet said that they are
children of God. Hear their names!' (We were distraught and
tearful, however, about those who slept.) 'The five wise are
Faith, Love, Grace, Peace and Hope,' he said. 'Those believers
who possess these will be guides for those who believe in me and
in him who sent me. For I am the Lord and I am the bridegroom
whom they have received, and they entered the bridegroom's
house and reclined with me in my wedding-chamber and slept.
But as for the five foolish ones who had fallen asleep, when they
woke up and came to the door of the wedding-chamber and
knocked, it had been shut against them. Then they wept and
grieved that the door was not opened for them.'

'Lord,' we said, 'didn't their wise sisters inside the bridegroom's house open the door for them? Didn't they grieve for
them or plead with the bridegroom on their behalf to open the
door for them?'

'They were not yet able to find favour for them,' he answered.

'Lord, when will they enter for their sisters' sakes?'

'Whoever is shut out is shut out,' the Lord replied.

'Lord, is this matter decided? Who, then, are the foolish?'

'Hear their names,' he said to us. 'They are Knowledge, Wisdom, Obedience, Patience and Mercy. For it is these that have
slept among those who believe and confess me. 44. Since those
who slept did not fulfil my commandments, they will remain
outside the kingdom and outside the fold of the shepherd and
his flock. And whoever remains outside the sheepfold will be
devoured by wolves: when he hears the wolves, he will die in
great pain, and continual distress shall come upon him. He
will be terribly tortured – lacerated and torn apart with severe,
agonizing punishment.'

45. 'Lord, you have revealed all things to us well,' we said.

'Do you not understand these words?' he replied.

'Yes, Lord, through the five they will enter your kingdom.
But surely those who stayed awake with you, the Lord and
bridegroom, do not rejoice over those who fell asleep?'

'They do rejoice that they entered with the bridegroom, the
Lord, but they grieve over those who slept, for they are their
sisters. The ten are all daughters of God the Father.'

'Lord, it is in your power to be gracious to their sisters.'

'This is not your concern, but the affair of him who sent me,' he said to us. 'And I agree with him.'

Disciplining sinful behaviour in the Church

46. 'But as for you,' he continued, 'preach and teach uprightly and well, showing partiality to no one and fearing no one, especially the rich, for they do not obey my commandments but delight in their wealth.'

'Lord,' we said to him, 'do you speak to us only of the rich?'

'If someone who is not rich but has a little property and gives to the poor and needy,' he answered, 'people will call him a benefactor. 47. But if he falls, bearing a burden because of the sins he has committed, his neighbour should rebuke him for what he has done to his neighbour. When his neighbour has rebuked him and he repents, he will be saved and the one who rebuked him will be awarded eternal life. But if a man who is in need sees his benefactor sinning and does not rebuke him, he will be judged with a woeful judgement. If a blind man leads a blind man, both will fall into a pit. Whoever shows partiality and whoever receives partiality will both be judged with the same judgement. As the prophet said, "Woe to those who show partiality, who justify the sinner for a bribe, whose stomach is their god."* Consider how the judgement takes place! For truly I say to you, I will neither fear the rich nor have pity on the poor on that day.

48. 'If you see a sinner, rebuke him privately. If he does not listen to you, however, take up to three others with you and instruct your brother. If he still does not listen to you, treat him as a gentile and a tax collector.

49. 'If you hear a rumour, do not believe anything against your brother and do not slander or relish listening to slanderous talk. For as it is written, "Let your ear not listen to anything against your brother."* But if you have seen it, rebuke, instruct and convert him.'

'Lord,' we said to him, 'you have taught us and warned us in every way. But, Lord, will there really be division, strife, jealousy, quarrelling, hatred and slander among believers who truly believe the preaching of your name? For you said that they will rebuke one another and show no partiality to those who sin and who hate whoever rebukes them.'

'Why then will the judgement take place?' he answered. 'It is for the wheat to be put into its barns and its chaff put onto the fire! 50. Those people hate whoever loves me and rebukes those who do not keep my commandments, and these will be hated, persecuted, despised and mocked. The wicked will speak what is untrue, taking counsel and conspiring together against those who love me, and these will rebuke them so that they may be saved. But these who rebuke, instruct and warn them will be hated, ostracized and scorned, and those who wish to do good to them will be prevented. Those who endure, however, will be witnesses before the Father, because they were zealous for righteousness, and it was not with a zeal for corruption that they were zealous.'

'Will this happen among us, then?' we asked.

'Do not fear what will not happen to many but to a few,' he said.

'Tell us how!'

'There will be strange teaching and strife, and people will desire their own glory, putting forward unprofitable teaching, and there will be a deadly stumbling-block within it. They will teach and turn those who have believed in me from my commandments, and deprive them of eternal life. But woe to those who falsify this my word and my commandments, and to those who listen to them and who are far from the life of the teaching! With them they will be eternally punished.'

Jesus' ascension

51. When he had finished saying this, he continued, 'Behold, on the third day, at the third hour,† he who sent me will come so that I may go with him.' And as he spoke there was thunder and lightning and an earthquake, and the heavens were torn asunder, and a bright cloud came and took him. And we heard the voices of many angels as they rejoiced and blessed and said,

'Gather us, O priest, into the light of glory!' And when he drew near to the firmament of heaven, we heard him saying, 'Go in peace!'

In the name of our Lord Jesus Christ.

36 The Questions of Bartholomew

(c. *fourth century* CE)

INTRODUCTION

The *Questions of Bartholomew* is a typical example of a post-resurrection dialogue, in that it represents Jesus and his disciples in conversation about speculative details of the heavenly and infernal realms. The first topic of the question-and-answer is Jesus' 'Harrowing of Hell', which interestingly is timed not after Jesus' death on the cross, but during the three hours when the sun stopped shining on Good Friday: Jesus, then, under cover of darkness, departed from the cross and went down to the underworld to rescue the faithful dead who had believed in him before his coming. Second, Bartholomew asks a series of questions about how many people die and enter Paradise (ch. 1). Third, Mary recounts how God revealed her destiny of conceiving Jesus (ch. 2). Then, after the insistence of the disciples, Jesus reveals the abyss to them – and they later regret having asked (ch. 3). Bartholomew subsequently is invited to have a dialogue with Satan, who tells him of his fall from heaven, how various angels control the winds and the sea, and how temptation takes place (ch. 4). The climax is a discussion of the deadly sins (ch. 5).

There are some nice literary touches in the piece. In Chapter 2, there is an argument between Mary and the group of disciples about who should pray to God for revelation about how the incarnation took place: the argument consists of a 'humility contest' in which each describes how the other is superior and should really be the one to pray. In Chapter 4, Satan is portrayed as a frustrated manager, who would love to be on the front lines but instead has to send out his minions to do the real work of tempting. The dialogue with Satan has comic touches similar to those in the comparable dialogues in Milton's *Paradise Lost* and C. S. Lewis's *The Screwtape Letters*.

The text is also rich in theological interest. Mary is a key focus of attention, especially in the scene depicting her early life in the temple (ch. 2). In this section, the young Mary receives a promise of her conception of Jesus in three years' time. When this promise comes, she is prepared for it by a vision of God himself. God sprinkles her with a cloud of dew, and then presents her with a colossal loaf of bread and an enormous cup of wine, which he ate and drank from first. These events probably symbolize Mary receiving a strangely pre-Christian 'baptism', as well as the sacraments of the bread and wine, which in the vision God himself consumes first before passing them to her.

The work survives only in three Greek manuscripts. The present translation is based on a Jerusalem manuscript, which preserves the beginning of the text and runs through to about the middle of Chapter 4, and a Vienna manuscript, whose beginning is missing but which runs through to the final Amen at the end. Hence a whole text is more or less preserved. The original composition of the work probably took place in about the fourth century, but it could be earlier or later.

DRAMATIS PERSONAE

JESUS CHRIST
MARY *The mother of Jesus*
BARTHOLOMEW *A disciple of Jesus*
JOHN *A disciple of Jesus*
PETER *A disciple of Jesus*
BELIAR (BELIAL) *Satan, Death, the serpent*
HELL *A personification of the underworld*
MICHAEL *The archangel*

TRANSLATION

1. Jesus' account of the Harrowing of Hell

After the resurrection of our Lord Jesus Christ from the dead, Bartholomew approached him.

'Reveal to me, Lord, the mysteries of the heavens,' he asked.

'If I put aside the fleshly body, I will not be able to speak to you,' Jesus replied.

Bartholomew therefore came closer to the Lord and said, 'I have something to say to you, Lord.'

'I know what you are going to say', the Lord said to him. 'Therefore say what you want to say. Ask, and I will answer you.'

'Lord, when you departed to be crucified on the cross,' Bartholomew said, 'I followed you at a distance. I saw that as you were being crucified on the cross, angels were coming down from heaven and worshipping you! Then, when it went dark, I looked and saw that you had disappeared from the cross, and I only heard a voice in the subterranean depths – a great wailing and gnashing suddenly sounded. Tell me, Lord, where you went from the cross.'

'You are blessed, my beloved Bartholomew,' Jesus replied, 'because you saw this mystery. Now everything which you have asked of me I will tell you. When I disappeared from the cross, I went down to Hell in order to bring up Adam and all those with him, in answer to the archangel Michael's request.'

'Lord,' Bartholomew then asked, 'what was the voice which sounded?'

'It was Hell, saying to Beliar, "It looks like God has come here!" Then Beliar said to Hell, "Look carefully at who it is. He looks to me like Elijah or Enoch, or one of the other prophets."

'And Hell replied to Death, "Six thousand years have not yet passed. Where have they come from, Beliar? The mark of the number is on my hands."

'Beliar said to Hell, "Don't get in a fluster. Secure your gates and fasten your bolts. Think about it – God does not come down to earth!"

'Hell said to him, "I can't hear your soothing words – my stomach is being torn up, and I'm going through my own innards! It can only be that God has come here. Woe is me! Where can I flee from the presence of the great King's power?"

'Then I said to Hell, "Let me enter you, because I was formed before you were." So I entered Hell, and I beat him, bound him with unbreakable chains, released all the patriarchs and then went back onto the cross.'

'Tell me, Lord,' said Bartholomew, 'Who was the one whom the angels carried up in their hands, that massive man?'

'That was Adam, the first formed,' Jesus replied. 'It was because of him that I came from heaven to earth. I said to him, "I was hanged on the cross because of you and your children." When he heard this, Adam lamented, and said, "Such is your will, O Lord."'

'Lord,' Bartholomew continued, 'I also saw angels coming up to Adam and singing. One of the angels was even more colossal than the others, and he refused to go up. He had a flaming sword in his hand and he acknowledged you alone.'

The number of souls dying and entering Paradise*

When Bartholomew had said this, Jesus said to the apostles, 'Stay with me in this place, because today a sacrifice is being offered in Paradise, and I must be present to receive it.'

'Lord,' he said, 'What is this sacrifice offered in Paradise?'

'The souls of the righteous which have come forth from their bodies today,' Jesus said, 'are entering into Paradise. But unless I am present, they will not be able to enter.'

'Lord,' Bartholomew asked, 'how many souls depart from the world each day?'

'Thirty thousand,' Jesus replied.

'Lord,' Bartholomew went on, 'how many souls enter Paradise each day?'

'Three,' Jesus replied.

'Lord, when you were among us teaching the word, were you receiving sacrifices in Paradise?'

'Truly I say to you, my beloved,' Jesus answered, 'I was at

the same time among you teaching the word, and also seated uninterrupted with my Father, receiving daily sacrifices in Paradise.'

'Of those that depart from the world,' Bartholomew asked, 'how many righteous souls are found? Is it only the three souls that come forth each day?'

'No, my beloved,' Jesus replied, 'but still just fifty-three.'

'How is it, then, that only three enter Paradise?'

'Of the fifty-three, three enter Paradise, that is, are deposited at the bosom of Abraham,' Jesus said to him. 'The others – not the three, but the fifty or so – go to the place of resurrection.'

'Lord,' Bartholomew said, 'how many souls are born in the world each day?'

'Just one more than the number of those who depart from the world,' Jesus said.

When he had said these things, he gave them peace and disappeared from them.

2. The apostles ask Mary about her conception of Jesus

The apostles were in Cheltoura, and Bartholomew approached Peter, Andrew and John.

'Let us ask highly favoured Mary how she conceived the uncontainable one, how she carried the one who cannot be carried, and how she gave birth to one of such great magnitude.' They hesitated to ask her, however.

'You are a kind of chief to us,' Bartholomew said to Peter, 'and a teacher to me. You can go and ask her.'

Peter said to John, 'You are a virgin, blameless, the beloved disciple – you go and ask her.'

Since the others were all hesitant, however, and refused, Bartholomew approached her, smiling.

'Greetings to you,' he said, 'O Tabernacle of the Most High! We apostles (they sent me) all want to ask you how you conceived the uncontainable one, how you carried him who cannot be carried, and how you gave birth to one of such great magnitude.'

'Are you really asking me about this mystery?' Mary said. 'If

I begin to tell you, fire will come forth from my mouth and set all the world ablaze.'

Nevertheless, they kept on asking her, and she was reluctant to disobey the apostles.

'Stand in prayer,' she said, so the apostles stood behind Mary.

'Peter, chief, and mightiest pillar,' she continued, 'why are you standing behind me? Did the Lord not say, *The head of a man is Christ*?* Now, then, stand in front of me, and you pray!'

'In you the Lord pitched his tent and willed that you contain him,' they said to her. 'So it should be you who stands in prayer!'

'You are shining stars,' Mary said to them, 'as the prophet said, *I raised my eyes to the hills, from where my hope will come.** You are those "hills", and so you should be the ones who pray.'

They said to her, 'You should pray, O womb for the heavenly king!'

Mary said to them, 'In accordance with your likenesses, the Lord made the sparrows and sent them into the four corners of the world.'

'But the one who is hardly contained by the seven heavens was pleased to be contained in you!' they said to her.

Mary prays and recounts the revelation of her destiny

Finally, Mary stood before them and spread out her hands to heaven and prayed.

'*Elphoue zarethra charboum nemioth melitho thraboutha mephnounos chemiath aroura maridon elison marmiadon sephon hesaboutha ennouna saktinos athoor belelam opheoth abo chrasar.*'*

That is, in Greek:

> God, surpassingly great and all-wise,
> king of the ages, unsearchable, ineffable,
> who sustains all the magnitude of the heavens by a
>   word,

who fitted from what is unknown the heavenly poles,
sustaining them and fixing them,
who formed the material vessel,
who brought the disparate elements into composition,
who separated the gloomy darkness from the light,
who upheld the foundations of the waters together,
who became the terror of the ethereal realm
and appeared as the fear of the earthly,
who fixed the earth and refused to let it be destroyed,
supplying the ground with rain
for the nourishment of all who are blessed by the Father.
You, whom the seven heavens can hardly contain,
yet were pleased to be contained painlessly in me,
you who are yourself the full Word of the Father,
and in whom all things were made!
Glorify your almighty name, Lord,
and command me to give utterance before these holy
*   apostles.*

When she had finished praying, she said, 'Let us sit down on the ground. Come now, Peter our chief, sit on my right and lay your left hand under my arm; and you, Andrew do the same on my left; and you, John the virgin, embrace my chest; and you, Bartholomew, press your knees against my back and push against my shoulders, in case, when I begin to speak, my bones come loose.'

When they had done this, she began to speak.

'I was in the temple of God, receiving my food by the hand of an angel. One day, an angel appeared to me. At least, he was angelic in shape, but his appearance was limitless in size, and he had no food or drink in his hand like the angel which had previously come to me. Suddenly the curtain of the temple tore and there was a terrible earthquake. I fell on my face, unable to bear the figure's appearance. He placed his hand under me and lifted me up, and I looked up to heaven, and a cloud of dew touched my face. He sprinkled me with it from head to foot, and dried me with his robe.

' "Greetings, you who are highly favoured, chosen vessel",

he said. Then he struck the right-hand side of his garment and a colossal loaf of bread appeared. He placed it on the altar of the temple, and first ate from it himself and then gave some to me.

'Then, again, he struck the left-hand side of his garment, and there appeared an enormous cup full of wine. He placed it on the altar of the temple, then drank from it first and after that gave some to me. I was watching – and I saw the cup full and the bread whole. Then he said to me, "In another three years I will send you my Word, and you will conceive a son, and through him all creation will be saved. Peace to you, my beloved, and peace will be with you forever." Then he disappeared, and the temple was just as it had been before.'

When she had said this, fire came forth from her mouth. It was about to engulf the whole world, but then the Lord quickly appeared.

'Do not speak this mystery,' he said to Mary, 'or all creation will come to an end today.'

Then the apostles were seized with terror, concerned that the Lord was angry with them.

3. Jesus reveals the Abyss to the apostles

He went away with them to Mount Maurei and sat down in the middle of them. In their fear they hesitated to ask him anything, but Jesus spoke to them.

'Ask me what you will, and I will instruct you and give you revelation. For there are still seven days until I return to my Father, and then I will no longer appear to you in this form.'

'Lord,' they said hesitantly, 'as you have offered, show us the Abyss.'

'It is better for you not to see the Abyss,' Jesus said. 'But if you wish to, follow me and look.'

He then led them off to a place called Chairoudek, which is the place of truth. He then beckoned towards the diving angels, and the earth was rolled up like a scroll, and the Abyss was revealed for them. When the apostles saw it, they fell on their faces, but the Lord raised them up.

'Did I not tell you it was better for you not to see the Abyss?' he said. Again he beckoned to the angels, and they covered the Abyss up.

4. Jesus' revelation of Satan

They he took them back up to the Mount of Olives.

'Most highly favoured one!' Peter said to Mary. 'Ask the Lord to reveal to us what is in the heavens.'

'O chosen rock!' Mary said to Peter. 'Did he not promise to build his church on you?'

'But you are the tabernacle formed for the Lord!' said Peter.

'And you are the impression of Adam!' Mary said. 'Was not he made first and then Eve? Look at the sun, because following the pattern of Adam it shines bright. Look at the moon, which is filled with clay because of Eve's transgression. The Lord has placed Adam in the east, and Eve in the west, and has appointed these luminaries to shine on the earth, giving the sun in fiery chariots for Adam in the east, and the moon as a milky white flame for Eve in the west. It was she that defiled the command of the Lord. Because of this, the moon became clay and does not give its light. Therefore you, the impression of Adam, ought to ask; I can only muster female strength.'

When they reached the peak of the mountain, the Lord departed from them for a little while. Then Peter said to Mary, 'You are the one who has destroyed the transgression of Eve, changing shame into joy! You should ask.'

When the Lord appeared again, Bartholomew said to him, 'Lord, show us man's Adversary, so that we may see what he is like, how he acts, where he comes from, and the nature of his power that he did not spare even you, but had you hanged on the cross.'

Jesus looked at him. 'Your heart is hard,' he said. 'You are not able to look at what you are requesting.'

Bartholomew was distraught and fell at Jesus' feet. 'Unquenchable illuminator,' he said, 'Jesus Christ, maker of eternal light, who granted the universal gift to those who love you, who granted the eternal light through your coming in the world to us through the virgin Mary. Grant us what we ask!'

After he had said this, Jesus lifted him up.

'Do you want to see man's antagonist, Bartholomew?' Jesus said. 'I declare to you, that not only you, but the other apostles and Mary will also fall on their faces and be like corpses.'

'Lord,' they all said to him, 'let us see him.'

Jesus then led them down from the Mount of Olives. After rebuking the angels of the underworld, he beckoned to Michael to sound his mighty trumpet. Immediately Michael sounded the trumpet, and Beliar came up, seized by 560 angels, bound in flaming chains. The serpent was 1,600 cubits long and 40 cubits wide.[†] His face was like a flaming bolt of lightning, his eyes were dark, from his nostrils came malodorous smoke, and his mouth was like a chasm in a precipice. And each of his wings was 80 cubits long.

When the apostles saw him, they fell flat on the ground and were like corpses.

Jesus went over to them and lifted the apostles up. He gave them a powerful spirit and said to Bartholomew, 'Go and stamp your foot on his neck, and ask him what his work is.'

Jesus stood at a distance with the apostles, and Bartholomew, though terrified, raised his voice and said to Jesus:

'Blessed be the name of your immortal kingdom from now and for ever.'

When he had said this, Jesus instructed him. 'Go off and trample on Beliar's neck.'

Bartholomew went at full speed and trampled on his neck, and Beliar shook in terror.

Bartholomew was also afraid, and ran away.

'Lord Jesus,' he said, 'give me a corner of your garments, to embolden me to approach him.'

'You cannot take a corner of my garments,' Jesus said, 'because these garments of mine are not what I wore before I was crucified.'

'I am afraid, Lord,' Bartholomew said, 'that he may not spare your angels and would eat me up.'

'Has not everything come to pass by my word and by the will of my Father?' Jesus said. 'The spirits submitted to Solomon.

You, then, at the word of my command – go forth and ask him what you want to know.'

Bartholomew made the sign of the cross and prayed to Jesus. On every side, flames were kindled and Bartholomew's garments caught fire.

'As I told you,' Jesus instructed him, 'trample on his neck as you are asking him what his power is.'

Bartholomew went off, then, and trampled on his neck, pushing his face into the ground up to his ears.

'Tell me who you are,' Bartholomew said to him, 'and what your name is.'

'Ease off my neck a little,' he said, 'and I will tell you who I am and how I came here, what I do and what my power is like.'

Bartholomew released some of the pressure and said, 'Now tell me everything you have done and are doing.'

'If you want to know my name, I was first called Satanael,' he replied, 'which means "angel of God". After I did not acknowledge the reflection of God, I became known as Satan, which means "angel of the underworld".'

'Reveal everything to me,' Bartholomew continued, 'and keep nothing hidden.'

'I swear to you by God's glory,' he replied, 'that even if I wanted to keep something hidden, I cannot, for my accuser is standing by me. If I were able, I would have killed you all as I did him before you. For I was formed as the first angel. For when God made the heavens, he took a handful of fire.

First, he made me;
second, he made Michael;
third, he made Gabriel;
fourth, he made Raphael;
fifth, he made Uriel;
sixth, he made Xathanael.

'He also made six thousand other angels whose names I am not able to speak, for they are God's staff-bearers. They beat me with their staffs seven times a day and seven times a night. They never leave me alone, and they dissipate my power. There are two avenging angels who stand in the presence of the throne of God – they are those who were first made. And after them the multitude of angels was formed.

> The first heaven has a million angels;
> the second heaven has a million angels;
> the third heaven has a million angels;
> the fourth heaven has a million angels;
> the fifth heaven has a million angels;
> the sixth heaven has a million angels,
> and the seventh heaven has a million angels.

'Outside the seven heavens is the first plate, where the authorities at work in people dwell. There are other angels who oversee the winds.

'One angel, appointed over the north wind, is called Khairoum. He restrains the flaming staff in his hand, and keeps his great power in check so that the earth is not scorched dry.

'Another angel, appointed over the east wind, is called Ertha. He has a flaming lamp, and attaches it to his sides and warms his coldness, so he does not freeze the earth.

'The angel appointed over the south wind is called Kerkoutha, and is kept calm so he does not make the earth quake.

'The angel appointed over the west wind is called Naoutha. He has a snowy staff in his hand and puts it to his mouth to quench the fire coming from it. If the angel had not placed the staff on his mouth, he would burn up the whole world.

'Another angel is over the sea, and controls it with waves.

'I will not tell you the others, for the one standing by does not permit me.'

'How do you punish men's souls?' Bartholomew asked.

'Do you want me to tell you the punishment,' Beliar said, 'for slanderous hypocrites, jokers, idolaters, money-lovers, adulterers, sorcerers, fortune-tellers, people who believe in me, and all those over whom I watch?'

'I ask you to be brief', 'said Bartholomew.

Beliar gnashed his teeth, and a breaking wheel came up from the Abyss, with a jagged-edged sword which flashed fire.

'What is that sword?' I asked him.

'This is the sword for the gluttonous,' he said. 'They are sent to this first jag because they discover all other sins through their gluttony. Slanderers who malign their neighbours behind their backs are sent to the second jag. Hypocrites – and others whom I dismember when I am so inclined – are sent to the third jag.'

'So do you do these things by yourself?'

'If only I could, I would go by myself through the whole world and rampage for three solid days,' Satan said. 'But I cannot, nor can any of the six hundred. We have other lesser minions to whom we give orders and whom we kit out with various hooks. We send them out hunting and they catch men's souls for us by baiting them with different delicacies – drunkenness, frivolity, slander, hypocrisy, indulgence, sexual immorality and other trifles from their stores.

'Let me tell you the other angels' names. The angel of hail is called Mermeoth, and he holds the hail over his head, and my servants adjure him and send him where they want. There are other angels over the hail, as well as other angels over the thunder, and still others over the lightning. But when a certain spirit wants to go off either through the land or the sea, the angels send fiery stones and set fire to their limbs.'

'Hush now, subterranean serpent!' Bartholomew said.

'I can tell you a lot about these angels,' said Beliar. 'These are the ones who roam together across the heavenly and earthly realms: Mermeoth, Honomatath, Douth, Melioth, Charouth, Graphathas, Hoethra, Nephonos and Khalkatoura. They spread over the heavenly, earthly, and subterranean realms.'

'Hush now – desist!' Bartholomew said. 'I must pray to my Lord.'

Bartholomew began to speak, falling on his face and hurling his head to the ground.

'Lord Jesus Christ, that great and glorious name. All the choirs of angels praise you, Master! My lips are not worthy, yet I am an instrument for your praise, Master. Hear me your servant, and as you chose me from my tax office and did not leave me to carry on living in my former exploits, Lord Jesus Christ hear me and have mercy on sinful men.'

After he had spoken, the Lord said to him, 'Get up and put to flight that figure uttering with a groan "Let me tell you the rest!" '

Bartholomew lifted Satan up. 'Go to your habitat, you along with your tests,' he said to him. 'The Lord is merciful to the whole world.'

'Let me explain to you,' the devil said, 'how I was cast here and how the Lord made man. I was going about in the world, and God said to Michael, "Bring me a clod of earth from each of the four corners of the earth, and water from each of the four rivers of Paradise." When Michael had brought them, God made Adam in the east of the world by shaping the formless earth, stretching his sinews and veins, setting them in harmony. Then Michael bowed down before him. Michael was the first to bow down to him, because Adam was the image of God.'*

'When I came from the edge of the earth, Michael said to me, "Worship the image of God which he made in his own likeness."

' "I am fire from fire!" I replied. "I was the first angel to be made! Am I to worship a material clod of earth?"

' "Worship him," Michael said. "Otherwise God will be angry with you."

' "God will not be angry with me," I said to him. "Instead, I will make a throne of my own, opposite his throne, and I will be like him." Then God was angry with me, instructed the trapdoors of heaven to open, and cast me down.

'When I had been cast down, he also asked the six hundred under my charge if they were willing to worship Adam.

' "As we have seen our first angel act," they said, "we also are not going worship a being who is so inferior to us." Then along with me he cast down the six hundred.

'After being cast down to the earth, we were in a deep sleep for forty years. Then, when the sun shone seven times more brightly than fire, I suddenly woke up. I looked about me and saw the six hundred under my charge who had fallen asleep. I woke up my son, Salpsan, and planned with him how to deceive the man whose fault it was that I was cast down from heaven.

'This was my plan. I took a jar in my hand and poured in the sweat from my chest and my hair. Then I dipped it in the water sources from which the four rivers* flowed. When Eve drank from the water, she discovered desire. If she had not drunk from that water, she would have been impossible to deceive.'

Then Bartholomew ordered him back into Hell.

Bartholomew came to Jesus and fell at his feet.

'Abba,* Father,' he said, in tears, 'unsearchable to us! Word of the Father, whom the seven heavens can hardly contain, but who willed to be contained contentedly and painlessly within the body of the virgin. She did not realize she was carrying you, but you in your mind had fully planned it to happen, giving your gifts willingly to us before ever being exhorted to do so.

'You wore the crown of thorns, to make the precious crown of heaven permissible for us who repent. You were hanged on a tree so we could drink the wine of contrition. Your side was pierced with the lance to that you might fill us with your body and blood.

'You named the four rivers: the first, the Pishon, because of the faith which you proclaimed when you appeared in the world; the second the Gihon, because of the earthly existence of man; the third the Tigris, so you could indicate to us the consubstantial Trinity existing in heaven; the fourth, the Euphrates, because when you were present in the world you gladdened every soul through your incorruptible word.*

'My God, most great Father, King, Lord – save sinful men!'

When Bartholomew had finished praying, Jesus spoke to him.

'Bartholomew,' he said, 'the Father called me "Christ" so that I might come down to the earth and anoint all men who come to the olive tree of life. He called me "Jesus" so that by the power of God I might heal every sin of the ignorant,* and to enable men to bear divine things.'

'Lord,' Bartholomew asked again, 'should I reveal these mysteries to every person?'

'My beloved Bartholomew,' Jesus replied, 'entrust these things to whoever is faithful and can guard them for themselves. There are some who are worthy, and others to whom it is not right to entrust these things – for they are boastful, drunkards, arrogant, merciless, participants in idolatry, initiators of sexual immorality, slanderers, self-promoting teachers, doing whatever the works of the devil may be, and for this reason they are not worthy to be entrusted with such matters.

'They are hidden because of those who cannot accept them. But whoever can accept them will have a share of them. The reason I have spoken to you on this matter, my beloved, is that you are blessed, and all your kin are willingly entrusted with this word, because all those who can accept them will receive whatever they wish on the [day] of my judgement.'

Then I, Bartholomew, inscribed these things in my heart and took the hand of the lover of man. I began to rejoice!

> Glory to you, Lord Jesus Christ,
>   who granted to all your grace which all had observed.
>   Hallelujah!
> Glory to you, Lord – the life of sinners.
> Glory to you, Lord – death has been put to shame.
> Glory to you, Lord – the treasury of righteousness.
> We praise God!

When Bartholomew had said these things, Jesus took off his cloak and took the scarf from Bartholomew's neck.

'You are [. . .] to us. Hallelujah!' Jesus said, exultantly. 'You are meek and gentle to us. Hallelujah! Glory to you, Lord, for I grant gifts to all who desire me. Hallelujah! Glory to you Lord, for ever and ever, Amen. Hallelujah!'

When he had finished, the apostles kissed him and gave him the sign of loving peace.

5. Dialogue about grievous sins

'Show us, Lord,' Bartholomew said, 'what sin is the most serious of sins.'

'Amen I say to you,' Jesus said, 'of all sins the most serious is hypocritical slander. Because of such people the prophet said in the Psalm, *"The godless shall not rise at the judgement, nor sinners in the council of the righteous."** Nor will the godless rise at the judgement of my Father. Amen, Amen I say to you, everyone will be forgiven for every sin, but the sin against the Holy Spirit will not be forgiven.'

'What is the sin against the Holy Spirit?' Bartholomew asked.

'Whoever declares a word against anyone who is a servant of my holy Father also blasphemes against the Holy Spirit. But anyone who serves God reverently is worthy of the Holy Spirit, while the person who speaks anything evil against him will not be forgiven. Woe to whoever swears "by God's head"! He is not even really forswearing him. For God Most High has twelve peaks, because he is truth and in him there is no deceit or false oath.

'As for you, then, go and preach the word of truth to all nations. You, Bartholomew, preach to everyone who wants this word, and whoever believes in it will have everlasting life.'

'Lord,' Bartholomew said, 'if someone commits a sin in the body, what is their punishment?'

'It is better if the baptized person keeps his baptism blameless. The pleasure of the flesh will become an attraction, however. Monogamy is a solemn matter. Truly I say to you, after a third wife, the sinner is unworthy of God. Preach to everyone the need to keep such instructions. I am inseparable from you, supplying you with the Holy Spirit.'

Epilogue

Bartholomew along with the other apostles glorified God earnestly. 'Glory to you, Holy Father, unquenchable sun – unsurpassable, abundantly flaming. To you be glory, to you be honour and worship for ever and ever. Amen!'

37 The Sophia of Jesus Christ

(late second to mid-third century CE*)*

INTRODUCTION

The *Sophia of Jesus Christ* is a clear example of a genre which
we have seen in the *Gospel of Judas* and will appear again later
in the *Gospel of the Egyptians*, namely a revelation of knowledge which consists of an elaborate myth (see pp. 200–203,
342–354). As in the *Gospel of Judas*, the myth is punctuated by
dialogue in which particular questions from the disciples draw
out what the author wants to communicate, but here the dialogue takes place after the resurrection.

In this myth, the supreme being ('He who is') is called eternal Light, or the Forefather, or the Great Invisible Spirit. In
other texts, like the Gnostic *Apocryphon of John*, this same
figure is said to be impossible to describe: words like 'God' or
'being' are illegitimate terms to convey such transcendence.
After this supreme being, various other deities come into
existence in a sequence. Out of his desire to create entities to
share in his goodness, the Forefather generated 'Man'. This
event is not a true parallel to the Judaeo-Christian creation
story, however, because this 'Man' is still a heavenly being,
and there is still some way to go before the earthly realms are
reached.

This 'Man', or 'Father' (as opposed to 'Forefather'), has a
female consort, 'Great Sophia', and together they generate 'Son
of Man', who is also called Christ and who therefore seems to
be the same being who reveals this knowledge in dialogue with
the disciples in this text. This 'Son of Man', although (or
because?) he is androgynous, in turn has a consort – who may

simply be his female aspect. She is Sophia, a female deity distinct from the superior 'Great Sophia'. Again, this is still all within the heavenly realms.

Son of Man together with Sophia generates an All-begetting Light. This seems to be what is called the 'droplet' of light, consisting of the divine spirits of the true disciples on earth: this droplet of light has descended into the lower realms, into the material world.

This material realm appears to be a creation of Sophia, but an illegitimate one, because 'she willed from herself alone, without her male partner' (codex p. 118). As a consequence of her unilateral activity, in this philosophical system – following some strands of Greek philosophy and medicine – the resulting creature has substance (the female contribution) but no form (the male contribution). It is therefore a chaotic, amorphous blob – attempting to imitate the heavenly realms, but in fact a hideous distortion of them. However, when the light enters the material world, it brings form in some sense: not form to the material world itself, but to the souls or lives of the authentic, elite disciples ('the perfect') who have come into possession of true knowledge.

This is not the complete picture of salvation, however. The further event that is needed is the advent of the Saviour, who awakens this light within (which has come from the droplet), or – in another metaphor – breathes upon the chilled, numbed soul: it is then 'warmed by the breath of the great Light of the male' (p. 120), and so the 'deficiency' of the female (a common idea in this literature) is resolved.

There is also a host of angels, and also very frequently mentioned in this kind of literature are 'aeons', which are both personal heavenly beings and regions beyond the material world. In some texts their relations are clearly defined, but here in the *Sophia of Jesus Christ* it is very hard to fit them together. This is also true of the dramatis personae of the myth presented here, which should be taken with a pinch of salt. Some of the apparent incoherence in the designations and operations of the different figures probably arises because the *Sophia of Jesus Christ* is a reworking of another book, *Eugnostos the Blessed*.

This reworking has led to the abbreviation and omission of some important detail.

This work was obviously produced by and for a small, intellectual circle of Gnostic or Gnostic-related disciples. The work survives in two fairly complete Coptic manuscripts, which represent different translations of an underlying Greek original. (The page numbers indicated below are those of the slightly more complete Berlin manuscript.) A very small fragment of a Greek copy, from Oxyrhynchus, also survives. The original Greek composition probably comes from sometime between the late second and the mid-third century.

DRAMATIS PERSONAE

In the dialogue:
JESUS   *Saviour or Lord (possibly = Son of Man or All-begetting)*
PHILIP, MATTHEW, THOMAS, BARTHOLOMEW, AND MARY   *The disciples of Jesus*

In the mythology:
FOREFATHER   *The Infinite, unnameable Light, the Great Invisible Spirit*
FATHER, MAN   *The self-begotten Father, Autogenes, First Man, Adam*
GREAT SOPHIA   *His consort*
CHRIST, SON OF MAN   *Their son, immortal Androgynous Man, Jesus*
SOPHIA   *His consort, or female aspect*
THE ALL   *The spiritual realm*
THE ALL-BEGETTING   *The great Androgynous Light, All-begetting Saviour/Sophia*
THE ALL-DOMINANT   *Ruler of Chaos*
YALDABAOTH   *Ruler of the material realm (possibly = the All-dominant)*

TRANSLATION

[p. 77] The Wisdom of Jesus Christ

1. The risen Jesus appears to the disciples

After Jesus rose from the dead, his twelve disciples and the
seven women continued to follow him, and went to Galilee, up
the mountain called 'Divination [p. 78] and Joy'. When they
gathered together, they were puzzled about the nature of the
All, the plan of salvation, holy providence, and the virtue of
the powers: in short, about everything which the Saviour was
doing with them in the mystery of the holy plan of salvation.

The Saviour did not appear to them in the form he had taken
before, but as an invisible spirit. His likeness was the likeness
of a great angel of light, [p. 79] but his form I cannot describe.
No mortal flesh could take such a form, but only the pure,
perfect flesh like his, about which he taught us on the mountain called the 'Mount of Olives' in Galilee.

'Peace be with you,' Jesus said. 'My peace I give you.' They
all were amazed, as well as afraid. The Saviour laughed.

2. The folly of philosophical ideas of God

'What are you thinking about, and why are you puzzled?' he
said to them. 'What are you seeking?'

'The nature of the All, [p. 80] and the plan of salvation,' said
Philip.

'I want you to understand,' the Saviour said to them, 'that
every person who has been born on the earth since the foundation of the world until now is dust. Although they inquire into
who God is and what he is like, they have not found him. The
wisest among them have drawn comparisons from the ordering
of the world and its movement, but their comparisons have
not got to the truth. [p. 81] Philosophers have taken three views
on how the ordering is directed, and so they do not agree with
one another. Some of them say that the cosmos is self-directed.

Others say that a providence governs it. Still others maintain that it is fate. But it is none of these. The three aforementioned views are nowhere near the truth, for they are from human beings.

'I, however, have come from the infinite Light, and I am in this place (for I know him, the Light) so that I can speak [p. 82] to you the exact truth. For whatever is from itself is defiled life, because it is self-created; providence does not contain wisdom; fate has no perception.

'As for you who are permitted to know, who are worthy of knowledge – you will receive it because you who have not been begotten from the seed of "impure caressing", but by the First who was sent. For he is an immortal in the midst of mortals.'

3. He who exists

[p. 83] 'Lord,' asked Matthew, 'no one can find the truth except from you. Teach us the truth, then!'

'He who exists is ineffable,' the Saviour replied. 'No principality or power, and no subject or nature of any kind, has known him since the foundation of the world until now, except himself alone and whoever he desires to know him through me, who came from the first Light. From now on he will bring revelation to you through me. I am the great Saviour.

[p. 84] 'He is immortal, he is eternal. He is eternal and unborn, for whoever is born will perish. He is unbegotten, and has no beginning, for whoever has a beginning has an end. No one rules over him: he has no name, for whoever has a name is a creature of someone else.

'He is unnamed, with no human shape, for whoever has human shape is the creature of someone else. He has a form [p. 85] of his own, such as you have never seen and such as you have never apprehended. Indeed, it is an unfamiliar form, surpassing everything, more excellent than the universals. He perceives on every side, seeing himself from himself alone. He is infinite. He is imperishable. He is incomprehensible, everlasting, incomparable. He is good, and immutable. He has no deficiency. He is eternal. He is blessed. He is unintelligible, while always directing his intellect to himself. He is immeasurable and [p. 86] untraceable, perfect with no deficiency, incorruptibly blessed, and is called "Father of the All".'

4. 'He who exists' reveals through Autogenes

'Lord,' Philip said, 'how then did he appear to the perfect?'

'Before anything visible is revealed,' the Perfect Saviour replied, 'greatness and authority exist within him, and he contains the entirety of the universals, although nothing contains him. For he is entirely intellect, reflection and thought, as well as wisdom, reasoning [p. 87] and power. These are all equal powers, sources of the universals. Their whole species from beginning to end was in the foreknowledge of the infinite, unbegotten Father.'

'Lord, Saviour,' Thomas said, 'why have these things come to be? And why have these things been revealed?'

'I have come from the infinite,' the Perfect Saviour replied, 'to speak to you of everything. The Spirit who exists was a begetter. He had a begetting power, and a forming substance, such that the power of his [p. 88] wealth hidden within him might appear. Because of his kindness and love, he desired of his own will to beget fruit, so that he would not be alone in enjoying himself in his goodness, but that other spirits of the immoveable generation would give birth to bodies and fruits, glory and honour in incorruptibility and his infinite grace, so that the Spirit's goodness would appear through the divine Autogenes,* the Father of all imperishability and of those who came into being after them. But they had not yet come to appear. [p. 89] There is considerable difference among the imperishable beings.'

He then called out, 'Whoever has ears to hear of the infinite ones, let him hear. I am speaking to those who are awake.' He continued further: 'Everything which has come into being from what is perishable will perish, because it has come from what is perishable. Whatever has come from imperishability will never perish; it will remain imperishable, because it comes from imperishability. As most men have gone astray and not known this difference, they have died.'

[p. 90] 'Lord,' Mary said to him, 'how then can we know these things?'

'Come away from what are invisible,' the Perfect Saviour said, 'to the perfection of what are visible, and this emanation of thought will reveal to you how faith in the invisible revealed is to be found through the thought which appears, which belongs to the unbegotten Father. Whoever has ears to hear, let him hear.

'The Lord of the All is not called "Father" but "Forefather". [p. 91] For the Father is the beginning of those that will be revealed, while the other is the Forefather without beginning.

'Seeing himself within himself, as in a mirror, he appears like himself. But his likeness appeared as God and Self-father, and facing the one he faced, namely the unbegotten pre-existent Father. He is coeval with the Light which is in front of him, but he is not equal with him in power. After him, an abundance appeared [p. 92] facing him – all the self-generated beings who are coeval and equal in power, and innumerable glories.

'Their race is called "the indomitable generation" from which you yourselves appeared from the other humanity. That entire indomitable multitude are called "sons of the unbegotten Father, Saviour, Son, God". His likeness is among you.

'He is the unfathomable one, filled with every imperishable glory and [p. 93] inexpressible joy. All these have their rest in him as they remain rejoicing in inexpressible joy in his immutable glory and immeasurable gladness. This has never been heard or thought in any of the aeons or their worlds until now.'

5. Autogenes and Sophia reveal Immortal Man

'Lord, Saviour,' Matthew said to him, 'how did man appear?'

'I want you to understand,' the Perfect Saviour replied, 'the one who appeared before the All in infinity, [p. 94] the self-produced, self-created Father, perfect in the shining light. He is ineffable, contemplating the beginning so that his likeness might come to be a great power. The principle of that light appeared immediately as an immortal androgynous man so that through that immortal man people might reach salvation, and sober up from their oblivion through the interpreter who has been sent. He is with you until the end of the poverty imposed by the robbers.

'His consort is [p. 95] Great Sophia, who has been ordained since the beginning within him for a union, by the self-generated Father himself. Through the immortal man, the name appeared as the beginning, divinity and rule. For the Father called "Man" and "Father in himself" revealed this. He created a great aeon, called the Octad,* a monument to his greatness.

'This aeon was given great authority, and ruled over the impoverished creation. From that light and the triple-male Spirit of Sophia, his consort, he created for himself innumerable myriads of divinities, angels, and archangels, [p. 96] which serve him. For from this God, divinity and rule originated.

'For this reason he was called "God of gods" and "King of kings", the First Man who has his own intellect and thought within him, as he is wisdom, reflection, reasoning and power. Every attribute [p. 97] which exists is perfect and immortal, equal in incorruptibility while different in power (like the difference between a father and a son, between a son and a thought, or between thought and other things). As I said before, the monad is the first among the generated beings. But finally, he who revealed everything revealed all things by his power.

'From what was created, everything which was fashioned appeared. From what was fashioned, [p. 98] what took form appeared. From what took form, what is named appeared. For this reason, a difference came into being among what were unbegotten from the beginning to the end.'

6. The distinction between the Father (Man) and the Son of Man

'Why is he called in the Gospel "Man" and "Son of Man"?' Bartholomew asked. 'From which of them does the Son come?'

'I want you to understand,' the Holy One said to him, 'that the First Man is called "Begetter, Self-Perfected Intellect".

[p. 99] He reflected with his consort Great Sophia, and revealed his first-born, androgynous Son. This Son's male name is "First-begetting Son of God", who is Christ. His female name is "First-begetting Sophia, Mother of the All". Some call her "Love". The First-Begetter is called "Christ" because he has authority from his Father, and he made for himself from Spirit and Light an innumerable multitude of angels to [p. 100] attend him.'

'Lord,' his disciples said to him, 'give us revelation about the Father, the one called "Man", so that we will understand exactly his glory.'

'He who has ears to hear, let him hear,' the Perfect Saviour replied. 'The first begetting Father is called "Adam, the Eye of Light", because he came from the shining light, as did his holy and ineffable angels – [p. 101] those who are without shadow, and who delight and continue rejoicing in the reflective thought which they received from their Father.

'The whole kingdom of the Son of Man, who is called the Son of God, is filled with unspeakable joy which has no shadow, and with unchanging delight, as they rejoice over his incorruptible glory which has never been heard of until now, and has not appeared in the aeons which came into being after them or in [p. 102] their worlds. I have come from Autogenes and the first, infinite light, in order to disclose everything to you.'

7. The Son of Man and Sophia generate All-begetting Saviour/Sophia

'Lord,' his disciples continued, 'teach us clearly how these came down from the unrevealed beings, from the immortal one, to the mortal cosmos.'

'The Son of Man consented with his consort, Sophia,' the Perfect Saviour said, 'and revealed a [p. 103] great androgynous light. Its male name is "All-begetting Saviour", and its female name is a "All-begetting Sophia". Some call her "Pistis"*.

'All who come into the world, as a droplet from the light from him, are sent by him into the world of the All-Dominant, in order to be guarded by him. The fetter of oblivion chained the All-Dominant by the will of [p. 104] Sophia, so that through it everything of his "Pride" and "Blindness" and "Ignorance" (as he was called) might appear to the entire impoverished world.

'But I have come from the higher places,
by the will of the great Light.
I have untied that fetter!
I have broken the work of the thieves!
I have raised up that droplet sent from Sophia,
so that it bring forth abundant fruit through me,
and be perfect and without [p. 105] deficiency
and be united by me, the Great Saviour,
so that its glory be revealed,
so that Sophia is justified from that deficiency,
so that her sons are never again deficient
but reach honour and glory,
and ascend to their Father,
and know the words of the male light.

As for you who have been sent by the Son who was sent, so that you should bear light, and [p. 106] withdraw from the principalities' forgetfulness so that the "defiled caressing" does not appear again because of you: that activity is from the fearful fire which came from their carnality. Trample upon its intentions!'

8. The great aeons

Then Thomas spoke to Jesus:

'Lord, Saviour,' he said, 'how many aeons are superior to the heavens?'

'I praise you, my disciples,' the Perfect Saviour replied, 'for you are asking about the great aeons, because your own roots are in the infinite beings. [p. 107] Now, when those whom I mentioned before appeared, the Self-begetting Father first made twelve aeons to attend the twelve angels, which are perfect and good. Through these, deficiency appeared in the female.'

'How many aeons are there, after the infinite of the immortals?' Thomas asked.

'He who has ears to hear, let him [p. 108] hear,' the Perfect Saviour replied. 'The first aeon belongs to the Son of Man, who is called "First-begetter", or "Saviour who has Appeared". The second aeon belongs to the Man who is called "Adam, the Eye of Light". That which embraces these is the aeon which admits no rule over himself, the aeon which belongs to the infinite, eternal god Autogenes, the aeon of the aeons of the immortals within him – those immortals which I mentioned before above the seventh [p. 109] which appeared from Sophia, which is the first aeon. He, the immortal man, revealed aeons and powers and dominions, and granted authority to all those which had appeared in him, so that they might do their will until the last things, which are above Chaos.

'For these consented with each other, and revealed every greatness, and from the Spirit came a multitude of lights below the innumerable glories. These were called [p. 110] "In the beginning", that is, the first aeon with the second and the third. The first is called "Unity and Repose". (Each one has its own name.) The third aeon was named "Church" because of the great multitude which appeared – in one, many appeared. It is because the multitudes [p. 111] gather together as one that they are called "Church",* after the Church beyond which surpasses heaven. Because of this the Church of the eighth appeared as androgynous. It was called part male and part female. The male is called "Church", while the female was called "Zoë", so that it might appear that from the female [p. 112] all the aeons' life came to be.*

'Every name was taken from the Beginning, for from his consent with his thought the first powers appeared: these were called "gods". Now the gods of the gods from their intention revealed gods. Then the gods from their wisdom revealed lords of lords. Then the lords of lords from their thoughts revealed lords. Then the lords [p. 113] from their power revealed archangels. The archangels from their words revealed angels. From them the ideas and shapes and forms appeared, along with names for all the aeons with their worlds. The immortals just mentioned have authority from the power of the immortal Man who is called "Silence", because by wordless reflection, [p. 114] he perfected all his greatness. Since the incorruptible beings had authority, they each created for themselves in the eighth in the firmament a great kingdom, along with thrones and temples to their greatness. For all these came into being by the will of the mother of the All.'

9. The completion of the aeons

'Lord, Saviour,' the holy apostles said, 'reveal to us what are in these aeons. We have to ask!'

[p. 115] 'Whatever you ask,' the Perfect Saviour replied, 'I will tell you. They created for themselves hosts of angels, innumerable myriads to attend them in their glory. They also created virgin spirits – ineffable, shadowless lights. They have no suffering or weakness, but only will. This is how the aeons were completed, in an instant, along with the heavens and the firmaments (which are for the glory of the immortal Man [p. 116] and Sophia his consort) from where every aeon and world, along with those that appeared after them, took the pattern for creating the images of the skies of Chaos and their worlds. But every nature since the appearance of Chaos is in the light which shines without shadow. They exist in unspeakable joy, ineffable exultation and everlasting pleasure, as they take delight [p. 117] in their immutable glory and in the immeasurable repose indescribable in any of the aeons (as well as their powers) which came into being after them.

'All these that I have just mentioned, I have described for you so that you can shine in the light, even more brightly than they do.'

10. Sophia's illegitimate creatures

'Holy Lord,' Mary asked, 'from where have your disciples come? Where are they going? And what are they to do here?'

[p. 118] 'I want you to understand,' the Perfect Saviour replied, 'that Sophia is the mother of the All, and the consort. She willed from herself alone, without her male partner, that these things should come into being. But the will of the Father of the All, so that his inconceivable goodness would appear, created the veil to separate the immortals from those that came into being after them, so that what is reckoned to come into being would follow every aeon and Chaos, and so that the deficiency of the female would appear and it would come about that Error would contend with her. These became [p. 119] a veil composed of Spirit.'

11. The descent of the light into the lower realms

'From the aeons above the emanations of light, as I mentioned before, a droplet from the Light and the Spirit came down to the lower realms in Chaos which belong to the All-Dominant, so that their shapes would appear from that droplet. This is a condemnation for the Arch-Begetter, called Yaldabaoth.

'That droplet revealed their shapes through the breath, as a [p. 120] living soul. It grew cold and fell asleep in a stupor of the soul. But when it was warmed by the breath of the great Light of the male, and contemplated with thought, those who were in the world of Chaos took every name and everything in it, through that immortal one when the breath blew into him. But when they came into being by the will of the mother, Sophia, such that [p. 121] the immortal man might fit together garments in this realm for them, in condemnation of the robbers, he too welcomed the exhalation from the breath. But because he is ensouled, he has not been able to receive that power for himself until the number of Chaos is complete and the time appointed by the great angel is fulfilled.'

12. The salvation of Man

'I have now taught you about the immortal Man, and loosened the robbers' fetters around him, and broken through the gate of [p. 122] the merciless in their presence. I have brought low their plotting and they are all humiliated. They have risen from their sleep. The reason I have come to this place is so that they might be united with the Spirit and the breath, and that the two would become a single one, just as in the beginning. Then you will bear abundant fruit, and will ascend to him who exists from the beginning with the ineffable joy, glory, honour and grace of [p. 123] the Father of the All.

'Whoever knows the Father with pure knowledge will go to the Father, and rest in the unbegotten Father. But whoever knows him deficiently will exist in deficiency and have his rest in the eighth. Whoever knows the immortal Spirit of light in the Silence, through reflecting and approval in the truth, should bring me symbols of the invisible one, and he will become a light in the Spirit of [p. 124] silence. Whoever knows the Son of Man with knowledge and love should bring me a symbol of the Son of Man and go to the places with those who are in the eighth.

'Behold, I have revealed to you the name of the Perfect one, the whole desire of the mother of the holy angels: this is so that the male multitude will become complete here so that they might appear in all the aeons, from [p. 125] the infinite ones to those who have come into being in the untraceable wealth of the Great Invisible Spirit; and so that they receive all things from his goodness and wealth, [the rest] which has no kingdom over it.

'I have come from the First who was sent, to reveal to you the one who exists from the beginning, because of the arrogance of the Arch-Begetter and his angels, for they say of themselves that they are gods. I [p. 126] have come to rebuke their blindness, so that I might teach everyone about the God who is over the All.

'As for you then, trample upon their tombs! Put their plots to shame! Shatter the yoke they have imposed! Raise up what is mine! I have given you authority over all things as sons of the Light, for you to trample their power underfoot.'

13. The disappearance of the Saviour

These are the things which the blessed Saviour said. He then [p. 127] disappeared from them, but all the disciples were in a state of great, inexpressible joy in the Spirit from that day on. Then his disciples began to proclaim the gospel of God, the eternal imperishable Father. Amen!

The Sophia of Jesus Christ

V

OTHER GOSPEL TEXTS

Beginning of the *Gospel of Philip*
Nag Hammadi Codex II (4th–5th cent.)

38 The Gospel of Truth

(mid-second century CE)

INTRODUCTION

Unlike some apocryphal Gospels, which appear to relish arcane detail and consist of ill-formed prose, the *Gospel of Truth* is a work of philosophical depth and developed literary style. Its literary and theological character has led some scholars to claim that the work was written by the second-century teacher Valentinus, because the style and content of the work fit most closely with the movement which he pioneered. Even if authorship by Valentinus himself is something of a speculation, the work almost certainly belongs to his school of thought (labelled 'Valentinian'). Moreover, the second-century Christian writer Irenaeus specifically states that the Valentinians published a 'Gospel of Truth', the opening words of the text below. The main Coptic manuscript, once in the possession of Carl Jung and now residing in the Coptic Museum in Cairo, hails from the Nag Hammadi hoard discovered in the 1940s.

The *Gospel of Truth* is notable for its use of metaphor, and the mixed metaphors are theologically productive for the author. In the New Testament book of Revelation there is a scroll which no one except Christ can open, and this motif is taken over into the *Gospel of Truth*, describing Jesus as clothed in this scroll on the cross. The scroll is also identical with the 'book of life', in which the names of all the saved are written (codex pp. 19–21). The author additionally delights in etymology as a theological device, as for example where the opening word 'gospel' is explained: it means 'the revelation of hope', because the Greek-Coptic word *euangelion* is formed from the prefix *eu-* ('good',

'well', hence 'hope') and -*angelion* ('announcement', hence 'revelation'). The name 'Christ', a Greek word meaning 'anointed',
sets in train an extended metaphor about how the anointing
from the Father's mercy fills good vessels, whereas other jars are
in danger of cracking and losing their oil (p. 36).

The theology of the *Gospel of Truth* takes as its starting
point a primeval fall, a fall not in a this-worldly Eden but in a
mythological realm. Here the fall is not so much a moral fail-
ure, as in the Bible, but more of an inevitability. It comes about
because the Father, the supreme divinity, is intrinsically incomprehensible as a result of his transcendence. He is even unknowable to the spiritual realm of the 'All', which is somehow
also part of him. (The 'All' is the supernatural substance
containing the spiritual identities of Christian disciples.) Hence
this 'All', in its unavoidable ignorance of the Father, secedes
from him and, going off on its own, lapses into catastrophe. It
falls prey to 'Error', who weaves a matrix of matter which
earthly people think is real but is in fact merely illusion. The
'All' enveloped in this web of deceit is afflicted by two main
predicaments: *ignorance*, because the All does not know the
Father, and *emptiness*, or *deficiency*, because it has become disconnected from its source of divine life.

The solution to this twofold plight is found in Jesus. He is
also called the 'Word', because he is the primordial expression
(before his appearance on earth) of the thought of the Father.
He is also the Father's Son, and the 'name' of the Father: the
Father is unknowable, but this 'name' is the symbol through
which thought about the Father can take place, and by which
people can call upon the Father. In terms of salvation, Jesus 'is
knowledge and perfection' (p. 20). He is *knowledge*, providing
the solution to the plight of ignorance: his revelation brings the
truth about the Father. He is *perfection*, not so much in a moral
sense but in a metaphysical sense, so that the deficiency or emptiness of the All can be filled up again. Eventually, then, the All
is liberated from Error, and restored to union with the Father.

Like the Coptic *Gospel of Philip* (see pp. 359–390), another
Valentinian Gospel, the *Gospel of Truth* operates on two, even
three, levels. First, the whole history of salvation is played out

on an abstract plane, in a primeval mythological drama. Second, it also takes place in real (or for the author, *unreal*) space and time. Jesus' teaching in his earthly ministry mirrors the revelation of the Father's thought in the myth, and Jesus' death in particular is of real significance for salvation: in attacking Jesus' physical body, Error is actually attacking her own substance, and so she effectively commits suicide. Third, there is also a ritual dimension to be worked out in the present life of the Valentinian community which used the text. This is not a focus in the *Gospel of Truth*, but the references to anointing point to the ritual practice going on in the time and place of the readers.

The *Gospel of Truth* only survives complete in Coptic translation in a manuscript probably from the fourth century, but it goes back to a Greek original written in the second century.

DRAMATIS PERSONAE

THE FATHER *The supreme transcendent being*

JESUS CHRIST *The Son, or Word; the revelation of the Father's thought*

THE HOLY SPIRIT *The Father's Spirit bringing life to dead souls*

THE 'ALL' *Spiritual substance from the Father*

AEONS *Individual elements of the All*

ERROR *Creator of the illusory material world*

TRANSLATION

1. Introduction

[p. 17] The gospel of truth is a joy for those who have received from the Father of truth the gift of knowing him by the power of the Word who has come from the fullness in the Father's thought and intellect. This Word is called 'Saviour', referring to the name of the work which he was to carry out for the redemption of those who did not know the Father. The term 'gospel' means 'the revelation of hope'. It is a discovery for those who seek him.

2. The All's fall and Error's creation

Since the All sought after the one from whom it had come forth, and the All had been within the uncontainable and inconceivable one who surpasses all thought, ignorance of the Father brought about turmoil and fear. Now turmoil condensed like a mist, such that no one was able to see. For this reason, Error became powerful, and she worked upon her own matter in vain. Not knowing the truth, she assumed a form which powerfully manufactured an attractive substitute for the truth.

This, however, did nothing to diminish the uncontainable and inconceivable one, because turmoil and oblivion and the deceitful form were nothing, while the secure truth is unchangeable, imperturbable and absolute beauty. Show nothing but contempt, then, for this Error!

Thus, because Error had no root, she was in a fog, ignorant of the Father, but still prepared her works of oblivion and fear, so she could use them to entice those in the Middle* and so imprison them.

Now Error's oblivion did not come into the open. She was not [p. 18] [named] by the Father, nor did oblivion come into existence in the presence of the Father, even if it did come into existence because of him. What comes into existence in him is knowledge: this appeared so that oblivion would evaporate, and the Father would become known. Since oblivion came to exist because the Father was unknown, so, when the Father comes to be known, oblivion will thenceforth no longer exist.

3. The Father's saving purpose

This gospel of the Father who was sought revealed his perfect ones by his mercy, the hidden mystery, Jesus Christ. Through him, the Father illuminated those who because of the oblivion were in darkness. He illuminated them and showed them a way, and this way is the truth which he taught them.

4. Jesus' crucifixion and the destruction of Error

For this reason, Error grew furious at Jesus and persecuted him, but she was afflicted by him and brought to nothing! He was nailed to a tree but became a fruit of the Father's knowledge! He did not wreak destruction in being eaten; rather, he brought those who ate of him into being! They rejoiced in the discovery: them he discovered in himself, and him they discovered in themselves.

5. The All's need for salvation by the Father

The uncontainable and inconceivable perfect Father is the one who made the All. The All was within him, and the All had need of him. He kept their perfection in himself and did not give it to the All. (Not that the Father jealously refused it! How could there be jealousy between him and his own 'limbs'?) [p. 19] For if the aeon* had received the perfection which belonged to them, they would not have been able to come [back] to the Father. Hence he retained their perfection in himself, granting it to them as a way back to him, and giving them uniquely perfect knowledge. He it was who made the All, and the All was in him, and the All had need of him. It is like when there is a person whom some do not know, and he wants them to know him, and to love him. In the same way, what was the All lacking except the knowledge of the Father?

6. Jesus at school

Jesus became a calm and serene guide. He came into the midst of a school and spoke the word as a teacher. Those wise in their own eyes came to him and tested him. But he confounded them because they were empty. They hated him because they were not truly wise.

7. Jesus' illumination of his disciples

After all of them, children came to him. To them belongs the knowledge of the Father. When they became strong, they learned the forms of the Father's face. They knew and were known. They received glory and gave glory. In their hearts appeared the living book of the living, which is written in the thought and intellect [p. 20] of the Father and from before the foundation of the All has been in his impenetrable places. This book no one is able to take, since it is ordained that the one who does take it will be slaughtered. Of those who have believed and so received salvation, none was revealed until that book had come into their midst. The reason the merciful and faithful Jesus was patient as he accepted his sufferings, until he took up that book, was that he knew that his death meant life for the many.

8. Jesus' revelation through the cross

Just as when before a will is opened the estate of the house-holder who has died is secret, so it is in the case of the All which is hidden as long as the Father of the All is invisible (since he is uniquely from himself, the one from whom every place comes). The purpose for which Jesus appeared, clothed himself with that book and was nailed to a tree, was to publish the Father's decree on the cross.

9. Jesus' death and descent into the void

What magnificent teaching! He drags himself down to death, though clothed in eternal life! He stripped himself of his perishable rags, and clothed himself with that imperishability which no one can take from him! He journeyed into the empty spaces of fear, and he passed by those who were stripped by oblivion, since he is knowledge and perfection, proclaiming the things which are in the heart [p. 21] [. . .] the teaching for those who learn. Those who learn are the living, who are written in the book of the living. They learn their own selves as they receive themselves from the Father when they return to him once again.

10. The need for the All's return to the Father

Since the All's perfection is in the Father, the All must ascend to him. Then, when each comes to know, he receives what are his and draws them to himself. For the one who is ignorant is deficient, and it is a great deficiency, since he is deficient in what will perfect him. Since the perfection of the All is in the Father, the All must ascend to him. Then each one receives what is his own and which the Father wrote down in advance when he prepared them to be given to those who came forth from him.

11. The ignorant destined for perdition

Those whose names he foreknew were called at the end, since each one who knows has a name which the Father proclaims. One whose name has not been spoken is unknowing. Indeed, how can someone hear if his name has not been called? For the one who is unknowing to the end is a fabrication of oblivion, and will be dissolved with that oblivion. Otherwise, why do these contemptible ones have no [p. 22] name and have no voice?

12. The illumination of those who are called

Therefore, whoever knows is from above. If he is called, he hears and makes reply. He turns to the one who calls him, he ascends to him and understands how he is called. Since he knows, he does the will of the one who called him. He wants to please him, and he finds rest. The name of each one comes to whoever knows, and so he understands where he has come from and where he is going. He understands as one who has been drunk but turns from his drunkenness. He returns to himself and establishes what is his own.

13. The mystery of the All's secession from the Father

He has turned many from Error and flew ahead of them to the places from which they moved away when they accepted Error because of the depth of him who surrounds every place (while there is nothing which surrounds him). It is a great wonder that they were in the Father but did not know him, and were able to depart of their own volition. Since they could not receive themselves and know the one in whom they existed unless his will came forth from him, he revealed it as knowledge with which all his emanations were in harmony.

14. The Father's revelation to the aeons

This is the knowledge of the living book which he [p. 23] revealed to the aeons at the end as his letters. When he reveals, they speak. They are not passages of vowels or consonants which are deficient in voice, and which a person could pronounce while thinking of something empty. They are letters of truth, and are spoken only when they are known. Each letter is a perfect thought, like a whole book, because they are letters written by the Unity. The Father wrote them for the aeons so they would know the Father by his letters.

His wisdom meditates upon the Word.
His teaching speaks it.
His knowledge has revealed it.
His patience is a crown upon it.
His joy is in harmony with it.
His glory has exalted it.
His form has revealed it.
His rest has received it to him.
His love made a body upon it.
His faithfulness has embraced it!

This is how the Father's Word, which is the fruit [p. 24] of his heart and the form of the face of his will, goes forth in the All and upholds it. He elects the All, and also takes the form of the face of the All, purifying it and returning it into the Father and into the Mother, Jesus who is boundless sweetness.

The Father unfolds his bosom – his bosom is the Holy Spirit. He reveals what is hidden of him – what is hidden of him is his Son – so that by the Father's compassion the aeons would know him and cease their toiling, and seek the Father, rest there in him, and know that this is rest.

15. Jesus brings perfection to what is deficient

When he filled up the deficiency, he dissolved its form – that form is the world in which he served. For where there is envy and strife, there is deficiency; but where there is unity, there is perfection.

Since deficiency came about because the Father was not known, when the Father comes to be known deficiency will thenceforth be no more. It is just as when a person is ignorant: when he comes to know, his ignorance is thereby dissolved. Or again, just as [p. 25] when light appears it dissolves darkness, so also deficiency is dissolved by perfection. The form, then, no longer appears, but will be dissolved by harmonious unity. For at present their works remain scattered, but in due time unity will fill the spaces. In unity each one will receive himself; in knowledge he will purify himself, from multiplicity into unity, consuming like a fire the matter in him, and the darkness by light, and death by life.

16. The illustration of moving house

Now if these things have come to pass for each one of us, then we must think on the All so the house will be solitary and quiet for unity. It is like when people move house, and have vessels which in places are not sound and get broken: the householder does not suffer loss but rejoices, because in place of those bad vessels there are full ones which are in perfect condition. For this is the judgement which has come forth from [p. 26] above: it pronounces a verdict upon everyone, and is a double-edged sword, drawn and slicing this way and that.

17. Jesus' incarnation in the material realm

When the Word, who is within those who speak him, came into the Middle, he was not a mere voice but took a body. A great disturbance occurred among the vessels, with some being emptied and others being half-filled, some being topped up and others being poured out, some being purified, others getting broken. All the spaces were moved and disturbed because they did not have fixture and stability.

18. Jesus' death destroys Error

Error grew anxious, not knowing what to do; she grieved and mourned, slashing herself because she had no understanding. Since knowledge, which brings destruction to her and all her emanations, approached her, Error proved empty because she has nothing in her.

19. The advent of truth in the world

Truth came into the Middle and all its emanations knew it and greeted the true Father perfect in power; this truth joined them with the Father. For everyone who loves the truth – truth which is the mouth [p. 27] of the Father just as his tongue is the Holy Spirit – and is bound to the truth, is bound to the mouth of the Father. From the Father's tongue, he receives the Holy Spirit since this is the revelation from the Father and his unfolding to his aeons.

20. The potential existence of those the Father will call

He revealed what was hidden of himself, and he explained it. For who can contain anything, except the Father alone? All the spaces are his emanations, which have come to know that they originated from him, like children from a grown man. They knew that they had not yet received form, nor had they yet received a name; but the Father begets each one, and then they receive the form of knowledge of him – otherwise they would be in him but not know him.

The Father is perfect in knowledge of all the spaces in him. If he wills, he reveals the one he wills, by giving a form and a name to him. And he gives him a name so that he might come to be. Those who have not yet come into being are unknowing of the one who made them.

I am not saying that these are nothing before they come into being. No, they exist [p. 28] in the one who is to will that they come into existence if he wills it, at a 'subsequent' moment, so to speak. Before all things are revealed he knows what he will bring forth. But the fruit which is not yet revealed neither knows anything, nor does anything. Therefore every space which exists in the Father is from him who exists, and who established it from what does not exist. For the one who does not have a root does not have fruit either. He may think to himself, 'I have come into being!' And yet he will be the cause of his own dissolution. For this reason, the one who has not existed at all will not come into being. What is it, then, that he wished this person to think? 'I have come into being as shadows and apparitions in the night do.' When the light shines upon the fear which that person experienced, he understands that it was nothing.

21. The consequences of ignorance of the Father

This is how it is for those who were ignorant of the Father. [p. 29] They did not look at him, since to them he was terrifying, disturbing, eviscerating, perplexing, and brought disintegration. They were subject to many illusions and vain, ignorant thoughts at work upon them because of him, like those who are fast asleep and find themselves in disturbing dreams – either running somewhere or unable to escape being chased, or hitting people or themselves being hit, or falling from heights or flying up through the air without any wings; still other times there are people killing them, though no one had been in pursuit, or they themselves are killing their neighbours with whose blood they are stained.

22. Awakening from ignorance of the Father

Up until the time when those who go about in all these things wake up, those in the thick of all these disturbances see nothing, because these things are nothing. So it is for those who have cast off ignorance like sleep, and do not think of it as anything, nor do they think of its [p. 30] events as events which are solid. Rather, they dismiss them as a dream in the night.

The knowledge of the Father they esteem as the dawn. Just as each person who was asleep acted in this way at the time when he was unknowing, so, conversely, he comes to know as if he has woken up. (Happy is the one who turns himself back and wakes up, and blessed is the one who has opened the eyes of the blind!) The Spirit, rushing from waking him up, ran after him and extended his hand to the one who was lying flat on the ground, and stood him up on his feet as he had not yet risen up. He granted them the means of understanding the knowledge of the Father and the revelation of the Son. For when they saw him and heard him, he granted them the taste and smell and grasp of the beloved Son.

23. The distinction between material and spiritual human beings

When he appeared, he declared the uncontainable Father to them. He breathed into them what is in Thought, doing his will. Receiving the light, then, many were turned [p. 31] to him. The material ones,* however, were strangers and did not see his likeness, and did not know him. For he came by means of the form of flesh, yet nothing blocked his path because his indestructibility meant that he could not be grasped. Furthermore, he spoke what was new because he spoke what was in the heart of the Father, and brought forth the word that had no deficiency. The light spoke through his mouth, and his voice gave birth to life. He gave them thought and wisdom, mercy and salvation, and the Spirit of power from the illimitability and sweetness of the Father.

24. The dissolution of Error and Bondage

He put an end to punishments and torments because they were leading some, who were in need of mercy, astray from him and into Error and Bondage: these two he dissolved with his power and rebuked with his knowledge. He became a path for those who had gone astray, and knowledge for those who were ignorant, a discovery for those who were seeking, stability for those who were insecure and purity for those who were defiled.

25. The parable of the lost sheep

He was the shepherd who left behind the [p. 32] ninety-nine sheep that did not go astray and went searching for the one that did go astray. He rejoiced when he found it! This is because 'ninety-nine' is a number which is on the left hand which holds it, but the moment he finds the one, the whole number transfers to the right.* Just as what is deficient in one unit (that is to say, the whole right hand) draws what it lacks and receives it from the left hand transferring it to the right, so then the number becomes one hundred. The sign of what is in the word is the Father.

26. Jesus' teaching about the meaning of the Sabbath

He even worked on the Sabbath for the sheep which he found had fallen into the pit. He saved the life of the sheep, bringing it up out of the pit so that you, sons of the understanding within, would have understanding within of the nature of the Sabbath – the day on which it is not right for salvation to be idle so that you might speak from the day which is above. That day has no night, and from it comes light which never sets, because it is perfect.

27. Instructions to the reader

Speak from your heart, therefore, for you are the perfect day, and the light which never fails rests in you. Speak of the truth with those who seek after it, and of knowledge to those who have sinned in their error. [p. 33] Strengthen the feet of those who have stumbled, and stretch out your hands to those who are sick. Feed the hungry, and to those who are weary give rest; raise up those who wish to rise; awaken those who sleep. For you are the wisdom which strengthens [. . .]. If strength is used in this way, it becomes even stronger.

Take thought for yourself, not for other things which you have cast aside. Do not return to eat what you have thrown away! Do not be moth-eaten! Do not be worm-infested! For you have already cast it off. Do not become places for the devil, for you have already subdued him. Do not set up obstacles for yourselves: these will collapse as a rebuke to you. For the unrighteous one is nothing, doing more harm to himself than to the righteous. For the former does his deeds as an unrighteous person; the latter, as a righteous person, does his deeds in the presence of others.

Do the will of the Father, therefore, for you are from him, and the Father is sweetness and in his will is the good. He knows what are yours so that you might take rest upon them. For by their fruits what are yours are known: the children of the Father [p. 34] are his fragrance because they come from the grace of his face.

28. The Spirit draws the Father's fragrance back

For this reason the Father loves his fragrance and reveals it in every place. And if it mixes with matter, he grants his fragrance to the light, and in his quietness he makes it surpass every form of every sound. For it is not ears which smell the fragrance! Rather, it is the Spirit who can smell the fragrance and draws it to himself, and so it sinks into the fragrance of the Father. Nourishing it, the Father receives it to the place from where it came, taking it out of the former fragrance, which is cold. This is an ensouled* form, like cold water which has flowed in soil that is not solid, but which those who see it think is just earth. Then afterwards, if a gust of wind draws it, it evaporates and warms up. The fragrances, then, which are cold derive from division. This is why faith came. It dissolved the division and brought the hot fullness of love so that the cold would not come again but there would be perfect unity of thought.

29. Salvation as the filling of deficiency

This is the word of the good news, the discovery of the fullness for those who are awaiting [p. 35] the salvation which is to

come from on high. The awaited hope which they are expecting is their image, the light which has no shadow in it. At that
time indeed the fullness is about to come. The deficiency
belonging to matter has not come into being from the illimitability of the Father: he is coming to give an opportunity to the
deficiency, even though no one is able to say that the incorruptible one will 'come' like this. Rather, the depth of the Father
abounded and the thought of Error was not in his presence.

This is a thing which has fallen but which is easily made to
stand again, through the discovery of what came to the one
who was to turn back. For that return is called 'repentance'.

The reason that incorruptibility breathed forth and went
after the one who had sinned was so he would come to rest. For
forgiveness is what is left for the light in the deficiency, the
word of the fullness. The doctor rushes to the place where
there is sickness, because that is the inclination within him.
The one who is deficient, then, does not hide, because the doctor has what he lacks. In the same way, the fullness (which is
not deficient at all) fills the deficiency by the gift [p. 36] of filling the one who is deficient of himself, so that he might receive
grace. For when he was deficient, he did not have grace. For
this reason there was a diminishing in the place where grace
did not exist. But the moment they received what had once
been diminished, what had been deficient appeared as fullness,
which is the discovery of the true light which has shone upon
it because it is unchanging.

The reason Christ was declared among them was so that
those who were disturbed could receive a returning, and he
might anoint them with the chrism. This chrism is the Father's
mercy which he will bestow upon them. Those whom he has
anointed are those who have become perfect.

30. Human beings as full or empty vessels

Vessels which are full are 'anointed' with a seal. But when the
anointing of one is broken, the vessel becomes empty; and the
cause of it becoming deficient is the fact that its anointing has
gone. For then a gust of wind can draw it off by the power of

what is with it. But no seal is ever removed from the person who is without deficiency, nor is he ever emptied. Whatever he may lack, the perfect Father replenishes. He is good; he knows those he has sown, for he sowed them in his Paradise. This Paradise is his place of rest.

31. The Word as the expression of the Father's thought

This [p. 37] is the perfection in the Father's thought, and these are the words of his contemplation. Each of his words is the work of his singular will in the revelation of his Word. Ever since these words have been the depths of his thought, the pre-existent Word has come forth and revealed them together with an intellect speaking the single Word in silent grace. This Word was called thought, since they were in him before they were revealed. And it came to pass that the will of the one who willed first came forth at the time when he was pleased to do so. In this will the Father is at rest, and with it he is pleased.

32. The will of the Father

Nothing comes to pass apart from him, nor does anything come to pass apart from the Father's will; but his will is incomprehensible. The will is his trace, but no one can understand it. Nor can anyone track it and thereby grasp it. Rather, when he wills, what he wills (even if the sight of it is not visible in any way) is desire for the Father in the presence of God. For he knows the beginning and the end completely, and at the end he will seek them out. The end is reception of knowledge of him who is hidden: this is the Father, [p. 38] from whom the beginning came forth, and to whom all who come from him will return. They are revealed for the glory and joy of his name.

33. The Son as the name of the Father

The Father's name is the Son. In the beginning, he gave a name to the one who came forth from him, namely himself. And he generated him as a Son. He, the Father who possessed everything else which existed with him, gave his name which he possessed to him. He possesses the name and he possesses the Son. It is possible for him to be seen, but the name is invisible, for it alone is the mystery of the invisible one which comes to the ears completely filled with it by him. Truly, the Father's name is not spoken, but appears in the Son.

Great, then, is the name! Who is able to speak a name for him, the powerful name, except for him alone whose name it is, and the sons of the name? Among them the Father's name is at rest, and they in turn are at rest in his name. Since the Father is unbegotten, he alone could generate a name for himself before he set the aeons in order, so the Father's name would be in command over them as lord. He is the [p. 39] true name which is secure in his command, in perfect power. For the name does not originate in speech and everyday naming. No, his name is invisible. He alone gave himself the name, he alone seeing it, and he alone being able to give himself a name. A 'someone' who does not exist has no name. For what name could be given to a non-existent person? But the one who does exist exists also with his name.

He alone knows it and alone gives him a name. He is the Father; the Son is his name. He, then, did not keep himself hidden somehow, but since he existed, the Son alone named him. The name, then, is what belongs to the Father, as the Father's name is the beloved Son, because where except with the Father could he find a name?

But someone will probably ask, 'Who can name someone who pre-existed him? Do not [p. 40] children receive their names from those who generate them?' It is right for us to think first about the question of what the name is, because it is the true name. It is not the name from a father of his, because this one is the principal name. He, then, did not receive the name by borrowing a name as others conventionally do, as is the case with each person who is created. This is the principal name, and the name he gave himself is not a name shared by others. Rather, he is unnameable and ineffable, at least until the perfect one speaks it, and he alone. And he it is who is able to speak and to see the name.

When it was his pleasure that his spoken name should be his Son, and this one who proceeded from the depth should provide him with the name, he uttered his secrets, knowing that the Father is without evil. The reason he brought this one forth was so he would speak of the place, his place of rest from which he came forth, [p. 41] and give glory to the fullness, the name's greatness and the Father's sweetness.

34. The place of salvation

Of the place they came from each one will speak, and about the share from which he received his position. He will run to return again and to receive from that place, the place where he stands, tasting from that place, and being nourished and growing. And his place of rest is his fullness.

35. The emanations proceeding from the Father

All the Father's emanations, then, are fullnesses, and all his emanations are rooted in the one who caused them all to grow from himself. He gave them a limit. Each appeared so that from their thought [. . .]. For the place to which they send their thoughts is the root which bears them all aloft in exaltation to the Father. They have his head, which is rest for them, and they are embraced as they approach him to declare that they have received kisses from his face.

[p. 42] These do not appear as those who exalted themselves. Neither were they deficient in the glory of the Father, nor do they think of him as small or bitter or angry but as without evil, imperturbable, sweet, knowing every path before it comes into being and having no need to be taught anything.

36. The blessings of restoration to the Father

This is how it is for those who have possessions from above, from the immeasurable greatness, and who wait for the one unique and perfect being, who is there for them. They do not go down to hell, nor do they have envy or groaning, nor is there death in their midst. No, they rest there in the one who rests, not growing weary or twisting around the truth. Rather they themselves are truth. The Father is in them and they are in the Father, since they are perfect and without division in the true good. They impart no deficiency to anything, but they impart rest since they are refreshed in the Spirit and they listen to their roots as they are occupied with them, since they are those amidst whom he finds his root. And he does not forfeit his soul. This place is the place of the blessed.

37. The perfect fullness of salvation

Finally, then, may they understand, in their places, that it is not fitting for me [p. 43] – since I have come into being in the place of rest – to say anything more. Rather, I shall be in him, and continually occupied with the Father of the All and the true brethren. The Father's love is poured out upon them and there is no deficiency of him in their midst. They appear in the truth, existing in true eternal life. They speak of the perfect light, full of the Father's seed, and which is within him and in the fullness in which the Spirit rejoices and gives glory to the one in whom he existed, because he is good. His children are perfect and are worthy of his name. It is children of this kind whom the Father loves.

39 The Coptic Gospel of the Egyptians

(c. 150–300 CE)

INTRODUCTION

The *Gospel of the Egyptians*, also known as the *Holy Book of the Great Invisible Spirit*, can be a rather baffling work. It may be helpful to divide it into four parts. First, it begins with the generation of a bewildering array of deities who come into being as part of the heavenly bureaucracy, beginning with the Great Invisible Spirit, who emanates a trinity of Father, Mother and Son, each of whom in turn becomes differentiated into eight elements, and the pattern of eights continues later as well. Here the influence of Egyptian mythology is evident, as the 'Octads' or 'Ogdoads' in the *Gospel of the Egyptians* often consist of four male and female pairs. Similarly, the Egyptian cosmological text *On the Primaeval Ocean*, from the first half of the second century CE, refers to the gods and goddesses of 'the Ogdoad according to their names . . . Here are their names: Amun, Amunet, Heh, Hauhet, Kek, Kauket, Nun and Naunet' (tr. Mark Smith). The expansion of the divine realm continues throughout the first half of the work (Codex III, pp. 40–56), and the result is a magnificently fecund supra-mundane plane. Much of this expansion takes place through a deity making a request for an assisting power, and then receiving it.

A second section, which begins after an interval of 5,000 years, describes the emergence of the demonic realm (Codex III, pp. 56–60). The demonic beings who arrive on the scene include figures such as Saklas (which means 'fool') and Nebrouel ('Nimrod-God').

In the wake of this threatening realm's appearance, third

(Codex III, pp. 59–64), the divine Seth undertakes to rescue his seed, who are the heavenly spirits or identities of disciples on earth. Seth passes through three 'parousias', or comings, which are tribulations he must endure. Eventually Seth comes to earth, fused with the person of Jesus.

The last section of the work (Codex III, pp. 64–67) is concerned with the ritual activities of the group, which involve baptism and a series of 'renunciations'. The recitation and the hymn addressed to Jesus are presumably voiced by the baptismal candidate. The most curious element of the hymn is the chanting of the sequences of vowels, echoing the praise which the three Octads give to the Great Invisible Spirit (Codex III, pp. 44, 66), where the heavenly praise runs through all seven Greek vowels (*a*, *e*, *ē*, *i*, *o*, *u*, *ō*) twenty-two times each, and since there are twenty-two letters in the Hebrew or Aramaic alphabet, there is probably a sense of linguistic completeness implied in the adulation. There are also some meanings suggested in the sequences of vowels in both the heavenly and baptismal litanies: IĒOU is the series of vowels in the name of Jesus; EI is Greek for 'you are' or 'you exist'; AEI means 'for ever'; and AIŌ probably refers to the Greek spelling of 'aeon'. (See further the endnotes.) What might appear at first as gibberish, then, does have some meaning in places.

A conclusion (Codex III, p. 68) describes how Seth himself wrote the Gospel, taking 130 years over the composition – a rather surprising amount of labour for a work which can scarcely be described as a literary masterpiece. A coda also contains the various titles and a scribal note.

The specific religious outlook of the *Gospel of the Egyptians* corresponds to what we know of the Gnostics. This is evident partly from what is said of the nature of the creator god and his creation. The two 'generating spirits of earth' are both evil figures, with Nebrouel explicitly called a demon. The other, Saklas, declares, 'I, I am God, and apart from me there is no other!', making it clear that the infernal realm which he inhabits is utterly separated from the higher plane of the Great Invisible Spirit and his emanations. An evil creator, rather than one who is good, or simply ignorant, is a hallmark of Gnostic sects. The cast of characters also resembles those in other Gnostic works: the Great Invisible Spirit and Barbelo on the one hand and Saklas, Nimrod and the list of the sentinels of hell on the other (Codex III, p. 58), correspond closely to the *dramatis personae* of, for example, the *Gospel of Judas* (see pp. 200–203 above). As in other such texts, then, the goal of salvation in the *Gospel of the Egyptians* is not the redemption of the world, but total liberation from the material realm, which – like its creators – is evil. The salvation of the individual involves both knowledge and the ritual practices which are delineated at the end of the Gospel.

The work survives in two manuscripts from the Nag Hammadi hoard, and both probably date to the fourth or fifth century. The translation here aims to select the best readings from these two texts. (The page numbers included are those of the manuscript in Codex III, unless Codex IV is specified.) The original work, composed in Egypt in Greek, dates in all likelihood to sometime between around 150 and 300 CE. While the text of the two manuscripts is Coptic, some small phrases at the end are preserved in Greek, and are presented in archaic English to show the different tone. The *dramatis personae* below is very selective, including only the major figures, because in a sense the entirety of the *Gospel of the Egyptians* is a *dramatis personae*.

SELECT DRAMATIS PERSONAE

THE GREAT INVISIBLE SPIRIT *The most transcendent deity*
THE VIRGIN *Spirit's androgynous companion (Yoel, or Barbelo)*
THE TRIPLE-MALE CHILD *Third deity after the Spirit and the Virgin*
FATHER *First of a second series of deities (possibly = the Spirit)*
  HIS OCTAD
MOTHER *Second of the second series (possibly = the Virgin)*

HER OCTAD

SON *Third of the second series (possibly = the Triple-Male Child)*

HIS OCTAD

DOMEDON DOXOMEDON *A glorious realm, containing the Triple-Male Child*

THE GREAT CHRIST *Father of the Triple-Male Child*

ESEPHECH *The keeper of glory*

AUTOGENES *'Self-generated', father of Adamas*

HIS OCTAD

ADAMAS, THE MAN *Heavenly paradigm of Adam*

SETH, THE SON OF MAN *Heavenly paradigm of Seth, son of Adam*

THE SEED OF SETH *The spirits of Gnostic disciples*

SAKLAS AND NEBROUEL *Creators of the earth*

THEIR ATTENDANTS

PROVIDENCE *Personification of an element in the divine plan*

REPENTANCE *Personification of an element in the divine plan*

BAPTISMAL ATTENDANTS

THE ALL *The totality of the spiritual realm*

TRANSLATION

Introduction to the Great Invisible Spirit

[p. 40] The holy book of the [Egyptians], the book of the Great Invisible [Spirit], the unnameable Father, [who is] from the heights, who is the perfect light, the eternal light of the aeons; light in the silence in the Providence and silence of the Father; light in word and truth; light incorruptible; [p. 41] light unbounded; the radiance from the aeons of the light of the invisible, untraceable, ageless, unproclaimable Father; aeon of the aeons; self-generated, self-generating, self-emanating; the stranger; uninterpretable power of the ineffable Father.

Part I: The generations of the divinities

1. The Spirit's emanation of Father, Mother and Son

From him came forth three powers – the Father, the Mother and the Son – from themselves, from the living silence, the radiance from the incorruptible Father. They came forth from the silence of the unseen Father.

2. A reflected emanation of Son, Mother and Father

From that place there came forth Domedon Doxomedon,* the aeon of the aeons and the [light] of each of their powers. In this way the Son emanated fourth, the Mother [fifth] and the Father sixth. He was [. . .] unknown, untraceable among all the powers and incorruptible glories.

3. The eightfold expansions of Father, Mother and Son

From that place three powers came forth, [p. 42] the three Octads which the Father brought out from within himself in silence and Providence. These are the Father, the Mother and the Son:

> The first Octad, for whose sake the Triple-Male Child came forth:
>> Thought,
>> Reason,
>> Incorruptibility,
>> Eternal Life,
>> Will,
>> Intellect,
>> Foreknowledge,
>> The androgynous Father.
>
> The second Octadic power:
>> The Mother,
>> Virgin Barbelo,
>> Epititioch[. . .],

Adonai,
Memenaimen appointed over heaven,
Akroboriaror,
The uninterpretable power,
The ineffable Mother.
She emanated from herself, came forth and assented with
the Father of the silent silence.

The third Octadic power:
The Son,
of the silent silence;
The crown,
of the silent silence;
The glory,
of the Father;
The virtue,
of the [p. 43] Mother.
He brings forth from within himself the seven powers of
the light-power of the seven sounds.* The Word is their
completion.

These are the three powers, the three Octads that the Father in
his Providence brought forth from within himself – that is the
place from where he brought them forth.

4. The realm of Domedon Doxomedon and the Triple-Male Child

Domedon Doxomedon, the aeon of aeons, came forth along
with the throne within him and the powers which surround
him – the glories and the incorruptibilities. The father of the
great light who came forth from the silence is the great Doxomedon aeon in which the Triple-Male Child rests, and in
which the throne of his glory is established. This is his imperceptible name which is written on the wooden tablet [. . .] The
Word, the Father of the light of the All, is one, and came forth
from the silence, reposing in the silence, he whose [p. 44] name
is an invisible symbol.

5. The praise, request and gift of the three Octads

A secret invisible mystery came forth:*

I I I I I I I I I I I I I I I I I I I I I I
Ē Ē
O O O O O O O O O O O O O O O O O O O O O O
U U U U U U U U U U U U U U U U U U U U U U
E E E E E E E E E E E E E E E E E E E E E E
A A A A A A A A A A A A A A A A A A A A A A
Ō Ō

This is how the three powers praised the Great Invisible Spirit, unnameable, virginal, upon whom no one can call, and his female-male virgin.

They requested a power.

A silence of living silence came forth, glories and incorruptibilities among the aeons [. . .] additional myriads [. . .], the three males [. . .] male generations born filled the great Doxomedon aeon with the power of the Word of the fullness of light.

6. The praise, request and gift of the Triple-Male Child

[IV p. 55] Then the Triple-Male Child of the Great Christ, whom the [Great] Invisible Spirit – whose power was given the name Ainon* – had anointed, gave praise to
   the Great Invisible Spirit
   and his female-male virgin Yoel
   and the silently silent silence
   and the greatness
[. . .] ineffable [. . .] ineffable [. . .] unanswerable and uninterpretable, the first who was revealed, unproclaimable [. . .] [IV p. 56] wonderful [. . .] ineffable [. . .] all greatnesses, the greatness of the silence of silence there.

Having given praise, the [Triple-Male] Child asked for [a power] from the [Great Invisible Virgin] Spirit.

Then [. . .] revealed the place which [. . .] who sees glories

[. . .] treasures in a [. . .] [invisible] mysteries [. . .] of silence [. . .] male virgin [. . .].

Then [. . .] child Esephech appeared [. . .].

7. The completion of the five seals

This is how the [Father]-Mother-Son came to completion, the five seals, the unconquerable power which is the great [. . .] of [IV p. 57] all the undefiled ones [. . .] holy [. . .] end [. . .] defile and [. . .] are powers and [. . .] and undefiled [. . .] they came forth [. . .] forth [. . .] which will [. . .] He brought [. . .] to the imperceptible hidden [. . .] hidden [. . .] him in the [. . .] aeons [. . .] and [. . .] each [. . .] innumerable myriads surround [. . .] [IV p. 58] [. . .] glories and undefiled ones [. . .] and they [. . .] the Father [and] the Mother [and] the Son and the whole afore-mentioned [. . .] and the five seals and the mystery of [. . .] They appeared [. . .] set over [. . .] and the aeons [. . .] truth [. . .] and the [. . .] eternal [. . .] and the truly eternal aeons.

Then Providence [came forth in the silence] and the living silence of the Spirit and a word [of] the Father and light [. . .] [IV p. 59] seals which the [Father] emanated from his own midst and Providence passed out of all the aforementioned aeons. And she established glorious thrones and innumerable [myriads] of angels surrounding them, powers and [undefiled] glories [. . .] and glorifying, all giving praise with one voice in an image [. . .] unsilent [. . .] the Father, the [Mother] and the Son [. . .] fullness [. . .] This is [. . .] Christ who is from [. . .] This is the undefiled child Telmael Telmachael Eli Eli Machar Machar Seth, [the] living power in [. . .] and the male virgin Youel who is with him, and Esephech the keeper [of the glory], the child of the child and the crown of his glory [. . .] of the five seals, the aforementioned Fullness.

8. Autogenes and Adamas

[IV p. 60] The great [. . .] living Autogenes, god in truth [. . .] there, the unbegotten nature. Speaking his name, I say '[. . .]

aia[. . .]thaothosth [. . .]', who is the son of the [Great] Christ, who is the son of the ineffable silence. He came forth from the Great [Invisible] and Undefiled [Spirit], the son of silence and silence. He appeared [. . .] invisible [. . .] secret [. . .] treasures [. . .] his glory. He appeared out of the [. . .] visible. He established the four [. . .]. With a word he established them.

He lifted up [praise] to
    the Great Invisible Virgin Spirit,
    [. . .] of the Father in the silence of the silence of living silence,
    where the Man rests [. . .] by [. . .].

Then [III p. 49] the great light-cloud came forth from there, the living power, the mother of the holy incorruptibles, the great power Mirothoë. She gave birth to the one whose name I will speak: 'You are one, you are one, you are one. EA EA EA three times.'*

For Adamas, the shining light, is from Man, the first Man through whom and for whom everything came into being, and without whom nothing came into being. The unthinkable, incomprehensible Father came forth and emanated from above to destroy the deficiency below.

9. The praise, request and gift of Autogenes and Adamas

Then the great Logos – the divine Autogenes – together with the incorruptible man Adamas, mingled with one another. A human word came into being, and the man came into being through a word.

He praised
    the Great Invisible, Incomprehensible Virgin Spirit,
    and the female-male virgin,
    and the Triple-Male Child,
    [p. 50] and the female-male [virgin] Youel,
    and Esephech the keeper of glory,
    the child of the child,
    and the crown of his glory,
    and the great Doxomedon aeon

and the thrones within him
and the powers which surround him – the glories and the
   incorruptibles
and their aforementioned complete fullness,
and the aerial earth – the receiver of god, the place where the
holy men of the great light, men of the Father (the living Father)
of the silent silence, take their image, and their aforementioned
complete fullness.

The great Logos, the divine Autogenes, along with the incorruptible man Adamas, both gave praise.

They requested power and eternal might for Autogenes for
the fullness of the four aeons, so that through them the glory
and the power of the invisible Father would be revealed [p. 51]
to the holy men of the great light. This is the light which comes
into the world which is in the image of the night.

The incorruptible man Adamas requested them to grant him
a son from himself so that that son might be the father of the
immovable, incorruptible generation so that in turn the silence
and the sound might be revealed by that generation, and by it
the dead aeon might raise itself up and be destroyed.

This is how the power of the great light came forth from
above. Luminescence gave birth to the four great luminaries,
Harmozel, Oroïael, Dauithe and Eleleth, along with the great
incorruptible Seth – the son of the incorruptible man, Adamas.

This is how the perfect Heptad became complete. It was in
the midst of hidden mysteries [p. 52] and when it receives the
glory, it is eleven Octads.

10. Consorts and servants for the luminaries

The Father nodded, and the whole Fullness gave approval, to
the luminaries. Therefore consorts came forth to complete the
Octad of the divine Autogenes:
   Grace for the first light, Harmozel,
   Perception for the second light, Oroïael,
   Understanding for the third light, Dauithe,
   and Wisdom for the fourth light, Eleleth.

This is the first Octad of divine Autogenes.

Again the Father nodded, and the whole Fullness gave approval, to the luminaries. Therefore servants came forth:

first, great Gamaliel for the first great light Harmozel,

then, great Gabriel for the second great light Oroïael,

then, great Samlo for the great light Dauithe,

then, great Abrasax for [p. 53] the great light Eleleth.

In turn, for them consorts came forth by approval of the Father's will:

Memory, for the first, great Gamaliel,

Love, for the second, great Gabriel,

Peace, for the third, great Samlo

Eternal Life, for the fourth, great Abrasax.

This is how the five Octads, forty in total, became complete, as an uninterpretable power.

11. The praise, request and gift of Autogenes and the Word

Then the great Logos Autogenes and the Word of the Fullness of the four lights praised

the Great Invisible Spirit, who is virginal and cannot be called upon,

and the female-male virgin,

and the great Doxomedon aeon,

and the thrones within them,

and the powers surrounding them,

and the glories,

and the authorities,

and the powers,

and the Triple-Male Child,

and the female-male virgin Youel,

and Esephech [p. 54] the keeper of glory,

[child] of the child,

and the crown of glory –

the entire fullness, along with all those glories, the boundless fullnesses and the nameless aeons.

This was so that they might name the Father 'the Fourth', along with the incorruptible generation, so that the Father's seed would be called 'the seed of the great Seth'.

Then everything shook, and the trembling gripped the incorruptibles. Then the Triple-Male Child came down from above to the ungenerated and the self-generating and those born from another generated being. The greatness, the entire greatness of the great Christ came forth, and he established thrones in glory, innumerable myriads in the four aeons surrounding them, innumerable myriads, powers and glories [p. 55] and incorruptibles. That is how they came forth.

12. The heavenly church

The incorruptible spiritual church grew in number in the four lights of the great Autogenes, living god of the truth. They praised and sang and gave glory, with one imaged voice, with mouths unresting, to the Father and the Mother and the Son and the whole aforementioned Fullness. The five seals, to which belong the myriads and those who rule over the aeons as well as those who bear the glory of the Governors, were instructed to reveal those who are worthy. Amen.

13. Seth's first praise, request and gift

Then the great Seth, the son of the incorruptible man Adamas, praised
the Great Invisible Virginal Spirit, who cannot be called upon or named,
and the female-male virgin,
and the Triple-Male Child
and the female-male virgin Youel,
and Esephech the keeper of glory,
and the crown of his glory,
the child of the child,
[p. 56] and the great Doxomedon aeons
and the aforementioned fullness with his seed.

And Seth requested that seed.

Then from that place came forth the great power of the great light Plesithea, the mother of the angels and mother of the lights, the glorious mother, the four-breasted virgin, who brings the fruit from the Gomorrah spring and 'Sodom', which is the fruit of the spring of Gomorrah within her. She came forth through the great Seth.

Then the great Seth rejoiced over the gift which had been given him through the incorruptible child. He received his seed from the four-breasted virgin, and placed it with him in the fourth aeon, in the third great light, Dauithe.

Part II: The emergence of the demonic realm

14. The realm of Chaos and Hell

After five thousand years, the great light Eleleth spoke.

'Let there be someone to reign over Chaos and Hell.'

And a cloud appeared, [p. 57] [whose name] was material Sophia. She looked out to [. . .], her face like [. . .] in appearance [. . .] blood.

And the [great] angel Gamaliel said [to the great Gabriel], servant of the luminary Oroïael, '[Let an] angel come forth to rule over Chaos [. . .].'

Then the cloud [. . .] from two Monads [. . .] single light. [. . .] which she placed [. . .] in the cloud above. [. . .]

Saklas the great [angel] saw the great demon Nebrouel, and they became a generating spirit of earth. [. . .] angels in attendance [. . .]. Saklas [. . .] to the great demon Nebrouel, 'Let there be twelve aeons in [. . .] aeon, worlds [. . .].'

The great angel [Saklas] said, by the will of [p. 58] Autogenes, '[. . .] seven in number [. . .].'

He said to the [. . .], 'Go all of you, [. . .] and reign over its [. . .].' So they each went [. . .] twelve.

The first angel is Athoth, whom human generations call [. . .];

The second is Harmas [. . .];

The third is [. . .];

The fourth is Yobel;
The fifth is Adonaios, called 'Sabaoth';
The sixth is [. . .], whom human generations call 'Sun';
The [seventh is . . .];
The eighth is Akiressina;
The ninth is Youbel;
The tenth is Harmoupiael;
The eleventh is Archir-[. . .];
The twelfth is [. . .].
These were stationed over Hell [. . .].
And after the establishment [. . .], Saklas said to his [. . .], 'I, I am God [. . .], and apart from me there is no other!' (He believed [p. 59] in his own nature.)

Part III: The salvation of Seth's seed

15. The descent of the voice and Repentance

Then a voice came forth from the heights. 'There is the Man and the Son of Man.' Because of the descent of the higher image which resembles its voice in the height of the image which looked out, through that higher image's looking out, the first form was constructed.

For this reason, Repentance came into being. She received her perfection and her power by the will of the Father and in the approval which he conferred upon the great, incorruptible and immovable generation of the great and powerful men of the great Seth. This was so that Seth would sow Repentance in the aeons which had been generated, so that through Repentance their deficiency would be replenished. For she came down from above to the world which is the image of night. When she came, she prayed for the defiled seed of the archon* of this aeon and of the authorities which had come into being from him, the defiled, perishable seed belonging to the god who generated the demons. She also prayed for the seed [p. 60] of Adam and of the great Seth, which resembles the sun.

16. The coming of Seth and his
seed among the aeons

Then the great angel Hormos came to establish the seed of the
great Seth in a holy vessel born of the Logos, both through
the virgins of the defiled seed of this aeon, and through the Holy
Spirit.

Then the great Seth came, and he brought his seed and
sowed it in the aeons which had been generated, whose number is the count of 'Sodom'. Some say that Sodom is the place
of the great Seth's pasture, and that Gomorrah is one and the
same, whereas others say that the great Seth carried his planting out of Gomorrah and planted it in a different place, which
he named Sodom.

This is the generation which came forth from Edokla, for by
a word she gave birth to truth and rightness, which are the
beginning of the seed of eternal life which exists with those
who persevere because they have knowledge of their emanation. They are the great, incorruptible generation which has
come forth through three [p. 61] worlds to the world.

17. The danger to Seth's seed

And the cataclysm came about as a type until the fulfilment of
the aeon. This will be sent into the world because of this generation. A conflagration will come about upon the earth, and
grace will be with those who are numbered among the generation through the prophets and the guardians who watch over
the life of this generation. Because of this generation there are
famines and plagues. These will occur because of the great
incorruptible generation. Because of this generation, trials
come – deception from false prophets.

18. Seth's second praise, request and gift

Then the great Seth saw the activity of the devil, his multitude
of forms, his machinations against the incorruptible and immovable generation, his terrible persecutions, his angels with

their trickery – all the ventures which were attempted against that generation.

Then the great Seth praised

the Great Invisible Virginal Spirit who cannot be called upon,

and the [p. 62] female-male virgin Barbelo,

and the Triple-Male Child Telmael Telmael Heli Heli Machar Machar Seth – the truly true living power,

and the female-male virgin Youel,

and Esephech the keeper of glory,

and the crown of his glory

and the great Doxomedon aeon,

and the thrones which are within him,

and the powers which surround them,

and the entire aforementioned fullness.

And Seth requested guards for his seed.

Then four hundred aerial angels came forth from the great aeons, and with them was the great Aerosiel and the great Selmechel, to guard the great incorruptible generation and its fruit, and the great men of the great Seth, from the time and season of truth and rightness until the fulfilment of the aeon and its archons – the archons whom the great judges have condemned to death.

19. Seth enters the fallen realm

Then the great Seth was sent forth by the four lights, by the will of Autogenes [p. 63] and the entire fullness, and by the gracious approval of the Great Invisible Spirit, and of the five seals and the entire fullness.

He passed through the three aforementioned advents – the cataclysm, the conflagration, and the judgement of the archons and powers and authorities, to save the generation that had gone astray; by the reconciliation of the world and by baptism through a body generated by the Logos which the great Seth mysteriously prepared for himself through the virgin. This was to bring to birth the holy ones:

through the Holy Spirit;

through the invisible, secret symbols;

by reconciling the world with the world;
through the renunciation of the world and the god of the
    thirteen aeons,
through the invocations of the holy ones,
        and of the ineffable ones,
        and of the incorruptible heart,
        and of the great light of the pre-existent Father,
        and of his Providence.

Through Providence, he decreed the holy baptism which surpasses heaven, by the incorruptible one generated by the
Logos [p. 64] and the living Jesus and the great Seth who
clothed himself with him. Through him he nailed the powers
of the thirteen aeons and confirmed those who bring forth
and those who take away, equipping them with the armoury
of knowledge of the truth in unconquerable, incorruptible
power.

Part IV: The baptismal ritual

20. The baptismal attendants

And there appeared for them:
    the great attendant Yesseus Mazareus Yessedekeus, the liv-
        ing water,
    the great governor James the great,
    Theopemptos,
    Isaouel,
    the overseers of the spring of truth – Micheus and Michar
        and Mnesinous,
    the overseer of the baptism of the living,
    the purifiers,
    Sesengenpharanges,
    the overseers of the gates of the waters – Micheus and
        Michar,
    the overseers of Mount Seldao and the olive trees,
    and those who receive the great Seth's great incorruptible
generation of powerful men,
    the servants of the four luminaries –

Gamaliel the great,
Gabriel the great,
Samlo the great,
and [p. 65] Abrasax the great,
the overseers of the sun and its dawning, Olses and Hypneus
and Eurymaeus,
the overseers of the entrance to rest in eternal life,
the presidents, Mixanther and Michanor,
the guardians of the souls of the elect, Akramas and
Strempsouchos,
the great power Telmachael Eli Eli Machar Machar Seth,
the Great Invisible Virgin Spirit who cannot be called upon
or named,
the Silence,
the great light Harmozel, the place of the living and true god
Autogenes,
and the incorruptible Man who is with him, Adamas,
the second light Oroïael, the place of the great Seth
and of Jesus to whom life belongs
and who came forth and crucified what is under the Law,
the third light, Dauithe, the place of the sons of the great Seth,
the fourth light, Eleleth, the place where the souls of those
sons rest,
the fifth light Yoel, who oversees the name of whoever is
permitted to baptize with the holy, incorruptible baptism
which surpasses heaven.

Henceforth, however, [p. 66] through the incorruptible man
Poimael and those who are worthy of invoking the renunciations and the five seals in the baptismal spring, they will know
those who receive them as they are taught of them. They will be
known by those who receive them, and will not taste death.

21. Baptismal hymn*

IE IEUS EO OU EO OUA – verily, verily!
O Yesseus Mazareus Yessedekeus,
Living water, child of the child,
Glorious name – verily, verily!

Aeon which existeth,
IIII ĒĒĒĒ EEEE OOOO UUUU ŌŌŌŌ AAAA – verily true!

EI AAAA ŌŌŌǪ existent one
seeing the aeons – verily true!

AEE Ē Ē ĒIII UUUUUU ŌŌŌŌŌŌŌ
Existent for ever and ever – verily true!

IEA AIŌ within, existent U!
Everlasting unto everlasting,
Thou art what thou art;
Thou art who thou art.

This great name of yours is upon me,
Autogenes with no deficiency,
who are not outside me.
I see you – you who are invisible before all,
For who can contain you with another sound?

22. The baptismal recitation

Now that [p. 67] I have known you,
I have mixed myself with the unchangeable one,
I have armed myself with an armoury of light,
and I have been illuminated.

The Mother was there because of the radiant beauty of grace.
Therefore I have spread out my closed hands.
I have received form in the circle of the riches
of the light which is within me,
which gives form to the multitude
born in the light where no accusation is brought.
I will speak of your glory truly, since I have comprehended you!

Thine, O Jesus – behold, everlasting O everlasting,
O Jesus, the aeon, aeon.
God of silence, I glorify you in your entirety.

You are my place of rest, O Son, ES ES O E,
formless one who exists among the formless beings,
existing, raising up the man in whom you will purify me for
    your life,
in accordance with your name which never fails.

For this reason I have mixed the fragrance of life within
with water as a type of all the archons,
so that I may live before you in the peace of the holy ones,
as one who exists for ever [p. 68] – verily, verily!

Conclusion

This is the book which the great Seth wrote, and which he
deposited in lofty mountains upon which the sun has not risen,
nor can it. Since the days of the prophets and the apostles and
the preachers, the name has in no way entered human thought,
nor could it, nor have human ears heard it.

The great Seth wrote this book letter by letter over one hundred and thirty years, and deposited it in the mountain called
'Charaxio', so that at the end of the times and the seasons – by
the will of the divine Autogenes and the complete Fullness,
through the gift of the Father's love which is untraceable and
inconceivable – it may go forth and appear to this incorruptible holy generation of the great Saviour and those who dwell
with them, in love, with the Great Invisible Eternal Spirit and
his only begotten Son and the eternal light [III 69] and his
great incorruptible consort and incorruptible Sophia and Barbelo and the entire fullness in eternity. Amen!

Scribe's epilogue

The Egyptian Gospel.
    The divinely written, holy and secret book.
    Grace, understanding, perception and wisdom be with him
who has copied it: beloved Eugnostus in the Spirit – in the flesh
my name is Concessus – and with my fellow luminaries in
incorruptibility.

Jesus Christ, the Son of God, and Saviour. ICHTHUS.*

The divinely written and holy book of the Great Invisible Spirit. Amen.

The Holy Book of the Great Invisible Spirit. Amen.

40 The Coptic Gospel of Philip

(second–third century CE)

INTRODUCTION

The *Gospel of Philip* is, frankly, a difficult text. This partly arises from its constant use of metaphor, which is characteristic of works from the Valentinian school (like the *Gospel of Truth*: see pp. 319–337). *Philip* also consists of disconnected sentences, rather than having a narrative structure or sequential argument, and so the statements can be hard to connect to one another. In form, it resembles the *Gospel of Thomas* and its series of 'logia'. Unlike *Thomas*, only a few of the sayings are attributed to Jesus (e.g. logia 54, 57, 69, 72), while most are presented as the authorial voice. The only apostle to whom a saying is attributed is Philip, in accordance with the naming of the work.

Like the individual sayings of *Thomas*, the statements in the *Gospel of Philip* are often either obscure ('God is a dyer') or truisms ('the dead cannot inherit'), but in both cases they are metaphors, as is the dominant style of Valentinian theologizing. Despite its discontinuous character, the *Gospel of Philip* does have a coherent theology along Valentinian lines. Four elements of this can be mentioned here.

First, understanding the nature of the cosmos is of central importance for the *Gospel of Philip*. In the Valentinian view, the world came about through a mistake, because the demiurge, or creator deity, did not have the power to make something everlasting, or the awareness to realize the problem with his handiwork (logion 99). In contrast to the orthodox view, where the creator is supreme and perfect, and the Gnostic view according to which the creator is evil, the view of the *Gospel of Philip* sits somewhere in between.

Second, unlike the Gnostic cosmos which is utterly devoid of truth, the *Gospel of Philip* teaches that this world below contains shards of truth which can be used, by those who have eyes to see, to understand the heavenly realm above. Hence, 'truth, which has existed from the beginning, is sown everywhere' (logion 16). A number of specific instances are given, hence for example the temple in Jerusalem is an image of the heavenly sanctuary above, sex is a picture of the celestial bridal chamber, and circumcision teaches the destruction of the flesh. These earthly signs are profoundly distorted, however, since demonic forces have got at them, persuading people that the material things and physical actions are the genuine article and concealing their true reference points. The institutions of our world require the Valentinian *savant* to decode them.

Third, in the *Gospel of Philip* as in the *Gospel of Truth*, Jesus is the Father's name. He is clearly a saviour figure throughout the Gospel, both in how he is depicted in his earthly ministry, and in what he accomplishes in the present ritual life of the group. As 'Christ', he is anointed by the Father; Jesus then in turn anointed the apostles who anointed others, and so on up to the present in an apostolic succession (logion 95). Again, even more so than in the *Gospel of Truth*, the Valentinian interest in decoding names such as 'Christ' is apparent.

Finally, the *Gospel of Philip* presents a multifaceted description of salvation. Salvation comes through Jesus' activity of redemption, rescue and ransom. It is being acquainted with the Father's name, but also involves a ritual process of a second baptism, an anointing with oil, or 'chrism' (logion 95). The disciple must come to know the truth and experience entry into the heavenly bridal chamber. The true disciple transcends this vale of tears and is reunited with the divine. This is referred to in logion 61 as the earth-bound 'image' (the female element) being united with the heavenly 'angel' (the male element), and this union with the divine is perhaps the dominant image of salvation in the work.

The *Gospel of Philip* survives only in a single manuscript, from Nag Hammadi, now housed in the Coptic Museum in

Cairo. The original Greek behind the Coptic text we now have is usually thought to come from the second or third century CE.

DRAMATIS PERSONAE

JESUS CHRIST
JOSEPH *The father of Jesus*
MARY (I) *The mother of Jesus*
MARY (II) *Jesus' sister*
MARY MAGDALENE *A female disciple*
THE APOSTLES *The twelve followers of Jesus*
PHILIP *One of the twelve, or possibly Philip 'the evangelist'*
LEVI *One of the twelve*
THE DISCIPLES *Other followers of Jesus*
FRIENDS OF THE APOSTLES *New Testament authors who were not apostles*

TRANSLATION

Logion 1

[p. 51] A Hebrew makes Hebrews, and those of this sort are called 'proselytes'. A proselyte, however, cannot make proselytes. [. . .]. Some are like [. . .] and they make others [p. 52] [. . .] It merely suffices for them that they exist.

Logion 2

The slave seeks only to be free. He does not seek his master's property. The son, however, not only is a son but also collects the inheritance from his father after him.

Logion 3

Those who inherit from the dead are themselves dead and inherit what is dead. Those who inherit from the living are alive and inherit what is living along with what is dead. Those who are dead do not inherit anything, for how could a dead person inherit? But if a dead person inherits from the living, he will not die: that dead person will have life in greater abundance.

Logion 4

A gentile does not die, for he has never lived such that he could die. The one who has believed in the truth has received life, and is at risk of dying because he is alive.

Logion 5

Ever since Christ came, the world has been created, cities have been adorned, and the dead have been carried off.

Logion 6

When we were Hebrews, we were orphans. We had our mother, but when we became Christians we possessed both Father and Mother.

Logia 7-8

Those who sow in winter harvest in summer – the 'winter' is the world, the 'summer' is the other aeon.* Let us sow in the world so that we might harvest in 'summer'. This is why it is not right to pray in winter. The consequence of winter is summer. But if someone harvests in winter, he will not really harvest but will only pick, [*Logion 8*] since it will be the kind of harvest which yields no produce. Not only does he come forth [. . .] but even on the Sabbath [. . .] it is unfruitful.

Logion 9

Christ came [p. 53] to ransom some, to rescue others, and to redeem still others. He ransomed strangers and made them his own. He set apart those who were his own, those whom he had laid down as deposits by his own will. It was not only when he appeared that he laid down his soul as he willed to do, but ever since the world began he has laid down his soul when he wills. Then he came early to take it up since it had been laid down as deposits. It fell among thieves and they took it captive. He rescued it, however, and redeemed both those who are good in this world and those who are evil.

Logion 10

Light and dark, life and death, right and left – these are siblings to one another and inseparable. For this reason the good are not good, nor are the evil evil; nor is life life or death death. Each one will therefore break down to its first principle. Those who transcend the world, however, are unbreakable and eternal.

Logion 11

The names which are given to things of this world are very deceptive. For they turn the mind from what is genuine to what is not. Hence the person who hears the word 'god' does not think of what is genuine but of what is not. This is also the case with the words 'Father', 'Son', 'Holy Spirit', and 'life', 'light', 'resurrection' and 'church', and everything else. People using these words are not thinking of what is genuine but of what is not genuine – unless they have learned what is genuine. The names which one hears are of this world [. . .]. [p. 54] They deceive. If they were in the aeon, they would never be named in the world, or be attached to things in this world. They would have their purpose in the aeon.

Logia 12-13

One name is not spoken in the world – the name which the Father gave to the Son. It is above everything: it is the Father's name. For the Son would not have been 'Father' unless he had put on the name of the Father. Those who possess this name think on it, but do not say it. Those who do not possess it cannot think on it.

The truth, however, has given birth to names in this world for our sake. We cannot learn about the truth without names. The truth is singular and is multiple, and for our sakes it teaches this singular thing in multiple ways, out of kindness to us. [*Logion 13*] The archons* wanted to deceive man, since they saw that he possessed kinship with what is truly good. Therefore they took the names of good things and attached them to what is not good, so that by the names they could deceive him and bind people to what is not good. In addition, as if they were doing them a favour, they removed the names from what is not good and set them upon what is good. They knew them, for they wished to take the free man and enslave him to them for ever.

Logion 14

There are powers existing which give [. . .] man, not wanting him to be saved, so they become a [. . .]. For if man is saved, sacrifices [. . .] and they offered up wild beasts [p. 55] to the powers. For those to whom they offered up sacrifices were beasts. The animals were offered up alive, but when they had been offered they were dead. Man they offered up to God dead, but he lived.

Logion 15

Before Christ came, there was no bread in the world, just as Paradise where Adam lived had many trees to feed the wild animals but had no wheat to feed man. Man fed like the wild animals. But when Christ, the perfect man, came, he brought bread from heaven so that man could be fed with human food.

Logion 16

The archons thought that it was by their own power and will that they did what they did, but the Holy Spirit was secretly working everything out through them as he willed! The truth is sown everywhere, and has existed from the beginning. There are many who see it being sown, but few who see it harvested.

Logion 17

Some say that Mary conceived by the Holy Spirit. They are deceived! They do not know what they are talking about! When did a woman ever conceive from a woman? Mary was a virgin whom no power defiled. She is a great anathema to the Hebrews who are apostles and friends of the apostles. This virgin whom no power defiled is [. . .] the powers defiled them. And the Lord would not have said 'My Father in heaven'* unless he had another father. Otherwise he would simply have said ['My Father'].

Logion 18

The Lord said to the disciples, [p. 56] ['Bring something] from every house into the Father's house, but do not steal what is in the Father's house and take it away.'

Logia 19-20

'Jesus' is a hidden name, 'Christ' is a manifest name. Therefore Jesus is not a word in any language, but Jesus is his name, by which he is called. His name 'Christ', however, is in Aramaic Messias but in Greek Christos. Perhaps everyone else has a word for it in their own language. 'Nazarene' is a manifestation of what is hidden.* [Logion 20] Christ has everything in him, whether man or angel or mystery or Father.

Logion 21

Those who say that the Lord first died and then rose are wrong. For he first rose and then died. Unless someone first obtains resurrection, he cannot die. As surely as God lives, he would [. . .].

Logion 22

No one hides an important and precious object in something important, but many times one casts countless thousands into something worth an *assarion*.† So it is with the soul. It is a precious thing, but has come to be in a despicable body.

Logia 23-24

Some are afraid of being raised naked. That is why they want to be raised in the flesh. They do not know that those who bear flesh are the naked ones! Those who [. . .] naked [. . .] are not naked. 'Flesh [and blood] cannot inherit the kingdom of God.'* What is that flesh which does not [p. 57] inherit? That which clothes us. What, though, is the flesh which does inherit? That of Jesus and his blood. That is why he said, 'Whoever does not eat my flesh and drink my blood has no life in him.' What is this flesh? His flesh is the word – and his blood is the Holy Spirit. Whoever receives these has food and drink and clothing.

I also object to others who say, 'The flesh will not rise.' A plague on both their houses! You say, 'The flesh will not rise.' Then tell me what will rise, so we may pay tribute to you! You say, 'It is the Spirit in the flesh,' or, 'It is this light in the flesh,' or again, 'It is word within the flesh.' But whatever you describe you are not talking about anything outside the flesh! Resurrection in this flesh is necessary, for everything exists in it. [*Logion* 24] In this world, those who wear clothes are better than their clothes. In the kingdom of heaven, the clothes are better than those who wear them.

Logion 25

By water and fire everywhere is cleansed, the manifest by the manifest, and the hidden by the hidden. Some are hidden by what is manifest. There is water in water, and there is fire in chrism.

Logion 26

Jesus took everyone by stealth. For he did not appear as he was, but in a manner in which he could be seen. He appeared to all: to the great he [appeared] great, to the small he appeared small; he [appeared] [p. 58] to the angels as an angel, and to people as a man. For this reason his word hid him from everyone. Some saw him and thought they were seeing their own selves, but when he appeared to his disciples in glory on the mountain, he was not small! He became great, but he also made his disciples great so that they could see him in his greatness.

He said on that day in the eucharist, 'You who have joined the perfect light to the Holy Spirit, join the angels also to us, the images.'

Logion 27

Do not despise the lamb, for without it, it is impossible to see the king. No one can go before the king naked.

Logia 28-31

The heavenly man has more sons than the earthly man. If the sons of Adam are abundant though they die, how many more will the sons of the perfect man be who never die but are continually begotten! [*Logion 29*] A father makes a son, but the son cannot make a son, for the one who has been begotten cannot beget. Rather the son acquires brothers, not sons. [*Logion 30*] All who are begotten in the world are begotten naturally, and others are [fed] by the one from whom they are born. A man is fed from being promised to the place above. [. . .] him from the mouth. If the word had come forth from there [p. 59], he would be nourished from the mouth, and would become perfect. [*Logion 31*] For the perfect conceive and give birth by a kiss. Therefore we ourselves kiss one another, and are conceived by the grace which is within one another.

Logion 32

There were three who walked with the Lord continually: Mary his mother, Mary his sister and Mary Magdalene, who was called his partner. For 'Mary' was his sister and his mother and his partner.

Logion 33

'Father' and 'Son' are simple names. 'Holy Spirit' is a double name, for 'they' are everywhere: they are above, they are below; they are hidden, they are manifest. The Holy Spirit is in what is manifest, and it is below; it is hidden, and it is above.

Logion 34

Evil powers serve the saints, because these powers are blinded by the Holy Spirit to think that they are serving a mere man when they are serving the saints. This is why, when the disciples asked the Lord on one occasion for something of this world, he said to them, 'Ask your mother, and she will give you what is somebody else's.'

Logia 35-36

The apostles said to the disciples, 'May our whole offering be accompanied by salt.' [Sophia] was called 'salt', and without it no offering can be acceptable. [*Logion 36*] But Sophia is barren and childless. That is why she is called '[. . .] of salt'. Wherever they [. . .] in their way, the Holy Spirit [. . .]. [p. 60] And her children abound.

Logion 37

What a father possesses is the property of the son, but while the son is a minor he is not entrusted with his property. When he becomes a man, however, his father gives him everything which he possesses.

Logion 38

Those whom the Spirit generated but have gone astray also go astray because of him. Hence by the one Spirit the same fire is kindled and extinguished.

Logion 39

One is Echamoth and the other is Echmoth.* Echamoth is simply Sophia, but Echmoth is Sophia of Death, who knows death. She is called 'Little Sophia'.

Logion 40

There are animals which can be tamed by man, like the bull and the donkey and others of this sort. There are others which cannot be tamed and are only found in the wild. Man ploughs the land with the tamed animals and from this both he and the animals (whether tame or wild) are fed. This is how it is with the perfect man: by the powers which he has tamed, he ploughs everyone as he prepares for them to come into being. It is because of this that everything stands, whether good or evil, right or left. The Holy Spirit feeds every one and he rules all the powers – tame, wild or otherwise. For in fact he [. . .] imprisons them so that they cannot escape at will.

Logia 41-42

The one who has been formed is [beautiful but] you would not find his sons to be [p. 61] noble forms. If he had not been formed but begotten, you would find his offspring to be noble. But now that he has been formed, he has begotten. What is the child's pedigree? [*Logion 42*] First adultery came, then murder: he was begotten in adultery – for he was a son of the serpent – and he so came to be a murderer like his father, and killed his brother. Every intercourse which has taken place among those not akin to one another is adultery.

Logion 43

God is a dyer. Just as the good dyes, called 'the true', dissolve
into what they are dyeing, so it is with those whom God is dyeing. Since his dyes are immortal, they too are made immortal
through his colours. Those whom he baptizes, God baptizes in
water.

Logion 44

It is impossible for anyone to see anything in reality unless that
person becomes like the object. It is not like this for the man in
the world. He sees the sun without becoming a sun and he sees
the sky and the earth and everything else without becoming
those things. But this is how it is in the truth: in fact, you saw
something of the beyond, and you became like those there; you
saw the Spirit, and you became Spirit; you saw Christ and you
became a Christ; you saw the Father and you will become
Father. Therefore, [in this realm] you see everything but you
do not see yourself, but there you see yourself. For what you
see is what you become.

Logia 45-46

Faith receives, love gives. [No one can [p. 62] receive] without
faith, no one can give without love. [*Logion 46*] For this reason, we have faith in order to receive, and we give in order to
love, since if someone does not give in love, he does not have
the benefit from what he gives. Whoever has not received the
Lord is still a Hebrew.

Logion 47

The apostles who came before us called him 'Jesus, Nazoraean, Messiah', which means 'Jesus, Nazoraean, Christ'. The
last name is 'Christ', the first is 'Jesus' and the one in the middle is 'Nazarene'. 'Messiah' has two meanings, both 'Christ'
and 'measured'. 'Jesus' in Hebrew means 'redemption'.

'Nazara' means 'truth', and so 'Nazarene' means 'truth'. The Christ is the one who is 'measured', and so the 'Nazarene' and 'Jesus' are measured.*

Logion 48

If a pearl is cast into the mud, it does not become worthless, nor if it is anointed with balsam oil does it become more precious. It always retains its value for its owner. So it is with the sons of God, wherever they may be. They are still precious in the eyes of their Father.

Logion 49

If you say, 'I am a Jew', no one will bat an eyelid. If you say, 'I am a Roman', no one will be disturbed. If you say, 'I am a Greek', or 'barbarian', or 'slave', or 'free man', no one will be distraught. But if you [say], 'I am a Christian', the [world] will shake! May it be that I [. . .] like that. The one who [. . .] will not be able to bear to [hear] his name.

Logion 50

God is a [p. 63] man-eater. Therefore the man is sacrificed to him. Before the man was sacrificed, wild beasts were sacrificed because the recipients of the sacrifices were not gods.

Logion 51

Glass vessels and earthenware vessels are made by fire. Glass vessels which break can be remade, for they came into being through breath; but if earthenware vessels are broken, they are ruined, for they came into being without breath.

Logion 52

A donkey turning a millstone walked for a hundred miles.† When it was released, it found itself still in the same place.

Some people make a number of journeys but make no progress. When evening comes, they see neither town nor village, neither creature nor nature, or power or angel. The wretches have laboured in vain.

Logion 53

The 'eucharist' is Jesus. For in Aramaic it is called *pharisatha*, which means 'spread out', for Jesus came to crucify the world.

Logion 54

The Lord went into Levi's dyeing works. He took seventy-two colours and cast them into the cauldron. He brought them up completely white. And he said, 'In the same way, the Son of Man has come as a dyer.'

Logia 55-56

Sophia who is called barren is the mother of the angels. And the partner of the [Saviour] is Mary Magdalene. He [. . .] her more than the disciples [. . .] kissing her on her [. . .] times. The other [. . .]

[p. 64] 'Why do you love her more than all of us?' the disciples asked him.

'Why do I not love you like her?' the Saviour replied. [*Logion 56*] 'When a blind man and someone who can see are both in darkness, there is no difference between them. But when the light comes, then the person who can see will see the light, but the blind one will remain in darkness.'

Logion 57

The Lord said, 'Blessed is the one who exists before he comes to exist. For the one who is has come to be and shall be.'

Logion 58

The exaltedness of man is not manifest but is hidden. For this reason he is master over the beasts even though they are stronger than he is and greater in both size and hidden powers. Yet man also ensures their survival. If he were cut off from them, they would kill one another and devour one another. They used to eat one another, unable to find any other food. But now they have found food because man works the land.

Logion 59

If someone goes down into the water and comes back up without receiving anything but says, 'I am a Christian', he has borrowed the name at interest. But if he receives the Holy Spirit, he has the name as a gift. A gift is not taken away from someone who has received it, but the person who has taken out a loan will have it exacted from him. This is how it is for us if one exists mysteriously.

Logion 60

The mystery of marriage is a great matter! For without it the world would [not] exist. The constitution of the world [. . .], but the constitution [. . .] marriage. Consider partnership which is [. . .] defiled, because it has [. . .] power. Its image [p. 65] exists in defiled form.

Logia 61-62

The forms of unclean spirits are male or female. The male ones have intercourse with the souls which go about in female form. The female ones for their part commingle with those who are male in form because they are not conjoined. And no one can escape from those who bind him unless he receives the male and female powers, which are the bridegroom and the bride. A person receives them from the imaged bridal chamber.

When ignorant females see a male alone, they jump on him

and sport with him and defile him. Similarly, ignorant men who see a beautiful woman alone seduce her and violate her in their desire to defile her. When they see a husband and his wife together, however, the females would never approach the male, nor the males the female. This is how it is if the image and the angel conjoin, in which case no one would dare to approach the male or the female.

Whoever comes out of the world can no longer be seized despite having been in the world. For it is clear that he transcends the desire of [. . .] and fear. He is master [. . .] He is superior to envy. But if [. . .] he comes, he is seized and strangled [. . .]. And then how could he be released from [. . .] power? How could he [. . .]? There are some who say, 'We are faithful', so that [. . .] [p. 66] unclean and demonic spirits. For if they had the Holy Spirit, no unclean spirit would cling to them. [*Logion 62*] Do not fear or love the flesh. If you fear it, it will gain mastery over you. If you love it, it will consume you and strangle you.

Logia 63-64

A person exists either in this world or in the resurrection or in the places in the Middle.* May it never be that I am found there! In this world there is both good and evil. Its goods are not good and its evils are not evil. After this world there is evil which is truly evil, namely what is called the 'Middle'. It is death. While we are in this world, we must acquire resurrection so, when we strip off the flesh, we may be found in 'rest' and not wander in the Middle. For many are deceived on the way.

It is good to come out of the world before one sins. [*Logion 64*] There are some who are neither willing nor able to do this. Others would be able if they were willing, but that is no benefit to them because they do not act. For what they actually wish makes them sinners, but if they did not wish, righteousness would be beyond them in either case, whether through lack of will or lack of action.

Logion 65

A friend of the apostles saw in a vision some people enclosed in a blazing house, bound with [. . .] blazing, as they lay [. . .] blazing [. . .] them in [. . .]. And they said to them, '[. . .] can they be saved?' [. . .] [. . .] they did not wish it. They received [. . .] punishment, which is called [p. 67] '[. . .] darkness' because he [. . .].

Logion 66

By water and fire the soul and spirit have come into being; from water and fire and light the son of the bridal chamber has come to be. The fire is the chrism, the light is the fire. I am not speaking of fire in this world, which has no form, but the fire beyond, whose form is white since it is beautiful and gives beauty.

Logion 67

Truth has not come into the world naked, but has come in types and images. The world cannot receive it any other way. There is rebirth along with an image of rebirth; truly one must be reborn by the image. What is it? The resurrection. The image must rise by the image, the bridal chamber and its image must come, by the image, into the truth which is the restoration.

This is necessary not only for those who have gained the name of the Father and the Son and the Holy Spirit but also for those who have gained them for you. If one does not gain them for himself, the name will also be taken from him. A person receives them in the chrism of the [. . .] of the cross's power. This power the apostles called 'the right' and 'the left'. For the person is no longer a Christian but is a Christ.

Logion 68

The Lord did everything symbolically – baptism and chrism and eucharist and redemption and bridal chamber.

Logion 69

[. . .] he said, 'I have come to make the [below] like the [above] and the outside like the [inside] and [. . .] in the place where [. . .] these places by types [. . .].'

Those who say, '[There is a man above] and one above [him' are] deceived. For the one who revealed [. . .] [p. 68] the one whom they call 'the lower one' and the one who possesses what is secret 'above' him. Strictly one should say 'the inside,' 'the outside' and 'outside the outside.' Hence the Lord called destruction 'the outer darkness',* and there is nothing outside that. He said, 'My Father who is in secret,' and, 'Go inside into your chamber and close the door and pray to your Father who is in secret'* – it is the Father who is inside everything. The one who is inside everything is the Fullness. There is nothing further inside after that. This is what they call 'the one above them'.

Logion 70

Before Christ, some came forth from where they could no longer go in, and others went into a place from which they could no longer come out. But Christ came, and those who had gone in he brought out, and those who had gone out he brought in.

Logion 71

When Eve was inside Adam, there was no death, but when she was separated from him, death came. If she goes back in and he thereby receives himself, there will be no death.

Logion 72

'My God, my God, why O Lord have you forsaken me?'* He said this on the cross, because he had left that place [. . .] begotten from the one who [. . .] by God.

[. . .] from the dead [. . .] exist, but those [. . .] he is perfect [. . .] flesh, but this [. . .] is true flesh [. . .] is not true, but [. . .] true image.

Logion 73

[p. 69] The bridal chamber is not for wild beasts, nor is it for slaves or defiled women. It is for free men and virgins.

Logia 74-75

By the Holy Spirit we are born again, and equally we are born through Christ – it is by both. We are anointed by the Spirit. When we are born, we are united. [*Logion 75*] No one can see himself either in the water or in a mirror without light. Nor, conversely, can you see yourself in the light without water or mirror. Hence baptism must be in both, in light and water – the light is the chrism.

Logion 76

Three houses were places of offering in Jerusalem: one facing west, called 'the holy place'; another facing south, which is called 'the holy of the holy', and a third facing east, called 'the holy of holies', where the high priest alone entered. The 'holy place' is baptism; 'the holy of the holy' is redemption, and the 'holy of holies' is the bridal chamber.

Baptism contains both resurrection and redemption. Redemption is in the bridal chamber, and the bridal chamber is in what is higher than [. . .]. You will not find its [. . .] those who pray are [. . .] Jerusalem [. . .] Jerusalem, they [. . .] Jerusalem, awaiting [. . .]. These are called 'the holy of holies' [. . .] curtain was torn [. . .] the bridal chamber, unless the image [. . .] [p. 70] above. For the reason its curtain tore from top to bottom is that it was necessary for some from below to go upwards.

Logion 77

Those who put on the perfect light are invisible and indomitable to the powers. A person is to clothe himself in light in the mysterious union.

Logia 78-79

Had the female not separated from the male, she would not have died with the male. His separation marked the beginning of death. Therefore Christ came to put right the separation which had existed from the beginning, to reunite the two and to give life and union to those who had died in the separation. [*Logion 79*] The woman is united to her husband in the bridal chamber, and those united in the bridal chamber can no longer be separated. The reason Eve separated from Adam was that she had not united with him in the bridal chamber.

Logion 80

Adam's soul came from a breath. The soul's partner is the spirit; the spirit given to Adam was his mother. His soul was taken, and he was given a spirit in its place. When he was united he spoke words too exalted for the powers, so they envied him. [. . .] spiritual union [. . .] hidden [. . .] themselves [. . .] bridal chamber, so that [. . .].

Logion 81

Jesus appeared [. . .] the Jordan, the fullness of the kingdom of heaven. He who [was born] before the All* was born again [p. 71], he who was anointed in the beginning was anointed again, he who was redeemed in turn redeemed.

Logion 82

We must speak in a mystery. The Father of the All united with the virgin who came down, and a fire illuminated him on that day. He appeared in the great bridal chamber and so his body came into being that day. He came from the bridal chamber as one born from a bridegroom and bride. This is how Jesus, through them, set right the All in the bridal chamber. And it is necessary for each disciple to go to his rest.

Logion 83

Adam came into being from two virgins, from the Spirit and from the virginal earth. The reason Christ was born from a virgin was so that the fall which came about in the beginning might be set right.

Logia 84-85

There are two trees growing in Paradise. One gave birth to the [wild animals], the other gave birth to man. Adam ate from the tree which produced the animals, and so became an animal and himself produced animals. This is why Adam's children worship animals. The tree [. . .] is fruit [. . .] This abounded [. . .] eat the [. . .] fruit of the [. . .] give birth to men [. . .] man [. . .]. [*Logion 85*] [. . .] God makes man [. . .] [p. 72] man makes God. Thus, men make gods in the world and they worship their creations. Presumably, then, gods should worship men!

Logion 86

Just as it is true of a man's deeds that they come from his power, that is why they are called 'powers'. Some of his 'works' are his children, but they have come into being from rest. For this reason, his power comes to expression in his works, but rest appears in the children and you find it permeating the image. And this is the imaged man who does his works from his power, but from rest begets sons.

Logion 87

In this world, slaves serve the free. In the kingdom of heaven, the free will serve the slaves. The children of the bridal chamber will serve the children of the marriage bed.

Logion 88

The single name which the children of the bridal chamber have is 'rest'. [. . .] They do not need to assume a likeness because they have contemplation. [. . .] they abound [. . .] in those [. . .] the glories of the [. . .] them not.

Logion 89

[. . .] go down into the water [. . .] redeeming it [. . .]. Those who [. . .] go forth in his name. For he said, '[This is how] we are to fulfil all [p. 73] righteousness.'*

Logion 90

Those who say that they first die and then rise are deceived. If they do not first receive resurrection while they are alive, then when they die they will not receive anything. The same applies also to those who say of baptism, 'Great is baptism, for those who receive it will live.'

Logia 91-92

The apostle Philip said, 'Joseph the carpenter planted a garden, for he needed wood for this woodwork. He it is who made the cross from trees which he had planted, and it was his seed who hung upon what he had planted.' His seed was Jesus, his planting was the cross. [Logion 92] In the middle of the garden, however, is the tree of life, the olive-tree from which came the chrism for resurrection.

Logion 93

This world is a corpse-eater! Everything else which is eaten in it dies itself. Truth is a life-eater! Therefore no one nourished by the truth will die. Jesus came from that place, brought sustenance from it and gives life to whoever wants it, so they do not die.

Logion 94

God [. . .] Paradise. Man [. . .] Paradise [. . .] with some [. . .] of God in [. . .] those in [. . .] I wish. Paradise [is the place] where I am told, '[Eat] this' or 'Don't eat that' [. . .] [p. 74] wish. The tree of knowledge is located where I eat everything. There it killed Adam, but here the tree of knowledge enlivens man. The tree was the Law. It can give the knowledge of good and evil, but it neither removed him from evil nor set him in the good. It brought death to those who ate from it, because by saying 'eat this' or 'don't eat that', it became the beginning of death.

Logia 95-96

The chrism is superior to baptism. For from the chrism we are called 'Christians' (not because of the baptism), and Christ was named after the chrism. For the Father anointed the Son, the Son anointed the apostles, and the apostles anointed us. Whoever is anointed has everything – the resurrection, the light, the cross [*Logion 96*] and the Holy Spirit. The Father has given him this from the bridal chamber, and the person received it. The Father was in the Son and the Son was in the Father. This is the kingdom of heaven.

Logia 97-98

Well has the Lord said, 'Some entered the kingdom of heaven laughing and came out [. . .].' [. . .] Christian [. . .]. And when [. . .] down into the water, he came [. . .] the All, because [. . .] it is a plaything, but [. . .] despises this [. . .] kingdom of heaven [. . .] if he despises [. . .] and has contempt for it as a plaything [. . .] he laughs. [*Logion 98*] It is the same [p. 75] with the bread and the cup and the oil, even if there is someone else greater than them.

Logion 99

The world came into being by a mistake. For its creator wanted to make it imperishable and immortal, but failed, and did not manage what he had hoped. For imperishability was not a property of the world, just as imperishability was not a property of the one who made the world. For imperishability is proper not to creations but to sons, and no creation can receive imperishability unless it is a son. And if someone cannot receive it, all the more is it true that he cannot give it.

Logia 100-101

The cup of prayer has wine and water. It is laid down as a type of the blood for which the eucharist is celebrated. It is filled by the Holy Spirit, and is a possession of the completely perfect man. Whenever we drink it, we receive the perfect man to ourselves. [*Logion 101*] The living water is a body. We must put on the living man. Hence when a person presents himself to go down into the water, he strips off so that he can put on that living man.

Logion 102

A horse begets a horse. A man begets a man. A god begets a god. So with the bridegroom as well as the bride: they come to be from the [. . .]. No Jew [. . .] from [. . .] comes to be, and [. . .] from Jews [. . .] Christians [. . .] These places are called [. . .] The chosen race of [. . .] [p. 76] and the true man, and son of man, and the seed of the son of man. In this world they are called 'the true race'. They are where the sons of the bridal chamber come into being.

Logia 103-104

There is union in this world between male and female, where there is power and weakness. In the aeon, the image of the union is something different. [*Logion 104*] We call them by the same names, but other names exist which are higher than any name by which we call things. They are higher than strength. For where there is force, there are those who are superior to power. Those are not different and yet are different. In fact, they are both one and the same. This the flesh cannot understand.

Logion 105

Must not everyone who possesses the All understand all things? Some do not understand them and so do not enjoy all the things which they possess. But those who have learned them do enjoy them.

Logia 106-107

It is not only that the perfect man is indomitable. He is also invisible. For if he were visible, he could be grasped.

No one can gain this gift for himself other than by putting on the perfect light and himself becoming perfect light. The one who has put it on will go [. . .] This is perfect. [*Logion 107*] [. . .] that we become [. . .] before we go [. . .] Whoever receives the All [. . .] to those places, he will be able to [. . .] that place. Rather, he will [. . .] the Middle, as imperfect. [p. 77] Only Jesus knows this one's end.

Logion 108

The holy man is completely holy even in his body. For whether he receives the bread or the cup or anything else at all, he sanctifies it, because he takes it and purifies it. How, then, could he not purify his body as well?

Logion 109

Just as Jesus perfected the water of baptism, so he also emptied out death. For this reason we go down into the water, but we do not go down into death, in case we are poured out into the spirit of the world. When that spirit breathes, it makes winter come.

But when the Holy Spirit breathes, summer comes!

Logia 110-111

Whoever has the knowledge of the truth is free, and the free man does not sin. For the one who sins is a slave to sin. Truth is the mother, knowledge is the father. Those who do not turn away from sin the world calls 'free'. Knowledge of the 'truth' puffs up those who do not turn away from sin – that is what makes them 'free' and superior to everything! Love, however, builds up. Whoever has become free by knowledge is a slave to love for those who have not yet been able to bear the freedom of knowledge. Knowledge, however, enables them to become free. Love [. . .] nothing as its own. [. . .] is its own [. . .] or, 'This is mine [. . .] are yours' [. . .]. [*Logion 111*] Spiritual love is wine and fragrance. [p. 78] All who anoint themselves with it enjoy it. Those who stand around the anointed ones also enjoy it while those who are anointed stand. If those who are anointed with ointment leave them and go away, however, those who are not anointed but only standing by are left in a stench.

The Samaritan gave nothing to the one who was wounded except wine and oil. There was nothing else except ointment, and he healed the wound. 'For love covers a multitude of sins.'*

Logion 112

Those to whom the woman gives birth resemble the one she loves. If she loves her husband, they resemble the husband. If an adulterer, they resemble the adulterer. Often if a woman has to lie with her husband, but her mind is on the adulterer with whom she usually has intercourse, the child she gives birth to resembles the adulterer. As for you who dwell with the Son of God, do not love the world, but love the Lord, so that what you beget does not come resembling the world but comes resembling the Lord.

Logion 113

A human has intercourse with a human. A horse has intercourse with a horse. A donkey has intercourse with a donkey.
Those of a particular species have intercourse with fellow
members of that species. Similarly, spirit has intercourse with
spirit, word has partnership with word, and light with light. If
you become human, the human will love you. If you become
spirit, spirit will unite with you. If you become word, word
[p. 79] will have intercourse with you. If you become light,
light will have partnership with you. If you become one of
those who exist above, those above will rest upon you. If you
become a horse or a donkey or calf or dog or sheep or any
other wild beast of the outer realm or from below, you will be
loved by neither human nor spirit nor word nor light. Neither
those who exist above nor those within will be able to rest
within you, and you will have no share within them.

Logion 114

The one who is an unwilling slave can be free. Someone who
has gained freedom by the good graces of his master but then
sells himself into slavery again can no longer be free.

Logia 115-118

Agriculture in this world is based on four elements. Bringing
the harvest into the barn comes as a result of water, soil, wind
and light.

In the same way, divine agriculture is based on four elements: faith, hope, love and knowledge. Faith is our soil in
which we take root. Hope is the water by which we are sus-
tained. Love is the wind by which we grow. Knowledge is the
light by which we ripen. [*Logion 116*] Grace is in four [. . .]
earth, it is [. . .] high heaven [. . .].

Blessed is the one who has not [. . .] [p. 80] a soul: that is
Jesus Christ. He has come everywhere but oppressed no one.

Blessed is the person of this kind, for he is a perfect man.

[*Logion 117*] The word tells us that it is difficult to achieve this. So how can we accomplish this great thing? How will it give rest to everyone? [*Logion 118*] Above all, one must do no harm, whether to the great or to the least, unbeliever or believer, and then give rest to those who rest in their good deeds. There are some who do good by giving relief to a person who is well-off. The person doing good cannot help such a person, for he is not bringing what the recipient wants; nor can he do harm, since he is not afflicting the person. But does the one who is well-off sometimes harm them? It is not so. Rather, their evil harms them. The one who has Nature gives the good to the one who is good. But others outside him grieve terribly.

Logion 119

A householder possesses all his property, whether children or slaves, livestock or dogs or pigs, wheat or barley or chaff or hay or [. . .] or meat or acorns. He is wise and he understands how to provide for each of them. Children he provides with bread [. . .], slaves he provides with [. . .] seed, the livestock [he provides] with barley and chaff and hay, dogs he throws bones, and to the [pigs] he tosses acorns [p. 81] and stale bread. So it is with God's disciple. If he is wise, he understands discipleship, and physical appearances do not deceive him. Rather, he looks out for the disposition of the soul of each person as he speaks with him. There are many beasts in the world who have human shape. If he recognizes them as pigs, he will toss them acorns, or if as livestock, he will throw them barley and chaff and hay, or if as dogs, he will throw them bones. If he recognizes them as slaves, he will give them a basic 'course', but if as children, he will give them a complete one.

Logia 120-122

The Son of Man exists, and the son of the Son of Man exists. The Son of Man is the Lord, and the son of the Son of Man is the one who creates through the Son of Man. The Son of Man has received the authority from God to create. He also has the authority to beget. [*Logion 121*] He who has received the authority to create is a creature, but he who has received the authority to beget is begotten. A creator cannot beget, but a begetter can create. It is said by some that the creator begets, but what he 'begets' is a creature. This is why his 'children' are not begotten but are [. . .]. The one who creates does a visible work, and he himself is visible. But the one who begets begets in secret and is himself hidden, being [. . .] the image. The one who creates creates in the open, but the one who begets [begets] his children in secret. [*Logion 122*] No one [can] know when [a man] [p. 82] and a woman have intercourse with each other except they themselves. For marriage in this world is a mystery for those who have married. And if marriage which is defiled is secret, how much more is the marriage which is undefiled a true mystery! For it is not fleshly, but pure. It is not attributed to lust but to will. It is not assigned to the darkness or the night but to the day and the light. If marriage is 'exposed' it is fornication. The bride is a harlot not only if she receives the seed of another man, but also if she is outside her bedchamber and is seen. She should appear only to her father and her mother, and the friend of the bridegroom and the sons of the bridegroom. They are granted entrance every day into the bridal chamber. As for the others, let them desire just to hear her voice and enjoy the fragrance of her ointment, and let them be nourished, like dogs, with the crumbs which fall from her table. Bridegrooms and brides belong to the bridal chamber; no one can see the bridegroom and the bride unless he becomes one.

Logion 123

When Abraham [. . .] to see what he was to see, he circumcised the flesh of his foreskin, thereby teaching us that we must destroy the flesh.

Most things in the world, which as long as it [. . .] hidden, they are secure and live [. . .] appear, they die as a visible man does [. . .] While [p. 83] a man is alive, his intestines are hidden, but if his intestines are uncovered and come out, the man will die. Similarly a tree blossoms and grows tall when its roots are hidden, but if its roots are exposed the tree withers. So it is with every begetting which is in the world, not only the manifest ones but also the hidden. For, as long as the root of evil is hidden, it is strong, but if it is known, it is destroyed. If it is exposed, it perishes. For this reason the word says, 'Already the axe is laid at the root of the trees.'* It will not merely cut, because what is cut will blossom again. Rather, the axe digs down until it brings up the root. Jesus pulled up the root of every place, whereas others did so only in part. As for us, let us each dig out the root of evil within, and pull up its root in our hearts. It will be pulled up if we come to know it, but if we do not know it, it takes root in us and produces its fruits in our hearts. It masters us and we are its slaves. It takes us captive to make us do what we do [not] want to do, but what we want, we do [not] do. It is powerful because we do not know it; as long as it exists, it is at work. Ignorance is the mother of [. . .].

Ignorance will lead to [. . .]. Those who exist by their ignorance neither were nor [are] nor will be. [. . .] [p. 84] will be perfect when the whole truth is revealed. For the truth, like ignorance, is hidden – and it gives rest within. But when it is revealed and is known, we glorify it because it is more powerful than ignorance and error. It gives freedom. The word said, 'If you know the truth, the truth will set you free.'* Ignorance is slavery. Knowledge is freedom. If we know the truth, we will find true fruit within us. If we are united with the truth, it will receive our fullness.

Logia 124–127

For now we have what can be seen in creation. We say, 'They are mighty and glorious, but contemptible weak things are obscure.' But this is how it is with what is revealed of the truth: they may be 'contemptible and weak', but it is 'the mighty and glorious' who are obscure. The mysteries of truth are manifest as types and images. [*Logion 125*] The bedchamber is hidden: it is 'the holy of the holy'. The curtain at first concealed how God managed creation. If the curtain tears, however, those within are revealed. Then this house will be left desolate, and indeed will be destroyed. All divinity will flee from these places, but not into the holy of holies. For it will not mix with the unalloyed light and the unfading fullness. Instead it will be under the wings of the cross and under its arms. This ark will bring salvation when the [p. 85] cataclysm of the flood overwhelms them. Those who belong to the priestly tribe will be able to enter behind the curtain with the high priest. This is why the curtain was not torn at the top alone: otherwise it would be open only to those of the upper realm. Nor was it only the bottom which was torn – then it would be revealed only to those in the lower realm. No, it split from top to bottom, and those above opened up for us below, so we could enter into the hidden truth. This is what is truly 'mighty and glorious', though we have access to it by means of weak and contemptible types. They are contemptible by comparison with the perfect glory. There is glory that surpasses glory, and power that surpasses power.

For this reason, the perfections and the secrets of the truth have opened up to us. The 'holies of holies' have been uncovered, and the bedchamber has invited us within. While that bedchamber is hidden, evil is idle but is not taken away from the Holy Spirit's seed; they are still servants of wickedness. But when it is uncovered, the perfect light flows out upon everyone, and everyone in the light will [receive] the chrism. Then the slaves will be free and the captives rescued. [*Logion 126*] '[Every] planting which the Father in heaven has not planted [will be] pulled up.'* Those who are divided will be united; [. . .] will be filled. All who [enter] the bedchamber will glow in the light [. . .]. For like marriages which [. . .] are in the night. The fire [. . .] [p. 86] in the night until it is extinguished. The mysteries of this marriage, however, are fulfilled by day in the light, and that day and its light never set. [*Logion 127*] If a person becomes a son of the bridal chamber, he will receive the light. If a person does not receive it while he is in these parts, he will not receive it in the place beyond. Whoever has received that light will be neither seen nor grasped, and no one will be able to trouble one of this kind, even while he lives in the world. Furthermore, when he goes forth from the world, he has

already received the truth in images. The world has become
aeons. For the aeon is fullness for such a person, and it exists
as it is revealed for him alone. It is not hidden in darkness and
night, but is hidden in the perfect day and the holy light.

The Gospel according to Philip

41 The Gospel of the Lots of Mary

(fifth to sixth century CE*)*

INTRODUCTION

This unusual text is very much a manual for everyday help, for the most part providing quotidian earthly advice rather than the good news of eternal life. The work fits most closely into the ancient genre of 'lots', in the sense of 'fortunes' or 'chances'. The owner of the book would seek advice either for himself or for a customer, randomly selecting an oracle in the hope of finding relevant guidance. In common with the horoscope genre, the references to both past and future events are notably vague: the instructions are usually of a general nature, such as 'take heart and endure' or 'do not be careless' (Lots 5, 6), as are the accompanying predictions ('you will be trusted', 'you will find joy', in Lots 5, 30). The work is not a mere crystal ball, however, but has a strong religious thrust, exhorting trust in God and suspicion of malign human influence. The text often provides a kind of therapy for the indecisive person – perhaps the sort of person who would seek this guidance in the first place: 'If you decide to do this thing, do it' (Lot 11), or 'Go ahead immediately' (Lot 34).

The use of the term 'Gospel' for this work is clearly little more than an attempt to confer authority on the text, as it bears little resemblance to any other Gospel-like works. It illustrates not a development in the portrayal of Jesus, but how potent the term 'Gospel' had become. There is not much reference to Jesus in the text overall, or even much that is distinctively Christian, although there are a number of allusions to the ethical content of the Gospels (e.g. Mk 7:6 in Lot 1; Jn 5:14 in Lot 3), and the rest of the New Testament. It is also clearly significant for the author that the mother of Jesus is the purported source of the oracles. As in the Beatles' song, mother Mary comes speaking words of wisdom, according to the Prologue. The Coptic text is contained in a miniature codex, approximately 8cm × 7cm in size and seventy-six pages long, and dates from the fifth or sixth century CE. It is held in Harvard University's Sackler Art Museum. Unusually, we probably have here an 'original' manuscript rather than a copy, because books of Lots like this one were probably adapted for each user.

DRAMATIS PERSONAE

JESUS CHRIST
MARY *Jesus' mother*
GABRIEL *The archangel*
MICHAEL *The archangel*

TRANSLATION

Prologue

The Gospel of the Lots of Mary, the mother of the Lord Jesus Christ and who received the good news from the archangel Gabriel. Whoever seeks with his whole heart will reach what he is seeking as long as he is not double-minded.

Lot 1

O man, you are greatly loved in how people speak of you, but their hearts are far from you. You know what happened to you before today when you nearly lost your life, and yet still you are being fiercely hunted.

Lot 2

Rejoice, delight, be glad, and give glory to God for what has happened to you! For a little while you were far from home. Afterwards you suffered loss, and were subjected to mockery and danger. But God had mercy on you!

Lot 3

Behold, you have been saved, so do not turn back to evil in case even worse things befall you. Can you not remember what happened to you before today? Yet God saved you from everything. Do not turn back to it!

Lot 4

It is only you loading a great wearisome burden on yourself. You are wanting to do something before its time has come. Endure a little while, and you will see the confidence in God that will come to you.

Lot 5

You will be trusted in this matter. Take heart and endure, because time is hastening on for you. Do not be distressed or slacken off or grieve, for you have a firm hope from God.

Lot 6

The Lord God has heard your request and will send his angel, and he will go ahead of you. Then you will see the confidence in God that will come to you. Only do not be careless, thinking that the thing will not happen to you. It will in fact happen.

Lot 7

You know, O man, that again you did everything you could. You did not gain anything except loss, dispute and conflict.

However, if you bear the burden for a little while, the matter will prosper through the God of Abraham, Isaac and Jacob.

Lot 8

Fight bravely in what has happened to you, for it is a human wickedness. Your enemies are not far off and have plotted against you again in the wickedness in their hearts. Yet trust in God, and walk in his commands forever.

Lot 9

Arise and go immediately. Do not dither from day to day, for this is the time which God has ordained [. . .] for you. They are only bringing a capital charge against you. But be patient for a little while.

Lot 10

The peace of God will be with you, and you will be saved from the affliction which has come upon you. What you have vowed, fulfil. For God does not tempt anyone: it is just that you are being disobedient.

Lot 11

If you decide to do this thing, do it. Do not neglect it, for God has established it. It is you alone holding it back. Truly the evil one will not come upon you. But trust in God and do not be double-minded.

Lot 12

Do not abandon the faith which is in your heart. You have God as a helper, and he will guide you on the path you will travel. Only do not doubt, for nothing is impossible with God.

Lot 13

Therefore do not think about strength, O man. You will not prevail now, but will receive great sufferings because the hard time has at present not yet passed. Do not trust in vain human words.

Lot 14

You will be trusted and will prevail in this. Strengthen your heart. This is from God. Do not be afraid! In your case, God is with you in everything you do.

Lot 15

O man, bear with everything and give thanks with remembrance of God, for the hand of God has made you firm. Do not doubt in your heart, and do not walk in vain human counsels.

Lot 16

Remember that you have come close to death again in the affliction which came upon you, for you returned to your former actions. Your enemies are plotting against you, though you think they care for you. You will understand my words. Abandon these people!

Lot 17

The peace of God will be with you all your days and you will rejoice when a great year's harvest comes to you. You will rejoice in the works of your hands, for the angel of the Lord will go ahead of you.

Lot 18

The king of heaven and earth, and God of all flesh, is fighting on your behalf. He will enable you to prevail over your enemies, for

God has accepted your request. God is concerned about all the sufferings which you have borne.

Lot 19

This is a victory from God! But be patient, and endure until the time comes and you receive the hope of your salvation, the crown prepared for you. Yet you are being attacked by people. Do not let them deceive you!

Lot 20

It is still a little while before you receive the completion of your life. For the Lord is your mediator. Endure and you will receive the hope of your salvation, for the power of God is greater than that of men, and they will marvel at you.

Lot 21

Behold, the hard time has passed for you! Behold, the time of rest has come to you! Just take heart. You will see the confidence in God which will come to you, and he will send the angel of peace to guide you. And he will give you rest.

Lot 22

You are being played false as before. Do not let yourself be completely robbed and die a violent death because of your disobedience and lack of attention.

Lot 23

I am amazed at you, O man, that you have no strength. You will be afflicted. Your hope vanished once before. Unless you fear God, you will not be saved from the wrath which has come upon you.

Lot 24

O man, stop being double-minded about whether this will come to pass or not. It will indeed come to pass! So take heart and do not be double-minded, for it will remain with you for a long time, and you will rejoice and delight.

Lot 25

Go and make your vows, and fulfil immediately what you have sworn to do. Do not be double-minded, for God is merciful. He will answer your request and release you from your heart's affliction.

Lot 26

Rise up and help yourself, for the time of crisis has come. Why are you sitting down? There will be a knock at the door, but you will be unaware of it! Do not think that you can escape from the danger which is upon you. Go and pray to God immediately!

Lot 27

Trust in the help of the Most High. Call upon his name with all your heart, and he will send his good angel to guide you. Do not be afraid of those who kill your bodies and then have nothing else they can do to you.

Lot 28

Take heart in all circumstances! For you are worrying about nothing. The Lord will help you with his right hand, and will send his angel Michael to help you. You will prevail over those who attack you, and he will humble your enemies in your presence.

Lot 29

Get away quickly! Do not stop and wonder, 'What have I done for these things to happen to me?' No – be patient in suffering for a little longer, until God resolves the matter. Only trust God with all your heart, and you will see what will happen in the end.

Lot 30

No evil will come upon you in this matter, and nor will grief or loss. For the Lord Jesus fights on your behalf. You will find joy, and will delight even in the course of your short life. Trust God and do not be double-minded.

Lot 31

Go and take yourself away immediately! Do not dither from day to day, because God is one who fights on your behalf. He will put your enemies under your feet. If you are patient in suffering for a little while, you will receive the hope of your salvation, and will rest.

Lot 32

Hurry, for behold – the time has come! Your heart will rejoice. Go ahead, for the matter is established by God for you. He will prepare a good path for you, and you will be rescued from the affliction which has come upon you.

Lot 33

Do not follow the desire of your heart, or pursue its fulfilment. Do not trust in the words of men, for you did all you could once before but were not able to make it happen. But you alone are turning back.

Lot 34

Go ahead immediately. This matter is from God. You know that – behold! – for a long time you have been bearing great sufferings. But do not be anxious for yourself, for you have come to the haven of victory.

Lot 35

You will not be able to trust them, nor will you be able to have confidence in their speech. They are deceivers and betrayers. Keep away from them! For they have played you false before with others.

Lot 36

O man, look at what you have done! Examine yourself to see whether there is some great transgression in you. Do not try your strength against the hand of God! No – go and give glory to God.

Lot 37

This is the day that God has prepared for peace and rejoicing to be in it. For Christ Jesus will grant you a good harvest and life in abundance.

VI

TWO MODERN FORGERIES

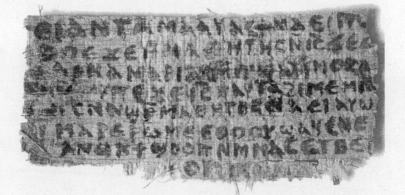

The Gospel of Jesus' Wife
(Walter Fritz/Harvard University)

42 The Secret Gospel of Mark

(twentieth century)

INTRODUCTION

Included here is what claims to be the beginning of a letter of Clement of Alexandria (*c.* 200 CE) and the quotations in it of a 'Secret' or 'Mystical' Gospel of Mark. Announced in 1960 and published in 1973, this text was accepted as authentic by most scholars for the rest of the twentieth century, and indeed a few still hold the view that the letter of Clement is genuine. There is very strong evidence, however, that it is a forgery, with the most likely candidate for its authorship being the 'discoverer' of the text, the late Professor Morton Smith of Columbia University in New York. This letter of Clement distinguishes between three versions of Mark's Gospel: (1) the public, canonical Gospel of Mark, written while Peter was still alive; (2) the 'spiritual' or 'mystical' version of the Gospel, written after Peter's death once Mark had moved to Alexandria; and (3) the heretical Carpocratians' corruption of this spiritual Gospel.

Various pieces of evidence converge to persuade scholars that the letter of Clement is a forgery, or – as some prefer to call it – a hoax. First, the manuscript can no longer be found, and so it cannot be tested properly for its authenticity. Only photographs survive.

Second, Smith's account of the discovery of the text, in the Mar Saba Monastery, has some remarkable details in common with the potboiler novel *The Mystery of Mar Saba*, published in 1940. In this story, Sir William Bracebridge talks of how he knew that many of the manuscripts had been removed from the monastery, but he could not help feeling that some might remain hidden there. After extensive searching, he became reconciled to the thought that he would go home empty-handed, when a monk told him that some books in his cell had been overlooked. Morton Smith similarly reported about his Mar Saba manuscript that he knew most of the manuscripts had been transferred to Jerusalem, 'but there was always a chance that something had been missed'. Again, after a long, fruitless search he was gradually reconciling himself to the idea that he would find nothing, when one day he found himself in his cell staring at a Greek text.

Thirdly, some have pointed out the oddities of this Letter of Clement to Theodore. The letter is curious because it attempts at the same time both to conceal and reveal the existence of the Secret Gospel of Mark and of Carpocrates' corrupt edition of it. Mark's 'Mystical' edition of his Gospel is a closely guarded secret in Alexandria, but Clement explains the details of its existence. Theodore has been effective in silencing the Carpocratians, but the letter reveals their modifications of the Gospel text. The manuscript also breaks off just where Clement really begins actually to answer Theodore's questions.

There has been considerable debate about the handwriting. Some have identified evidence of a 'forger's tremor', where blobs of ink or shaky letters appear because the author is tracing the letters very slowly. Other analyses of the handwriting have been used to argue for authenticity. As in the case of the Hitler Diaries, however, graphology is an unreliable guide. Many have observed that the portrayal of Jesus as a magician conveniently fits some of the scholarly theories Smith had advanced before his discovery of the manuscript. Others have noted that the overtones of homosexual behaviour towards the end of the passage fit a twentieth-century environment much better than a second-century one.

Overall, there is now considerable scepticism among scholars about this text, and it was probably written by Morton Smith in the twentieth century. It is also possible, however, that it is an eighteenth-century forgery, because the text was written on the end-papers of an early modern book in a handwriting style of that period.

TRANSLATION

From the letters of the most holy Clement, author of the *Stromateis*.

To Theodore.

You have done a fine job of silencing the unmentionable teachings of the Carpocratians. They are the subject of the prophecy about the 'wandering stars', who stray from the narrow way of the commandments into a boundless abyss of carnal, bodily sins. For since they are puffed up with the knowledge, so they claim, of 'the deep matters of Satan', they neglect the fact that they are hurling themselves into the dark gloom of falsehood. While they pride themselves on being 'free', they have in fact become enslaved to servile passions. They are to be resisted completely by all means. Even if they were to say something true, the lover of truth should not agree with them on the point. For not all true things are the truth, nor should one prefer the apparent truth in accord with human opinions, over the true truth in accord with the faith.

About their babblings about the divinely inspired Gospel according to Mark, then. Some of what they say is entirely false. Some is not truly reported even though it contains some true material. For truth mixed with fabrications is debased, such that, as the saying goes, 'the salt loses its saltiness'.

Mark's two editions of his Gospel

Now Mark, during the time of Peter's stay in Rome, wrote up the deeds of the Lord. He did not record all of them, nor of course did he point out the mystical acts. What he did was to choose those which he considered most useful for the growth of the faith of catechumens.

When Peter was martyred, Mark moved to Alexandria, bringing both his own notes and the memoirs of Peter, from which he transferred into his first book teachings which are appropriate for those advancing in knowledge. He thereby composed a more spiritual Gospel for the use of those seeking perfection.

Nevertheless, he still did not publish the secret doctrines, nor did he record the mysterious teaching of the Lord, but merely included other deeds along with those he had recounted previously. Yet he did add some oracles whose interpretation he knew would initiate its hearers into the mystery of the truth of the seven veils.

This is how he earlier prepared his Gospel, neither jealously nor unguardedly in my opinion. When he died, he left his account to the church in Alexandria. It is still now kept there very securely indeed, read only to those who are initiated into the Great Mysteries.

Carpocrates' corruption of the Mystical Gospel

Carpocrates was taught by those foul demons which ever contrive destruction for the human race. He utilized deceptive arts to take captive an elder of the church in Alexandria, and thereby acquired from him a copy of the Mystical Gospel, which he also interpreted in accord with his own blasphemous, carnal opinion. Yet he added to this pollution by mixing shameless lies with the undefiled holy writings. It is from this mixture that the teaching of the Carpocratians derives.

As a result, as I said before, nothing should ever be conceded to them, nor should one agree with them, when they offer their falsehoods, that the Mystical Gospel of Mark exists. In fact, it should be denied on oath, for not all truths should be spoken to everyone. This is why the wisdom of God proclaimed through Solomon, 'Answer the fool according to his folly,' teaching that the light of truth should be concealed from those with blind minds. After that, Scripture says, 'from him who has not, it will be taken away', and, 'let the fool walk in darkness'. We, however, are children of the light, illuminated by the dawn of the Lord's Spirit from on high. 'Where the Spirit of the Lord is,' it says, 'there freedom is,' for 'to the pure all things are pure.'

Therefore I have no qualms about answering the questions

which you have asked, refuting through the actual words of the Gospel what they have falsified. One example is a passage after 'They were going up on the road to Jerusalem etc.', up to 'after three days he will rise'. Here it adds (I quote verbatim):

And they came to Bethany and there was a woman there whose brother had died. She came and worshipped Jesus, and said, 'Son of David, have mercy on me!' The disciples, however, rebuked her. Jesus, angered by them, went away with her to the garden where the tomb was, and immediately a loud voice was heard from the tomb. Jesus approached it and rolled away the stone from the tomb's entrance. Immediately he went in to the place where the young man lay. He stretched out his hand, took the young man's hand, and raised him up. When the young man looked at Jesus, he loved him and started to implore Jesus to remain with him. Having gone out from the tomb, they went to the young man's house, for he was rich. After six days, Jesus instructed him, and when evening fell the young man came to him wearing only a linen cloth on his naked body and stayed with Jesus that night. For Jesus was teaching him the mystery of the kingdom of God. From there he got up and returned to the other side of the Jordan.

In addition to this is the following: 'And James and John came to him', along with the whole paragraph. But the phrase 'naked together' and the other things about which you wrote are not present. After 'and he went to Jericho', there follows only 'and the sister of the young man whom Jesus loved, his mother, and Salome were present, but Jesus did not receive them'. The many other statements of which you have written appear to be, and indeed are, falsehoods. While, then, interpretation which is true and accords with the true philosophy . . .

43 The Gospel of Jesus' Wife

(twenty-first century)

INTRODUCTION

The *Gospel of Jesus' Wife* is a credit-card sized piece of papyrus with eight partial lines of text (with a few letters on the other side). The key sentence that has attracted attention is line 4: 'Jesus said to them, "My wife . . ."' – unfortunately the line breaks off here. The text is in Coptic, and refers specifically to 'Mary', and so there is probably an implied claim in the fragment overall that this wife of Jesus is supposed to be Mary Magdalene.

The manuscript initially came to public attention on 18 September 2012, and it was announced as an unquestionably genuine fourth-century manuscript, a translation of a Greek original from the second century CE. Almost immediately after the initial announcement, however, questions were raised about it by leaders in the field. The manuscript was then subjected to scientific testing, in the hope that this would decide the matter.

There was then a frustratingly long delay, during which time some scholars wondered whether the scientific examination would ever really happen. In March 2013, however, an analysis of the ink (by Micro-Raman Spectroscopy) showed that the ink composition was consistent with types of ink from the ancient world. In June and July 2013, the papyrus was carbon-dated – to a date-range of 404–209 BCE! Further tests were conducted in March 2014 in another laboratory, producing a more likely timeframe of seventh–eighth century CE. This ancient date for the papyrus, and the reports about the ink, appeared to confirm the opinion of those who had initially judged that the text was part of an ancient work.

Almost as soon as these scientific reports appeared, however, evidence began to mount up against the authenticity of the fragment, with the result that scholars now agree that the manuscript is a modern fabrication. First, the lack of archaeological provenance and the coincidental appearance of such a fragment in our post-*Da Vinci Code* era are elements which should have raised concerns from the beginning. Second, it was guilty by association: a fragment of the Gospel of John accompanying the Jesus' wife fragment was almost identical to a Cambridge manuscript of John, though it turned out to be based not on the actual fourth-century John manuscript, but copied from a twentieth-century book in which the text was presented. Third, the carbon-dating certainly confirmed that the piece of papyrus was ancient (as noted, from the seventh or eighth century), but the problem was that the dialect of Coptic in which the text was written was no longer used at this time. Fourth, the text is a patchwork of quotations from the *Gospel of Thomas* (see pp. 45–70). Worse still, it is a copy of a particular version of *Thomas* on the internet; this version contained a mistake in the copying of the Coptic, a mistake which the author of the *Gospel of Jesus' Wife* text reproduced. The final nail in the coffin was the discovery in 2016 by investigative journalist Ariel Sabar of the identity of the forger – a German Coptic student who, via curating a museum, working in a car-parts business and a stint in online pornography, became a dealer in fake manuscripts.

TRANSLATION

'[. . .] not. My mother has given me [life].' [. . .]

The disciples said to Jesus, '[. . .] deny . . . Mary is worthy of it . . .' [. . .].

Jesus said to them, 'My wife [. . .] She will be able to be my disciple, and [. . .] Let an evil man bring forth [. . .]. I am with her because [. . .] an image [. . .].'

Notes

The Protevangelium of James

Prot. 5: *the high priest's crown.* The high priest's golden crown, or perhaps a reference more narrowly to the front piece of the crown on which the sacred name of God (YHWH) was engraved (Exodus 28:36–38).

Prot. 8: *The high priest then went in and took the twelfth bell into the Holy of Holies.* According to the prescription in Exodus 28: 31–35, the high priest must wear bells when he goes in and out of the Holy of Holies, the inner sanctum of the temple.

Prot. 15: *the Lord my God lives, and his Messiah lives, and the Witness of the Truth lives.* A reference to the Trinity of the Father ('the Lord my God'), the Son ('his Messiah') and the Holy Spirit ('the Witness of the Truth'); cf. John 14:17; 15:26–27; 16:13.

Prot. 16: *the water of the Lord's judgement to drink.* The water used in the ritual to identify an adulterer (cf. Numbers 5:11–31).

Prot. 21: *the Praetorium.* The headquarters of the governor of a Roman province.

The Infancy Gospel of Thomas

IGT 17: *Passover.* The Jewish festival commemorating the Israelites' deliverance from the Egyptians recorded in the book of Exodus.

The Gospel of Thomas

Gos. Thom. 2: *the All.* The entirety of the spiritual realm, or perhaps the physical universe.

Dura Parchment 24

the Judaean town of Erinmathaea. A variant spelling of 'Arimathaea'.

Marcion's Gospel

Gos. Marc. 6:1–5: *shewbread.* The twelve loaves of bread laid out on the golden table in the Tabernacle, replaced every Sabbath when the existing bread was eaten by the priests (see Exodus 25: 23–30).

Gos. Marc. 20:41–44: *The Lord said to my Lord . . . for your feet.* A quotation from Psalm 110:1.

Gos. Marc. 23:26–31: *They will say to the mountains . . . Cover us!* A quotation from Hosea 10:8.

The Greek Gospel of Philip

Gos. Phil. (Gk): *The archon.* A standard Gnostic term for a demonic power.

The Jewish Anti-Gospel

Anti-Gos. 8: *ichor such as flows in the blessed gods.* Quoted from Homer, *Iliad* 5.340.

Vienna Greek Papyrus 2325 (The 'Fayyum Gospel')

I will strike the shepherd and the sheep will be scattered. A quotation from Zechariah 13.7.

The Gospel of Nicodemus

Gos. Nic. Prologue: *the ninth indiction.* The ninth year (running 1 September–31 August) of a fifteen-year cycle. The cycles began in (September) 312. Therefore the cycle referred to here ran from the year 417–418, making the ninth indiction the year 425–426.

Gos. Nic. Prologue: *principate.* The period of a Roman emperor's 'reign', although Romans had for centuries despised the idea of kings. The principate of Tiberius ran from 14 to 37 CE, and so the fifteenth year was 28 CE (cf. Luke 3:1).

Gos. Nic. 1: *Hosanna membromē barouchamma Adonai.* A corrupt rendering of the words of Psalm 118:26, shouted at Jesus' entry into Jerusalem: '*Hosanna*! Blessed is he who comes (*baruch haba*) in the name of the Lord (*Adonai*).' *Membromē* is an approximation of the Aramaic *bamromē*, 'in the heights'. Compare Mark 11:9–10.

Gos. Nic. 1: *Praetorium.* The headquarters of the governor of a Roman province.

Gos. Nic. 9: *Passover.* The Jewish festival commemorating the Israelites' deliverance from the Egyptians recorded in the book of Exodus.

Gos. Nic. 11: *baddach ephkid rouel.* An approximation to the original of 'Into your hand I commit my spirit', spoken by Jesus on the cross (Luke 23:46), in quotation of Psalm 31:5. The Hebrew of the Psalm reads *byadka aphkid ruchi*, in Aramaic *baydak amanei ruchi*. Possibly the word *rouel* is supposed to mean 'Spirit of God [*El*]'.

Gos. Nic. 12: *Vengeance is mine, and I will repay, says the Lord.* A quotation of Deuteronomy 32:35, via Romans 12:19.

Gos. Nic. 14: *Go into all the world . . . make them well.* A quotation of Mark 16:15–18, from the later 'longer ending' of Mark's Gospel.

Gos. Nic. 14: *We shouldn't trust gentiles.* Possibly an allusion to the fact that Galilee had historically been dominated by gentiles. See Matthew 4:15, quoting Isaiah 9:1. The apocryphal book of 1 Maccabees records the liberation of the Jews in 'gentile Galilee' (1 Macc. 5:9–44).

Gos. Nic. 16: *Now dismiss your servant in peace . . . laid bare.* A quotation of Luke 2:28–35.

Gos. Nic. 16: *On the word of two or three any matter rests.* A quotation of Deuteronomy 19:15.

Gos. Nic. 16: *And Enoch walked with God, and he was not, because God took him.* A quotation of Genesis 5:24.

Gos. Nic. 16: *And Moses died by the command of the Lord, but to this day no man knows where he is buried.* A quotation of Deuteronomy 34:5–6.

Gos. Nic. 16: '*What is it that Rabbi Simeon said when he saw Jesus?*' *Rabbi Levi said.* '*He is set for the falling and rising of many in Israel, and as a sign to be rejected.*' A quotation of Luke 2:34.

Gos. Nic. 16: *Behold I send my messenger ahead of you who will go before you to protect you on every good path, because my name is invoked in it.* A quotation of Exodus 23:20.

Gos. Nic. 16: *If this is from the Lord and it is marvellous in our eyes ... Cursed is everyone who hangs on a tree ... The gods who did not make heaven and earth will perish.* The three quotations come, respectively, from Psalm 118:23, Deuteronomy 21:23 and Jeremiah 10:11.

Gos. Nic. 16: *the year called Jubilee.* In the Israelite calendar, the fiftieth year in a fifty-year cycle.

The Narrative of Joseph of Arimathaea

Narr. Jos. 3: *the Patriarchs.* In Jewish and Christian tradition, a reference to Abraham, Isaac and Jacob.

The Gospel of Mary

Gos. Mary codex p. 9 (§1): *the lawgiver.* Probably Moses, or perhaps a reference to the Old Testament god as a deity below the supreme God in the *Gospel of Mary*'s view of the divine.

Gos. Mary codex p. 15 (§4): *the All.* The material universe.

The Epistle of the Apostles

Ep. Ap. 11: *As for an appearance of a demon, its foot is not in contact with the ground.* Original source unknown.

Ep. Ap. 15: *my Memorial and my Agape.* These terms probably refer to two 'meals'. The Memorial probably refers to the eucharist, which is done 'in memory' of Jesus according to Paul and the Gospel of Luke. The Agape (a Greek word for 'love') referred to a communal meal among Christians. These were not always separate, but around the same time as the *Epistle of the Apostles* the church father Tertullian refers to them as distinct.

Ep. Ap. 19: *Lord, many are those who afflict me ... upon his people.* A quotation from Psalm 3:1–3, 5–8.

Ep. Ap. 33: *Behold, from the land of Syria ... him who sent me.* Although apparently presented as an Old Testament quotation, it does not resemble any known form of a biblical passage. The sentence about the barren woman resembles Isaiah 54:1, and other parts of the prophecy seem to derive from the New Testament book of Revelation.

Ep. Ap. 35: *Swift are their feet to shed blood ... I am like you?* A composite of various biblical passages, some from Psalms attributed to David, but also containing, for example, Isaiah 59:7.

Ep. Ap. 47: *As the prophet said, 'Woe to those who show partiality, who justify the sinner for a bribe, whose stomach is their god.'* A loose combination of Isaiah 5:23 and Philippians 3.19.

Ep. Ap. 49: *Let your ear not listen to anything against your brother.* Source unknown.

The Questions of Bartholomew

Gos. Bart. 1: *The number of souls dying and entering Paradise.* The following section is textually corrupt, and the numbers of souls born, dying or entering Paradise are hard to determine.

Gos. Bart. 2: *The head of a man is Christ.* Quoted from the apostle Paul in 1 Corinthians 11:3.

Gos. Bart. 2: *I raised mine eyes to the hills, from where my hope will come.* Quoted from Psalm 121:1.

Gos. Bart. 2: *Elphoue zarethra charboum . . . chrasar.* This section alleged to be Aramaic or Hebrew is in fact gibberish.

Gos. Bart. 4: *Michael was the first to bow down to him, because Adam was the image of God.* The Greek of this sentence is corrupt, and may have originally had a different meaning.

Gos. Bart. 4: *the four rivers.* The four rivers in the Garden of Eden according to Genesis 2:10–14.

Gos. Bart. 4: *Abba.* Aramaic for 'father'.

Gos. Bart. 4: *the Pishon, because of the faith . . . the Gihon, because of the earthly existence . . . the Tigris, so you could indicate to us the consubstantial Trinity . . . the fourth, the Euphrates, because when you were present in the world you gladdened every soul . . .* The Hebrew names of the four rivers are given these interpretations because Pishon, Gihon, Tigris and Euphrates resemble the Greek words *pistis* ('faith'), *gēinos* ('earthly'), *trias* ('Trinity') and *euphrainō* ('gladden').

Gos. Bart. 4: *the Father called me 'Christ' . . . so that I might come down to the earth and anoint all men . . . He called me 'Jesus' so that by the power of God I might heal every sin of the ignorant.* 'Christ' in ordinary Greek means anointing or ointment, and the name 'Jesus' sounds like some forms of the Greek word for 'heal'.

Gos. Bart. 5: *The godless shall not rise at the judgement, nor sinners in the council of the righteous.* A quotation from Psalm 1:5.

The Sophia of Jesus Christ

SJC 88 (§4): *Autogenes.* The name in Greek means 'self-generated'.

SJC 95 (§5): *the Octad,* or Ogdoad. An eight-part spiritual realm, a motif derived from Egyptian mythology. (See the introduction to the Coptic Gospel of the Egyptians, pp. 338–340.)

SJC 103 (§7): *Pistis.* A Greek word meaning 'faith'; the names Sophia and Pistis in other Gnostic literature are sometimes paired, to designate a female divinity as 'Pistis Sophia'.

SJC 110–111 (§8): *because the multitudes gather together as one they are called 'Church'.* The Greek-Coptic word for 'church' has the meaning 'assembly' or 'gathering' in normal Greek.

SJC 111–112 (§8): *'Zoë', so that it might appear that from the female all the aeons' life came to be.* The Greek *zoē* means 'life'.

The Gospel of Truth

Gos. Tr. codex p. 17 (§2): *the Middle.* This world, seen as an illusory and negative entity.

Gos. Tr. p. 19 (§5): *the aeon.* Here another way of speaking of the All.

Gos. Tr. p. 31 (§23): *The material ones.* In Valentinian theology, a distinction was drawn between 'the spiritual' (truly enlightened disciples), 'the ensouled' (ordinary Christians), and 'the material ones' (doomed non-Christians).

Gos. Tr. p. 32 (§25): *the whole number transfers to the right.* This refers to a Roman technique of counting on the fingers, in which ninety-nine different manipulations of the left hand can signify the numbers from one to ninety-nine. Then for numbers 100 and above the right hand is employed.

Gos. Tr. p. 34 (§28): *ensouled.* A condition midway between 'material' and 'spiritual' in the Valentinian system. (See note on 'material ones' above.)

The Coptic Gospel of the Egyptians

Gos. Eg. codex III, p. 41 (§2): *Domedon Doxomedon.* The name has connotations of 'house (*dōmē*) of glory (*doxa*)'.

Gos. Eg. III, p. 43 (§3): *the seven sounds.* The seven vowels in Greek and Coptic, important in the *Gospel of the Egyptians*: alpha (*a*), epsilon (*e*), eta (*ē*), iota (*i*), omicron (*o*), upsilon (*u*) and omega (*ō*). Epsilon and omicron are short vowels; eta and omega are long.

Gos. Eg. III, p. 44 (§5): *A secret invisible mystery came forth.* The ensuing rows consist of the seven vowels (see above) in sets of twenty-two (perhaps because this is the number of letters in the Hebrew alphabet). The unalphabetical order I Ē O U E A Ō is probably because IĒOU are the vowels of Jesus' name in Greek (*Iēsous*), then 'E' may be an abbreviation for the Greek verb 'to be', and finally 'A and Ō' (*alpha and omega*) is a divine title meaning 'the first and the last', applied to Jesus in the biblical Book of Revelation. See further the note to *Gos. Eg.* III, p. 66 below.

Gos. Eg. codex IV, p. 55 (§6): *Ainon.* The word means 'praising', and is also a place name in John's Gospel, where John the Baptist was active (Jn 3:23).

Gos. Eg. III, p. 49 (§8): *You are one, you are one, you are one. EA EA EA three times.* Here 'EA' probably is an abbreviation of the Greek *ei a*, which means 'you are one', since Greek letters are used for numbers.

Gos. Eg. III, p. 59 (§15): *the archon.* A standard Gnostic term for a demonic power.

Gos. Eg. III, p. 66 (§20): *Baptismal hymn.* At least some of the vowels in this hymn have significance: IE and IEUS suggest the name of Jesus (or YESSEUS as he is called in the hymn). The sequence of vowels, I Ē, E, O, U, Ō, A (each four times) is the list of all the Greek vowels, the order of the first five suggesting Jesus' name. The last two are *omega* and *alpha*, which in reverse order are a divine title in the Book of Revelation, where Christ declares, 'I am the Alpha and the Omega, the First and the Last, the Beginning and the End' (Rev. 22:13). As the first (*alpha*) and the last (*omega*) letters of the Greek alphabet they imply divine eternity. The same is true of the phrase EI AAAA Ō Ō Ō Ō, which means in Greek, 'you are the *alpha* (four times) and the *omega* (four times)'. The sequence A, E, Ē, I, U, Ō is the alphabetical order of the vowels (minus *omicron*). Finally, AIŌ is probably an abbreviated form of *aiōn*, the Greek spelling of 'aeon'.

Gos. Eg. III, p. 69 (*Scribe's epilogue*): *ICHTHUS.* The Greek word for 'fish', a common Christian symbol in antiquity because it was and an acrostic for *Iēsous CHristos THeou Uios Sōtēr* ('Jesus Christ, God's Son, Saviour').

The Coptic Gospel of Philip

Gos. Phil. logion 7: *the other aeon.* The world beyond, understood both temporally and ontologically.

Gos. Phil. logion 13: *The archons.* A standard term for demonic powers.

Gos. Phil. logion 17: *My Father in heaven.* A common phrase attributed to Jesus in Matthew's Gospel (Mt. 7:21; 15:13; 16:17; 18:10).

Gos. Phil. logion 19: *'Nazarene' is a manifestation of what is hidden.* This interpretation may be derived from a Semitic word *nistar,* meaning 'hidden'.

Gos. Phil. logion 23: *Flesh [and blood] cannot inherit the kingdom of God.* A statement of the apostle Paul in 1 Corinthians 15:50.

Gos. Phil. logion 39: *One is Echamoth and the other is Echmoth.* Aramaic *chokma / chokmata* means 'wisdom' (*sophia* in Greek); *eyk mot* is Aramaic for 'like death'.

Gos. Phil. logion 47: *The Christ is the one who is 'measured', and so the 'Nazarene' and 'Jesus' are measured.* Aramaic *mashach* is the origin of the term 'Messiah', 'anointed one' (translated into Greek as *Christos*). This root has two separate meanings, 'to anoint' and 'to measure'.

Gos. Phil. logion 63: *the Middle.* Understood here as a future realm, a place entirely evil.

Gos. Phil. logion 69: *the outer darkness.* See Matthew 8:12; 22:13, and 25:30. *'My Father who is in secret,' and, 'Go inside into your chamber and close the door and pray to your Father who is in secret.'* Quoted from the Sermon on the Mount, in Matthew 6:6.

Gos. Phil. logion 72: *My God, my God, why O Lord have you forsaken me?* Quoted from the words of Jesus on the cross, slightly modified by the addition 'O Lord' (Mt. 27.46; Mk 15.34). Jesus is in turn quoting the first verse of Psalm 22.

Gos. Phil. logion 81: *the All.* A reference either to a spiritual realm below the supreme deity, or to the physical universe.

Gos. Phil. logion 89: *[This is how] we are to fulfil all righteousness.* Said by Jesus of his baptism in Matthew 3:15.

Gos. Phil. logion 111: *For love covers a multitude of sins.* Quoted from 1 Peter 4:8.

Gos. Phil. logion 123: *Already the axe is laid at the root of the trees.* Spoken by John the Baptist in Matthew 3:10. *If you know the truth, the truth will set you free.* Spoken by Jesus in John 8:32.

Gos. Phil. logion 126: *Every planting which the Father in heaven has not planted will be pulled up.* Spoken by Jesus in Matthew 15:13 (cf. also *Gos. Thom.* 40).

Times, Measurements
and Currencies

Days (Starting the Preceding Evening)

First day of the week, the Lord's day:	Sunday
Second day of the week:	Monday
Third day of the week:	Tuesday
Fourth day of the week:	Wednesday
Fifth day of the week:	Thursday
Day of Preparation (for Sabbath):	Friday
Sabbath:	Saturday

Dates

The Passover Meal:	15th of the Hebrew month Nisan (usually in March or April)
The Passover Feast: (or Feast of Unleavened Bread)	The week beginning on 15th Nisan
Pentecost: (or the Feast of Weeks)	6th of the Hebrew month Sivan, fifty days after Passover (usually in May or June)

Times (Approximate)

First hour (of daylight):	7 a.m.
Second hour:	8 a.m.
Third hour:	9 a.m.
Fourth hour:	10 a.m.
Fifth hour:	11 a.m.

Sixth hour:	12 noon
Ninth hour:	3 p.m.
Tenth hour:	4 p.m.
Eleventh hour:	5 p.m.
Twelfth hour (last hour of daylight):	6 p.m.

(An 'hour' is a twelfth part of the daytime.)

Measurements (approximate)

cubit	45 centimetres
stade	180 metres
mile (Roman)	1,500 metres
seah	7.5 litres (dry)
bath	22 litres (liquid)
bushel	36 litres (dry or liquid)
kor (*30 seahs*)	220 litres (dry)
mina	560 g
talent (*60 minas*)	34 kg

Currencies

lepton (*prutah*)	1/128 denarius
quadrans	1/64 *denarius*
assarion, or *as*	1/16 denarius
denarius (16 *assaria*)	labourer's daily wage (3–4 grams of silver)
obol	1/6 drachma
drachma	skilled worker's wage (4–5 grams of silver)
mina (560g of silver)	150 denarii/100 drachmas
talent (34 kg of silver)	60 minas/10,000 denarii

Original Language Sources

1. *The Protevangelium of James:*
Émile de Strycker, ed. *La forme la plus ancienne du Protévangile de Jacques,* Subsidia Hagiographica 33 (Brussels: Société des Bollandistes, 1961), 64–191.

2. *The Birth of Mary:*
Karl Holl, ed. *Ancoratus und Panarion haer. 1–33,* Die Griechischen Christlichen Schriftsteller, vol. NF 10 (Berlin: Walter de Gruyter, 2013), 290–91 (Epiphanius, *Panarion* 26.12.1–4).

3. *Cairo Papyrus 10735:*
Thomas Kraus, Michael Kruger and Tobias Nicklas, eds. *Gospel Fragments,* Oxford Early Christian Gospel Texts (Oxford: Oxford University Press, 2009), 244–6.

4. *The Apocryphal Book of Seth:*
Jacques-Paul Migne, ed. *Ioannis Chrysostomi Omnia Opera, Patrologia Graeca,* vol. 56 (Paris: Imprimerie Catholique, 1859), cols. 637–8.

5. *The Infancy Gospel of Thomas:*
Tony Burke, ed. *De infantia Iesu Evangelium Thomae Graecae,* Corpus Christianorum Series Apocryphorum 17 (Turnhout: Brepols, 2010), 304–37.

6. Justin's Account of Baruch's Appearance to Jesus:
David Litwa, ed. and tr. *Refutation of All Heresies* (Atlanta: SBL, 2016), 348. (Pseudo-Hippolytus, *Refutation of All Heresies* 5.26. 29–31).

7. *The Gospel of Thomas:*
Bentley Layton, ed. 'The Gospel according to Thomas', in B. Layton, ed., *Nag Hammadi Codex II,2–7, together with XIII,2*, Brit. Lib.*

Or.4926(1), and P. Oxy. 1, 654, 655, vol. I, Nag Hammadi Studies
20 (Leiden: Brill, 1989), 52–93.

8. *Tatian's Diatessaron*:
P. Augustinus Ciasca, *Tatiani Evangelium Harmoniae Arabice*
(Rome: Vatican Library, 1888); J. Hamlyn Hill, *The Earliest Life of
Christ Ever Compiled from the Four Gospels. Being the Diatessaron
of Tatian* (Edinburgh: T&T Clark, 1894); Hope W. Hogg, 'The Dia-
tessaron of Tatian', in A. Menzies, ed. *The Ante-Nicene Fathers,* vol.
IX (New York: Charles Scribner's Sons, 1896), 33–138, and other
scholarly treatments.

9. Dura Parchment 24:
Matthew R. Crawford, 'The Diatessaron, Canonical or Non-
canonical? Rereading the Dura Fragment', *New Testament Studies*
62 (2016), 253–77 (258).

10. *Marcion's Gospel:*
Dieter Roth, *The Text of Marcion's Gospel,* New Testament Tools,
Studies and Documents 49 (Leiden: Brill, 2015), 411–36.

11. Jesus' Correspondence with Abgar:
Kirsopp Lake, ed. *Eusebius: Ecclesiastical History, Volume I: Books
1–5* (Cambridge, MA: Harvard University Press, 1926), 88, 90
(Eusebius, *Ecclesiastical History* 1.13.5–10).

12. *The 'Unknown Gospel', or Egerton-Cologne Papyrus*:
Lorne R. Zelyck, *The Egerton Gospel (Egerton Papyrus 2 + Papyrus
Köln VI 255): Introduction, Critical Edition and Commentary* (Lei-
den: Brill, 2019).

13. Oxyrhynchus Papyrus 210:
Andrew Bernhard, *Other Early Christian Gospels* (London: T&T
Clark, 2007), 108–12.

14. Oxyrhynchus Papyrus 840:
Bernhard, *Other Early Christian Gospels,* 120–24.

15. Oxyrhynchus Papyrus 1224:
Bernhard, *Other Early Christian Gospels,* 114–18.

16. Oxyrhynchus Papyrus 4009:
Bernhard, *Other Early Christian Gospels,* 54.

17. Oxyrhynchus Papyrus 5072:
'P. Oxy. 5072. Uncanonical Gospel?', in *The Oxyrhynchus Papyri*
vol. 76 (2011), 1–19.

18. Merton Papyrus II 51:
Bernhard, *Other Early Christian Gospels*, 106.

19. Berlin Papyrus 11710:
Bernhard, *Other Early Christian Gospels*, 126.

20. *The Gospel According to the Hebrews*:
Andrew F. Gregory, ed. *The Gospel According to the Hebrews and the Gospel of the Ebionites* (Oxford: Oxford University Press, 2017), 31–168 (various sources: see details in Gregory).

21. *The Gospel of the Ebionites*:
Gregory, ed. *The Gospel according to the Hebrews and the Gospel of the Ebionites*, 169–261. (Epiphanius, *Panarion* 30.13.2–8; 30.14.3, 5; 30.16.5; 30.22.4–5).

22. *The Gospel of Eve*:
Karl Holl, ed. *Ancoratus und Panarion*, 278 (Epiphanius, *Panarion* 26.3.1).

23. *The Greek Gospel of Philip*:
Holl, ed. *Ancoratus und Panarion*, 292–3 (Epiphanius, *Panarion* 26.13.2–3).

24. *The Greater Questions of Mary*:
Holl, ed. *Ancoratus und Panarion*, 284 (Epiphanius, *Panarion* 26.8. 2–3).

25. *The Gospel Used by Apelles*:
Jürgen Dummer, ed. *Epiphanius II. Panarion haer. 34–64*, GCS NF 10 (Berlin: Akademie-Verlag, 1980), 92. (Epiphanius, *Panarion* 44.2.6).

26. *The Greek Gospel of the Egyptians*:
Otto Stählin, ed. *Clemens Alexandrinus II. Stromata I–VI* (Berlin: Akademie-Verlag, 1985), 225–6, 238, 225 (Clement, *Stromateis* 3.9.64.1–66.3; 3.13.92.2; 3.9.63.2).

27. The Gospel/Traditions of Matthias
Stählin, ed. *Clemens Alexandrinus II. Stromata I–VI*, 137 and 208 (Clement, *Stromateis* 2.9.45.4; 3.4.26.3); idem, *Stromata, Buch VII und VIII. Excerpta ex Theodoto – Eclogae propheticae quis dives salvetur – Fragmente*, GCS (Berlin: Walter de Gruyter, 1970), 58 (Clement, *Stromateis* 7.13.82.1).

28. The Jewish Anti-Gospel:
Paul Koetschau, *Origenes Werke: Buch I–IV, gegen Celsus*, GCS (Berlin: Walter de Gruyter, 1899), 56–125.

29. Vienna Greek Papyrus 2325 (The 'Fayyum Gospel'):
Bernhard, *Other Early Christian Gospels*, 104.

30. *The Gospel of Judas*:
Lance Jenott, ed. *The Gospel of Judas: Coptic Text, Translation, and Historical Interpretation of 'the Betrayer's Gospel'*, STAC 64 (Tübingen: Mohr Siebeck, 2011), 136–86.

31. *The Gospel of Peter* (incl. Oxyrhynchus Papyrus 2949):
Paul Foster, ed. *The Gospel of Peter: Introduction, Critical Edition and Commentary*, TENTS 4 (Leiden: Brill, 2010), 64, 178–208.

32. *The Gospel of Nicodemus* (or, *Acts of Pilate*):
Constantin von Tischendorf, ed. *Evangelia Apocrypha* (Leipzig: Mendelssohn, 1876), 210–86.

33. *The Narrative of Joseph of Arimathaea*:
Tischendorf, ed. *Evangelia Apocrypha*, 459–70.

34. *The Gospel of Mary*:
Christopher M. Tuckett, ed. *The Gospel of Mary* (Oxford: Oxford University Press, 2007), 86–103, 108–109, 112–15.

35. *The Epistle of the Apostles*:
See Francis Watson, *An Apostolic Gospel: The Epistula Apostolorum in Literary Context* (Cambridge: Cambridge University Press, 2020).

36. *The Questions of Bartholomew*:
Gottlieb Nathanael Bonwetsch, 'Die apokryphen Fragen des Bartholomäus', *Nachrichten von der königlichen Gesellschaft der Wissenschaften, Philol.-hist. Kl.* (1897), 9–29, and E. Tisserant and A. Wilmart, 'Fragments grecs et latins de l'Évangile de Barthélemy', *Revue Biblique* 10 (1913), 185–90, 321–33.

37. *The Sophia of Jesus Christ*:
Douglas M. Parrott, ed. *Nag Hammadi Codices III,3–4 and V,1 with Papyrus Berolinensis 8502,3 and Oxyrhynchus Papyrus 1081: Eugnostos and The Sophia of Jesus Christ*, Nag Hammadi Studies 27 (Leiden: Brill, 1991), 37–215.

38. *The Gospel of Truth*:
Harold W. Attridge and George W. MacRae, 'The Gospel of Truth', in H. W. Attridge, ed. *Nag Hammadi Codex I (The Jung Codex)*, vol. I, Nag Hammadi Studies 22 (Leiden: Brill, 1985), 82–116.

39. *The Coptic Gospel of the Egyptians*:
Alexander Böhlig and Frederik Wisse, eds. *Nag Hammadi Codices III, 2 and IV, 2: The Gospel of The Egyptians (The Holy Book of the Great Invisible Spirit,* Nag Hammadi Studies 4 (Leiden: Brill, 1975), 52–167.

40. *The Coptic Gospel of Philip*:
Bentley Layton, ed., 'The Gospel according to Philip', in B. Layton, ed. *Nag Hammadi Codex II, 2–7, together with XIII,2*, Brit. Lib. Or.4926(1), and P. Oxy. 1, 654, 655,* vol. I, Nag Hammadi Studies 20 (Leiden: Brill, 1989), 142–214.

41. *The Gospel of the Lots of Mary:*
AnneMarie Luijendijk, *Forbidden Oracles? The Gospel of the Lots of Mary,* STAC (Tübingen: Mohr Siebeck, 2014), 98–144.

42. *The Secret Gospel of Mark:*
Morton Smith, *Clement of Alexandria and a Secret Gospel of Mark* (Cambridge, MA: Harvard University Press, 1973), 448–53.

43. *The Gospel of Jesus' Wife:*
Harvard Magazine, 18 September 2012. Photograph of Coptic text at: https://harvardmagazine.com/2012/09/new-gospel.

Index